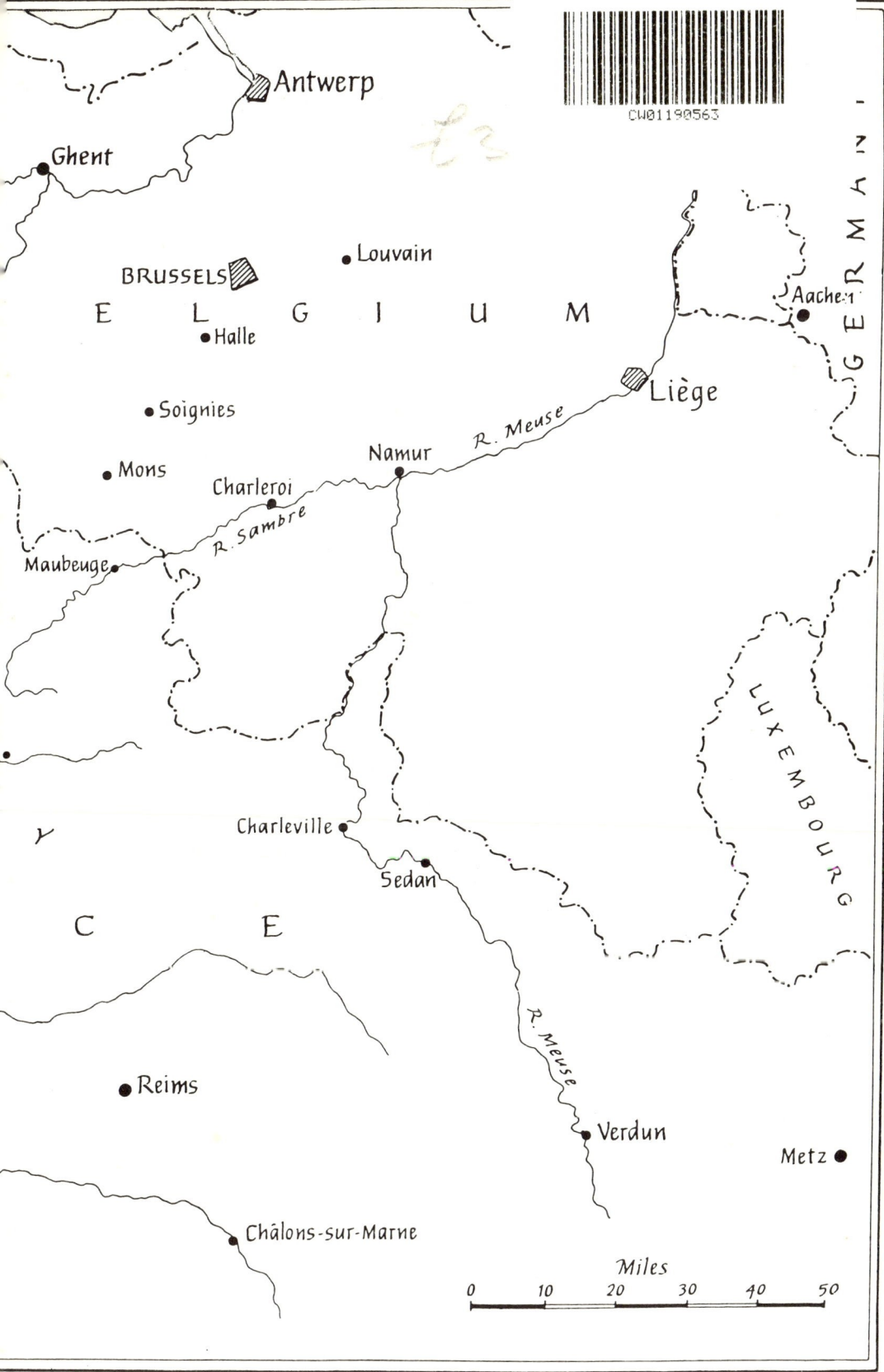

A HISTORY OF THE
BRITISH CAVALRY
1816 to 1919
VOLUME 8

THE WESTERN FRONT 1915–1918;
EPILOGUE 1919–1939

By the same author

THE CAPEL LETTERS, 1814–1817 (CAPE, 1955)
ONE-LEG (CAPE, 1961)
SERGEANT PEARMAN'S MEMOIRS (CAPE, 1968)
LITTLE HODGE (LEO COOPER, 1971)
A HISTORY OF THE BRITISH CAVALRY, 1816–1919
   VOLUME 1: 1816–1850 (LEO COOPER, 1973)
   VOLUME 2: 1851–1871 (LEO COOPER, 1975)
   VOLUME 3: 1872–1898 (LEO COOPER, 1982)
   VOLUME 4: 1899–1913 (LEO COOPER, 1986)
   VOLUME 5: EGYPT, PALESTINE AND SYRIA
     1914–1918 (LEO COOPER, 1994)
   VOLUME 6: MESOPOTAMIA, 1914–1918
     (LEO COOPER, 1995)
   VOLUME 7: THE CURRAGH INCIDENT AND THE
   WESTERN FRONT, 1914 (LEO COOPER, 1996)

A HISTORY OF THE BRITISH CAVALRY
1816 to 1919

by

THE MARQUESS OF ANGLESEY
F.S.A., F.R.HIST.S.

VOLUME 8
THE WESTERN FRONT, 1915–1918;
EPILOGUE, 1919–1939

LEO COOPER
LONDON

First published in Great Britain in 1997 by
LEO COOPER
190 Shaftesbury Avenue, London WC2H 8JL
an imprint of
Pen & Sword Books Ltd
47 Church Street, Barnsley, South Yorkshire, S70 2AS

© The Marquess of Anglesey, 1997

A CIP record for this book is
available from the British Library
ISBN 0 85052 467 9

Typeset in 11/13pt Linotype Sabon by
Phoenix Typesetting, Ilkley, West Yorkshire.

Printed by Redwood Books Ltd.,
Trowbridge, Wilts.

DEDICATED TO MY WIFE WHOSE PATIENCE OVER
A QUARTER OF A CENTURY HAS MADE IT POSSIBLE
FOR THIS WORK TO REACH COMPLETION

CONTENTS

Acknowledgements		xvii
Preface		xix
1	Life in trenches and billets – bus transport – trench improvements – recreations – working parties – leave	3
2	Neuve Chapelle – 2nd Ypres	19
3	Loos – Dismounted Division formed from Cavalry Corps – Haig succeeds French – Robertson appointed CIGS – Churchill's resignation	25
4	Introduction of steel helmets – Verdun – Hindenburg replaces Falkenhayn – reduction of cavalry proposed – arrangements for cavalry in 1916 campaigns – cavalry tracks – battle of the Somme – Bazentin Ridge – Flers Courcelette – tanks – Morval	34
5	*L'Affaire Nivelle* – French mutinies – German withdrawal to Hindenburg Line – Villers Faucon – opening of battle of Arras – Monchy	65
6	3rd Ypres – Messines – 1st Cambrai	97
7	Reduction and re-organization of the cavalry – the German spring offensives – Falvy – Collézy – Gough sacked – Morcuil Wood	161
8	The advent of the Americans – Amiens	220
9	End of battle of Amiens – 2nd Cambrai and 2nd Le Cateau	247
10	Last days on the Western Front – administrative chaos – the Armistice	270
11	Horses: forage supply – remounts – types of horse – veterinary service – weights on cavalry horses	284

Contents

Epilogue		305
Envoi		347
Appendix 1	'The Last Charge'	349
Appendix 2	Old Soldiers	353
Abbreviations used in footnotes and source notes		355
Source notes		365
Index		383

LIST OF ILLUSTRATIONS

1. London buses transporting troops to the front
   Murray, Rev. R.H. *The History of the VIII King's Royal Irish Hussars, 1693-1927*, 570 — 38
2. Brigadier-General Sir Philip Chetwode, commanding 5th Cavalry Brigade, with his staff, Zillebeke Woods, February, 1915
   Charrington, Maj. H.V.S. *The 12th Royal Lancers in France, 1914-1918*, 6 — 38
3. A typical shelter for cavalry horses, winter, 1915
   Coleman, Frederic *With Cavalry in 1915*, 1916, 32 — 39
4. A cavalry horse shelter being built, winter, 1915
   Coleman, Frederic *With Cavalry in 1915*, 1916, 33 — 39
5. 'B' Squadron, the Bays, in the earliest type of gas masks
   Whyte, F. and Atteridge, A.H. *A History of the Queen's Bays (the 2nd Dragoon Guards), 1685-1929*, 1930, 336 — 70
6. German gas masks: horse and man, 1916
   Hartcup, G. *The War of Invention: Scientific Developments, 1914-1918*, 1988, 132 — 70
7. Horse gas masks being fitted
   (Imperial War Museum) — 70
8. The 19th Lancers (Fane's Horse) watering, 1915
   Hudson, Gen. Sir H. *History of the 19th King George's Own Lancers...*, 1972, 160 — 71
9. The 4th Dragoon Guards, June, 1915. Note the fly-fringes
   Photograph by Captain Roger Chance — 71
10. Cavalry horses waiting for water, winter, 1916
    Galtrey, Captain S. *The Horse and the War*, 1918, 72 — 102
11. Horses being treated for mange in gas chambers
    Galtrey, Captain S. *The Horse and the War*, 1918, 91 — 102
12. The Fort Garry Horse crossing a cavalry track bridge, June, 1916
    (Imperial War Museum) — 103
13. Part of a taped cavalry track
    (Imperial War Museum) — 103
14. Indian cyclists with cavalry, July, 1916
    (Imperial War Museum) — 134
15. Men of the 20th Deccan Horse, 14 July, 1916
    (Imperial War Museum) — 134
16. Brigadier-General J.E.B. Seely (left), commanding the Canadian Cavalry Brigade, with General Hughes (centre) and Sir Max Aitken, Amiens area, August, 1916
    Nicholson, Col. G.W.L. *Canadian Expeditionary Force, 1914-1919 (Official History....)*, 1962, 178 — 135
17. The Bays entering the Carnoy Valley, 18 September, 1916
    (Imperial War Museum) — 135

Illustrations

18. Cavalry crossing the Yser to enter the battle zone
Galtrey, Captain S. *The Horse and the War,* 1918, 76 — 166
19. Cavalry crossing a log bridge over a communication trench, 7 May, 1917
(Imperial War Museum) — 166
20. Horses of the 3rd Cavalry Division waiting in the snow behind Arras, April, 1917
(Imperial War Museum) — 167
21. Cavalry waiting to go forward near Arras, 1917
Nicholls, J. *Cheerful Sacrifice: The Battle of Arras, 1917,* 1990, 84 — 167
22. Cavalry crossing a trench on their way to Monchy, 13 April, 1917
(Imperial War Museum) — 198
23. The scene after the action at Monchy, April, 1917
Nicholls, J. *Cheerful Sacrifice: The Battle of Arras, 1917,* 1990, 85 — 198
24. Brigadier-General Sir Archibald ('Sally') Home, 1915
Photograph by Frederic Coleman. (Ed.) Briscoe, Diana *The Diary of a World War One Cavalry Officer,* 1985, 64 — 199
25. General Byng
By J.S. Sargent (National Portrait Gallery) — 199
26. General Rawlinson
By J.S. Sargent (National Portrait Gallery) — 199

between pages 214 and 215

27. Cavalry horses tethered behind a line of dugouts in a dip in the ground, in front of Zillebeke, September, 1917
(Imperial War Museum)
28. 4th Dragoon Guards on the way up to Cambrai, November, 1917. Note the man, seated right, with a pigeon basket on his back. Photograph by Captain Roger Chance
29. A disabled Mark IV female tank, marked WC for Wire Cutter being used as a vantage point, photographed near Ribécourt, 23 November, 1917
(Tank Museum)
30. A grapnel used by wire-cutting tanks at Cambrai
(Tank Museum)
31. 'Flying Fox', a Mark IV male tank which broke the bridge at Masnières, falling into the canal, photographed by German troops
(Tank Museum)
32. 'Flying Fox' helping to support a replacement bridge built by the Germans over the canal at Masnières
(Tank Museum)
33. Lieutenant Harcus Strachan, VC, Fort Garry Horse
Williams, Captain S.H. *'Stand to Your Horses': Through the First World War with the Lord Strathcona's Horse,* 1961, 160
34. After Cambrai, 'B' Squadron, Fort Garry Horse, led by Lieutenant Harcus Strachan, who won the VC in the battle, passing through Epéhy, 30 November, 1917
(Imperial War Museum)

Illustrations

35. Field Marshal Erich von Falkenhayn
    Livesey, A. *Great Battles of World War I*, 1989, 72 — 230
36. General Henri Pétain
    Livesey, A. *Great Battles of World War I*, 1989, 72 — 230
37. General Sir Hubert Gough, in 1932. By Sir William Rothenstein
    (National Portrait Gallery) — 230
38. Field Marshal Sir Henry Wilson in 1919. Painted by Sir William Orpen
    (National Portrait Gallery) — 230
39. Brigadier-General A.E.W. Harman
    Bickersteth, Lieutenant J.B. *History of the 6th Cavalry Brigade, 1914-1919*, [1920], 51 — 230
40. Brigadier-General Ewing Paterson
    Bickersteth, Lieutenant J.B. *History of the 6th Cavalry Brigade, 1914-1919*, [1920], 107 — 230
41. Haig inspecting a guard of honour with the King of Montenegro, 1916
    May, Col H.A.R. *Memories of the Artists' Rifles*, 1929, 238 — 231
42. Haig talking to a French resident at a Horse Show near Arras, May, 1917
    (Imperial War Museum) — 231
43. Haig with Dominion journalists, September, 1918. Note his hand holding a journalist's arm in friendly embrace
    (Imperial War Museum) — 231
44. Cavalry waiting to advance near Trescault, battle of Cambrai, 20 November, 1917
    (Imperial War Museum) — 262
45. No.4 Remount Depot, near Boulogne, February, 1918
    (Imperial War Museum) — 262
46. The aftermath of the charge of the Canadians at Moreuil Wood, 30 March, 1918. Photograph taken on 3 April
    (Imperial War Museum) — 263
47. The Scots Greys behind the line, May, 1918
    (Imperial War Museum) — 263
48. An armoured car held up by fallen trees on the Villers Bretonneux to Brie road, 8 August, 1918. Photograph taken by Australians
    Montgomery, Maj.-Gen. Sir A. *The Story of the Fourth Army in the Battle of the Hundred Days...*, 1919, 42 — 294
49. Canadian cavalry passing German wounded, September, 1918 (Imperial War Museum) — 294
50. 21 August, 1918. The 18th Hussars advancing
    (Imperial War Museum) — 295
51. 21 August, 1918. An officer of the 18th Hussars steadying his horse under shell fire
    (Imperial War Museum) — 295
52. General Kavanagh, Cavalry Corps Commander, watching his troops passing through Spa, the General Headquarters of the German Army, on 29 November, 1918
    Briscoe, Diana (ed.) *The Diary of a World War One Cavalry Officer*, 1985, 128 — 326

Illustrations

53. The 9th Lancers enter Spa, the General Headquarters of the German Army, on 29 November, 1918
Sheppard, Major E.W. *The Ninth Queen's Royal Lancers, 1715-1936,* 1939, 309   326
54. Five 'bull-nosed' Morris motor cars bought and converted into machine gun carriers by an officer of the Inns of Court Regiment, 1933. Private enterprise mechanization!
Hatton, Major D.M. *'The Devil's Own': A History of the Inns of Court Regiment,* 1992, 77   327
55. Serving and former Life Guards officers during the Cavalry Memorial Weekend, 1988
Guards Magazine, Summer, 1988   327

TEXT ILLUSTRATIONS

Dismounted cavalryman *Punch*, 1 September, 1915	5
How various military branches go to War! May, Col H.A.R., *Memories of the Artists' Rifles*, 1929, 224	10
Programme of 'D' Squadron Horse Show Keith-Falconer, A., *The Oxfordshire Hussars in the Great War*, 1927, 135	12
In Billets Carnock, Lord, *History of the 15th Hussars 1914–1922*, 1927, 99	16
"'Ere you! What are you doin' there, ridin up an'down like a general?" *Punch*, 23 June, 1915	28
A Private of the 3rd Hussars in the Great War Willcox, Lt-Col N.T., *The 3rd Hussars in the Great War*, 1925, 168	35
"Why have you put that cloth over his head?" *Punch*, 22 August, 1917	39
"Stop that bad language" *Punch*, 20 January, 1915	44
"Tank walking up the High Street at Flers" Mitchell, F., *Tank Warfare*, 1933, 32	61
"What do you mean by feeding that horse?" *Punch*, 7 February, 1917	66
Two patterns of Caltrops or "Crows' Feet" Blenkinsop, Maj.-Gen. Sir L.J. & Rainey, Lt-Col J.W., *History of the Great War ... Veterinary Services*, 1925, 556	69
A Whippet Tank Mitchell, F. *Tank Warfare*, 1933, 166	228
"Stop whisperin' to 'im in public!" *Punch*, 13 February, 1918	257
Top deck passengers. Interest in the hay ration by Lionel Edwards, Galtrey Capt. S. *The Horse and the War*, 1918, 55	284
From the ship to the Remount Depot by Lionel Edwards, Galtrey Capt. S. *The Horse and the War*, 1918, 28	285
Humours of a Remount Depot *Punch*, 14 July, 1915	289
Branding a British Government purchase in North America by Lionel Edwards, Galtrey Capt. S. *The Horse and the War*, 1918, 31	290
Testing an alleged riding horse before a British Government purchaser by Lionel Edwards, Galtrey Capt. S. *The Horse and the War*, 1918, 29	292
Humours of a Remount Camp *Punch*, 7 November, 1917	293
Landing of American horses at an English port by Lionel Edwards, Galtrey Capt. S. *The Horse and the War*, 1918, 21	294

The transport safely docked
by Lionel Edwards, Galtrey Capt. S. *The Horse and the War*,
1918, 59   298
"Don't you worry. It'll be a long time before they can do without us"
Cavalry Journal, July, 1927, 418   316
"What the Cavalry thought they would do"
Martel, Lt-Gen Sir Giffard, *An Outspoken Soldier*, 1959, 34   319
"Still the same spirit"
by Gilbert Holiday
Stewart, Capt. P.F., *History of the XII Royal Lancers*, 1950, 320   337
"I don't care if you have been mechanised"
Cavalry Journal, XXVIII, 1938, 418   343

MAPS

Battle of the Somme, 1 and 14 July, 1916	46
Battle of Bazentin Ridge, 14 July, 1916	46
German withdrawal from Hindenburg Line, battle of Arras and *L'Affaire Nivelle*, 1917	67
Action at Villers Faucon, 27 March, 1917	71
Battle of Arras, 1917	75
Monchy, 11 April, 1917	82
Cambrai area, 20 November to 1 December, 1917: The battle area	109
Battle of Cambrai, 20 November, 1917	118
Action of Lieutenant Strachan's Squadron, 20 November, 1917	130
Cambrai, 30 November–2 December, 1917	144
Action of the Mhow Cavalry Brigade, 1 December, 1917	144
The German Offensive, 21 March–5 April, 1918	167
Area of Third and Fifth Armies, 21 March, 1918	171
2 Cavalry Division and Harman's Detachment: area of operations, 25–27 March, 1918	181
Situation south of Falvy, 23 March, 1918	
Action of 9th Cavalry Brigade at Falvy, 23 March 1918	187
Action of part of 6th Cavalry Brigade at Collézy/Villeselve, 24 March, 1918	192
German offensive: area South-East of Amiens, 28–30 March, 1918	199
Moreuil Wood, 30 March & Rifle Wood, 30 March–1 April, 1918	202
Battle of Amiens, 8 August, 1918	224-5
The Allied Advance, 1918	250
Second battle of Le Cateau, 9 October, 1918	262
The area of Mons/Maubeuge, 11 November, 1918	277

ACKNOWLEDGEMENTS

In compiling this volume, numerous people have given me assistance, asked for and given voluntarily. Every one of them warrants my sincere gratitude. The following have been particularly helpful: Dr S.D. Badsey, Professor Brian Bond, Mr J.M. Brereton, Mr Michael Burn, MC, the late Sir Roger Chance, Bt, Mr Peter Chapman, Mr B.J. Crichton, Mr G.J. Crump, Mr Andrew Francis, Lord Jenkins of Hillhead, OM, PC, Mr H. Keown-Boyd, Mr Peter Kirby, MC, Mr I.D. Leask, Colonel A.L. Mallinson, Mr S.E.H. Robinson, Mr T.J. Schadler, DVM (of Columbus, Ohio), Mr M.G. Sims (Librarian, Staff College, Sandhurst), my son, the Earl of Uxbridge, Mrs Theresa Whistler and Mr Patrick D. Furse, and the curators of the cavalry and yeomanry regimental museums.

Expert advice has been given me by numbers of institutions, as also has unrestricted access to their papers and books. Chief amongst these stands the Ministry of Defence Whitehall Library, the successive Chief Librarians and the splendid staffs of which never fail to provide answers to the trickiest of questions.

The helpfulness, both in the Reading Room and in correspondence, of the various sections of the Imperial War Museum, has been essential, for without it I could not have proceeded with the work. For a number of years the sympathetic help given me by Mr Roderick Suddaby, the Keeper of Documents, has been vital. To him my thanks know no bounds. The Department of Photography, too, has given me all that I asked for in the way of illustrations.

To the National Army Museum I offer my very real gratitude for assistance in a number of areas. To the London Library, for books as well as information, to the India Office Library and indirectly to the Liddell Hart Centre I am also much indebted. Mr David Fletcher, Librarian of the Tank Museum, has enlightened me in an area hitherto little studied by me. He has always come up with complete answers to my ignorant questions, thus earning my sincere appreciation.

Were I to list all the living authors from whose books I have unashamedly purloined and pilfered much material, it would be almost as impossibly lengthy as would be a list of all of those who are no longer alive. To both categories I acknowledge my deep obligation. Without their succour, I should have had to consult many more primary sources than I have done.

Acknowledgements

For the excellence of the maps I thank Neil Hyslop, whose ability to produce meaning out of the confused sketches with which I presented him, never miscarried.

Once again I register with undying gratitude the names of my two chief assistants over many, many years: Tom Hartman, the very model of an editor, and Mrs Pat Brayne, the doyenne of the typists' profession. For quite a time after she retired Pat Brayne nobly continued to make sense of my first and numerous subsequent drafts. Accuracy and speed have ever been her hallmarks. These have inspired in me appreciative and affectionate admiration. For nearly thirty years, whilst these eight volumes have been in gestation, Tom Hartman has overseen, in the mode of a skilful midwife, each successive birth. His patience has equalled that of my wife, to whom this volume is dedicated, and for whose long-suffering sympathy I am eternally grateful.

Finally, to the ever patient impresario of the whole enterprise, Leo Cooper, the foremost publisher of military history in Britain, I give my very fullest gratitude for his unfailing encouragement and forbearance.

PREFACE

Justice has never been done to the part played by the cavalry in France and Flanders during the years 1915 to 1918. This volume attempts to do just that. It tries to show that the portrait so often painted by historians, both good and bad, of the cavalrymen sitting in comfort, a numerous pampered and useless body of mounted men, waiting well behind the front line, while the poor bloody infantrymen die horrible deaths in the unutterable misery and fear of the trenches and of the great offensives, is not a picture which corresponds with the facts.

Much of the cavalry's time was indeed spent far from the battlefields in vigorous training for the culminating moment of truth that never came – 'the ride for the G'.* Yet at least as many days were devoted to training in an infantry role. Further, large numbers of cavalrymen were extensively employed in taking their turn in the trenches, (much more often than is generally conceded), not of course as constantly as the infantrymen, but sharing to the full the horrors and dangers experienced by them. Those experiences are little touched upon here since they have been discussed in Volume 7 and because they varied hardly at all from the endlessly repeated accounts of them given elsewhere from the infantry's point of view.

That the cavalry was frequently employed upon every conceivable sort of task which no one else was prepared to undertake is another aspect which is usually neglected. These 'odd jobs', many of them involving great danger, were far from glamorous, but after initial disgruntlement were embarked upon with good grace. They included pioneer work, constructing and mending roads, often close to the front, and numerous other 'non-combatant' duties,

---

*The 'G' stood for gap. The phrase originated in the Boer War. It evolved from the practice of describing a featureless location on a sketch map lacking grids, by using the lettering appearing on it as if it actually existed on the ground, thus: 'A mile NE of the first o in Tiger Kloof Spruit.'

Full marching order for the cavalry came to be known on the Western Front as 'gap organization'. (Whyte and Atteridge, 344)

By early 1917 the word 'gap' had been officially dropped 'as it had become almost a term of derision'. In its place '"operations beyond the trench system" or some such phrase came into use.' (Darling, 73)

There were jokers who purported to believe that 'G' stood for 'Gee-gees'.

such as digging reserve trench lines. These were chores the like of which cavalrymen had never dreamed of being called upon to perform, for which they had certainly never been trained and which they carried out with exceptional efficiency.

Inevitably, for most of those terrible years, their lot was to be preferred in purely physical ways to that of most of the infantrymen (as, too, was that of many of the gunners). The comparative brevity of their casualty lists is proof enough of this. That many of them were eating their hearts out in frustration is evidenced by the large number of all ranks who tried to get and often succeeded in getting into the infantry, air force and other more active arms such as the tanks and armoured cars.

More important than any of this was the truly vital part played by the mounted troops of the BEF at the worst moments of crisis. Acting as a 'fire brigade' they time and again stopped up gaps as only the sole speedily movable element of the force could do. It is not too much to claim that on a number of occasions catastrophes of major dimensions were averted by such action. In this volume overdue recognition of this aspect of their work is given in full.

There is one particularly pernicious myth that needs banishing from the minds of future historians. Even most of the authoritative and reliable of those who have written about the Western Front repeat time and again the fallacious idea that vast quantities of shipping had to be devoted to the provision of forage for the cavalry's horses. This is nonsense. If the disquisition on p. 286 will not dismiss once and for all this too often propagated falsehood, the present author presumes to believe that nothing will. Though the proportion of cavalry to the other arms was by the end of the war a great deal less than it had been at the beginning of 1915, the actual numbers of cavalrymen became (until the very last phase) considerably greater. At no time, though, did they constitute more than a very small percentage of the total manpower. The same applies to their horses.

Yet another legend has been assiduously propagated by writers of all sorts. No one today accepts Lloyd George's *Memoirs* as being anything but economical with the truth. It does not surprise therefore to find him affirming that 'the army chiefs were mostly horsemen'.[1] The fact is that out of the top twenty-six First World War commanders (including the five CIGS, and all the BEF's Army commanders and Chiefs of Staff) only eight were cavalrymen. Fourteen were infantrymen and four artillerymen. Of the four

CIGS only Robertson came from the mounted arm. Of the twelve Commanders-in-Chief (including those who commanded the 'sideshows') only three came from the cavalry. Out of the four Chiefs of Staff who served French and Haig, two were cavalrymen, while five of the ten generals who commanded Armies in the BEF at various times come into that category. In 1918 there were seventeen corps commanders. Only one of these, and, out of the fifty-one commanders of divisions, only five came from the cavalry. So much for A.J.P. Taylor's 'most British generals were cavalrymen',[2] which soon became, in the words of Robert Graves, 'All our generals were cavalrymen'![3] As John Terraine has put it: 'The fact that the BEF's Commanders-in-Chief were both cavalrymen is seen to be a most unusual circumstance. The overwhelming majority of the generals actually handling troops in battle came, as one might expect, from the arm which produced the overwhelming majority of those troops: the infantry.'[4]

Denigration of generals who were cavalrymen in the war occurs in two celebrated works of fiction. Siegfried Sassoon in his semi-fictional *Memoirs of an Infantry Officer* of 1930 describes a 1916 Army commander thus: 'He had taken the salute from four hundred officers and N.C.O.s of his Army. How many of them had been killed since then, and how deeply was he responsible for their deaths? Did he know what he was doing, or was he merely a successful old cavalryman whose peace-time popularity had pushed him up on his present perch?'[5] C.S. Forester's *The General*, published in 1936, has on more than one occasion been quoted in serious works on the war,[6] as showing the mentality of the typical cavalry general, especially is this so respecting what is supposed to be a portrait of Allenby and which Wavell rightly condemned as 'a grotesque caricature'.[7]

From whatever arm they originated, there is evidence that, contrary to received notions, there were men on all sides who were of the calibre of the much-lauded Second World War generals. Cyril Falls puts this well:

'Generals from the Western Front who got fresh chances elsewhere – Falkenhayn in Rumania, Allenby in Palestine, Franchet d'Esperey in Greece, Serbia and Bulgaria – manoeuvred fast and brilliantly. The wiseacres conclude that they were bad, hide-bound, mud-bound generals in the west and became good, creative, fertile generals in changed scenes. Is it likely? No, it was the circumstances of the Western Front that shackled them.'[8]*

---

*There was a time, some thirty or forty years ago, when there was a spate of what Terraine calls 'Instant History' concerning the First World War. The most contemptible of this genre is Alan Clark's *The Donkeys* (1961). This was designed to denigrate at all costs both French and Haig during 1915. That it is full of deliberate falsification of simple facts is not to be wondered at. What is more pitifully despicable is that by selectivity and omission, he perverts the meaning of numerous quotations from important documents. A typical example of Clark's intentionally misleading method concerns the cavalry. 'In the Expeditionary Force,' he writes, 'it seemed that there were nearly as many regiments of horse as of foot.' In a footnote to this extraordinary statement he adds, 'Actually the proprtion was eighteen cavalry to seventy-eight infantry, but seventeen cavalry regiments were in the line compared with only forty-two infantry battalions.' (p.15) If this makes any sense at all it indicates that the assertion in the text is (to be charitable) meaningless! The funniest specimen of Clark's ignorance is his 'polished Shakos' of the French cuirassiers. (p.14)

The most unfortunate thing about this deplorable travesty of history is that it was influential in the making of a sensational and amusing film, *Oh! What a Lovely War*, thus spreading a totally false story to millions of people.

It is distressing, but, alas, no surprise, to learn that Clark received 'the greatest help at every stage of the development of the book' from Liddell Hart, as well as assistance from Captain Bickersteth, whom he describes as 'the historian of the Cavalry Brigade', thus again displaying his ignorance or carlessness. Bickersteth's book dealt with the *6th* Cavalry Brigade, only one, of course, of those engaged.

Terraine's brilliant criticism of *The Donkeys* ('Instant History', *JRUSI*, CVII, 1962, 140–44) ought to be read by everyone who embarks on works connected with the Western Front. (So, too, ought Bond, B. 'Judgment in Military History', *JRUSI*, Spring, 1989 and Mearsheinzer, J. *Liddell Hart and the Weight of History*, 1988, as well as Wolff, L. *In Flanders Fields*, 1958).

In 1927, thirty-four years before Clark's book appeared, Captain P.A. Thompson of the RASC wrote one entitled *Lions Led by Donkeys, Showing How Victory in the Great War was Achieved by Those Who Made the Fewest Mistakes.* Unlike Clark's, Thompson's book is dull but honest. In an 'Apologia' he wrote

> 'If you, who read this, were one of the Lions, do not forget that throughout those four years you were unable to find any others more capable of leading you. Nor do I intend to confine the meaning to ourselves alone, for while we made some bad mistakes we never equalled the grand miscalculations of the German High Comannd. So for my sub-title I have adapted Napoleon's definition of the best General.' (p.iv)

In 1961 there were many old lions left. If they believed Clark's parodies of those who led them, their consternation and distress must have been harassing indeed – everything they endured wasted by incompetence. Another aspect of his service to historical truth!

Preface

There has been much unthinking criticism of the high command for keeping in being a respectable mounted force throughout the years of trench warfare. Yet it would have been highly irresponsible of Haig had he failed to do so. Whether the actual numbers were at times needlessly large is a question incapable of an assured answer. Even with hindsight it is difficult to be certain that they were. No one was to know that the time was never to come when the pursuit of a broken, thoroughly demoralized enemy was to be the order of the day. Indeed, had the armistice not intervened to put an end to operations when it did, had, instead, the incipient breakdown of discipline in the German armies during the late summer and autumn of 1918 been given time for full exploitation, a considerable mounted force might well have come into its own.*
Certain it is that the tank with its mechanical unreliability, its very slow speed and the small number of the latest improved marks available, would have proved no substitute for mounted men supported by adequate fire power had the conditions for a pursuit ever materialized. It would, though, have taken a large degree of demoralization to silence the amazing efficiency and persistence of the German machine gunners, only a few of whom in the right place and at the right time could make cavalry pursuit suicidal. As it was, with defeat staring them in the face, their performance must command enormous respect.

It has been argued, among others by Ludendorff (though in his case it may have been special pleading), that had the Germans not drastically reduced their mounted troops and dissipated what were left by attaching regiments and squadrons to infantry units instead of keeping at least a few divisions in being as such, the great offensives of March and April, 1918, might have succeeded even better than in fact they did. This argument, though, can only be fully sustained had there been a more universal breakdown of Allied morale than in fact there was. In short, with no mobile alternative to the cavalry, Haig's decision to hold in hand significant numbers of mounted units was undoubtedly correct.

* * *

---

*But see p. 272. Chronic supply difficulties, which were not, and perhaps could not have been foreseen, would probably have made any far-reaching exploitation impossible.

Preface

As in previous volumes, except rarely and for obvious reasons, only *mounted* actions have been recounted in detail. Further, those of the other arms have been described only cursorily, except where an understanding of the cavalry's part demanded a fuller account.

Equally, the numerous controversial decisions taken at political and top military levels, the intrigues, the battles between 'Westerners' and 'Easterners', the jealousies existing between senior personages, not least among the generals, if mentioned at all, are only lightly touched upon except in those instances where they had a special bearing on the use of cavalry. The operations of the French, often concurrent with those of the British, also receive only passing treatment, unless, again, they particularly illuminate British cavalry actions.

* * *

Much in the way of first-hand evidence is lost, especially at the lower levels of rank, from the activities of the censors, which for the first time in history were comprehensively effectual.

* * *

While the first four volumes made some modest claim to be definitive (in so far as any accounts of human activities in which large numbers are killed and of which the majority of participants fails to give an account can be), the same cannot be asserted for the last four, least of all for this one. The quantity of material is so vast that any possibility of completeness within a reasonable compass, even with respect only to the mounted arm, is quite out of the question. The degree of selectivity which has had to be exercised is prodigious. For example, it has proved impossible even to mention every one of the mounted units of the BEF.

* * *

In Chapter 5 of Volume 7 there appears a considerable amount of information concerning types of officers and men of the BEF, throughout the war on the Western Front, including 1914.

Note. Mons. Christophoros C. Matiatos has kindly pointed out to me that contrary to the footnote on p. 391 of Vol. 4, no regiments of the Austrian cavalry still carried the lance 'up to and well beyond 1914'. He provides convincing 'chapter and verse'.

'War, which used to be cruel and magnificent, has now become cruel and squalid.'
– CHURCHILL in *My Early Life*

'The war was decided in the first twenty days of fighting, and all that happened afterwards consisted in battles which, however formidable and devastating, were but desperate and vain appeals against the decision of fate.'
– CHURCHILL in Foreword to Spears' *Liaison, 1914*

' "No longer like Frederick at the end of the day do we hurl our jingling squadrons upon the tottering foe." No indeed; better not: they might still have one of those machine-guns with them which refuses to totter.'
– IAN HAMILTON in Introduction to Seekt, Hans von *Thoughts of a Soldier*, 1930

'The latest joke on the front is to call the cavalry the M.P. because they sit and do nothing.'
– CAPTAIN COLWYN PHILIPPS, Royal Horse Guards in a letter home, 29 April, 1915

'C for the cavalry who (so I've heard it say)
Have not seen their gee-gees for many a day.
But soon they will mount them and gallop away
And we'll all say goodbye to the trenches.'
– *The Wipers Times*, 5 March, 1917

'There seems to be nothing to look forward to – only trenches. Nothing one has learnt seems to be of any use to one. We can only exercise the horses in half sections along a road, as the men are away digging. Nobody knows how to use us or where. Indeed, cavalry in this sort of war seems to be an anachronism.'
– An officer of the 18th Lancers, July, 1915

'Young officers feel that they are not pulling their weight and want to go where there is more fighting. It is only natural – yet one does not want to lose the best cavalry soldiers we have got.'
– BRIGADIER-GENERAL ARCHIBALD HOME, late in 1915

'It would be quite easy in a short time to fit up a number of steam tractors with small armoured shelters, in which men and machine-guns could be placed. . . . The caterpillar system would enable trenches to be crossed quite easily, and the weight

of the machine would destroy all wire entanglements.'
  – CHURCHILL to Asquith, Jan., 1915, quoted in Fuller, *Cav. Jnl*, 1920

'It was the *only war* ever fought without voice control; which came back in World War II with Walkie-Talkie and without which the modern soldier is as completely lost as we were.'
  – LIEUTENANT-COLONEL C.F. JERRAM, GSO 1, 46th Division, to General Sir Alan Bourne, GSO 1, 8th Division, quoted in Terraine: *WW1*, xi

'That cavalry proved to be an ineffective exploiting arm does not alter the fact that that is what it was. A general who launches what he hopes will be a decisive offensive without an arm of exploitation (as Ludendorff did in 1918) strikes me as criminally culpable. It was in the hope that infantry lives might thereby not be vainly expended that British and French generals brought cavalry up behind their offensive fronts.'
  – JOHN TERRAINE in *The Smoke and the Fire*

'There is a melancholy comfort in reflecting that if the British and French commanders were shortsighted, the ablest soldier in Germany was blind.'
  – CHURCHILL in *The World Crisis, 1916–1918*, Volume 2

Those who still [in the mid-1930s] speak and write of the fruitless slaughter in the west ought to remember that it was in the west that the war was won and that all that tragic slaughter bore its victorious fruit in the end.'
  – DUFF COOPER in *Haig*, Volume 1

'The history of this war will never be written. Those who could write it will remain silent. Those who write it have not experienced it.'
  – BINDIN, Rudolf (German officer) in *A Fatalist at War*

1

> 'They were short of troops and no cavalry were wanted by then, so they dismounted us. It was a terrible come-down. To be turned into infantrymen was like being pole-axed. Of course, we weren't very good at walking at the best of times, never mind in those conditions. We'd just arrived in France and they gave us a couple of weeks' infantry training at the Bull Ring until we were ready for the slaughterhouse. We went up to relieve the Canadians. We'd never seen anything like it. Going up through this area it was just as if an earthquake had been there. It was all mud and I was frightened to death.'
> – TROOPER REG LLOYD, Cheshire Yeomanry
> (attached to 8 Bn, S. Lancs Regt), early 1916[1]

Life in trenches and billets – bus transport – trench improvements – recreations – working parties – leave

At the conclusion of Volume 7 of this work the first battle of Ypres had come to an end and the Indian Cavalry Corps had been formed. The cavalry had already learned what trench warfare involved, for it had taken its share of the manning of the trenches. From these it had been gradually withdrawn so as to form a mobile reserve south-west of Ypres, but only for a short period. At the beginning of 1915 it found itself again sharing trench duties with the infantry.

On 31 January the Cavalry Corps relieved the French for a month in the trenches near Zillebeke, each division doing ten days in turn. In Flanders the fighting was limited throughout the winter to sniping and long-range duels between the rival gunners. The chief enemy was the weather. 'The whole situation,' wrote the 4th Hussars' Commanding Officer, 'is most weird. The landscape just one big shambles; not a soul to be seen because everyone is hiding in a trench.... But law! The filthiness of it all: knee deep in mud and debris of every description – not excluding corpses, which seem to be everywhere.... The trenches are all ditches and half the parapets are falling in.'[2] Early in January the cavalrymen found themselves being transported to the front in London buses, with their windows boarded up and complete with their own drivers and conductors. It took eleven buses to move a regiment and thirty-six to move a brigade. For the first time in its history, instead of moving on horseback, by foot or by train, the cavalry was being carried along by means of internal combustion engines. From this time dates the military term 'to embus'.

At this stage the trenches were still very primitive. The parapets were far from being bullet proof, the traverses*, too, where they existed, were insufficiently thick. There were very few communication trenches which meant that men had to climb over the top to get from one trench to another – a dangerous business which could only be undertaken at night. In spite of an overall acute shortage of sandbags, the 1st Cavalry Brigade alone used over 10,000 of them during its week in the line in February. The brigade also in that time managed to drain their trenches of two feet of water and to 'corduroy' their floors with faggots. Only by continual pumping, day and night, were the trenches made habitable.[3]

These appalling conditions took their toll in a decline in the men's health. Many of the 13th Hussars after only twenty-four hours had 'to be lifted out of the trenches owing to being cramped with standing in the mud and water for so long,' and within a fortnight the 17th Lancers had sixty-five men admitted to hospital with what was at first called frost-bite but later trench feet. In due course this joined the list of military offences. It was caused chiefly by the shrinkage of the men's long woollen pants round the knee and calf and by too tight puttees. Long gumboots did not arrive in numbers until late February. Both cod-liver oil and whale oil were soon issued. Applied to the feet and up to the waist, these certainly helped to keep men warm and effected a marked decrease in trench feet.[4]

The nastiest ingredient in the nasty business of trench warfare was the nightly ration party. It was very hard labour and the men hated it:

'The enormous weights to be carried – heavy ammunition boxes, biscuits, bully beef, beside of course each man's own rifle and ammunition and many other things such as parcels, rum jars, extra entrenching tools, etc. – the darkness and difficulty of keeping touch, the rough ground, pitted with shell holes, the extreme probability of being shelled or sniped or both....

*Parapets thrown across exposed passages, designed to intercept enfilade fire.

A regular trench organization devised for cavalry

Dismounted Cavalryman (on way back from trenches, seeing Officer's servant exercising a horse). 'Well, if anything gives me sore feet it's seein' an 'ighlander ridin' where I've got to pad the 'oof.'

'Throughout the war', says the historian of the Oxfordshire Hussars Yeomanry, 'the men always preferred the front line, where the strain was frequently broken by spells of comparative peace, to the incessant and wearing fatigues of the support and reserve trenches.'[5]

* * *

During First Ypres the strain placed upon cavalry units in the trenches as compared with that experienced by the infantry had been manifest. It was now exacerbated by the increasing shortage of officers and by the fact that by early February there was also a shortage of men. In the Oxfords, for instance, each squadron was short of nearly sixty and could only find fifty-seven or so rifles, 'forty men being required as horse-holders, cooks, shoeing smiths, transport drivers, etc.' Cavalry Corps headquarters devised a regular trench organization to avoid the absurdity of 200 men going into the line with twenty officers where the infantry took only a third of that number for an equivalent number of men. Each brigade now provided a dismounted *battalion*, each regiment finding a dismounted *company*, battalion headquarters being found by each regiment in turn. Later on this system was modified, it being found that it was more convenient to occupy the trenches in the cavalry formations. 'It was soon realised by infantry staffs that a dismounted cavalry brigade was only slightly stronger than an infantry battalion.' Appropriate arrangements were henceforth made. There is some evidence, incidentally, that the officers took a full share in the work of improving the trenches, 'handling pick and spade with their men and helping to fill and carry up sandbags'. The 'infantry-ization' of the mounted arm was proceeding apace! This process, beside requiring a radical change of outlook on cavalrymen's part, presented other difficulties.

'You can see,' wrote home Captain Eve of the 13th Hussars, 'what it is, trying to make us do two jobs at the same time, cavalry and infantry. The men are simply worked off their legs and haven't a minute all day. . . . We do all our cavalry parades, all these infantry ones, route-marches, afternoon parades, fatigues, evening classes, &c., &c., and they complain if the men don't turn out smartly on parade. In spite of all this we are to organise games and let the men train for cross-country runs and so on. Whenever can they possibly have time? And I must help the country people in their farming in my spare time.' (See p. 17).

During the following winter Major Charrington of the 12th Lancers, in describing life at that time, took a more relaxed view:

'The men sleep in little farms and cottages round about, with, of course, the usual night guard over the horse lines. We have early morning stables at 6.30 when we rub the horses down and try and restore a little circulation in the poor brutes after these cold wet nights; so they are well hand-rubbed, and if wet wisped down with straw, then fed; breakfast for all ranks is at 7.30. At 8.20 we go for two hours' exercise or training. . . . At 10.30 the horses are watered, for though they are watered at early morning stables they very seldom drink except after a very hot night; they can think of nothing but the nosebag that awaits them. Then at 11 we have stables till

Mine exploded under the 16th Lancers' trench, 21 February, 1915

I and the horses are given a really good grooming and are watered and fed. Then dinner, after which the men generally are free till 4 or 4.30 when they come and groom and water and feed the horses, finishing about 5.30. Evening meal at about 6. Of course if there has been bad weather or we have been a lot on the march we always seize the afternoons to clean saddlery, arms and kit. And what with bomb-throwing parties, classes for signallers and M.G.'s, fatigues for drawing forage, digging latrines and cleaning up generally, it is not often that we get much rest in the afternoon. . . . The hours all depend on circumstances.'[6]

Almost the greatest pleasure afforded troops coming out of the line was the provision of baths. The men of the 2nd Life Guards enjoyed 'a hot bath in a brewery at least once a month', while the 11th Hussars, in the aptly named *Ecole de Bienfaisance* at Ypres, found it 'a queer experience lying in a hot bath with the deafening noise of shell-bursts echoing down the corridor'.

There occurred on 21 February what the 16th Lancers called 'the worst day of the war'. At 6 a.m. the first large mine of the war was exploded under the front trench occupied by a squadron of the 16th Lancers. Immediately afterwards two more were detonated, completely destroying the trench. The Germans at once followed these up by a strong attack. Confusion and hand-to-hand combat ensued. The three reserve squadrons counter-attacked but failed to regain the lost trench. Eventually the 20th Hussars and some French infantry tried again, but failed to recapture it. No further attempts were made and a new trench was dug in rear of it. The 16th lost five officers killed, one wounded and one (blown into a German trench) made prisoner. Seven other ranks were killed and forty wounded or missing.[7]

By the last half of February immense improvements had been made in many of the trenches. The Oxfords on their second visit to the front found that 'dugouts, traverses, fire-steps, communication trenches, were now universal' and that 'weak points' were 'revetted with timber and the bottom floored with duck boards'. Some of the finest trenches were those occupied by the Northumberland Hussars Yeomanry. The skill of the pitmen who formed a considerable part of the regiment proved invaluable for construction and drainage. By the end of the year a further transformation had taken place. Even the trenches

> 'which had so impressed us a year before,' according to the regimental diary of the Oxfords, 'were primitive when compared with these. Battalion headquarters were in the biggest dugout we had ever seen. You went down about ten steps which brought you to a narrow corridor, leading to a kitchen on the left and to the officers' quarters on the right. . . . Down another flight of twenty steps was the officers' sleeping-room, containing three bunks and a stretcher. The rooms were about the size of the cabins on a good cargo steamer and the kitchen was as big as many kitchens in small private houses. There were two pretty good officers' dugouts, high enough to stand up in and all the men had dugouts also. One of the dugouts actually contained a wicker-work armchair, a luxury very rarely found even in billets. Our trenches were 800 yards behind the front line, with which they were connected by a perfect labyrinth of communication trenches, turning and twisting in all directions, crossed by six other lines. . . . There were signboards at most of the crossroads, but even with their help it was very easy to get lost, especially at night. In fact the whole sector resembled nothing so much as the maze at Hampton Court magnified 100 times, with walls of chalk instead of shrubbery. . . .
>
> 'The trenches were very good, mostly boarded and quite dry. There were no dugouts in the front line, but shelters here and there made of half a dozen stout logs thrown across the trench and covered with plenty of earth and a sofa-shaped seat for two cut out underneath.'[8]

The first home leave started in November, 1914. At first batches of four or five officers and eight men from each squadron went every five days for ninety-six hours. This liberal arrangement did not last long. 'This is the Week-End War with a vengeance,' wrote Captain Philipps of the Blues in optimistic mood. The officers, in those early days, travelled 'in comfort to Boulogne in our own motor-cars, unharassed,' as an officer of the Oxfordshire Hussars put it, 'by officious RTOs [Railway Transport Officers].' In the 5th Dragoon Guards, the men's leave was temporarily cancelled, 'there being cases of overstaying leave'. From the following winter, 1915–1916, leave was generally granted for seven days, sometimes for eight.* As the war wore on all sorts of different arrangements were made, much less generous than in 1915, but officers rarely had less than two leaves a year and other ranks seldom more and sometimes less than one, generally for eight full days at home. In August, 1917, the men of the 5th Dragoon Guards were granted ten whole days. None of them had been on home leave for 'at least eighteen months'. By the winter of 1917 the men who had been in the BEF up to the end of 1915 were granted in principle seven days every six months, while those who had arrived after the Somme were allowed fourteen days after fifteen months, yet by 1 January, 1917, there were some 4,000 of all ranks who were awaiting leave after eighteen months. There were two main reasons for this paucity of home leave: an acute shortage of cross-Channel transport and, especially during the months before the great German Spring Offensive in late March, 1918, the crying need to employ fighting troops for the purpose of constructing strong defensive systems behind the front line – a need much exacerbated by Lloyd George's persistence in holding back at home large numbers of men in an effort to curb Haig's use of them in offensives. (See p. 169)†[9]

* * *

For most of the time the cavalry regiments were in billets. 'We have quite gone back to peace conditions,' wrote an officer of the 12th Lancers early in 1915. 'All bits and steelwork are burnished. The winter training which we are going to do will be very dull for those who have seen the real thing.' Before that training got fully going sports were arranged for the men: football, of course, while the Oxfords played hockey, 'introduced into the regiment about this time [March, 1915]'.[10]

The officers organized some traditional recreations for themselves. The first regiment to play polo in France were the

---

* 'As late as Easter, 1916, leave trains from France were stopped for five days so as not to interfere with holiday traffic.' (Taylor, A.J.P. *English History, 1914–1945*, 1965, 5)

†After the French army mutinies, Pétain had conceded ten days' leave every four months. This involved 350,000 men being away *en permission* at any one time.

FRANCE, 1915
(An Infantryman's libellous idea of how various military branches go to War!)

Oxfords – on troop horses. Enterprising officers in other regiments 'brought back a few couples of harriers and beagles from leave in England and started hunting hares', while the officers of the 17th Lancers found relaxation 'through the medium of some hounds, the property of M. Maillard, whose kennels were in the neighbourhood.... The pack was mixed Artois hounds, English fox hounds, beagles and Basset hounds, about sixty couple in all. But they afforded excellent fun.' The Leicestershire Yeomanry were naturally to the fore where hunting was concerned. 'A pack of foxhounds, four and a half couple, were sent to them from the Quorn, Cottesmore and Lord Harrington's, and the regiment hunted hares and sometimes a drag over the country about Cassel.' In February, 1918,

> 'hares were extraordinarily abundant in the district around Peronne, but in deference to French susceptibilities the use of hounds or dogs of any description, for purposes of sport, had been forbidden very early in the war. Some genius, however, evolved the pastime of coursing hares on horseback. The element of danger was considerable, as the country was very rough, and there were many sunken roads, while the numerous old camping-grounds, naturally a favourite resort of the hares, were covered with every variety of pitfall. The intense fascination of the sport, however, made it more and more popular, and with increasing numbers taking part in it the roll of casualties began to mount up alarmingly. At last, when three brigadiers were hors de combat at one and the same time, it was impossible to keep the secret any longer and the practice was at once forbidden.'

Throughout the war various forms of hunting, mostly illicit, were indulged in. The 12th Lancers, in May, 1916, organized a boar hunt. 'As the kill took place right under the windows of the château which harboured Cavalry Corps HQ, by whom la chasse was forbidden, none of the field of six, which included two masters of fox hounds and two whips of the Pytchley, lingered on the scene.' Horse shows were arranged at all formation levels. On 15 August, 1917, a divisional horse show took place which was, as the historian of the Deccan Horse put it, 'an unique occasion, as never before had there been such a gathering of cavalry regiments drawn from all quarters of the Empire; no fewer than twenty-six

Recreations: horse shows

Programme of 'D' Squadron Oxfordshire Hussars Yeomanry's Horse Show

British, three Canadian, five Yeomanry and eleven Indian regiments being present.' These horse shows sometimes included esoteric races, such as one for 'two-horsed water-carts'. There were foot races too. Private Batchelor of the Oxfordshire Hussars in June, 1917, described some of them: 'competitors had to run fifty yards, drink a mess-tinful of beer, undress, run back and light a cigarette and run back and dress and then run to starting-place. Winner, J. Boyles. Cook's Race. Run fifty yards, light a fire, cook an egg, eat it, and run back to starting-point. Winner, Taylor, fifteen francs and a bottle of whisky.'[11]

12

Recreation: officers' clubs

An officer of the 4th Dragoon Guards found that 'the best method of getting partridges for dinner was to find a covey and gallop them, particularly in the snow, when after about three flights they were exhausted and one could dismount and wring their necks.' Milder amusement was procured through the gramophone. Major Valentine Fleming* of the Oxfords brought one out from England, 'at that time rather a rarity, though afterwards to be found in almost every mess in the British army'. Officers' clubs were set up in the bigger towns. In 1916 the 10th Hussars found the one in Béthune 'excellently managed'. There was also in the town 'an excellent oyster shop in the Square'. In Ypres well into 1915 Fortnum and Mason maintained a shop. 'Everything we want,' wrote an officer of the 18th Hussars, 'seems to be available.' In the Essex Yeomanry 'a military and string band was formed and admirably trained by R.Q.M.S. Joscelyne; it was only after the serious casualties at Monchy [see p. 81], in which engagement many of the band were killed, that it became impossible to keep it going.' When at long last trench warfare came to an end in late 1918, the VI Corps Club, and no doubt others, moved continually forward

> 'at a safe distance from the front line, but not too far back to be out of reach of the fighting troops when in rest. It was a godsend to tired officers. It consisted of a large marquee and one or two smaller ones near by. Comfortable armchairs and a large selection of newspapers were provided; meals were to be had by passing officers, and camp beds by those stranded late at night on their way to or from England; above all, one could get one's hair cut there, cleanly, efficiently and in comfort. It was of course impossible to provide anything on so elaborate a scale for the men, but for them also baths, cinema shows, pierrot troupes and other sources of comfort and amusement travelled permanently in the wake of the Corps. Things,' wrote an Oxfordshire Hussar, 'had changed indeed since 1914.'

---

*Member of Parliament for South Oxfordshire since 1910 and father of Peter and Ian Fleming. He was killed in 1917.

Recreations: concerts and dramatic performances

In 1917 the 5th Lancers were entertained by 'the ladies of the Lena Ashwell Concert Party from Abbeville'.* They gave a concert in the Maintenay village hall, 'which was much appreciated by all ranks'.[12]

The historian of the Bays gives a good description of life behind the lines of a winter's evening:

'The Divisional Supply Column at Arneke, officers and men of the R.A.S.C., made a very welcome and successful contribution to the recreation of all ranks by organising a concert and dramatic company, known as 'Les Choses.' They had some musicians amongst them, including an exceptionally good amateur violinist in the person of their French interpreter. There were two or three who had had the advantage of experience behind the footlights of London variety theatres before the call to arms made them soldiers. One of them proved to be a first-rate stage manager. A large shed at Arneke station was converted into a theatre. The Royal Engineers supplied the electric lighting. An artist, with large tarpaulins for his canvasses, provided very fair scenery. The orchestra started with a troop of mouth-organ performers, but soon developed into something more ambitious, and long before the season at Arneke ended there was an array of violins, wood and brass wind instruments, and drums, directed by a conductor in a dress-suit imported from London!

'The audience came from all parts of the billeting area. Officers arrived in motor-cars, rank and file in lorries. There were gala nights, when the front seats were crowded with officers of all ranks, with a General in the middle of the first row. There would be a good programme, and everything was so well organised that it was strange to realise that the whole show was within hearing of the distant mutter of gun-fire round the Ypres salient. A standing joke in one of the comic interludes was the question: "Is it true there is a war going on?" and the reply, "Well, I have heard rumours of something of the kind".'

---

*Lena Ashwell was an actress and theatre manager of some distinction. She was awarded the OBE for her 'concerts at the front'. She died in 1957 at an unknown age.

'The arts of billeting'

On 25 October, sixty-one years after a famous battle, the 13th Hussars held a 'Balaclava sing-song for the men'. At Christmas, 1915, the Cavalry Benefit Association sent 'cardigan jackets, vests, gloves and plum puddings', while, out of the canteen proceeds, each man received 1 Fr. 50.[13]

* * *

Between November, 1914, and December, 1915, the headquarters of the 17th Lancers occupied thirty different French villages. The same sort of number applied to most other units. The regiment's historian describes well 'the arts of billeting':

'The advanced party, consisting of the second in command of the regiment and of the four squadrons, with an N.C.O. each and an interpreter, went on in advance of the main body. The primary object of the second in command on arrival was to find a château for headquarters, if available. This, or a *pis aller*, having been obtained, a tour round the various areas to be allotted to squadrons was undertaken. Should the area under inspection seem salubrious, with large farms where a troop or more could be put, every effort was made by squadron representatives to "catch the Speaker's eye"; if, on the other hand, only poor accommodation seemed available, it was with difficulty that anyone could be seen on the horizon to whom the area could be allotted. By the time the Regiment had arrived, the squadron areas had been subdivided into troop areas, which were as often as not rearranged by the squadron leader and again surreptitiously changed by the squadron sergeant-major.

'The allotment having been done from the top, complaints forthwith started *de profundis*. The scattered musketry of section commanders, supported by the light artillery of troop leaders, with finally the heavy bombardment of squadron leaders, was lulled to rest by the pacific efforts of the adjutant, a very Solomon, who could gaze on the battle with equanimity from his castle walls. Much practice soon taught every man where to find a suitable "hangar" for the horses and space for saddles, and, in spite of the billet-snatching propensities of every officer and man, order soon reigned where chaos had been.'[14]

Householders were given an allowance of a franc a day for putting up an officer. This inducement and 'the honour of entertaining an officer, thus proving their house of a status above that of a vulgar cottage', usually ensured that rooms for officers were willingly provided. An officer of the 2nd Lancers (Gardner's Horse) reported that it was

> 'always difficult to find rooms for messes and kitchens, as no government allowance was given for them, and the inhabitants found it very inconvenient to have strange servants

In billets

sharing their kitchens and freely borrowing their pots and pans. The regiment had been authorized to buy a two wheeled cart at Orleans as a mess cart. This was a yellow and black hooded cart capable of carrying a good quantity of stores, and invariably forced to carry an excess. It is almost incredible that it lasted for the whole of the regiment's time in France, but its frequent breakdowns furnished a constant source of employment for that most ingenious artificer Armourer Dafadar Bishen Singh.'[15]

* * *

From time to time throughout the war cavalrymen assisted local farmers. Volunteers of the Oxfords helped to gather in the harvest of 1915. 'They felt very much at home!' In May, 1917, the cavalry cut and stacked '150 tons of good hay'. The following January at a time when the effects of the German submarine offensive were being painfully felt, regiments 'found time between training, working parties and looking after the horses' to plough up several hundred acres and sow them with wheat and oats and to prepare land for potato growing. But it was the Germans who, after their great offensives in the spring of that year, reaped *that* harvest.[16]

Increasingly the authorities came to use the cavalry for every odd job that there was no one else to undertake. The resulting working parties were often far from pleasant. Trench-digging parties were peculiarly repulsive since 'they were generally on ground that had already been fought over, and dead bodies in varying stages of putrefaction', as the 5th Dragoon Guards found, 'were lying about all over the place.' In July, 1915, the 12th Lancers took part in building 'defensive works around La Clytte which after a trifling set back when one redoubt was found facing the wrong way were so well done that Plumer [see p. 99] ordered them to be known as "the 12th Lancer works".' That same month Brigadier-General Frank ('Scrubbs') Wormald, who as a major in the regiment had led a famous forced march during the Boer War (see Vol. 4, p. 257), was killed by a shell while commanding a divisional working party. 'If they will send up brigadiers to superintend 800 men burying dead,' wrote an officer bitterly, 'what do they expect?' After the 1916 battle of the Somme (see p. 36) 'working parties,' wrote an officer of the 3rd Hussars, 'were our fate through October on that battle-field. Here are a few of them: an ammunition dump devoid of great interest at Windy Docks one day took 2 officers and 47 men; upon another day the same dump at the same heaven-inspired spot took a similar party; yet another day that dump claimed 4 officers and 154 men. One night a cable was to be buried for the XIV Corps at what had once been the village of Guillemont and 6 officers and 186 men went to bury it; but someone had forgotten the promised tools – some men were wounded, and the party returned in the early hours of the morning. A couple of nights later 2 officers and 101 men again journeyed forth to bury that cable, the tools were there this time, and the cable planted with the loss of some more wounded men. Trônes wood, too, had a dump which asked for 4 officers and 150 men, who rode forth one night only to find that they were not required; but they built a section of a light railway instead, and the mud pulled the shoes off their horses on the return journey. Another party sallied forth to help "J" Battery dig their guns in near Flers. And so on, and so on, the dismounted parties taking a steady toll in wounded.'

In November, 1916, the cavalry was ordered to form pioneer battalions. These were originally intended for work in the line or close behind it in order to supply fresh experience of trench conditions, but before long most of them came under the Director-General of Railway Construction. 'Nothing,' wrote an officer of the 11th Hussars, 'could have been devised to damp the spirit of cavalrymen more than to use them as labour battalions on work about which there was no danger.' These battalions were made up of eight officers and 260 men from each regiment. In January and February, 1917, their chief task – 'slaving as coolies' – was the doubling of the railway between St Pol and Arras for the great offensives of that year. They were also employed extensively on road-making. The 7th Dragoon Guards ('The Black Horse'), for instance, 'sweated on a new supply road near Montauban' which they of course christened the *Chemin des Chevaux Noirs*.[17]

2

'The difficulty came, not with the initial break [-in] – provided preparations had been good – but with exploitation of it. The defenders' reserves would arrive by rail and road; the attackers would be moving up through mud, pitted with shell-holes and their every movement could be painful. Hence, the defender would have time to construct a new line, and the process would have to begin again.... The defenders' reserves were the key to the problem.'
– NORMAN STONE on the British and French offensives in 1915

'The cavalry will I fear do no good when they do get through for they are certain to be held up by wire and trenches in whatever direction they may attempt to go.'
– RAWLINSON to Wigram, 25 March, 1915

'If we had not tried to do too much our losses would have been one quarter what they were and we should have gained just as much ground but the idea of pushing through the cavalry which has seized hold of our leaders, all cavalry officers, was the origin of our heavy losses.
– RAWLINSON to Kitchener, after the battle of Neuve Chapelle

'We made our first acquaintance with the poisonous fume shells!! Although what one hears is rather exaggerated they are not nice. They smell a sort of mixture of ether, chloroform and turpentine. Your eyes, nose and mouth smart and you weep and splutter and feel rather as if you had dipped your face in turpentine and had a mouthful.'
– CAPTAIN J.A.T. PRICE, 5th Lancers on 25 April, 1915[1]

Neuve Chapelle – 2nd Ypres

During the whole of 1915 the cavalry was virtually never employed in action other than as infantry or pioneers, though there were occasional opportunities for mounted patrols. In the course of the year's three large-scale Allied offensives of Neuve Chapelle, Festubert and Loos, it had to look on impotently, for nothing approaching an exploitable breakthrough was ever achieved. On 11 April, 1915, Haig wrote in his diary: 'Allenby and Howell (A's Chief Staff Officer) of Cavalry Corps seem very despondent regarding the possibilities of cavalry action in the future. MacAndrew [see p. 50] thinks that if these two had their way, cavalry would cease to exist as such. In their opinion, the war will continue and end in "trenches". I told them that we cannot hope to reap the fruits of victory without a large force of mounted troops.' Commenting in his diary on 14 March upon the battle of Neuve Chapelle, which had started four days previously,* Rawlinson, commanding IV Corps, thought that Haig, commanding First Army and in charge of operations, 'looked for too much. He expects to get the cavalry through with the next push, but I very much doubt whether he will succeed in doing more than kill a large number of gallant men without effecting any very great triumph. I should be content with capturing another piece out of the enemy's line of trenches and waiting for the counter attack. I am not a believer in the cavalry raid, which even if it comes off will not effect very much.'

After the battle Rawlinson wrote that he believed Haig 'would have been better advised to content himself with the capture of the village [of Neuve Chapelle] instead of going on with the attack on 11th, 12th and 13th [March] for the purpose of trying to get the cavalry through. I advised him to do this in the first instance but he and Sir John were so obsessed with the cavalry idea that he would not listen. Had he been content with the village we should have gained just as much ground and reduced our casualties by three-quarters.' To the King's Assistant Private Secretary, Rawlinson wrote on 22 April that the cavalry even if it had got through would not 'have been able to effect much and would have suffered very heavily'.[2]†

Haig had asked for Hubert Gough (see Vol. 7, p. 20) to be

---

*In the three first days as much ammunition was fired as in the whole of the South African War.

†There is evidence from his own diary written up on the first three days of the battle that Rawlinson was initially just as enthusiastic about going beyond Neuve Chapelle to the Aubers Ridge as was Haig. Indeed he blamed one of his divisional generals for his 'failure to press on in the early stages of the attack' and tried to get him sacked. The full story, unedifying to Rawlinson, is well told in Prior and Wilson, 70–73.

attached to his staff during the operations 'so as to be able to take advantage of any suitable situation which may arise'.[3] French, two days before the battle commenced, 'cautioned Rimington against risking his troops mounted too close to the enemy. He is not experienced,' he wrote in his diary, 'in this kind of warfare and thinks he may be able to do some dashing cavalry work.' This perhaps indicates that French was not as optimistic as was Haig about the possibility of a breakthrough. Both men soon learned the lesson of Neuve Chapelle: the intense difficulty of converting a break *in*, meaning that nothing living would be left on a given stretch of the enemy's line, (which was in fact almost achieved on the first day of the battle) into a break *through*. In planning for the battle Haig had insisted on 'an operation of considerable magnitude'. He did not want 'to capture a trench here or a trench there'. Indeed he hoped to 'carry [the enemy] right off his legs' and to use the cavalry to 'exploit the success thus gained'. It took longer for him to realize that this was never likely to happen than it did for Rawlinson to do so.[4] In fact, the Germans were very thin on the ground at Neuve Chapelle and a certain measure of surprise was achieved there by the British. The whole concept of surprise was from now until 20 November, 1917, to lie in abeyance. On that date at Cambrai something near to complete surprise was consummated, yet still no real breakthrough proved possible. (See p. 111).

* * *

When on 22 April, 1915, the enemy made a serious attempt to capture Ypres, there started what is known as Second Ypres, the 'most dolorous and unsatisfactory', as Wavell has put it,[5] of the three battles of that name (1914, 1915, 1917 (Passchendaele)). It lasted, on and off, till 14 May. In its early stages the Germans employed poison gas for the first time in warfare. Its use did not have the devastating effect that it might have done had they waited to employ it until more lethal forms had become available.* The cavalry were not directly affected. The first that was heard of it was an 'appreciation of the situation', typewritten on a piece of

---

*In March Haig recorded that 'Lord Dundonald [see Vol. 4, p. 71 *et seq.*] arrived.... He is studying the conditions of war in the hopes of being able to apply to modern conditions an invention of his grandfather for driving a garrison out of a fort by using sulphur fumes. I asked him how he arranged to have a favourable wind.' (Terraine, 65)

The first use of poison gas: primitive gas masks

paper which was passed round. It said, 'The Germans attacked at dawn, using asphyxiating gas and broke the line for several miles round Langemarck. The situation does not appear in any way critical.'! There were many conjectures as to 'how the gas had been employed – pipes, tunnelling, etc., being among the suggestions – a gas cloud was not guessed at.' The earliest gas masks consisted of 'some cotton wool attached to white gauze on which one was supposed,' wrote Captain Adrian Carton de Wiart of the 4th Dragoon Guards, 'to urinate and then tie over the nose.' They 'resembled nothing so much as what we older folk would remember,' wrote another officer of the regiment 'was the fashion among ladies in the latter part of the last century, called a dress improver.' The next type of mask involved 'mufflers with both edges turned over and 2½ inches cotton waste stitched lightly inside: to be soaked before use.' The first efficient box respirators were not issued until well into 1916, but by May, 1915, every man possessed 'a mask soaked in hyposulphide of soda', while in August gas helmets first appeared. 'These were merely hoods impregnated with chemicals which irritated the skin and fitted with talc eye-pieces which were apt to cloud over, making observation and shooting difficult.' It was not long before horses were also given gas masks (see illustration no. 7). These were issued on a basis of 33% of a unit's animal strength. They proved useless, as they were not proof against mustard gas – only against the rarely employed chlorine gas. Further by the time that the man, who of course took priority, had fitted his mask 'it was too late to protect the horse'. Consequently horse masks were soon abandoned.[6]*

* * *

*Between July, 1916, and the war's end 211 horses had died from gas poisoning and 2,220 had been wounded from the same cause. (Clabby, 17). The German cavalry also devised a horse gas mask.

An anonymous cavalry officer, writing in the *Cavalry Journal* in early 1938, wondered 'what progress has been made in gas protection for the horse. It may well be,' he continued, 'that gas and not the tank will render the horse out of date in modern war. It is believed, however, that a horse gas mask has been produced and means of dressing the feet have proved satisfactory. There still remains the problem of spraying mustard gas on the horses' skins.' (Anon 'Oil and Oats', *Cav. Jnl*, Jan., 1938)

Second Ypres: 13 May, 1915

Like every battle until the great German offensives of March, 1918, Second Ypres provided virtually no opportunity for anything approaching major mounted action. On 13 May, a day of tempestuous weather, those cavalry regiments which were in the line, including some that only the previous night had taken over a stretch of trenches, were subjected to a fourteen-hour bombardment of unprecedented ferocity: 'At 4 a.m.,' wrote Sergeant Brunton of the 19th Hussars, 'the Germans started their usual "Hymn of Hate" which finished up in an inferno. Our trenches were blown in some parts to atoms.' The succeeding attack drove them from these trenches. The three brigades of the 3rd Cavalry Division on that single day of fighting lost ninety-one officers and 1,500 men.* These casualties were nearly as heavy in proportion as those of either of the infantry divisions which fought alongside them, and these had been in the line for a week. The 1st Cavalry Division, not taking the full brunt of the attack, lost fewer – fifty-four officers and 650 men.†

* * *

Those regiments which were not taking their turn in the trenches showed what it meant to be a mobile reserve. They were

---

*The Leicesters (7th Cavalry Brigade), out of 281 of all ranks, lost ninety killed and ninety-three wounded. (Codrington, Col G.R. *An Outline of the History of the Leicestershire Yeomanry*, 1928, 31–2). The casualty lists for the other five regiments of the division were, whilst not quite so great, of much the same order.

The total casualties of the 1st, 2nd and 3rd Cavalry Divisions between 22 April and 31 May were 3,065. Of these fifty-two officers were killed and 126 wounded.

†Conan Doyle thought that 13 May showed that

> 'the blue blood of the land was not yet losing its iron. The casualty list in this and the succeeding action of the 24th [Festubert] read like a society function. Colonel Ferguson of the Blues, Colonel the Hon. Evans-Freke, Lord Chesham, Captain the Hon. J. Grenfell, Lord Leveson-Gower, Sir Robert Sutton, Lord Compton, Major the Hon. C.B. Mitford, the Hon. C.E.A. Phillips, Viscount Wendover – so runs the sombre and yet glorious list. The sternest of Radicals may well admit that the aristocrats of Britain have counted their lives cheap when the enemy was at the gate.' (Conan Doyle, *The British Campaign in France and Flanders, 1915*, 1917, 102).

Second Ypres: cavalry 'doing fire brigade'

constantly on the move throughout the battle, marching and countermarching, often leaving their horses to go into the line when a dangerous gap appeared and as speedily getting back to them so as to answer the call of some hard-pressed infantry commander elsewhere. The process was known as 'doing fire brigade'.[7] It demonstrated that soldiers on horseback still had their uses. There were other occasions, though not a large number, during the rest of the war when the cavalry acting as infantry covered themselves with equal glory and suffered almost as many casualties. From now forwards they will not be mentioned or will be only lightly touched upon since they were dismounted actions. On this account their importance as showing that the cavalryman was at least as able to cope with the hideous problems of trench warfare as was the infantryman, should not be under-estimated.

3

'"Wully" [Robertson, CIGS] gave me his views on the use of cavalry during an advance.... [He] evidently feared we might lack push after all our trench work. As he put it, it was a good opportunity "to comb out our brains".'
– BRIGADIER-GENERAL ARCHIBALD HOME, newly appointed BGS, Cavalry Corps, 15 September, 1915

'Loos showed very plainly what we were "up against".'
– SIR FRANK COX in *G.H.Q.*

'A mysterious operation described as "going through the gap" was sometimes mentioned, generally in a spirit of rather incredulous levity.'
– An officer of the Oxfordshire Hussars in 1915

'One would not mind waiting in the least, if only one could feel sure that there would be a good fat piece of work at the end of the wait. But what I feel about it is that we shall wait *years* and then (possibly) get a thin piece of work.'
– An officer of the 1st Dragoons, 1915

'On balance, 1916 had been a successful year for the Allies, though that did not mean that victory was in sight.'
– KEITH ROBBINS in *The First World War*[1]

Loos – Dismounted Division formed from Cavalry Corps – Haig succeeds French – Robertson appointed CIGS – Churchill's resignation

In the late summer of 1915 Kitchener stated that eleven 'new army' infantry divisions had been sent to France. This enabled the BEF on 15 September to take over seventeen miles of the French trenches. This was ten days before there opened on the 25th the great Anglo-French offensive, known as the battles of Loos and of Champagne. The British would have much preferred to remain on the defensive. The need to build up the BEF's strength, especially in shells, of which the acute shortage earlier in the year was not

The battle of Loos, September to November, 1915

yet fully made good, ought to have been paramount, so that a really massive stroke could be delivered in 1916. Unfortunately the combination of recent setbacks on the Russian front and overwhelming pressure from the French forced a premature commitment of the British troops. 'Not even in the matter of locale,' as John Terraine has observed, 'was the British Commander in Chief able to assert his views. Joffre insisted that the British attack side by side with the French, through the ruined mining villages and slag heaps of Loos and Lens, instead of further north, as both French and Haig preferred.' Keith Robbins sums up the resulting battle thus: 'Thrust and counter-thrust in a conventional manner continued until early November when the line stabilized. The British had advanced about two miles.'[2]*

The arrangements made by Haig for the cavalry should a breakthrough occur marked a step forward in cavalry doctrine. One brigade, the 7th of the 3rd Cavalry Division, was split up into detachments which were allotted to the infantry divisions. These supplemented the yeomanry squadrons which in April had replaced the 15th and 19th Hussar squadrons as divisional cavalry. These two regiments which, as has been stated, provided the first six infantry divisions' cavalry had been withdrawn in April to form, together with the 8th Hussars, the 9th Cavalry Brigade. Once the enemy's second line had been broken, these regular and yeomanry troops were to be employed with their machine guns and cyclists to fight their way forward in the wake of the infantry, rather than wait for a perfect gap.[3] This to a degree they did, incurring heavy casualties to little purpose.

The 1st and 2nd Cavalry Divisions and the two remaining brigades of the 3rd were ordered 'to prepare for alternative roles, according as the breakthrough occurred first opposite the French attack or the British'. Cavalry tracks (see p. 42) across the rear line of trenches, consisting of bridges and specially sign-posted, were carefully prepared. The Indian Cavalry Corps was to be ready to support either the British or the French cavalry as might be decided. Initially, as one officer wrote in his diary, 'everyone was

---

*There were unfortunate moments during the counter-attacks. One of these was 'a very trying experience' for the Royals. They witnessed a disorderly retreat by the infantry from enemy machine guns. 'It was a most pitiful and appalling sight: the officers in great many cases seeming as frightened as the men.' (Royals, 125–7)

very optimistic about the "push"; our [8th Cavalry Brigade] brigade-major told us "it was all worked out from A to Z" [a gross exaggeration!] and we were told wonderful things about the new gas which was to be used against the Germans (see below). One young officer actually threw away his maps of the back area, as he was quite certain we should only be going forward in future.'

An officer in the 2nd Dragoon Guards reported on the second day of the battle:

> 'Here we are waiting in a "position of readiness" to go through the "gap". The horses are pegged down in mass on a sloping field.... The men are living and sleeping in among the horses. On these occasions they manage to make themselves quite comfortable. They put their saddles up on end to form a sort of head rest, and at night sleep on waterproof sheets, covered with their blankets, which are carried under the saddle with the horse blankets when on the move. As long as the weather is fine they are all right if it is not too cold, but in cold, wet weather it is far from pleasant.
>
> 'We did not move from here all day. All officers of the regiment crowded into an estaminet for meals.'

Later on an officer in the 7th Dragoon Guards found it 'difficult to understand why we were kept "standing to" constantly at short notice, sometimes with the horses saddled up all night, when the scene of the action was thirty-five miles away as the crow flies, and we were twenty-two miles from the nearest point of our front line.'* Though later in the battle the cavalry was brought up to take part in it dismounted,† on the first day two mounted patrols of the Northumberlands 'went out', according to the regiment's historian, 'to find a gap.... As they were within about fifty yards

---

*Nevertheless, on 25 September, it seems, according to Cruttwell (167), a reliable authority, that the cavalry was moved much closer to the front: 'Though the cavalry had been massed in villages so close behind the front as to be visible to the enemy, whose *communiqué* derided this futile parade, not an infantry reserve was available throughout the day.'

†The distinguished and useful part played by the 3rd Cavalry Division, dismounted, (less the 7th Brigade), is well recounted in Preston: 'Loos'. The division's losses amounted to 151, including twenty-seven killed.

of the Boche front line, most of their horses were killed and one man. Although they failed to find "the gap" they at least brought back a clear report of the situation, which was badly wanted.'[4]

An officer of the 1st Dragoons in the 3rd Brigade summed up the feelings of the cavalry: 'It was rather disappointing to start for the G in *Gap* [see p. xix] and end up by being the sort of last buffer against the enemy.' When the battle, in which incidentally the British used 'chlorine gas clouds' for the first time, was over, 2,000 men of the Cavalry Corps were sent to clear up the battlefield 'and put the German trenches into a state of defence. It is a beastly job,' as Home wrote in his diary, ' – especially that of clearing the battlefield as there are many unburied dead lying about. But of course one must do all one can to help.'[5]

* * *

In late October, 1915, GHQ began making out establishments for a Dismounted Division to be formed from the Cavalry Corps. It came into being in December. Each division provided a brigade of three battalions, one from each brigade. Every battalion was

Sergeant (to recruit wandering about at the will of his horse), "'Ere, you! What are you doin' there, ridin' up an' down like a general?'

made up of three companies, one from each regiment. Home supposed that 'England threatens to have the cavalry home and we have to show that we are doing something'. Numbering about 8,200 bayonets, the division went into the line on 30 December, 1915. When it came out of the trenches after seven weeks, it had suffered nearly 1,000 casualties. Home believed that 'the officers and men feel that they have done their share and there is not that restless feeling in the Corps. We are all busy training now in real cavalry work in the hope that if the day comes we may be ready.'6

* * *

On 15 December French was relieved of his command and Haig appointed in his place. Captain Eve of the 13th Hussars (See Vol. 6, p. 87) thought it would 'make little or no difference. He is one of French's men and both are first-class.'7 Except in the same sense that both men were cavalrymen and that they had served in South Africa together, Eve was wrong in thinking that Haig had ever been 'one of French's men'. Certainly ten months later he could not have been described as such. Haig wrote in his diary on 10 October, 1916: 'I would not receive Viscount French in my house. I despise him too much personally for that.'8 He was widely, and by no one more than Haig, blamed for delaying until too late the ordering up of the reserves at Loos. It seems that Kitchener too, after Loos, and perhaps long before that battle, was disillusioned with French. Further, as Roy Jenkins has put it, 'Few of those whose opinion counted were much in doubt that the time had come for French to go. The King thought so; Lloyd George thought so; Bonar Law thought so.'9*

There can be little doubt that French, never perhaps of the temperament necessary for large-scale modern war, was at sixty-four

---

*He might have added that Robertson, his Chief of Staff since January, had also lost confidence in him. On 23 June he wrote to the King's Private Secretary:

'He has never really, sincerely and honestly concerted with the French; while they regard him as by no means a man of ability or a faithful friend, and therefore they did not confide in him. Joffre and he have never yet been a mile within the heart of each other. Further he has never fully laid his opinions before the Government. He has too much taken the stand of doing as he wishes and telling the Government nothing.' (Royal Archives, Q.832, 276, quoted in Nicolson, 266). (*continued over*)

pretty well worn out.* Nevertheless, confronted as he was by problems of a complexity and scale hitherto unknown to military man, he did not do too badly. Compared with von Moltke, he comes out of the furnace as the slightly better general. He now, reluctantly, took the post of Commander-in-Chief of the Home Forces. In 1922 he was promoted from Viscount to Earl of Ypres, having been Lord-Lieutenant of Ireland during the unsatisfactory years 1918–21.

Haig, being some ten years younger, a great deal tougher and a far more 'modern', scientific soldier, appeared at the time, and later proved, that he was the finest soldier available, with the possible exception of Rawlinson. No serious historian now doubts that, with all his faults, Haig was largely responsible for the final victory. He compares not unfavourably with the majority of the senior generals produced by the Germans especially Ludendorff. He got on well, on the whole, with Joffre, Pétain and Foch. On 1 January he recorded in his diary that he had shown the French liaison officer the instructions which he had received from the Secretary of State for War. He pointed out that he was '*not under General Joffre's orders, but that would make no difference*'. His intention, he added, was to do his '*utmost to carry out General Joffre's wishes on strategical matters, as if they were orders*'. Still, a fortnight later, he confided to his diary that there was no doubt in his mind 'but that the war must be won by the Forces of the British Empire'.[10] His relations with 'the frocks' were notoriously bad, but by, for the most part, getting the better of Lloyd George,

---

Typical of his feelings for his allies is a letter he wrote to Kitchener in which he said: '*Au fond*, [the French officers] are a low lot, and one always has to remember the class these French generals mostly come from.' (15 Nov., 1914, Holmes, 202)

He was an insufferable snob. Of that there is abundant evidence. For example, of 'Wully' Robertson, who had risen from the ranks (see Vol. 3, 55) and was arguably one of the most efficient generals in the army of his time, he sneered that there were 'half a dozen corporals in Chelsea barracks who could do as well'. (Farrar-Hockley, 194). (But see p. 32)

---

*He seems to have had a heart attack in early November, 1914, and his health had certainly become doubtful a year later. (21 Nov., 1914 Haig: diary; Blake: *Haig*, 111; Esher, M.V. *Journals and Letters of Reginald, Viscount Esher*, III, 1938, 287–8)

he served his country well. Though it might be said that French was near to being the typical British cavalry general (and his career as illustrated in the earlier volumes of this history may help the reader to form a view on the matter), it is certain that Haig, (who on 27 December, 1916, was promoted to the rank of field marshal), was not.*

---

*A junior staff officer at GHQ 'fell immediately under the spell of [Haig's] personal magnetism.... With him I felt such a longing to gain a word of praise from him that I would have liked him to ask me to do some impossible exploit that I might prove my devotion to him.... He exhales such an atmosphere of honour, virtue, courage and sympathy that one feels uplifted like as when one enters the Cathedral of Beauvais for the first time.' (Lytton, N. *The Press and the General Staff*, 1920, quoted in De Groot, 237)

Young Furse of King Edward's Horse, when Haig rode unexpectedly into the lines, wrote, 'I shall never forget his warm smile as he leaned down from his horse and shook my hand.' Asking for the commanding officer, the Commander-in-Chief said, '"Is Dick here?" Just the name, as of an old acquaintance, without any "Major"; that was so characteristic of a born leader. Dick came up soon and Haig rode round our lines and chatted. "I'm glad you've got nice small horses, they do better out here." Then he was gone. We never saw him again – nor did I ever hear a fighting soldier say one word against him.' (June, 1915, Furse)

General Archibald Murray (see p. Vol. 5, p. 8, *passim*), a minnow by comparison, found Haig 'a man of mediocre ability, slow to absorb, tenacious of what he had learnt; not a very pleasant man to deal with, though he tried to be pleasant'. (Travers, T. *The Killing Ground...* 1987, 101) Of more interest is Chetwode's view imparted to Liddell Hart in 1937: 'I always regarded Haig as a very stupid man.' (LHC, Liddell Hart Papers 11/1937, 45). This may well have been the reaction of one who did not know him well, indeed Haig's well known awkwardness in speech (but not in writing) must often have struck those with the gift of the gab as denoting stupidity.

Major-General Guy Payan Dawnay (see Vol. 5, 125, 225) wrote a moving poem on Haig's death. It well sums up much post-war feeling about the man:

'Our country laid her burden upon you;
   Which bearing set you in high solitude,
   Whence the clear flame of your stark fortitude
Burned as a rallying beacon in our view.
A mighty burden – the colossal sum
   Of all our myriad smaller tasks, pains, fears;
   You bore the ultimate weight through those grim years,
Inflexible until the hour should come.
Unmoved by murmurings of pettier men,
   Of heart less single and of faith less firm;
You gave to comrades' service voice and pen,
   Careless your own achievement to confirm.
Set we a Brazier, symbol of your fame,
In iron Courage Faith's unwavering flame.'
(*Army Quarterly*, XVI, Apr., 1928)

It has been asserted that Asquith, who in Kitchener's absence at Gallipoli had temporarily taken over the War Office, told French that he was needed at home to advise against Kitchener.[11] Certainly there was a general feeling that the war had become too vast for Kitchener to continue as army supremo with only the vestige of a staff. On his return from the Dardanelles, confronted by Asquith, he reluctantly accepted Robertson (whom French, incidentally, had recommended as his successor) as CIGS with such extensive powers as to make Kitchener from now onwards, (until he met his watery death on 5 June from a German mine on his way to Russia at the Czar's invitation), not much more than 'the symbol of the nation's will to victory'.[12]

* * *

'Everyone discussing Winston Churchill's resignation,' noted Home writing up his diary at Cavalry Corps headquarters on 13 November. 'We got a wire asking if he could come back to the Oxfordshire Hussars, of which he is second in command.' Some twenty days later Prince Arthur of Connaught went in to see French 'and found Winston Churchill as aide-de-camp on duty!! It is rather funny,' thought Home. 'He will end by commanding the British Army!'[13]*

---

*Churchill's resignation from the Admiralty was a condition for Bonar Law's Opposition joining the coalition which Asquith seized the opportunity to form after Fisher's resignation in May. From his 'well-paid inactivity' as Chancellor of the Duchy of Lancaster he soon resigned, crossing to France on 18 November. In January, 1916, he assumed command of the 6th Battalion, Royal Scots Fusiliers. Four months later he returned to England. It was not until 17 July, 1917, that he resumed office, becoming Minister of Munitions under Lloyd George.

4

'The action of mounted troops under existing trench warfare conditions follows on the actions of infantry and artillery, who must first effect a breach in the enemy's outer system of defence. This breach will at first be narrow in comparison to the great extent of the enemy's front, and in making it we attain only to a local success. But having attained that success we must at once endeavour to exploit it without a moment's delay and to the utmost of our resources.'
— HAIG to his Army commanders, March, 1916

'So once more the mounted troops confidently expected the ride through a "gap" in the enemy lines. The force available for this was the largest army of horsemen that had been seen in European war for more than a hundred years. Between Amiens and the long lines of our batteries the country was full of billets, camps and bivouacs of the cavalry,'
— The historian of the 2nd Dragoon Guards

'My strongest recollection: all those grand-looking cavalrymen, ready mounted to follow the breakthrough. What a hope.'
— PRIVATE E.T. RADBAND, an infantryman

'[The Battle of the Somme's] four and a half months constituted undeniably the most destructive experience hitherto inflicted by human beings on each other.'
— JOHN TERRAINE in *The Road to Passchendaele*

'1.30 p.m. The cavalry found the ground so slippery from the wet that they could not get along, so did not go through the line. . . .

'10.30 p.m. Our mounted men have been seen chasing Bosches with spears. I hope this is true.'
— RAWLINSON in his diary, 14 July, 1916

'On 14 July a dawn attack towards Bazentin-le-Grand led to a local success and the world was eagerly informed that a squadron of the 7th Dragoon Guards had actually ridden on their horses as far as High Wood, whence they were withdrawn the next day.'
— CHURCHILL in *The World Crisis, 1916–1918*

'It was [the Prime Minister's] intention ... to raise the question of whether we need these cavalry in France. Was there ... the slightest chance that the cavalry could be used for a breakthrough? He was told that on the Eastern Front, where cavalry had several times gone through, they had invariably been roughly handled and driven back often badly shattered by a few machine-guns.'
– The War Committee Minutes, 6 November, 1916

'Officers and men are both fed up. We have been expecting to go through "the gap" so many times and have been so often disappointed that we have lost interest for the present.'
– CAPTAIN 'ARCHIE' WRIGHT's diary, September, 1916[1]

Introduction of steel helmets – Verdun – Hindenburg replaces Falkenhayn – reduction of cavalry proposed – arrangements for cavalry in 1916 campaigns – cavalry tracks – battle of the Somme – Bazentin Ridge – Flers Courcelette – tanks – Morval

Manganese steel (sometimes called shrapnel) helmets – coloquially known as 'tin hats' – were first issued in early 1916.* In the Indian cavalry

'the Sikhs, owing to their religious scruples, were allowed to retain the lungi. The Pathans applied, through their Risaldars for the same concession, which, however,' according to the historian of the Central India Horse, 'was not granted since, unlike the Sikhs, they had no real scruple of any sort. They simply considered the new helmets to be ugly. After being made to wear them as long as they were in the trenches they seem to have changed their minds concerning their aesthetic value. Before long they took to wearing them on all occasions, and nearly every man in the squadron had his photograph taken in his smart new head-dress.'[2]

---

*The French steel helmet preceded the British design by a year. The latter weighed 2 lbs and was said to be proof against shrapnel at 750 ft per second. The first million had been manufactured by July, 1916.

Steel helmets

'The appearance of these helmets,' says the Greys' historian,

'was not such as to predispose the British, as opposed to Indian troops to receive them with favour, and they were also heavy and uncomfortable to wear, being made only in three sizes and depending principally on the chin strap for their precarious balance on the head. As every mounted man knows, the proper control of one's horse is, for some inscrutable reason, very much affected by the proper sitting of one's head-gear, and in one cavalry regiment the commanding officer was so appalled at their appearance and the difficulty of fitting them to the head, that it was not till he had tested the real utility of them by setting his own up on a stick and having six shots at it with his revolver, that he could bring

A Private of the 3rd Hussars in the Great War
From a sketch by Captain Adrian Jones, MVO

himself to order his men to wear them. In the case of the Greys, however, they were at once received into favour, and for rather a curious reason. A certain number of them had been issued at Vermelles to the dismounted battalion as trench stores. Naturally Private McConnachie had to try one on at once and his comrades were still laughing at his antics, when a piece of anti-aircraft shell fell full on the helmet. Everyone was horrified, but the helmet remained undented and Private McConnachie, except for a slight headache, was not a ha'porth the worse. This incident effected more, in the way of propaganda in the helmet's favour, than could have been done by twenty lectures with diagrams. The Greys painted on theirs the yellow St Andrew's cross which was the badge they wore on their khaki helmets in South Africa, where a distinctive badge had been found very useful for identifying detachments of the Regiment. Later on they further improved on the idea, having red for regimental headquarters, yellow for "A" squadron, dark blue for "B" squadron, and light blue with a circle round the centre for "C".[3]

* * *

The first battle of the Somme which opened with the horrors of the infamous 1 July, 1916, lasted for four and a half months, involved some 3,000,000 men of whom nearly a third became casualties, including over 400,000 British, and achieved at its deepest an eight-mile advance. In the course of it Haig's army gained its first major, post-1914 victory over the Germans and carried forward (at vast cost), the process of grinding-down which ultimately helped to bring about Germany's collapse.

A result of the battle was the fall of von Falkenhayn after his other failure at Verdun and his replacement as Chief of the General Staff by von Hindenburg. In a sense it was a continuation of the great French battle of Verdun which had started on 21 February and which had an even greater psychological impact on the French nation than the Somme had on the British. 'British confidence,' as Keith Robbins justly observes, 'rested in the anticipated effectiveness of the preliminary bombardment. It would range over a wide front rather than concentrate on specific strong points. Some three-quarters of a million men were assembled – roughly seven British to one French – ready to clear a gap through which cavalry divisions would gallop to untold excitements in the interior.' The 57,000 British casualties on that first day proved that a whole week of unprecedented artillery barrage had utterly failed to smash the elaborate German defences. Further, by the end of that day it is clear with hindsight that the cavalry's 'untold excitements' were once again, except for a single very minor one (see below), to be denied it.[4]

For Haig, especially, this was disappointing. He was anxious, by showing London that mounted troops had been employed to some purpose in the great battle, to prove that they were still an essential part of his armies. On 9 January he had deprecated the closing of recruiting for the cavalry and had pressed Robertson to re-open it. In May, 1916, heavy pressure had been put on Robertson by the War Committee in Downing Street to find ways and means of reducing the cavalry in France. The King, too, asked Haig whether he could not cut the arm down. To this royal plea Haig replied that the mobility of the cavalry was essential 'to shorten the war and reap the fruits of any success'. He admitted to Robertson, who, like the War Committee, was worried about the increasing shipping losses from submarines and mines, that if 'we can't effect economy then some must go, but,' he added, 'I have an inward feeling that events will make us regret the reduction in mounted troops. It seems to me that troops and material are so embedded in the ground in trench warfare that a general retreat will be most difficult. We ought therefore to be prepared to exploit a success on the lines of 1806.' This was a reference to the pursuit by Murat after the battle of Jena.[5]*

One of the sillier proposals made by the War Committee came

---

*In May, 1916, GHQ sent out a letter, from which the following is an extract:-

'In consequence of the growth of the Army and the development of the Corps organization, much of the independence of action and movement formerly belonging to the Division has passed to the Corps. It has been found necessary, therefore, to reconsider the organization and distribution of the mounted troops hitherto allotted to Divisions.

'The allotment of these troops was originally made with a view to providing the Divisional Commander with a small mobile force under his immediate control for reconnaissance, protective and escort duties; and on the assumption (originally correct) that the Division would be moving either independently, or with one or more roads allotted to its exclusive use. (*continued over*)

Efforts to reduce the numbers of cavalry

in November. It was suggested that the cavalry should be wintered at home, thereby saving the shipping which was needed to supply forage. Haig's reply, based on much research by GHQ, made sure that the proposal was never made again. He pointed out that rations and forage for the cavalry for three months in France would require 74,620 ship tons, while to move the divisions to and from England would take 480,000 ship tons.[6]

Lord Curzon, who chaired the Shipping Control Committee, wanted the Indian cavalry to be sent to Egypt. 'The consequent saving,' he said, 'would be eight ships of 4,000 tons for two months and eight ships a year for forage. This,' he added, 'might appear a negligible quantity, but he wished the War Committee to realise that we had come to such a pass that we had literally to scrape up ships.' As will be seen the Meerut Cavalry Brigade was soon sent off, while the rest of the Indian cavalry, which constituted nearly half the total mounted troops in France, was shipped to Egypt early in 1918 (see p. 163), just before it was, for almost the first time, really needed. It is interesting to note that Haig's efforts to 'effect economy', chiefly by 'combing out' the ammunition columns of the BEF, managed to cut down the number of horses by 18,000, more than would have been saved by sending the whole of the Indian cavalry to Egypt. Further, to save the transport of forage, 'by arrangement with the French', the five divisions of the Cavalry Corps spent much of the winter of 1916 near the coast. There, based chiefly on summer resorts, intensive training took place. Among the exercises practised was co-operation between contact aeroplanes and the cavalry. For the first time schemes and lectures in conjunction with the RFC took place and, in preparation for the forthcoming battles, cavalry officers were attached to air squadrons.

'These conditions are unlikely to recur; any future movement will be by Corps, marching and fighting in depth on a comparatively narrow front. The mounted troops belonging to the Corps must, therefore, be assembled under the direct control of the Corps Commander, and organized as Corps units.

'The Commander-in-Chief has accordingly decided:- (a) To convert the squadrons of Divisional Cavalry into Corps Cavalry Regiments ... one regiment being allotted to each Corps.'

(Preston: '1918' (2), IV, 8)

1. London buses transporting troops to the front. (See p.3)

2. Brigadier-General Sir Philip Chetwode, commanding 5th Cavalry Brigade, with his staff, Zillebeke Woods, February, 1915.

3. A typical shelter for cavalry horses, winter, 1915.

4. A cavalry horse shelter being built, winter, 1915.

Haig's directive on the use of cavalry, January, 1916

A flavour of what life was like at this time is given by the Household Cavalry's historian: 'On the march down to the sea the 7th Brigade saluted the 8th and saw to their amazement that the Blues – admittedly emulating the example of the 10th Hussars – had collar-chains shining like silver; the Life Guards, reddening with vexation, at once set about their self-imposed task of removing two and a half years' rust from this item of equipment.'[7] It is easy to scoff at the attitude which could produce such seemingly pointless 'spit and polish' engendered by regimental rivalry and pride, yet they were probably needed to keep up discipline and morale at a time when frustration and feelings of guilt were prevalent in the inactive mounted arm.

* * *

Haig had not long been in the saddle before he had issued his Army commanders with some thoughts on future strategy with particular reference to the coming summer offensive. The first part of it was to be a wearing-out struggle. Only when that had succeeded would a cavalry breakthrough be on the cards. He now, in January, 1916, postulated that it could not be achieved

Major: 'Why have you put that cloth over his head?'
Private Mike O'Flannagan (harassed by restive horse): 'So as he won't know he's being groomed, Sore.'

'by at once pushing mobile troops through the breech to operate *at any great distance* beyond it. The first gap will probably not be wide enough to pass great forces through, even if they were immediately available; while small forces, however mobile, pushed through beyond supporting distance would, under the existing conditions of the enemy's reserves, certainly be held up, and eventually enveloped by superior numbers. . . . The operation to be undertaken will entail both attack and defence, mounted and dismounted, and the closest cooperation between cavalry and the other arms will be essential.'

The old, strongly held, principle that the cavalry should always, (except in the case of the small quantities required for infantry divisional cavalry), act independently of the other arms, was thus overthrown. In April all the cavalry was withdrawn to be "fatted up", as the phrase was, for the impending battle of the Somme. From the 1st and 3rd and the 2nd Indian Cavalry Divisions, together with some infantry, Haig now formed a 'striking force'. This he put under Gough. It was to be at the disposal of Rawlinson's Fourth Army which was responsible for the main attack.* Haig urged Gough to get rid of incompetent commanders – in the Indian cavalry alone he removed eleven British officers of the rank of major upwards[8] – and 'above all to spread the "doctrine" and get cavalry officers to believe in the power of their arm when acting in co-operation with guns and infantry. I am told,' he confided to his diary, 'that there are some officers who think that cavalry are no longer required!'[9] Though Rawlinson was told by Haig to make sure that corps commanders were prepared to make use of their mounted troops, he was determined, in spite of their 'dying to get at the Bosches', that they should not be employed 'unless there is a really good chance for them'.[10]

---

*In March the Cavalry Corps had been done away with (though only temporarily (see p. 58 below)) and a cavalry division had been allotted to each of the four Armies, the 3rd Cavalry Division being retained under the hand of GHQ. (Edmonds, *1916*, I, 39). Over the Corps' demise Home was 'heartbroken. . . . The 3rd Division,' he recorded, 'sent us [at Corps headquarters] a wreath, so we sent it on to the Cavalry Club as a souvenir.' (7 Mar., 1916, Home, 101)

Gough's force was the nucleus of Fifth Army which was formally constituted under his command on 30 October.

The cavalry's orders for 1 July, 1916

Gough's force was to fight its way forward immediately behind the chief infantry attack. Differing from earlier ideas, the advance of the leading cavalry division, once it had broken through, was now to be limited in the coming battle to Bapaume, a mere ten miles beyond the start line.

* * *

Part of GHQ's operation orders for the battle included these hopeful words: 'The enemy's resistance may break down, in which case our advance will be pressed eastwards far enough to enable our cavalry to push through into the open country beyond the enemy's prepared lines of defence. Our object will then be to turn northwards, taking the enemy's lines in flank and reverse, the bulk of the cavalry co-operating on the outer flank of this operation while suitable detachments should be detailed to cover the movement from any offensive of the enemy from the east.'[11] There was, as it turned out, to be, of course, no breakdown of resistance and no pressed advance, yet in one part of the front on that first terrible day something resembling a break-in did take place, but neither infantry nor cavalry reserves were close enough to take advantage of it, for Rawlinson had, it seems, made up his mind that there was little use for the cavalry, while he sent off Gough with his reserve infantry 'to restore order to the shattered left wing of 4th Army'. Rawlinson's early views on the use of cavalry in the battle were that in its second phase it could well be used but only 'if we succeed in inflicting on the enemy a serious state of demoralization'. Ten days before the battle started he called his corps commanders to a conference. That morning he had received very optimistic orders from Haig, including such phrases as 'a dash on Miraumont' by the cavalry. Before he read them out he said that he 'had better make it quite clear that it may not be possible to break the enemy's lines and push the cavalry through at the first rush.... A situation may supervene later ... for pushing the cavalry through; but until we can see what is the course of the battle, it is impossible to predict at what moment we shall be able to undertake this, and the decision will rest in my hands to say when it can be carried out.' Not surprisingly, Rawlinson's cautious attitude was not reflected in the officers' messes of the cavalry. Captain T.S. Irwin of the Royals, for instance, asserted with confidence that the cavalry's objective of the night of 1 July was to be Cambrai.[12]

'Cavalry tracks'

On that frightful first day, as the cavalry passed some of the infantry reserves marching towards the holocaust, a soldier shouted ''Ullo, cavalry! So you've broken yer neutrality at last!' To which the speedy, almost accurate retort was 'Garn! We was here years before you was fetched!' On 4 July Lieutenant Alan Lascelles of the Bedfordshire Yeomanry was writing: 'Here we wait – today, tomorrow, tomorrow week or month; no one knows; all we do know is that our time is not yet. . . . It is an odd life; every day people – staff and suchlike – motor down the road and watch the battle; every evening they motor back and tell us what is going on. It is like staying somewhere for Ascot and not going to the races.'[13]

* * *

As always, a chief difficulty when cavalry was to be brought up to a position near enough to take advantage of a 'gap' was how to get it there. The two words 'cavalry tracks' soon became as familiar and a great deal more real than the word 'gap'. The incessant pounding of the artillery invariably produced a wide belt of terrain which was virtually impassable by men on horses. They were therefore confined to these cavalry tracks. For weeks before an offensive, working parties from the mounted regiments were set the gruelling task of constructing them. It was work of much toil and considerable danger, often under heavy shell fire, most of it carried out at night. It consisted initially in the filling up of shell holes and the reconstruction of shattered roads and tracks between the billets in the far rear and the beginning of the trench system. The tracks were marked by an elaborate arrangement of coloured flags. An officer of the 15th Hussars remembered that during three weeks in September his working party

> 'were night workers. Each evening we would parade at 4.30 p.m. with rifles and 100 rounds in the bandolier, and march along a smooth track made by our predecessors, thirty feet wide, flanked occasionally by short stakes painted red and white, and inscribed "1st Cav. Div." – a track just inviting a horseman to gallop along it. The weather had been dry and the mud was baked hard. . . .
>
> 'At about midnight we would arrive at the R.E. dump, help ourselves to picks and shovels and drive the track forward. . . .

'Remembering that our tools consisted of nothing but picks & shovels, no steam rollers were issued, we did not do too badly, facing a mess of twisted barbed wire, half-flattened trenches, shell cases both empty and an occasional "dud" needing careful handling, poor dead that no one else had time to bury, broken rifles, machine guns, equipment and all the debris of what was perhaps the fiercest fighting the world had up to then known, the men (I, of course, was only an onlooker) proceeded to turn a width of thirty feet of desolation into a level track for cavalry.'

Over the rear trenches specially made portable trench bridges had to be erected. (See illustration no. 12 for a sophisticated example). They had no side rails and 'woe betide the wretched horse and its rider who got a couple of feet off the track, for there were yawning chasms and shell holes full of water and mud, to say nothing of loose and fixed barbed wire.'[14] More of these plank bridges had to be carried forward on the day of the infantry's assault, supplemented by working parties' efforts at temporary filling in of sections of the front line trenches (as well as any captured enemy ones, generally at this point only wide enough for one or at most two horses), all directly behind the front line. The 7th Dragoon Guards found that 'with a few shovels the parapet of a trench already damaged by shell-fire can be easily dug away sufficiently to enable horses to get over, while a gap can be made in the wire at the same time. Loose bits of wire, often rusty and saturated with the contents of gas shells, are bound to be met with and a few nasty cuts about the fetlocks are unavoidable. At these gaps, and when crossing ground that has been heavily shelled, pack-horses cause a certain amount of delay, unless they are allowed to follow in rear and catch up later.'[15]

A cavalry division had to march along these tracks 'in column of half sections [two men abreast] and the fighting troops were stretched out to a length of twelve miles. It therefore took,' as the 15th Hussars' historian puts it, 'nearly all day to deploy the rear regiments for action, as it was impossible to move along these tracks except at a slow pace.'[16]

As the battle dragged on there were a few limited infantry advances, but, as a reconnaissance by Second Lieutenant Freer of the 12th Lancers revealed, 'the cavalry tracks were, with constant [enemy] shelling, only passable in single file and the whole countryside, under the assaults of man and nature, was rapidly dissolving into slime and becoming impossible for the use of the cavalry arm.'[17]*

* * *

Throughout the battle, as an officer of the 5th Dragoon Guards wrote:

'the bulk of the cavalry had a very restless time, being constantly moved up to the vicinity of the front line in the hope of a break through, and then when the chance failed to materialize, being moved back to the west or north of Amiens so as to be out of the way. Most of these marches were made by night and the vile weather that seemed the almost invariable accompaniment of our offensives made them a very unpleasant experience. To add to the discomfort, it was of course necessary to mass the mounted troops in very confined spaces where they could obtain concealment from view preparatory to an attack, and the condition of these bivouacs after several days of heavy rain can be imagined.'

*For further references to cavalry tracks, see p. 113

N.C.O. *(passing squadron that has been halted, men resting).* 'Stop that bad language. What do you mean by it?'
Voice from darkness. 'You'd give tongue if you'd an 'orse's 'oof on yer face an' still 'alted!'

As was noted in the Greys: 'Jammed up together almost as close as if they were in a railway truck, exposed to the incessant rain..., standing up to their hocks in mud, and with their rations cut down to the veriest minimum, the wretched horses took many weeks to get over the hardships that they incurred, and the conditions for the men were very little better. Small wonder,' muses the Greys' historian, 'that the cavalryman got to display but a modified enthusiasm when he was informed by his superiors that his energies were again going to be directed towards the "G" in "gap".'[18] 'Of danger,' wrote the Adjutant of the Oxfords, 'there was none [not always quite true!], discomfort a great deal, boredom even more.'[19]

By 4 July there was so little hope of a breakthrough that only the 2nd Indian Cavalry Division remained in the battle zone east of Amiens. The 1st and 3rd Cavalry Divisions were withdrawn to the Abbeville region. This withdrawal had become imperative. The strain upon the railways 'which found the transport of bulky forage a great burden'[20] and upon the water supply was becoming too great. Further, the amount of space required by two cavalry divisions caused gross overcrowding and congestion in an area through which urgent infantry reinforcements, as well as supplies of all sorts, especially ammunition, were trying to reach the front.

* * *

Haig's second major assault took place a fortnight after the start of the battle. Rawlinson, in charge of it, wrote in his diary 'Kig[gell] says it will be one of the sixteen decisive battles of the world and certainly, if we are wholly successful, it will have far-reaching results – especially if I can get the cavalry through and catch the guns and break up their commands.' In the early hours of 14 July there took place a real penetration of the enemy's position. The second line had been breached over a distance of 6,000 yards. This was achieved by a combination of a dawn attack (proposed by Rawlinson and reluctantly agreed to by Haig) and the use of a new version of the 'creeping' technique employed by the gunners. 'The intensive five minutes artillery attack was devastatingly accurate and many of the attacking infantry were into the enemy trenches without a shot being fired at them.'[21] More than 1,400 prisoners were taken and the Ginchy-Pozières Ridge (see map p. 46) was speedily secured. Here, at last, there seemed to be

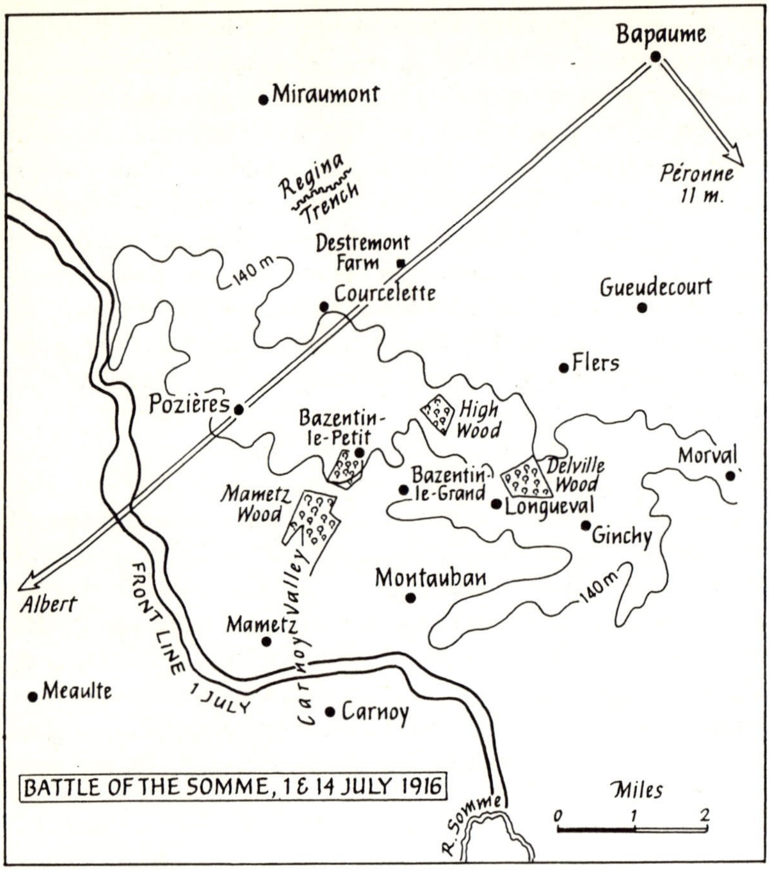
Bapaume
Miraumont
Regina Trench
Péronne 11 m.
Destremont Farm
140 m
Courcelette
Gueudecourt
Flers
Pozières
Bazentin-le-Petit
High Wood
Morval
Bazentin-le-Grand
Delville Wood
Mametz Wood
Longueval
Ginchy
Carnoy Valley
Montauban
140 m
Albert
FRONT LINE 1 JULY
Mametz
Meaulte
Carnoy
BATTLE OF THE SOMME, 1 & 14 JULY 1916
Miles
0 1 2
R. Somme

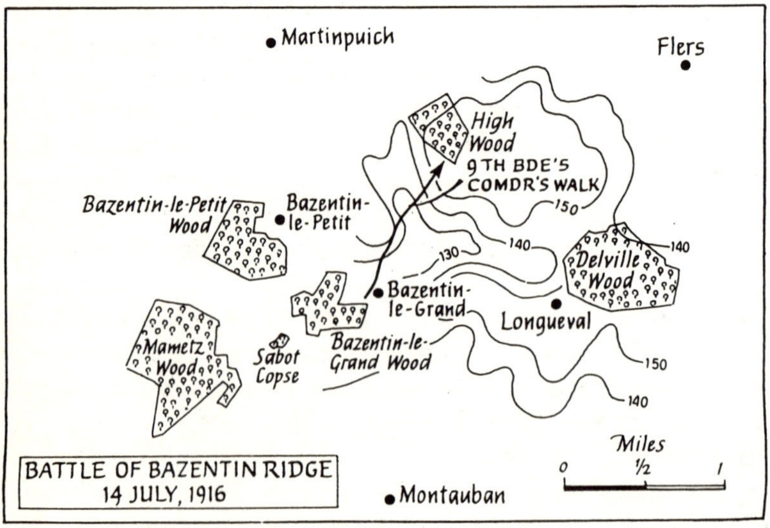
Martinpuich
Flers
High Wood
9TH BDE'S COMDR'S WALK
150
Bazentin-le-Petit Wood
Bazentin-le-Petit
140
130
140
Delville Wood
Bazentin-le-Grand
Longueval
Mametz Wood
Sabot Copse
Bazentin-le-Grand Wood
150
140
Miles
0 ½ 1
BATTLE OF BAZENTIN RIDGE
14 JULY, 1916
Montauban

the chance for exploitation which Haig and Rawlinson had been anxiously awaiting. As the Official Historian puts it, 'before 10 a.m. all opposition on this front appeared to have melted away.'[22] Proof that this was so was provided by the commander of 9th Brigade. 'I walked out alone,' he told the Official Historian, 'to examine the ground in front. It was a lovely day; the ground was very open and sloped gently up to a high ridge in front, so I wandered on until I found myself approaching a large wood which continued over the crest of the ridge. There was no sign whatever of the enemy, so I walked into the edge of the wood but saw no sign of a German, nor any defensive works.... The wood reached by me [after walking 'about a mile'] I afterwards knew as High Wood.' Here there seemed to be irrefutable evidence that a genuine 'gap' had for the first time been punched in the enemy's line: a breakthrough at last. There were two fresh infantry brigades whose commanders were ready and willing to commit them immediately 'for pursuit'. Neither was allowed either by Corps or Army headquarters to do so. The operation was to be left to the cavalry. It is easy to say with hindsight, as does the Official Historian, that it was obvious that 'the infantry should have been encouraged to exploit its success to the uttermost, since the more progress it made ... the more favourable would be conditions for the cavalry when, and if, mounted troops were able to come through'.* However, in view of the reasons given for holding up the mounted troops when they did eventually arrive (see below), it is perhaps wiser to entertain some measure of doubt as to the latter part of that sentence. Nevertheless, the capture at this point of High Wood, a chief objective of the operations in view of its commanding position over the surrounding countryside, would almost certainly have impaired the enemy's ability to defend Delville Wood and Longueval and perhaps even to hold on to them. It is interesting to note that it was Haig and not Rawlinson who on this occasion warned against premature use of the mounted arm. His view was 'that large bodies of cavalry should not be employed until the situation clearly admits of it; there would be too much danger of their coming unexpectedly under heavy fire from the enemy's rallying points

---

*'There were plenty of fresh infantry who had not taken part in the initial assault.... During the morning infantry commanders were waiting for the cavalry to arrive.... It took the Deccan Horse four hours to cover the six-seven miles to Montauban.' (Croft, quoted in Liddle, 74)

and being thrown back in confusion on our infantry.' These views were paid scant attention to by Rawlinson who did not in consequence of them alter his original orders which were that, if a 'gap' appeared, mounted troops were to seize High Wood and go beyond it.[23]

The 2nd Indian Cavalry Division was waiting in its place of assembly, no less than twelve miles to the rear, when at 7.40 a.m. it received its orders to advance. Within forty minutes it was on the move. By midday the Secunderabad Cavalry Brigade, acting as advance guard, ought to have reached Carnoy (see map p. 46) just behind the old front line of 1 July and about seven kilometres from High Wood. Attached to the brigade were a squadron of the Fort Garry Horse from the Canadian Cavalry Brigade,* (carrying with it portable trench bridges), a field troop of Royal Engineers, 'N' Battery of the RHA and two Rolls-Royces of the 9th Light Armoured Car Battery ('Lamb'). These last got irretrievably stuck in the mud near Montauban and therefore took no further part in the action.[24] It was now that the daunting nature of progress by

---

*On 1 February, 1915, Kitchener had formed a cavalry brigade consisting of the Royal Canadian Dragoons, Lord Strathcona's Horse (Royal Canadians) and the 2nd King Edward's Horse. (Later this regiment was replaced by the Fort Garry Horse from Winnipeg.) The brigade had arrived in France as infantry. In late January, 1916, it had left Canadian Corps and become mounted. With the brigade were a battery of the regular Royal Canadian Horse Artillery and the other usual auxiliaries.

To command it Kitchener had appointed 'Jack' Seely, an ex-Secretary of State for War (see p. 73 and Vol. 4, p. 377). This appointment much displeased the Canadian Prime Minister, who thought that there were Canadians capable of the job. 'I shall see to it,' he fumed, 'that the next mounted corps that goes from Canada is placed in command of one of our own men as brigadier.' In fact no further cavalry formations were sent out. (Nicholson, 39). Seely was succeeded in late June, 1917, by a Canadian, Brigadier-General Robert Walter Paterson, who had commanded the Fort Garry Horse. His command outlasted the war. Seely did not impress Home, the Cavalry Corps BGS when he visited the brigade in October, 1916. 'The whole thing,' he wrote in his diary, '[is] a failure. The material is excellent but with such a brigadier the thing is impossible. We asked him to review the operations and he made a speech which was useless from a military point of view. He ought to go back to politics, that is his proper sphere. Honest downrightness is what is wanted with soldiers, not fine phrasing and verbiage.' Ten days later the Corps Commander addressed the brigade 'on the subject of discipline – they want it badly,' wrote Home. 'It was a good straight talk of a soldier and must have been very different from the political jargon of Seely. I think it will do a lot of good.' (Home, 125)

The 7th Dragoon Guards send out patrols, 14 July, 1916

mounted troops across soft and slippery terrain cut up by the elaborate trench system and pitted with innumerable shell-holes made itself painfully clear. It was a long time past midday before the leading squadrons began to show near Montauban. Indeed, when at 1.30, the German guns on the left, expecting a further, immediate infantry attack, began to retire to new positions further back, Rawlinson, forgetting perhaps his previous lukewarm approach to the use of cavalry and misled by GHQ's optimistic reports on 'the proximity of a German collapse if the pressure could be continued immediately', exclaimed, 'If only we could get the cavalry through to charge them!'[25]

Although earlier reports that parts of Longueval to the north-east of the 'gap' and of Bazentin-le-Petit Wood to the north-west of it had been captured, these proved to be untrue. This was confirmed when the 7th Dragoon Guards, leading the brigade, on arrival on Montauban, sent out two patrols, one to each of these places. They reported back that

> 'they were unable to get on. Longueval was held by the enemy, and our patrol,' as an officer who was present relates, 'had come under a heavy fire on approaching it; while a strong German counter-attack was being delivered from the vicinity of Bazentin-le-Petit,* and our infantry was fighting in the valley between the two Bazentins. Brigade headquarters was therefore informed that it was impracticable to advance.'

At 9.30 two further patrols were sent out in different directions with similar results.[26]

The regiment therefore moved to a position near Carnoy. The brigade now awaited further orders. For more than five hours it awaited them. During this time the Germans filtered back into High Wood and crawled out to lie low in the cornfield between Longueval and Bazentin-le-Grand. At 3.10 p.m. the capture of the whole of Longueval was reported. On the strength of this news, which in fact was again false, the infantry was ordered to advance upon High Wood at 5.15. The cavalry was to co-operate. Brigadier-General Gregory, commanding the Secunderabad

---

*This wood was eventually taken at 7 p.m., 'and even then the enemy clung to a machine-gun post fifty yards beyond the edge.' (Edmonds, *1916*, II, 85–6)

14 July, 1916

Brigade, now received his orders. He was telephoned by MacAndrew, 2nd Indian Cavalry Division's commander, outlining what his brigade was expected to do. Before tying things up with the infantry headquarters near by, he recalled his working parties from bridging trenches and filling in shell holes. While he had been speaking to MacAndrew they learned that the attack was to be postponed to 6.15.* A little later he was ordered to send two of his regiments to Sabot Copse. He selected the 7th Dragoon Guards and the Deccan Horse. The Poona Horse was to be in reserve.†

The plan was this: while two infantry attacks were launched, one towards High Wood and the other towards Delville Wood (in spite of the fact that Longueval had not yet been taken), the 7th Dragoon Guards would attack towards the east side of High Wood, working on the infantry's right flank, and the Deccan Horse, operating on the 7th's right, would first assist in securing the high ground in its front and then wheel eastwards and raid Delville Wood. The artillery which was already playing upon High Wood would lift punctually at 6.15. It was essential that the

---

*There is a great deal of conflicting evidence as to timing. The above is based more on Norman (99) than on Farrar-Hockley (162) who states that: 'all agreement in principle was completed by 3.40 p.m. We now know that no orders of any sort reached the cavalry brigade commander [no evidence is given for this statement] ... before 5.40. ... The order to advance the reserve brigade of 7th Division did not reach the brigade commander until about 5.20.' This is just as likely, however, to be correct as is Norman.

†Jemadar Abdul Gafur of the Poona Horse was sent during the course of the day (unfortunately no time is given) with a patrol to examine the roads to Longueval. The regiment's adjutant wrote of this Indian officer;

> 'He, a man of very little education, went straight to the right spot and got an excellent report of the route back to headquarters within an hour. ... He then proceeded to find out the situation at Longueval, and found the village partly held by the enemy ... and a fierce fight in progress. Many a man would have been content to send in this information, but not Abdul Gafur.
>
> 'Leaving his patrol under cover, he worked his way on foot into the village and eventually found a British officer who pointed out to him the position of the opposing forces, and, having sent back this information, the Jemadar remained in touch with the infantry until all chance of a breakthrough was gone, when he was recalled. It is hard to imagine a finer instance of liaison between infantry in the front line and cavalry hoping to get through.' (Wylly, 115–6)

The first cavalry advance since trench warfare began

ground immediately to the cavalry's and the infantry's front should be crossed at speed if maximum benefit was to be gained from the barrage.

* * *

At 5.40 2nd Lieutenant H.W. Pope led his troop of 'B' Squadron of the 7th Dragoon Guards from the Carnoy Valley towards Bazentin-le-Grand, via Montauban. The rest of the regiment and the Deccan Horse followed in column of sections, the Deccan Horse in due course breaking off to the right. (See below). One squadron of each of the Secunderabad Brigade's regiments was armed with the lance. In both regiments the lancer squadron was placed, for obvious reasons, in front of the sabre squadrons. In the valley south of Mametz Wood, Pope, as recorded by Captain F.J. Scott, commanding 'C' Squadron, which was directly behind 'B' Squadron,

> 'crossed the trench line by one or two gaps.... It was a memorable occasion, as it was the first cavalry advance since the beginning of trench warfare. Gunners, infantry and returning wounded all paused to give us a cheer as we went past them.* The valley showed the intensity of the fighting: there was not a square yard of ground that was not broken up with shell holes; the trees in the woods stood blackened and broken, stripped of all their leaves and branches; dead and wounded, British and German, lay on every side; here and there a wrecked German gun, with the mangled remains of a team that had striven in vain to withdraw it; further on, three or four burnt-out railway trucks stood among the *debris* of a siding. Passing Bazentin-le-Grand, the regiment advanced into the valley to the west of Longueval, which was joined at this point by another valley, sloping down from the south-western side of High Wood.'[27]

---

*Private Anthony Brennan of the 2nd Royal Irish Regiment, engaged with a burial party, looked up from his grave-digging duties to watch this unaccustomed sight. 'We gave them a cheer as they passed,' he wrote, 'for we really believed that it was a sign that the breakthrough had come at last.' (Norman, 101)

The battle of Bazentin Ridge, 14 July, 1916

It seems that the time of arrival of Pope's troop in the concentration area was 6.25.[28]* None of the accounts of what came to be called the battle of Bazentin Ridge indicates whether the artillery bombardment lifted at the originally appointed time of 6.15. It is probable that its lifting was postponed, for there is conclusive evidence that the mounted attack did not start until 7.00. The reason for the delay was that 6.15 was an entirely unrealistic target for the two infantry battalions. One authority suggests that the staff had assumed that they would march as speedily as the cavalry.[29] As it was, and in view of the failing light, the cavalry and what infantry had managed to assemble, were ordered forward before all the infantry had arrived. It was more than nine hours since the infantry divisional commanders, discovering the amazing fact that the 'G' in 'Gap' was staring them in the face, had begged to be allowed to push through it.

* * *

'B' and 'C' Squadrons of the 7th now galloped across the junction of the two valleys, coming under machine-gun fire from both flanks, suffering remarkably few casualties. The gunners were probably overcome with amazement at such exotic targets presenting themselves travelling at a thoroughly unusual speed. Second-Lieutenant F.W. Beadle of the Royal Artillery found it

> 'an incredible sight, an unbelievable sight. They galloped up with their lances and with pennants flying, up the slope to High Wood. . . . Of course they were falling all the way because the infantry were attacking on the other side of the valley furthest away from us, and the cavalry were attacking very near to where we were. So the German machine-guns were going for the infantry and the shells were falling all over

---

*Between 6.15 and 8.27 p.m. an airman, flying at 1,000 feet and later at 500, observed the mounted troops moving from Montauban towards Bazentin-le-Petit and then on to Bazentin-le-Grand. He saw them retire to Bazentin-le-Petit when shells began to fall among them. In his log he wrote: 'Having trotted along the E. edge of Mametz Wood they dismounted in troops, at a point halfway down the E. edge of the wood.' At a crossroads south of High Wood they took cover. 'From here a mounted troop was sent out N.E. . . . They came across the Hun infantry in a field and a small scrap took place when a few prisoners were taken.' (Lieutenant T.L.W. Stallibras, RFC log, 14 July, 1916, Liddle, 75–6)

the place. I've never seen anything like it! They simply galloped on through all that and horses and men dropping on the ground, with no hope against machine-guns, because the Germans up on the ridge were firing down into the valley where the soldiers were. It was a magnificent sight. Tragic.'

Two hundred yards further on Pope's troop reached the shelter of a bank on the further side of the Longueval valley, beyond which a field of standing corn 'sloped upwards, convex in shape'. Pope's men jumped up the bank, and, wheeling to the right, charged some German machine gunners who were taking cover in the shell holes among the corn. 'About fifteen of the enemy', says Captain Scott, 'went down before the lances'.[30] Another thirty-two, no doubt demoralized by this unaccustomed eruption of spearmen, immediately put up their hands and surrendered.

There is confusion as to exactly what happened next, but there is no doubt that the 7th was soon forced to retire some way up and dismount, taking cover behind the bank. From the front and from the right came sustained machine-gun and rifle fire. Its chief source, though the height of the crops prevented it from being seen, was the Germans' reserve line, now the 'Switch Line', a new trench which had been begun some time earlier and which during the course of the day had been improved. It followed the reverse slope of the ridge and cut through the northern part of High Wood (see map p. 46).* A troop was sent out to try to locate it, but soon returned frustrated.

> 'Lieutenant Pope,' according to Scott, 'rode out three times into the corn and brought in two of his wounded men across the saddle. For his gallantry he received the immediate award of the Military Cross.'† Scott's account continued: 'Lieutenant [D.J.] Hartley's section of the Machine-Gun Squadron, which was attached to the regiment, advanced too far on the right, and one detachment got caught under heavy

---

*It was further improved and wired during the coming night. (Edmonds, *1916*, II, 89)

†It was the first MC the regiment received during the war.
  Pope had been a squadron sergeant-major in the Bays. He was commissioned into the 7th in 1915.

machine-gun fire. The gun horse was killed while making a very gallant attempt to save the gun. Lieutenant Anson took charge of the detachment and succeeded in withdrawing it from an awkward position, being wounded while doing so.'

Four machine guns of the squadron were with the 7th, while the other four were with the Deccan Horse. It seems that those with the 7th were unable to give effective support to the regiment, 'for their field of fire was much restricted by the corn'.[31]

Between 3.30 and 4 p.m. aeroplane reconnaissance had reported that High Wood and its northern approaches seemed to be lacking any signs of the enemy. Now the observer in another aeroplane – a two-seater Morane monoplane – saw quite another scene. What he thought to be about a company occupied shell holes to the wood's east and a similar number he guessed were in the switch trench and in front of the wood to the south-west. 'Flying very low,' as Scott observed, the aeroplane 'swooped down along the German trench, firing tracer bullets into it: this manoeuvre was repeated several times'[32] and drew enemy fire which made holes in the canvas sides of the aeroplane. This showed the 7th from where most of the fire was coming. The observer made a quick sketch of the enemy's positions and dropped it in a bag which was picked up by the commander of 'N' Battery, who without delay began registering his guns upon the switch trench. This aerial action – an early example of successful air co-operation – probably saved the regiment from considerable casualties. At about this time the German artillery began shelling in a big way, but all the shells fell well behind the position taken up by the cavalry.

* * *

Lieutenant-Colonel E. Tennant, commanding the Deccan Horse, tells how his regiment fared. On arrival at Sabot Copse, he received orders to

' "move at once . . . into a position to attack Delville Wood from the N. and N.W., so as to enable the 9th Division to complete the capture of that place. . . . Be sure to maintain communication with the 7th Dragoon Guards on your left and also with the 9th Division on your right. G.O.C.

[Gregory] will move slightly to the rear of and between you and 7th Dragoon Guards."

'In compliance with these orders "A" Squadron [the lancer squadron], under Captain F. Jarvis, was detailed as advance guard. Unfortunately the only passage through our lines from the assembly position at Sabot Copse was over a rough and narrow track which necessitated the advance being made in half-sections for a considerable distance and, as the 7th Dragoon Guards were leading, there was some delay before the regiment could get through.

'As each squadron cleared the defile it formed line and advanced at a gallop in the direction taken by the advanced guard, which lay through a broad belt of standing corn, in which small parties of the enemy lay concealed. Individual Germans now commenced popping up on all sides, throwing up their arms and shouting "Kamerad", and not a few, evidently under the impression that no quarter would be given, flung their arms around the horses' necks and begged for mercy – all of which impeded the advance ...

'When the advanced guard reached its objective, a German trench to the north of Delville Wood, occupied by infantry, could be seen clearly and German artillery (located by the flash of the guns) opened fire....

'During the whole period of the advance the regiment had been exposed to flanking machine-gun fire from Delville Wood; consequently "C" Squadron was ordered to form a defensive flank upon the right of "A" Squadron, and "D" Squadron was moved up to occupy the gap between the regiment and the 7th Dragoon Guards, who appeared to be held up some distance south of High Wood. "B" Squadron was retained in a central position as a support in case of unforeseen eventualities ...

'As no touch could be obtained with the 9th Division, whose whereabouts were unknown, and as any further advance of the regiment to a position from which to attack Delville Wood from the north would separate it still further from the 7th Dragoon Guards, messages were sent back to the Brigadier asking for instructions, but unfortunately he could not be found.

'Captain Jarvis now reported that bodies of Germans were massing on his right front, as though preparing for a counter-attack, and consequently "B" Squadron was warned to be ready to act at any moment. The German attack, however, did not materialize. It had now become dark and as the left flank of the regiment was in the air, whilst the right flank, "C" Squadron, was under heavy fire from Delville Wood, and not being able to get in touch with the Brigadier, Lieutenant-Colonel Tennant [the writer himself] ordered the regiment to fall back and take up a position extending from the right flank of the 7th Dragoon Guards along the valley, where it was hoped contact would be made with the infantry.

'This retirement was carried out in the nick of time, for shortly afterwards the enemy opened heavy artillery fire upon what had been the regiment's advanced position, and as no cover of any sort was available for either men or horses the casualties would have been extremely heavy. About midnight the enemy once more opened heavy artillery fire over the valley, but failed to locate the position, and the night passed without further incident except that a German patrol, advancing from Delville Wood, ran into one of the regimental listening patrols and was fired on, two prisoners being taken, both belonging to the 16th Bavarian Regiment. At 3.30 a.m. the Brigade was ordered to retire. Fortunately the morning was misty, which enabled the troops to ride back, undetected by the enemy, through the artillery positions (which were saturated with tear gas) to the valley of Montauban, where horses were watered and fed, and the Brigade returned to bivouac at Meaulte.'[33]

The evacuation of the wounded proved to be a tricky problem. The cavalry regiments had no stretchers with them. These 'had to be improvised with blankets slung on lances, but they were very unsatisfactory, as the lances,' according to Scott, 'bent and the blankets sagged.... The wounded had an uncomfortable journey to the nearest dressing station.'[34]

Next morning the cavalry was ordered to remain in its bivouacs ready for action – action that was not to materialize in mounted form for another sixteen months.

* * *

14 July, 1916

At about the time that the 7th Dragoon Guards were employing their lances, the infantrymen on their left were approaching High Wood. When the light began to fade, as they threaded their way through the thick undergrowth, they came up against increasing opposition. Before long they were finally held up by the enemy manning the switch trench. Two-thirds of High Wood was now in British hands. To the right the South African infantry was striving and failing to get forward through the ruins of Longueval. Delville Wood was still in German hands. Night fell with the Germans pouring in reinforcements for the inevitable counter-attacks in the morning. Two months of bloody conflict were to pass before High Wood and the switch trench fell into British hands.

* * *

The 7th Dragoon Guards lost on 14 July one officer and two other ranks killed, one officer and twenty other ranks wounded, while fourteen horses were killed, two missing and twenty-four wounded. The Deccan Horse suffered a greater number of casualties: two Indian officers wounded, nine other ranks killed and thirty-nine wounded. Nineteen horses of the regiment were killed and fifty-three wounded.*

The fact that cavalry had actually been in mounted action was made much of in the press at home. That it had had only a very minor effect on the battle was not, of course, mentioned. It is pleasing nonetheless to learn that the appearance of the cavalry near High Wood 'gave rise to alarmist reports at German corps and army headquarters: "The British had broken through northwards between Longueval and Pozières, and by 8.40 p.m. had

---

*Edmonds, 1916, II, 94, gives casualties of 102 British and Indians of all ranks and 130 horses. These figures probably include, beside the two regiments, the machine-gun squadron, the horse artillery and the Fort Garry Horse. The 7th received a few days later the following telegram forwarded from GHQ:
'French Active Army, English Front The Royal Guards Dragoons.'
  'Guard Dragons are delighted to congratulate our Glorious Brothers with the last brilliant charge.
  'Imperial Guard Dragons Commander, Major-General Djonkovsky.'
To this the regiment replied:
'Imperial Guard Dragons Russia.
  'All ranks Princess Royal's Dragoon Guards highly appreciate kind congratulations from their renowned comrades.
  'Princess Royal's Dragoon Guards.'

reached the line Flers-High Wood-Martinpuich, and were still advancing."'35

Foch described the events of 14 July on the British front as 'a blessing and a miracle'! The part played by the cavalry certainly gave a boost to the morale of the mounted arm. Young Lascelles's view was that it showed that the authorities meant 'to use us soberly, not gamble with us'. He added that 'a month ago the very idea of one troop galloping at the Germans and getting back alive – indeed of ever *reaching* the Germans at all – was unthinkable. Now two squadrons can charge, inflict loss and retire in good order.' He was told by an infantry colonel: 'You can't imagine how glad it makes me to see glimmerings of cavalry work again, and what tremendous encouragement it gives our men.' As for the battle as a whole Liddell Hart thought it 'the most brilliantly conceived and executed day's work of the British army since it first went to France'. Yet though the preparation for and performance of the assault were indeed brilliantly conceived, there was little sign of well worked out arrangements for the exploitation of the morning's successes.

Whether, even had there been less confusion at most levels of command, there ever existed a real, massive opportunity of a true breakthrough must remain in very considerable doubt. To say, as one commentator has, that the operation 'came within an ace of achieving a great victory' is surely to exaggerate.[36]

* * *

Early in September the Cavalry Corps was resuscitated. Home wondered 'if the old cavalry will come into its own at last. To be with it if it does will be stupendous. I am glad,' he added, 'that Kavanagh is going to command as he is a real leader of men and knows his job, has a mind of his own.'[37]

There were at least four occasions on which hopes were rekindled for a breakthrough. The first came on 15 September.* On this day tanks were used for the first time in history. There were forty-nine of the cumbersome Mark Is available and Haig has been much criticized for not waiting for large numbers to be assembled before

---

*Since 1 July Rawlinson's Fourth Army's small territorial gains had cost some 200,000 casualties. Two enemy trench systems had been overrun, but now two new ones confronted the attackers.

employing them.* He paid no attention to the advice given to French nine months before by Churchill: 'None should be used until all can be used at once.' As they were eventually, but certainly not in the First World War, to replace the cavalry as the army's chief instrument of fighting mobility, it is worth saying something about them and considering why these first few machines were used in what came to be known as the battle of Flers-Courcelette. First, to wait another year (as would have been necessary) would have dangerously risked the secrecy of their existence. As it happened they were a total surprise to the Germans on 15 September. Second, as Joffre told Haig on 28 August, the impending offensive was 'a great Coalition battle' in which, at much the same early September date, the French, the Russians and the Italians were also to launch large-scale attacks. Three days later Haig told his Army commanders that the battle was 'to be planned as a *decisive* operation'. With this in mind, as John Terraine has put it, 'it was unthinkable that Britain should hold anything back, no matter how small, unready or untried it might be.' Third, it was considered right to see how they actually worked in battle. Indeed it was only on account of the practical experience gained on the Somme that the jump between the primitive Mark Is and the much improved Mark IVs, which were the tanks chiefly employed at Cambrai fourteen months later, was possible. It is interesting to note that in retrospect a number of Tank Corps officers believed that the disclosure of the tanks' existence on 15 September was outweighed by the experience gained.[38]

Except that the initials would have been an embarrassment, it had been originally intended to christen the 'caterpillar machine-gun destroyers' (known to their designers as 'Little' and 'Big' 'Willies') *Water Carriers*! In March, 1915, Churchill, then at the Admiralty, had given the order to 'proceed as proposed' and eleven months later the first trials of the 'landships' had been held. In April Haig had high hopes of receiving 150 in time for 1 July, but production problems and the difficulties of crew training were holding up the desired results. Seven

---

*Concomitant with this criticism was the familiar one which accused Haig of being a dyed-in-the-wool, old-fashioned cavalryman who could not see any use for this new-fangled weapon. That the two criticisms contradict each other is obvious.

The Mark I tank

months after their first employment there were still only sixty in existence.

The Mark I, powered by a six-cylinder 105-horsepower Daimler engine, could, with luck, move over rough ground at just over ½ mph, its maximum speed on level roads being 3.7 mph. It was 32 feet 6 inches in length and 7 feet 4½ inches high. The 'male' version possessed two six-pounder guns in projecting sponsons and four of the cavalry model strip-fed light automatic Hotchkiss guns, while the 'female' version had five such Hotchkisses. There was a crew of eight, three of whom were required to effect a change of gear. It took four men to swing the starting handle. Because of their slowness, 'unless they go in front of the infantry', as one staff officer put it, 'they are never able to catch them up in time. If they go in front it prevents us using our barrage and on the other hand gives away the attack and brings down a terrific barrage on our trenches which wipes out our infantry as soon as they begin to climb out. . . . At present most people who've seen them in action say they'd rather do without.' Under these circumstances it is absurd to imagine that tanks, even the later improved ones, could take the place of cavalry in a pursuit. Kitchener dismissed tanks as 'pretty mechanical toys', but Home thought them, when he first laid eyes on one, 'wonderful machines – real ironclads on land'. More important, Rawlinson, whose responsibility it was to employ them, when they were first demonstrated to him, in spite of reservations, was 'on the whole rather favourably impressed'.[39] Captain 'Archie' Wright of the 4th Dragoon Guards, when he heard, two days before they went into action, that 'caterpillar forts are being used for the first time' thought that 'they should be a great success'.[40] He could hardly have been more right very long term, but in their first battle there were few who thought that they had done well. Haig was an exception. 'Though the tanks had not achieved all that had been hoped,' he wrote to Colonel (later Major-General Sir) Ernest Dunlop Swinton,* 'they had saved many lives and had fully justified themselves.' He wanted, he added, 'five times as many'.[41] What actually happened was that seventeen of the forty-nine either became 'ditched' or had mechanical breakdowns before they could get into action. Of the

---

*The chief originator of the tank and first commander of what was first called Heavy Branch, Machine Gun Corps and retitled in July, 1917, the Tank Corps.

The battle of Fleurs-Courcelette, 15 September, 1916

'Tank walking up the High Street at Flers, with the British Army cheering behind it.'

remaining thirty-two, thirteen were for a short time engaged in mutually supporting combat.*

* * *

As usual Haig and Rawlinson intended to create a gap through which the cavalry — in this case two divisions — was to pour so that it could interfere 'as much as possible' with the railways by which enemy reinforcements might arrive and also to raid German corps and divisional headquarters. 'If the cavalry does not get a chance this time,' wrote Home in his diary, 'it will be the end of them. I suppose,' he reckoned, 'that people at home are howling about expense and so on.'[42] On the first point he was not quite right. On the second, as has been shown, he was entirely correct. Rawlinson's orders added that 'any attempt to push too much cavalry through at one time will only lead to confusion and delay' and that

---

*A message from a combat aeroplane was translated by an enthusiastic press correspondent as 'Tank walking up the High Street of Flers with the British Army cheering behind.' (Quoted in Terraine: *WW1*, 120; see also Moyne, 117)

its advance must be continuous and methodical. For the construction of the cavalry tracks beyond the front line special parties were detailed. That work was to be begun as soon as the attack started. None of this was in the event to come about. Rawlinson, who thought that there was 'a fair chance of getting the cavalry through', had been 'a little anxious lest Kavanagh should act prematurely and thus compromise the actions of the other arms'.[43] He need not have worried. The cavalry received no orders. In the late evening of the following day three of the five cavalry divisions were ordered to move back (from whence, laboriously, on the 14th they had come, riding then in keen anticipation of action) 'across country so as to add nothing to the volume of battle traffic on the roads'.[44] The two Indian divisions remained in their forward positions. On the 18th, as Home wrote in his diary, 'came the news that Morval was unoccupied and so two squadrons were sent up. Of course when they got there they found it was occupied. . . . It raised a great flutter in the dovecotes.'[45]

* * *

A new assault was planned for 25 September. It came to be known as the battle of Morval.* After the first day one of the few squadrons left in the forward area was Captain FitzGerald's 'D' Squadron of the 19th Lancers. Such visits as he made from time to time to the infantry headquarters under whose command he had been placed 'did not point to any demand being made on the squadron'.[46] Suddenly, though, the unexpected happened. That morning, the 26th, the Welsh Guards reported that near Gueudecourt it was possible to walk about in the open with impunity, and that the few Germans encountered had surrendered.[47] Gueudecourt itself had been taken. FitzGerald was ordered 'to seize the high ground some 600 yards east of the village and establish a strong point in that area'. Proceeding mostly at a trot, he brought his squadron along a track east of Flers and turned towards

---

*This battle proved to be the most successful of those on the Somme. It was the first in which the creeping artillery barrage was really well employed. British casualties were less than one-fifth of those incurred on 15 September.

For an excellent, convincing account of how the combination of creeping barrage and clear passages for tanks employed on 15 September was such a failure, see Prior and Wilson, 242 *et seq.*

Gueudecourt, crossing without difficulty two trenches filled with British infantry. He was now joined by a troop of the South Irish Horse which was acting as corps cavalry. The infantry brigadier to whom he reported could not confirm that the village was in British hands, so FitzGerald continued his advance on Gueudecourt 'with the object of clearing up the situation there and, if able to do so, to carry out his mission. . . . Feeling painfully conscious of the exposed stretch to be crossed, the advance continued and, thanks to the comparative immunity given by rapid movements, the squadron reached the shelter of the village without a casualty,' though the South Irish Horse suffered quite a few. Once into the village, which was entered at about 2.15 p.m., the débris of its ruins prevented any further mounted movement. At the eastern end of the village heavy enemy fire from the high ground which was FitzGerald's objective stopped further progress. He decided to hold on to the village until the infantry relieved him. This it did at about 6 p.m. Before this his men and those of the South Irish Horse 'were engaged with enemy infantry' and with the help of the artillery broke up two attempted counter-attacks on the village. The squadron lost in this minor action three other ranks killed and seven wounded, but the loss in horses was thirty-five killed. This was because the exact position in which they had been left was 'identified by the enemy'. FitzGerald received the MC and four Indian other ranks were awarded the Indian Order of Merit (2nd Class).[48]

'I suppose,' moaned Home, 'we shall now move backwards until the next big attack. I am certain that D. Haig means to go on pushing and if so our chance may come yet.' He was right on Haig's intention, if not on the other points. 'Kavanagh,' he added, 'is a brick, he is very disappointed but does not show it at all.' It was 29 October before Home could bring himself to admit to his diary: 'I am sorry to say that I came to the conclusion that the cavalry as a mass cannot be employed before next spring. I don't believe horses would get through the mud and, if they did, they would be stone cold after a very short time.' Early in November, even in billets, there were numerous horse casualties, owing in part to the mud pulling their shoes off. Some even got so stuck in the mud that they had to be shot.[49]

The minor mounted actions in the battle of the Somme have been comprehensively recounted because it is so very surprising that they took place at all at a time when the real possibilities of a

The battle of the Somme ends

breakthrough did not exist.* Especially is this so, since the Germans during this same time were busy permanently dismounting the vast majority of their cavalry units. Those that were left were chiefly employed on the Eastern front.

* * *

As the battle of the Somme dragged on, the cavalry was mostly withdrawn so as to be out of the way. However, a forward concentration of the 1st and 3rd Cavalry Divisions was ordered for the period of 4 to 12 October. Neither division, of course, came into action. That the battle was really over was made clear when on 17 November GHQ ordered the Cavalry Corps to furnish four pioneer battalions, each 850 to 870 strong, to Fourth Army and another two to Fifth Army.[50]

---

*On 28 September patrols from the 19th Alberta Dragoons and the 1st Canadian Hussars (both Canadian Corps cavalry regiments) rode out of 'Courcelette to probe deep into enemy territory. Two patrols reached Regina Trench; others moving up the Bapaume road were repulsed by machine-gun fire from Destremont Farm.' (Nicholson, 179; see also Steele, Capt. H. *The Canadians in France, 1915–1918*, [1920], 77)

5

'The advance of our men to the Hindenburg Line proved the work of the first quarter of 1917.'
- THE REV. R.H. MURRAY in *The History of the VIII King's Royal Irish Hussars*

' "Pursuit" by the Allied Armies, no matter how vehemently ordered by their higher commanders, was hardly more than a pious hope.'

* * *

'Cavalry proved quite useless for this type of pursuit against an unbroken enemy.'
- JOHN TERRAINE, on the follow-up to the German withdrawal to the Hindenburg Line

'The still largely volunteer British Army of early 1917 was committed to action – as so often – in conjunction with a French attack elsewhere. The French failed and the morale of their army broke, and the British thereafter had to shoulder the major burden of sacrifice on the Western Front.'
- MARTIN MIDDLEBROOK in his Foreword to Jonathan Nicholls's *Cheerful Sacrifice: The Battle of Arras, 1917*

'There was much talk of what [cavalry divisions] could achieve and a great deal of complicated staff work was concentrated on the extremely difficult problem of pushing great masses of horsemen through the infantry and of feeding men and animals in the desert beyond the German trenches, supplies depending upon what could be squeezed through the bottle-neck of the precarious passages over the trench system.'
- SPEARS in *Prelude to Victory*

'The astonishing spectacle was seen of cavalry trying to charge in crater-fields; the result, as one might suppose, was high mounds of dead horses, much wasted gallantry and no progress worth mentioning.'
- JOHN TERRAINE in *Douglas Haig, the Educated Soldier*

'In one place the horses were lying so thick that it was necessary to climb over them in order to pass along the street.'
- LIEUTENANT-COLONEL F.H.D.C. WHITMORE, in Monchy, 11 April, 1917[1]

L'Affaire Nivelle

L'Affaire Nivelle – *French mutinies – German withdrawal to Hindenburg Line – Villers Faucon – opening of battle of Arras – Monchy*

During the winter of 1916 Robertson had been sending to France as infantrymen, and sometimes as engineers, recruits who had enlisted for the cavalry. This was dismaying to Haig, especially as the cavalry reserve at home which was meant to number 15,000 had fallen by early February to less than 5,000 and some of the regiments in France were so much below strength that they could not even train properly. Thus the BEF's mounted arm entered the year of *L'Affaire Nivelle* and the battles of Arras, Third Ypres (Passchendaele) and Cambrai noticeably weak. The debility of the horses was considerable, too, because the forage ration had been cut down since the year's beginning to nine pounds of oats and six of hay a day, due partly to the submarine menace. It was not restored to twelve pounds of both oats and hay until late April, when 'in addition a certain amount of bran and linseed was issued as a supplementary ration'.[2]

Officer: 'What do you mean by feeding that horse before the call sounded?'
Recruit: 'I didn't think as'ow 'e'd start eating before the trumpet blew, sir.'

L'Affaire Nivelle

This work need make no more than passing reference to the replacement of Joffre by Général Robert Georges Nivelle in late December; nor to that sanguine general's plan to smash through the enemy's lines in a lightning forty-eight hour offensive, its failure,* his consequent dismissal and replacement by Pétain and the 'mutinies' in the French armies which followed. Nor need it be much concerned with the political and military conferences, machinations, intrigues and conflicting views which characterized the mode of formation of the plans for the various campaigns undertaken by the BEF in conjunction with the French. Haig seems to have been not entirely unhappy about launching the major diversionary offensive which Nivelle's plan required and which was to start a week before his. This thirty-nine-day battle turned out to

---

*The puny success of its first day was very much less than that of the British at Arras.

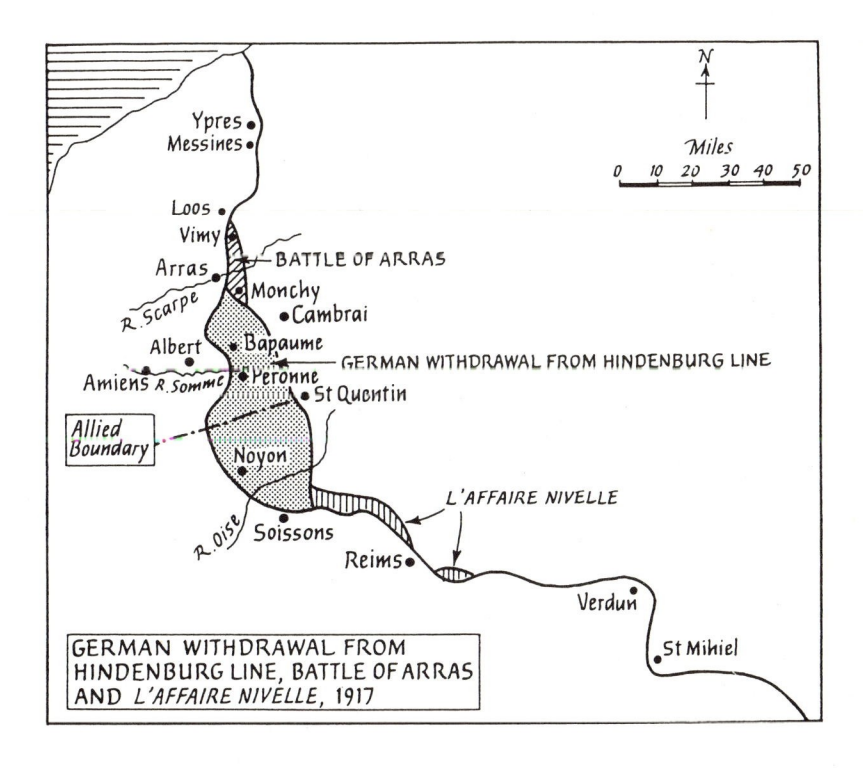

GERMAN WITHDRAWAL FROM HINDENBURG LINE, BATTLE OF ARRAS AND *L'AFFAIRE NIVELLE*, 1917

The Germans withdraw to the Hindenburg Line

be the most lethal of all the BEF's offensives. The daily average casualty rate was far higher than that of either the Somme or Third Ypres.[3] It took place in the icy spring which succeeded the coldest winter in European memory. Its epicentre was the town of Arras which gave the battle its name. Ever sensitive to the need to clear the coastal sector, Haig's original intention, as soon as the key position of Monchy-le-Preux, a village standing some 90 feet above the plain, had been captured, was to turn northwards so as to take the Messines and Passchendaele ridges (see endpapers), but the failure of Nivelle's main attack and the state of the French armies thereafter made it too dangerous not to continue the British battle so as to keep up the pressure against the enemy. Thus Haig's hope that Arras could be regarded merely as a preparation for the season's main campaign in Flanders was dashed and that main campaign imperilled.

※ ※ ※

As early as 5 February secret orders were issued by the enemy to prepare for a massive withdrawal to a new, immensely strong, about seventy mile-long defensive line, known to the Germans as the *Siegfried Stellung* and to the British as the Hindenburg Line. The actual withdrawal began in a small way seventeen days later. The greatest engineering feat of the war, the idea it is believed of Crown Prince Rupprecht, and initially much opposed by Ludendorff, was completed in five months. By giving up their vast salient, which ended in the south at Noyon, the Germans shortened their line by twenty-six miles, thus saving ten divisions. Once the retirement, which in a sense was a confession of a measure of defeat, had been completed, the intention was to stand on the defensive 'in order to let the U-boat commanders show what they could do'.[4]

As Churchill put it, the Germans 'left their opponents in the crater fields of the Somme, and with a severity barbarous because far in excess of any military requirements, laid waste with axe and fire the regions which they had surrendered.'[5] It is important to stress the extent of the devastation wreaked over the whole area evacuated by the enemy. The larger towns were literally razed to the ground. In hundreds of villages virtually every building was either blown up or burned down, trees were felled across the roads, huge mines were exploded at important road intersections, every bridge

The withdrawal to the Hindenburg Line

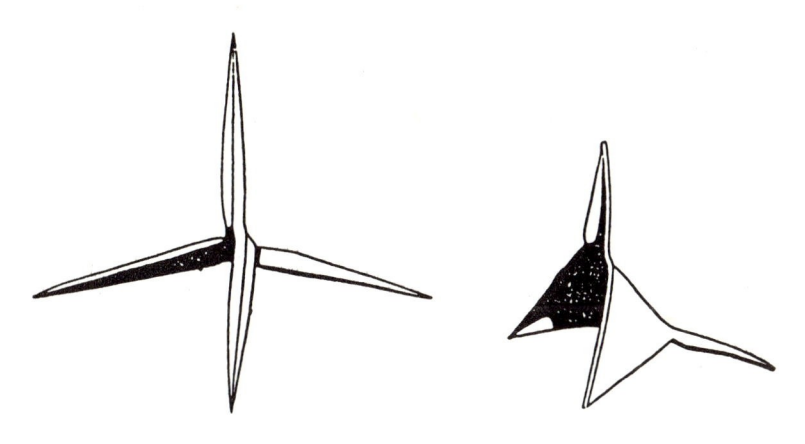

Two Patterns of Caltrops or 'Crows' Feet'

over the Somme and other rivers was destroyed, railway lines were torn up, no supplies of any sort were left behind; delayed-action bombs were planted, thousands of booby-traps were laid, three- and six-inch 'crow's feet' were sown in the river bottom at every ford, designed to puncture horses' hooves, nearly every well had been defiled, every pond polluted. This was especially serious for the horses of mounted units. The cavalry, both British and French, has sometimes been scoffed at for not effecting a major pursuit of the retreating enemy. Not only was the land in front of the Hindenburg Line excessively unpromising territory over which to attack, but the withdrawal was as unlike a rout as any in history. It was slow, measured and calculating. Further, rearguard strongpoints were manned throughout by nests of machine gunners. It is not surprising therefore that it was followed up with deliberation tempered by extreme wariness. 'Our difficulty,' observed Home, 'is the crossing over the bad lands of the battle of the Somme.' A chief inhibiting factor was the difficulty of getting up supplies. In consequence, though the various corps cavalry regiments sometimes got on well ahead – sometimes as much as ten miles ahead* –

---

*It is hardly fair to say, as does Terraine in *Haig*, 276–7, that the British cavalry was 'not well handled'. He does, however, add that the French cavalry, held 'in heavy massses', was handled less well, and goes on to say that 'cavalry and infantry alike, after years of trench warfare, had lost the habit and art of movement.'

the infantry and artillery were kept back until supplies could reach them. After a while the supply of cable gave out – another restricting factor. 'Telegraphic communication,' writes the Official Historian, 'was maintained by means of German wire insulated on wine bottles with the bottoms knocked out, which were fixed on pea-sticks – bottles and sticks having been obtained from Aurior Chateau.' Equally hampering was the inability to bring forage forward. The Wiltshire Yeomanry reported that, due chiefly to this cause, it had lost, between 20 and 29 March, twenty-two horses dead and thirty-five evacuated, some because of wounds. In an attempt to seize Sorel-le-Grand – an attempt held up by machine-gun fire – the horses were 'hock deep in the mud' and 'almost worn out'.*

There was never at any time anything but the most minor of opportunities for mounted action, though the German divisional cavalry were at times active as rear guards, being careful to avoid for the most part close contact with their British counterparts.† Typical of the kind of mounted action at that time was that of a non-commissioned officer's patrol of King Edward's Horse. Consisting of six men, it came across enemy horse lines in a wood. Being at once cut off by a troop of German cavalry 'with odds of four or five to one' in its favour, the patrol 'promptly charged with their swords drawn and the enemy fled'. The patrol continued its reconnaissance but was again attacked by an enemy troop. 'The patrol charged again,' the enemy fled again and the patrol returned unscathed. On 23 March a less successful NCO's patrol of the same regiment was caught by a burst of machine-gun fire on entering another wood. The sergeant commanding and three of his men were wounded and all their horses killed. A German account states that 'our hussars surprised a patrol and took prisoner four riders of the King Edward's Horse regiment'.[6]

---

*The horses' condition had been much reduced due to the exigencies of the shipping situation. As has been seen, the forage ration had to be severely cut. The 9th Lancers, for instance, 'had to utilize old straw, grass and the thatch of their billet standings as part substitutes for ration hay. . . . At the opening of the battle of Arras, they seemed fit enough in appearance when leaving winter quarters, but the lack of stamina soon made itself felt under test.' (Sheppard, 279).

†The German cavalry scouts employed trained dogs. These would approach the British outposts and (apparently) on seeing khaki uniforms race back to warn their masters.

5. 'B' Squadron, the Bays, in the earliest type of gas masks. (See p.22)

6. German gas masks: horse and man. (See p.22)

7. Horse gas masks being fitted. (See p.22)

8. The 19th Lancers (Fane's Horse) watering, 1915.

9. The 4th Dragoon Guards, June, 1915. Note the fly-fringes.

ACTION AT VILLERS FAUCON, 27 MARCH, 1917

* * *

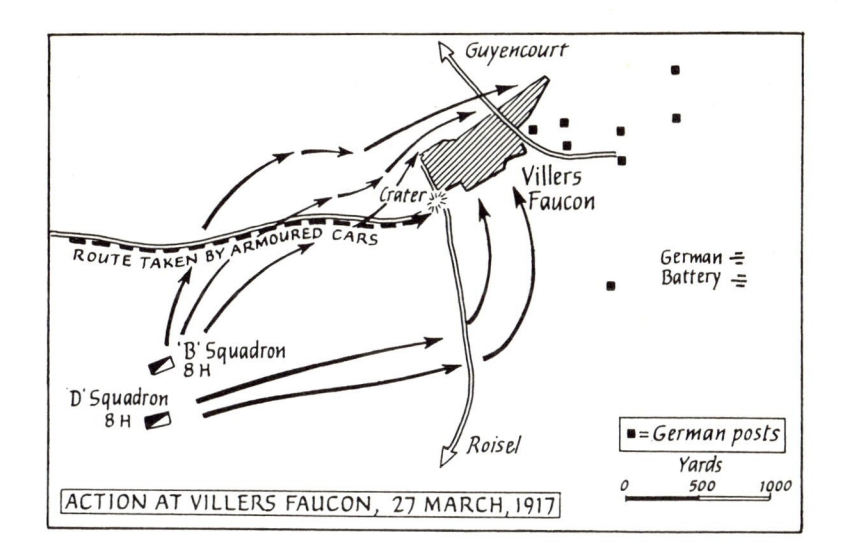

The only mounted actions of much interest took place on 27 March, a fortnight before the opening of the Arras offensive.* At 1 p.m. on that day 'B' and 'D' Squadrons of the 8th Hussars of the Ambala Brigade, 5th Cavalry Division, were ordered to take the village of Villers Faucon at 5 p.m. Two armoured cars were to come under the command of 'D' Squadron while 'X' Battery of the RHA and a howitzer battery were to support the attack by concentrated fire on the village. This was to lift to the ridge beyond it at 5 p.m. A sixty-strong rearguard with five machine guns was

---

*Two troops of Jacob's Horse of the Lucknow Brigade, the one at Boyelles and the other at Ecoust St Mein, on 19 March, ably supported by sections of the 12th Machine Gun Squadron, galloped into both villages ejecting the enemy, both infantry and cavalry patrols. (Preston: 'MG', 490).

Full descriptions of a reconnaissance made by King Edward's Horse, the IV Corps cavalry regiment, on 22 March, in which four men were killed and twelve wounded with 50% of the horses dead or maimed, are given in James: *KEH*, 180–3 and in detail in Furse, 74–87. It seems that a junior staff officer from 32nd Division's HQ reported that there was minimal enemy opposition to be expected. This contradicted the very full report made the previous day by a squadron of the regiment which stated in detail that strong enemy forces were in place. This, of course, was the truth. Against the second totally unnecessary reconnaissance, the regiment's commanding officer had protested to Corps HQ – but in vain.

71

thought to be holding the village. 'The country was open downland with no wire so far as was known.' This fortunately proved to be the case. Major John Van der Byl,* commanding 'D' Squadron, taking his troop leaders with him, was quickly disabused of any notion that he might reconnoitre the 1,700 yards or so of ground between the start line and the village. 'German artillery fire rendered this impossible.' He had therefore to make his plan on the information provided by his map. Conferring with the commander of the armoured cars, and Captain Edric George Weldon, commanding 'B' Squadron, he decided that

> 'The armoured cars were to start in their own time, advance rapidly down the road leading to the south-west end of the village, arriving there as the artillery lifted. Then they were to act in the village according to the situation. "B" squadron was to gallop to the area about the two copses shown in the sketch [see map p. 71], and to come into dismounted action, and to support by fire the mounted attack of "D" squadron from the south. As soon as "C" squadron was seen to be successfully approaching the village, "B" squadron was to move mounted against the north side of the village. "D" squadron was to start at a trot and move east on a line half way between Roisel and Villers Faucon, covered by one troop.'[7]

The map on p. 71 shows the actual directions taken by the two squadrons and the armoured cars. At exactly eight minutes after 5 p.m. the advance started – in a snow storm. Both the armoured cars became stuck at a huge crater which had been made at the road junction just outside the village. Both were put out of action, the three members of the leading one being killed by armour-piercing bullets fired from machine guns. This was very bad luck because the same two armoured cars had the previous day, when helping the 18th Bengal Lancers to capture Roisel, proved to be proof against ordinary bullets. But the enemy, speedily realizing how dangerous the cars could be, had rushed up armour-piercing

---

*Van der Byl had joined the 8th Hussars from Sandhurst in 1898, aged twenty, and served in the South African War with distinction. From 1927 to 1931 he commanded the 1st (Risalpur) Cavalry Brigade. He was Colonel of the 8th Hussars from 1930–47 and died, aged seventy-five, in 1953.

Action at Guyencourt, 27 March, 1917

bullets, just in time for the action the following day. From the point of view of the two squadrons, however, the armoured cars' action was well timed. The majority of the enemy machine-gun fire was directed at them, thus enabling both squadrons to enter the village with only two fatal casualties and 'a few wounded'. Most of these in fact occurred from shell fire after the village had been occupied. Both squadrons dismounted soon after entering the village and then fought on foot through its ruins as planned. It was cleared of the enemy and held for a night. Two enemy machine guns were captured intact and parts of another. One German officer and fifteen other ranks were taken prisoner.[8]*

The previous day Strathcona's Horse of the Canadian Cavalry Brigade had captured Equancourt by a surprise attack. Now, on the 27th, Brigadier 'Jack' Seely, commanding the brigade, (referred to by Liddell Hart as 'ex-War Minister turned Murat'), was ordered to take the village of Guyencourt. In the course of doing so, Lieutenant F.M.W. Harvey, who commanded the leading troop of Strathcona's Horse, won the Victoria Cross. Having galloped, as ordered, to a position behind the village, he came across an unsuspected wired trench full of Germans firing from a machine gun and with their rifles. Realizing that his horse would 'never jump the thin and almost invisible wire', he dismounted and 'ran forward well ahead of his men and dashed at the trench, still fully manned, jumped the wire, shot the machine-gunner and captured the gun.'[9]

* * *

Throughout the move up to the Hindenburg Line there were a few instances of mounted units being badly mauled by hidden machine guns. Typical of these was one witnessed by a field artillery officer. He saw the Irish Horse advancing in extended lines. 'They came upon a belt of wire and, unwisely converging towards an opening or passage which had been cut through the

---

*Van der Byl was awarded the DSO and Private Garvey the MM. 'The German officer, when interviewed, laid special stress on the point that his defensive measures simply contemplated preparations against a slow infantry attack, and he added that he would certainly have rendered such an attack both slow and difficult, resulting in many casualties. . . . The speed with which the squadrons effected their entrance from the south and north completely upset his plans, which he had no time to alter.' (Murray, 603)

The battle of Arras, 9 April, 1917

entanglements, suffered very heavy casualties when bunched together. The fire was disastrous to both horses and men.'[10]

* * *

As so often before the battle of Arras (and as often after), the Cavalry Corps* was to be employed to exploit a gap, should one be made. Haig, nevertheless, issued on 20 March a caution: The cavalry, he insisted, 'should be carefully handled so that its value may remain unimpaired; it is essential that the Cavalry Corps should be in a condition to deliver an effective blow against the enemy in battle; this moment has not yet arrived.'[11]†

As usual, to get the regiments forward cavalry tracks had been made. To complete the last sections of them, even as the battle was starting, working parties 'mixed irretrievably', as one 12th Lancer put it, 'dismounted Lancers, Dragoons and Hussars, with rifles slung, spade in hand, filled sandbags or hurled debris and all the flotsam and jetsam of battle into the shell-holes in the track.'[12] As the days wore on the tracks became 'well nigh impassable and, to make matters worse,' as a 3rd Hussar noted, 'were the number of dead horses upon it – horses which had fallen exhausted and in their weak state prevented by the clinging mud from rising again; a merciful bullet had ended the suffering of many of them.'[13]

* * *

The first moment at which it might have been possible for mounted troops to go through a gap (between the road to Cambrai and Feuchy) came on the first day of the offensive, 9 April, Easter Monday, but no units of the closest brigade – the 9th – were near enough to take advantage of the brief opening. Brigadier Adrian Carton de Wiart (4th Dragoon Guards), who

---

*To it were attached a squadron of the Royal Flying Corps and one observation balloon.

†An appreciation issued by First Army on 28 March specified the use of the 1st Cavalry Division 'to push forward and secure important rail and canal crossings in the Douai plain.' ('Battle of Arras, Considerations of Probable Action after the Attack on Vimy Ridge, First Army, 28 Mar., 1917', Appx 29, Edmonds, *1917*, I, 258)

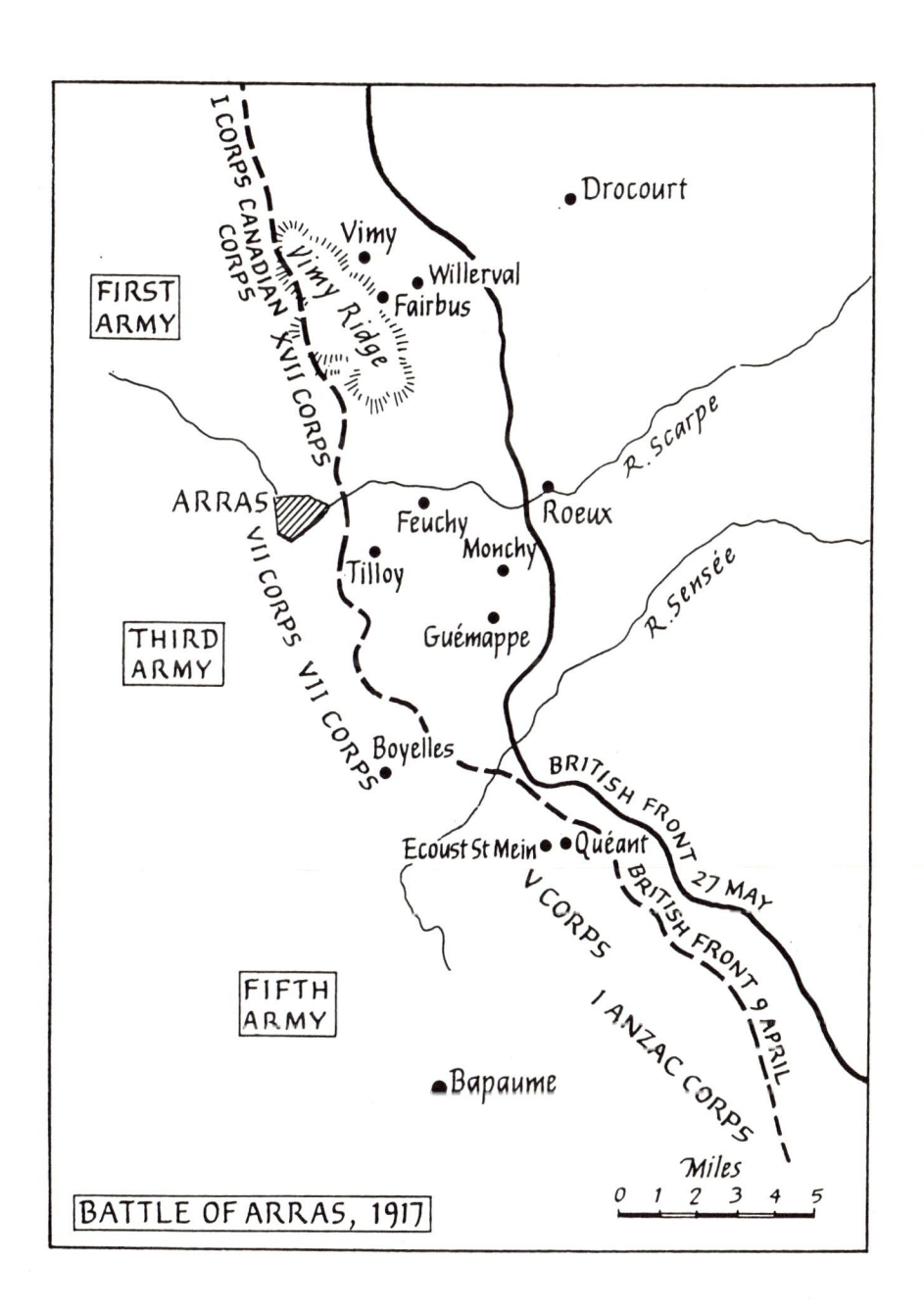

BATTLE OF ARRAS, 1917

now commanded the 12th Infantry Brigade, on learning that the cavalry was some twelve miles in the rear and could not get up till next day, told his cavalry liaison officer, 'Tomorrow will be too late'. The commander of a battalion of the 9th Infantry Division at the same time telephoned his brigade headquarters with the same message. He was asked, 'Are the Boches on the run?' He replied, 'Yes'. To 'Is cavalry good business?' he answered, 'Yes, ten thousand times yes, but it must be done *now*.'[14]*

At about this time the Northamptonshire Yeomanry, VI Corps cavalry, accompanied by horse artillery, further to the south, managed to gallop forward a good three thousand yards before meeting opposition at the last German trench line. 'It then drove off some snipers, captured six guns and made good the road and railway bridges.' This seems to have been the sole use of cavalry on the battle's first day, a truly splendid feat of arms, details of which seem to be almost entirely absent. It is worth pondering whether, had another regiment or two been available, it would not have been just possible to wheel southwards for the area of Monchy and to have taken that vital high point. On that same day, which was one of numerous sleet and snow squalls, Trooper Sam Bailey of the 1st Life Guards, waiting in the open on a race-course near Arras, 'a bleak, bare plain, with but one tiny hut-like structure on its surface', with their horses pegged down, awoke to 'a pitiful sight. The horses had pulled up their heel pegs and were huddled together. Some were dead through exposure, others had chewed their saddle blankets to pieces. It was impossible to release the head chains as they were completely frozen, and so were our fingers.... After a while came the order to saddle up and mount. What with the freezing night which had weakened the horses and our combined weight, many of them just collapsed and died.'[15]

A consequence of large masses of cavalry being concentrated behind the infantry, but not far enough up to be of use, was a

---

*Spears was told by a battalion commander that late in the evening 'the cavalry could have galloped to Monchy and occupied the place without great difficulty.... A little more luck,' Spears added, 'and a little more drive would certainly have given us the key position of Monchy by nightfall.' (Spears: *Prelude*, 594) There is, however, a good deal of evidence that this was not really the case.

On this day the Canadians captured the vital ridge at Vimy, one of the great feats of the war, and an advance of three and a half miles was achieved – the longest since the start of trench warfare.

Arras, 10 April, 1917

severe clogging of the advance of the other arms. This was exacerbated by the need in the late evening to withdraw them so that their horses could be watered.* Altogether 9 April was a very unsatisfactory day for the mounted arm.

* * *

The next day, during which elements of an infantry division advanced to within 500 yards of the western side of Monchy, due to the general confusion caused by the appallingly unseasonal weather and apparently to poor staff work, it was uncertain whether any British infantry had actually entered the village.† In the late morning one squadron of the 10th Hussars and two of the Essex Yeomanry, both of the 8th Cavalry Brigade, 3rd Cavalry Division, sent out patrols. All three ran up against intense machine-gun fire and suffered a number of casualties. At the same time, but in slightly different directions, the 3rd Dragoon Guards, leading regiment of the 6th Cavalry Brigade, commanded by Brigadier-General (Sir) Wentworth Harman, sent out one patrol mounted and another dismounted. Between them the five patrols established beyond doubt that parts of Monchy (which, since it had housed a German headquarters, had not yet been much knocked about) were still held in some strength. The patrols were able to retire without further casualties by the merciful intervention of a blinding snow storm.

Both the 3rd and 5th Cavalry Brigades advanced in the early evening. 'We trotted through Tilloy les Moufflains,' wrote Major the Hon. John Clive Darling of the 20th Hussars, 5th Brigade,

> 'in column of route. We then formed "line of troop columns" and broke into a gallop. The Greys were on the right, 20th on the left with the 12th Lancers in support. The 3rd Cavalry Brigade was on our right. . . . It was a fine sight, these large bodies of cavalry moving forward at a gallop over the

---

*'Congestion of the roads had made the return to bivouacs on the night [of 9 April] so laborious that the greater part of the 2nd Cavalry Division had not got in until 3 a.m., and "E" Battery, R.H.A. not until 5.30.' (Edmonds, *1917*, I, 252; see also Cruttwell, 407)

†In fact quite a few had, but by next morning these were completely exhausted by continual exertion and strain. (Edmonds, *1917*, I, 265)

open country, the columns closing in to pass through a defile where a gap in the wire had been negotiated,* and immediately deploying again when the obstacle was passed. Squadrons took the trenches in their stride. This time we really felt we were off and expected shortly to be passing through the infantry. . . . Patrols and advanced guards were all told off, and one word would be sufficient to despatch them on their missions.'[16]

The same snow storm that had covered the withdrawal of the 8th Brigade's patrols now put a temporary stop to the shelling which the enemy by this time was inflicting on these massed horsemen.

'It was marvellous,' wrote an officer of the Greys, 'how the leaders were able to keep their direction at top speed in the blinding snow storm, and the way that the troops managed to thread their way through the trenches and shell holes showed what a very handy and flexible formation line of troop columns is for an advance over rough ground. On their arrival at the new position, the Greys found that they were only about 150 yards behind our infantry, who were facing the Germans at about 200 yards range. The horses were distributed in batches of four to six, and the men took shelter in shell holes.'[17]

As with the 3rd, 6th and 8th Brigades, there were numerous casualties during the night.†

* * *

*The small numbers of tanks employed seem to have been successful in crushing the wire. 'A few tanks could be seen squatting in sinister immobility across the trenches they had cleared.' (Stewart, 284)

†When the Canadians' advance on Vimy to the north was so speedily successful, Byng, their commander, telephoned 1st Army pointing out the possibility of using a cavalry regiment to exploit the success of his two right-hand divisions. (2.40 p.m., 9 April 1917, War Diary, General Staff, Canadian Corps, quoted in Nicholson, 257–8). But, as the Canadian Official Historian puts it, 'the emphasis had been upon treating Vimy Ridge as a limited objective, and the rigid time-table required for effectively coordinating artillery and infantry in the attack had resulted in the exclusion from the Canadian Corps' scheme and the First Army's artillery plan of any participation by the cavalry.' (Nicholson, 258; see also Edmonds, *1917*, I, 333) (*continued over*)

Arras, 10 April, 1917

The 8th Brigade, commanded by Brigadier-General Charles Bulkeley-Johnson, a well-known big game hunter, spent the night at Feuchy Chapel (see map, p. 82), which had been captured the previous evening. There was desultory but heavy shelling with high explosives throughout the night. The Essex Yeomanry had sixty-one horses hit and the 10th Hussars lost ten men and fifty horses. The 6th Brigade bivouacked about a mile further back. 'It was impossible,' noted an officer of the 3rd Dragoon Guards, 'to picquet the horses owing to the mud and shell holes and they remained saddled up all night. As there was no water the horses had to go without for over thirty-six hours.'[18] A trooper of the Essex Yeomanry described the hardships of that night:

'Snow lay everywhere on the ground; the air was keen. Our horses were restless with cold and hunger, for we fed them sparingly, not knowing when fresh supplies might be available. Extra guards were, therefore, posted to control them. Then we manoeuvred for sleep, lying to the lee of the horses, deep in slush and wrapped in snow-soaked blankets, from which, however, a deal of warmth was to be got. The slush yielded to the pressure of our forms, became moulded to our shapes and thus provided partial protection. Our saddles we placed at our heads to keep off the wind.'

The men of the 20th Hussars, further north, spent the night sitting in big shell holes, holding their horses, which 'stood in circles

---

The only cavalry activity in the Canadian sector took place when the Corps Commander soon after 2 p.m. ordered a squadron of the Canadian Light Horse to 'push on to Willerval'. The Canadian Official Historian recounts how it fared:

'At 4.20 p.m. two mounted patrols, totalling twenty men, set out from Farbus for Willerval, a scant mile to the east. One patrol captured ten Germans in the village, but was in turn engaged by a machine-gun and lost half its men and horses; the other was all but wiped out by rifle fire. The main body of the squadron was shelled and half its horses were killed. Nevertheless the action, though costly and unsuccessful, was not without effect on the enemy: German reports that "a strong force of English cavalry had broken through into Willerval" led to orders being issued for a three-battalion counter-attack on the village.... [This however] failed to develop'.

(Report by CO, Canadian LH, Appx 'C' to War Diary, Canadian LH, April, 1917; *Die Osterschlacht bei Arras 1917*, I, 64, both quoted in Nicholson, 258)

round the edges. Pack horses brought up six pounds of oats per horse.' Private P.J. Batchelor of the Oxfordshire Hussars, remembered, many years later, that it was

> 'terrible cold and we pegged the horses out in the field in the snow, and we had no hay brought up for them for about three days, and one night I remember we walked the horses about all day till about four o'clock, round and round in a little circle, one after another, to keep them warm and to keep warm yourself. It was about a foot of snow there. We got in an old house with part of the roof on, and we sat down in there. There was a road outside and some lorries went up the road and they'd got some boxes of ammunition in, so our old cook says, "Here, we'll have some of them, we'll have a fire." We clambered up the back of these lorries, of course the drivers didn't know anything about it, threw these old boxes out, got about twenty, carried them inside this old house. The cook got his axe and he knocked them up and we sat all round this fire all night and we were warm in front and cold behind. Then we'd turn round and warm our backs. We never had any sleep – there was nowhere to sleep, we'd got no blankets (well, the horses had blankets) and it was wet and snowy. We'd saddle the horses up in the morning and they were so weak they went down with the weight of us. They'd had no grub! Some of the regiments lost a lot of horses up there. Died, they did.'[19]

* * *

The critical day of the battle was 11 April. It was thought by Allenby, commanding the Third Army, that the time had come to pursue 'a beaten army and that risks must be taken'. Indeed Ludendorff in his *Memoirs* says: 'April 10th. . . . A breach 12,000 to 15,000 yards wide, and as much as 6,000 yards or more in depth, is not a thing to be mended without more ado'.[20] Largely because the filthy weather had prevented air reconnaissance from detecting the speedy arrival of enemy reserves, there was no basis for Allenby's optimism. In fact the only success on that day worth mentioning – not an inconsiderable one – was the capture of

Monchy, 11 April, 1917

Monchy-le-Preux.* In this the cavalry took a prominent part, but not, as will be seen, an entirely happy one.

* * *

The infantry attack went in at 5 a.m. and nearly two hours later the 3rd Dragoon Guards reported that Monchy was 'held by us but our troops apparently have not gained eastern edge'. Bulkeley-Johnson, on learning this news, although he had not heard that the sunken road leading north-east from the village had also been taken, (a condition imposed by the divisional commander) decided to advance. At 8.30 the Essex Yeomanry, followed by the 10th Hussars, with the Royal Horse Guards, the third regiment of the 8th Cavalry Brigade, in reserve, received the order.† The

---

*Monchy, nearly three miles behind the German front line, dominated the central battlefront. 'Standing on a high plateau, with its odd sentinel-like church spire surrounded by a tight cluster of red brick houses, it appeared safe, serene and remote. To the north-west it was protected by two natural barriers, first Orange Hill and then Observation Ridge, and between the two lay a deep depression which the Germans called *Artillerie Mulde* – "Battery Valley" to the British. From this sheltered spot, German batteries lobbed shell after shell into Arras.' (Nicholls, 22). No wonder that Allenby was determined to take it before the first day of the battle was over.

†Officers of the Blues were heard singing the Eton Boating Song as they marched. (James: KEH, 101)
   Bulkeley-Johnson's message to 3rd Divisional headquarters read: 'I am sending off Tenth and Essex to try and get objectives. They are both going south of Orange Hill as M.G. fire from the river is as bad as ever and holding up the infantry. My report centre will be south end of summit of Orange Hill.'
   His verbal orders to his assembled commanding officers were:

'Seize the ridge Bois des Aubepines to Pelves Mill; Essex Yeomanry on right, Tenth Hussars on left. When this is achieved, proceed to first objective, namely Bois du Sart – east end of Pelves, including Hatchet and Jigsaw Woods. Dividing line between Essex and Tenth, north side of Keeling Copse – north end of Hatchet Wood – south edge of Jigsaw Wood. To each leading regiment, two subsections machine guns. Rest of brigade to follow in the order, G. Battery R.H.A., Blues, remainder of Machine Gun Squadron.'
(Preston: *Arras*, 529–30)

MONCHY, 11 APRIL, 1917

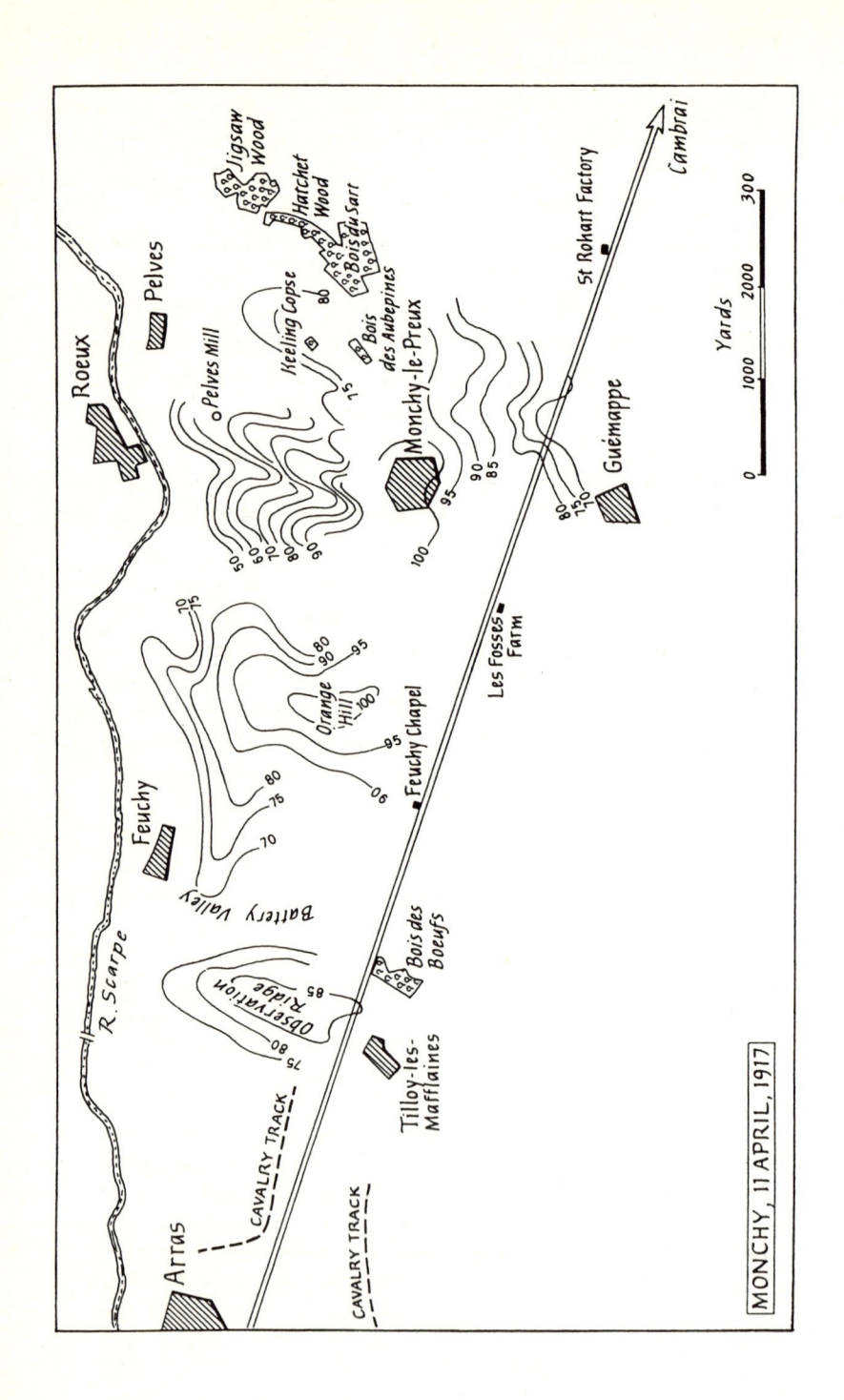

3rd Dragoon Guards also did so at about the same time. It was the leading regiment of the 6th Cavalry Brigade. It and the Essex Yeomanry, their commanding officers having conferred together, advanced more or less parallel to each other. The leading squadron of the 3rd soon reached its first objective, the ridge south of Monchy, under slight shelling. It was followed by a second squadron. Both squadrons were 'subjected to heavy shell and machine-gun fire, suffering a good many casualties both in men and horses'. After one intermediate bound, they reached their objective, encountering an enemy party digging in in front of four guns which they speedily abandoned.[21] By 9.5 a.m. the leading troop of the 3rd had reached the main road to Cambrai at the southern exit of Monchy. Here it dismounted in a partially completed enemy trench and was soon joined by most of the rest of the regiment. Hotchkiss posts were pushed forward to deal with a threatened German advance from the north-east and machine-gun fire from Guémappe to the south. Two sections of 'C' Battery, RHA soon joined in, as also did a machine-gun section. Later two squadrons of the North Somerset Yeomanry, the VI Corps Cavalry, arrived to strengthen the line.* By midnight fresh infantry came up to relieve the 3rd Dragoon Guards, the North Somerset Yeomanry and the attendant machine-gun squadron. These withdrew to spend another miserable night in the quagmire of the Arras racecourse.

* * *

The Essex Yeomanry and the 10th Hussars, meanwhile, were told by Bulkeley-Johnson that, should they come under machine-gun fire from the north-east (which had been experienced the previous day), they were to ignore their orders to move to the north of Monchy. Instead they should go straight for the western entrance to the village. In the event the advance squadrons of both regiments, each with two Vickers machine guns, (riding forward 'in line of troop columns, preceded by one troop, which in its turn threw out patrols to gallop to local objectives'), did, as expected,

---

* An airman, 'who made a forced landing about 11 a.m., reported that the Germans were digging in on the line St Rohart Factory – Keeling Copse – Pelves, and this was confirmed . . . by patrols of the 3rd Dragoon Guards.' (Preston: *Arras*, 532)

Monchy, 11 April, 1917

encounter intense fire from the area of Roeux. This came not only from machine guns but also from artillery, and it hit the horsemen as they emerged upon the crest of Orange Hill about 1,500 yards from the village. The Adjutant of the yeomanry wrote home: 'As soon as we topped Orange Hill the shells began to fall, first in ones and twos, then in half-dozens, then in a continuous stream. We started trotting, then galloping, in a sort of loose open formation. . . . I should think we galloped like this for a mile until we arrived at the north-western edge of Monchy.'[22] Some of the Northamptons, seeing what was going on, came in from the north and joined in the gallop. One of them, Trooper Bertie Taylor, in old age remembered that

> 'We got over the top of the rise and there it stood, red bricks showing – Monchy! The snow was laying thick and I remember at this point some of our horses collapsed, buckling the swords of their riders. We extended into one long line, a bugle sounded and we charged! Over open ground, jumping trenches, men swearing, horses squealing – a proper old commotion! The bugle sounded three times – and we had come under quite heavy shell fire and some of the saddles had been emptied. But the horses knew what to do better than we did, and galloping by me came these riderless horses. Mine, poor devil, had been wounded badly in the coronet so I pulled him up and dismounted and had a look at him. Well, he looked at me, there were tears in his eyes. Poor devils, they know you know. Another one came flying past me with half his guts hanging out, I'd never seen anything like that. Well, my horse perked up, so we galloped off after the others. The riderless horses were still leading the charge. Eventually I caught up with our officer, Mr Humphriss, who was riding a few yards ahead when a shell exploded just beneath his horse and split him like a side of beef hanging up in the butcher's shop. Both horse and rider were killed instantly. Next we got into the village and the streets were so narrow that tiles from the roofs were raining down on us – that's what caused a lot of injuries. The shell fire was so hot that the bugles sounded the retirement and back we went, led by the riderless horses!'[23]

Monchy, 11 April, 1917

Even more graphic is the account of Trooper Clarence Garnett of the 8th Machine Gun Squadron of the Essex Yeomanry:

> I was riding a little horse called Nimrod and leading another with a pack saddle on his back loaded with boxes of machine-gun ammunition. We had not gone far when a huge shell burst to my right. Someone yelled, 'Garnett's pack-horse has broken its leg!' Our [lance-] corporal, Harold Mugford,* shouted at me to keep going but the pack-horse fell, and as I was holding on to him so tightly, he pulled me out of the saddle. I let go and managed to stay on Nimrod, regaining my balance, but then my saddle slipped under his stomach. I rode on, hanging on for dear life, on his bare back. All the rest of the column had left me and seeing a huge hawthorn tree, I got behind it and adjusted the saddle. I remounted and rode on alone to where the others had gone and quickly entered the village where I saw a dead pack-horse with ammunition on his back, so I dismounted and took a box. Galloping along the street I soon reached the building marked 'Château' on my map, where I was stopped by our officer who demanded my box of ammunition and told me to follow him. By now there were a few of us and the shelling had become very heavy, so the officer ordered us to lie down under the shelter of a wall. As I was lying in a gap between two cottages, I immediately got up, still holding my horse, and lay down under the wall of a cottage opposite. I had not been there long when a light shell came through the gap in the cottages and cut down the officer and most of the others. Nimrod was terrified and he reared up violently, dragging me along the street for some yards until I was forced to let go. I never saw him again after that. As it was pointless staying in that spot, I wandered along the street and into the main square which was simply covered with dead horses and men. To my horror, I saw one of our blokes cut in two at the waist. One half

---

*Mugford was wounded in the jaw by a shell fragment whilst firing his Vickers gun. He continued firing it until another shell broke both his legs (which were later amputated). His men started to carry him to the rear, but he urged them to leave him and go on firing. Later when lying outside the dressing station he was again wounded – in the arm. He was awarded the VC. In 1929 he is recorded as having attended the Prince of Wales's dinner given to all winners of the VC. (Preston: *Arras*, 539)

of him was on one side of the street, the other on the other side. Later that morning it started to rain and I swear the streets of Monchy ran red with blood.'[24]

The two leading troops of the Essex Yeomanry were almost annihilated. The survivors and the rest of the regiment swerved to their right and found some cover from the trees and some houses which were still standing. The hussars, seeing the yeomanry's wheel, divined the reason and 'bent its course southward ... and entered the village at the same moment, having suffered little loss'.[25] 'We went full tilt,' said one begrimed subaltern, 'with a cheer for a good half mile into the funny old town.'[26]

Lieutenant-Colonel (Sir) Francis Henry Douglas Charlton Whitmore (Bart), commanding the Essex Yeomanry,* describes what happened next:

'At the N. Western entrance to the village only shell fire was met with, but many casualties occurred on account of the buildings and the hard roads offering greater resistance to the high explosive shell. The two advanced squadrons then proceeded as follows:- Essex Yeomanry via central road leading to the Square and thence by the sunken road leading N.E. towards Pelves, the 10th Hussars following the Essex Yeomanry to the centre of Monchy, thence turning due N. until they reached the outskirts of the village. On emerging from the village, both these squadrons were held up by machine-gun fire.

'By this time the remainder of the two regiments were already in the village and the whole force of the German artillery seemed to be concentrated upon it, causing many casualties to officers, men and horses.†

'Machine guns and Hotchkiss automatic rifles were brought up at once from both regiments and distributed in

---

*Whitmore had commanded the Essex Imperial Yeomanry in the Boer War. In 1918 he exchanged his command of the Essex Yeomanry for that of the 10th Hussars, becoming the only yeomanry officer to command a regular cavalry regiment. He became Colonel of five different units between 1926 and 1948 and had a distinguished career in local government, being created a baronet in 1954, eight years before he died at the age of ninety. For many years he was the yeomanry sub-editor of the *Cavalry Journal*.

†The concentration of fire was, according to the Official Historian, 'such as few observers had ever witnessed.' (Edmonds *1917*, I, 264)

positions surrounding the South-East, East and North of the village. At this time Lieutenant-Colonel [Philip Edward] Hardwick* commanding 10th Hussars, with one squadron ... endeavoured to make his way round the northern flank, but again met with severe machine-gun fire on the Northern outskirts of the village and was forced to turn in a South-Easterly direction through the wood [where he and his adjutant were both wounded]. ...

'The scattered remnants of the 111th and 112th Infantry Brigades were occupying isolated places in and W. of the château.† These were collected and they, together with the 10th Hussars and Essex Yeomanry [all by now dismounted], the whole being under [my command], consolidated the positions gained on the Northern and Eastern outskirts of Monchy.'

The led horses were then concentrated in the centre of the village. This was, of course, observed by the enemy, who 'put every gun he had on the village and,' according to Kavanagh in a letter written on 17 April, 'the losses in horses were very heavy indeed.'[27] A trooper of the Essex Yeomanry described the scene at this time: 'Bodies of men and horses lay in the streets and the ping-ping of the sniping came more and more frequently, the lead whistling past one's head on each side alternately. ... Their bullets flew too low, nine out of every ten that struck anything hitting an animal.'[28] At this point a number of the machine guns and Hotchkiss rifles were put out of action. 'Amidst the general turmoil,' wrote a yeomanry officer, 'it was refreshing to hear Colonel Whitmore remonstrating with his Adjutant, Captain [Sir] Richard George Proby [1st Bart],§

---

*Hardwick, who was twice wounded, died aged forty-four in 1919. He had joined the Royal Dragoons aged twenty-two and served with that regiment in the Boer War. He had taken over command of the 10th Hussars in 1916.

†According to Kavanagh these 'were reduced to about seventy men, who were mostly dead tired and taking cover in cellars and no officer to be seen.' (Crichton, 3)

§Proby, who later had a distinguished career in agriculture and forestry, receiving the Bledisloe Gold Medal in 1967, died, aged ninety-three, in 1979.

for not taking cover. "My dear Dick," he said, "if you continue to stand there you will be hit and I cannot afford to lose you".'[29]

At this critical moment, when it looked as if the enemy was massing for a counter-attack, a party of the Northamptons arrived in the village. Some indeed had already been there for quite a time (see p. 84). These and the few infantrymen available helped to consolidate the positions held while keeping in touch with the infantry to the north of Monchy. Whitmore sent at least eight separate messages to brigade headquarters. These were taken by mounted dispatch riders, the only remaining means of communication since all the signalling equipment had been destroyed. These intrepid officers and NCOs had to gallop through the barrage which swept the ground between the village and the rest of the brigade. The fourth message read: 'What remains of [our two] regiments are holding on to N-E, E and S exits of village. Require both M.G.s and Ammunition. Am afraid we have had many casualties. Counter-attack expected. . . . Reinforcements required as reserve. Majority of horses casualties.' His fifth message was sent at 11.45 a.m., thirty-five minutes after the fourth one. A yeomanry trooper saw Whitmore dictating these messages to the Adjutant 'as coolly as if in a club in Piccadilly'. As a result of one of them a squadron of the Royal Horse Guards, with four machine guns, was sent up. It failed, however, to get into the village and suffered many casualties, losing two of the machine guns.* At this moment, as

---

*'Soon,' wrote a young officer of the regiment, 'we got the orders to mount. Orders were given to go through the gap in half sections, form sections when over the front line trenches and then form line of troop column. . . . It was very heavy going to gallop over. A bomb went off in front of my troop, probably struck by a horse's hoof. Packs fell over from the Hotchkiss gun pack-ponies. The plateau on top was a mass of shell-holes. We galloped right into a terrible barrage. . . . Duddy Hardy (Brigade-Major) galloped at us shouting "File about", thereby saving all our lives. We galloped back.' (Buckmaster, 161).

The Blues' squadron was commanded by Major the Earl of Pembroke 'who crawled into Monchy on foot, just before 3 p.m., "but", [as a yeomanry officer said] "it cheered us to see him, because it showed that the Blues were trying to get up help to us".' (Burrows, 134–5)

Captain Lord Gerard of the regiment was wounded in seven places, having one arm and one leg broken. His horse was 'split straight up as if cut in half with a razor'. (Whitmore, 102; Arthur, 168)

one observer put it, 'seen from Orange Hill, Monchy village looked like a smoking furnace, and it seemed incredible that anything could be alive in it.'[30]

For some time it had been certain that a further advance to the original objective which had been set the brigade, some high ground about 4,000 yards to the east of Monchy, was impossible. The led horses could therefore be removed from the village, but the operation was made extremely difficult because of the casualties which blocked the roads and 'the fact that so large a number of horses of so many units were seeking the same shelter outside the village thus attracting the fire of the enemy's artillery'. Indeed those horses that escaped death or maiming rushed back into Monchy 'in a wild, panic-stricken gallop'.[31]

At about this time Bulkeley-Johnson, anxious to see at first hand what the situation was, against the advice of an infantry officer whom he asked to show him the enemy disposition, went forward on foot. Before he had gone far he was struck on the cheek-bone by a bullet. The officer who was accompanying him never forgot 'his piercing shriek as he tumbled down and rolled over on the ground'.[32]* The next most senior officer in the brigade was Lieutenant-Colonel Lord Tweedmouth, commanding the Royal Horse Guards. He at once, but only temporarily, assumed command of the brigade.

To the privations of horses and men was added the lack of water. The men had to collect snow and to melt it in order to make tea, mostly in the cellars of the crumbling houses, in one of which Whitmore after a time set up his headquarters. 'It was a common sight,' he wrote, 'to see the horses licking the snow off each others' backs in order to quench their thirst.'[33]

---

*An infantry officer described Bulkeley-Johnson as 'a tall fine-looking elderly man, the perfect type of pre-war regular soldier'. He remembered him as 'wearing one of those new-fangled two-piece trench suits over his uniform – a sort of short waterproof trench coat with separate trousers reaching to below the knee – under which his gold-laced tabs and cavalry boots could be seen.' (Cuddeford, D.W.J. 'Senseless Slaughter of Men and Horses: Blood and Snow and Confusion at Monchy', Hammerton, Sir J. *The Great War: I Was There!*, XXVII, 1939)

Fortunately the feared counter-attack never materialized. Kavanagh says that the Germans 'did assemble for an attack but our guns broke them up before it could mature'. This was especially lucky, for the digging of emplacements and trenches on the outskirts of the village was much impeded because 'a large number of the tool packs had been destroyed'.[34]

By now most of the officers of the hussars and yeomanry had been either killed or wounded and so had many other ranks. The not very numerous survivors of the 111th and 112th Infantry Brigades, the remnants of at least five battalions, were employed in taking the wounded to the dressing stations set up by the medical officers of the two regiments chiefly in the cellars of Monchy. Communication with the 3rd Dragoon Guards on the right and the infantry brigade on the left was now fully established. To add to the continuing shell fire which was rapidly reducing the village to a heap of pink rubble, 'there were constant visits over the lines from enemy aeroplanes during the day. . . . Enemy aeroplanes,' wrote Whitmore, 'swooped down and shot at the led horses with their machine guns.'[35]

Both regiments, just as night was falling, sent out foot patrols. These established that the Germans were digging themselves in about 300 yards from the north-eastern outskirts of Monchy. At 6.30 p.m. Whitmore made a situation report in which he estimated that the combined strength of the 10th Hussars and the Essex Yeomanry did not exceed 170, and that the shelling had 'died down'.[36]

Most of the village's defences were taken over by infantry at about midnight. 'The officer commanding the battalion at Monchy,' however, according to Kavanagh, 'said he could not hold it without some of the cavalry and machine guns staying, so two squadrons and the machine guns stayed.'* The rest of the cavalry – parts of two squadrons of the 10th Hussars and a few men of the 8th Machine Gun Squadron – were relieved during the next two days. 'The order rang out,' wrote Lance-Corporal G.W. Davis of the hussars, ' "Cavalrymen line up in the road."

---

*Lorries arrived at Les Fosses Farm on the 12th to take away the machine guns for which, the massacre of the horses being so vast, there were none left to carry them. (Burrows, 137)

So goodbye and good luck. Captain Stokes led us away from Monchy-le-Preux past the place where the bodies of our horses lay. Dumb, dead horses.'[37] In his diary that night Haig wrote sadly of 'the numbers of cavalrymen marching back on foot having had their horses killed'.[38] One officer of the relieving force, as he 'turned the bend of the road to go up the hill' stopped in his tracks.

> 'The sight that greeted me was so horrible that I almost lost my head. Heaped on top of one another and blocking up the roadway for as far as one could see, lay the mutilated bodies of our men and their horses. These bodies, torn and gaping, had stiffened into fantastic attitudes. All the hollows of the road were filled with blood. This was the cavalry. I walked up the hill, picking my way as best I could and often slipping in the pools of blood, so that my boots and the lower parts of my puttees were dripping with blood by the time I reached the top. Nor, I discovered on my way up, were all the men and animals quite dead. Now and then a groan would strike the air – the groan of a man who was praying for release. Sometimes the twitch of a horse's leg would shift the pattern of the heaped-up bodies. A small party of stretcher-bearers, obviously unequal to their task, were doing what they could to relieve the suffering.'[39]

* * *

The difficulty in attending to the seriously wounded left in Monchy, who could only be evacuated after dark because in daylight the approaches to the village were under constant enemy observation and fire, was compounded by what seems to have been a deplorable breakdown in communications between the divisional medical officers and the Cavalry Field Ambulances (CFAs). These had last been properly tested during the advance to the Aisne in 1914, proving more or less satisfactory. Later on, motor cars had replaced the horse-drawn ambulances of the main dressing stations, while the advanced dressing stations had remained horsed.[40]

In February, 1917, some of the CFAs had formed 'pack mounted sections'. 'It was anticipated,' as the official medical history puts it, 'that occasions might arise when cavalry would advance through a gap rapidly and far, over a trench system where ambulance transport could not follow.' These sections were designed to carry most medical needs right up with the advancing brigades, in close touch with regimental medical officers and aid posts.[41]

The sections employed on this occasion consisted of two officers, one NCO, five mounted orderlies, two pack horse leaders, ten riding and two pack horses. One of the latter carried eight jointed stretchers and the other six gallons of water in three petrol tins, dressings and medical comforts. In the saddle bags of the orderlies various medical equipment and further dressings were also carried.[42]

On 11th April, the first time they were tested in action, these sections proved sadly wanting. Beside one of them having three of its horses killed and two wounded, the petrol tins in the others broke through the wooden boxes carrying them; to get at one stretcher the whole bundle had to be removed from the pack horse; the poles of the jointed stretchers failed to fit into the canvas when it got wet and different parts of stretchers were carried on two pack horses which, when wanted, were often not together.[43]

The original orders had stipulated that an advanced dressing station should be established near Les Fosses Farm.[44] Because of the heavy shelling this proved impossible, even apparently after dark. The light sections of two of the CFAs managed to reach Bois des Boeufs, about three miles from Monchy, but for some reason were unable to get closer.[45]

At 4.30 p.m. the Deputy Assistant Director of Medical Services (DADMS) of the division spoke to the officers commanding these CFAs with their pack mounted sections. 'Heavy casualties were then known to be west of Monchy *but neither of them told him that they required further assistance.*' One of them stated, almost unbelievably, that by 9 p.m. 'all casualties in the brigade had been evacuated'.* The official medical historian points out, not surprisingly, that

> 'there were neither pack mounted sections nor light sections of the 3rd Cavalry Division nearer than the race course on the west of Arras during the night of 11th/12th April.... The [division's] A.D.M.S. first received information of wounded

---

* 'Poor Dawson Damer,' wrote Kavanagh, 'was badly hit and died in Monchy about twenty-four hours after, as he could not be got away.' (Crichton, 4)

still being in Monchy from the D.A.D.M.S. of *the Cavalry Corps* at 3 p.m. on the 12th April and at 6 p.m. of that day [the latter officer] himself went into Monchy with a stretcher party, bringing back the O.C. of the 10th Hussars and thirty other wounded during the night of the 12th/13th and reporting that some forty more were in the cellars there. These were eventually got *the following night* by a large party of officers and dismounted men and by motor ambulance cars which went forward to Feuchy Chapel. About eighty wounded were brought back.'[46]

As a result of this fiasco pack mounted sections were done away with. Instead, it seems, the intention for future operations was that some seventy-five stretchers and blankets would be carried 'in the lorry of the divisional sanitary section'. These were to be distributed 'to men obtained from regiments, for collecting and removing the wounded'. To what degree this idea was implemented it is hard to say. Certainly at Cambrai in November pack mounted sections were still to some extent being employed.[47]

* * *

An assessment of the losses incurred by the whole Cavalry Corps during the first three or four days of the battle of Arras is difficult to effect, especially as regards horses.* There can be little question that an important part of the horse casualties was due to the 'softness' of nearly all of them. From being under cover in back areas for months on end, pretty well pampered, they were suddenly hurled into endless marching in extreme cold with no night-time shelter and often under shell fire. Added to that was a sudden reduction in forage rations and many hours without water. It really was asking too much of equine endurance. A good example is provided by the Greys. They lost 'about twenty' horses during the night of 11 April alone. Though never much in contact with the enemy their total losses during the three days, 9 to 11 April, were 116, of which thirty-one died from exhaustion or had

---

*Edmonds, *1917*, I, 272, gives the total cavalry casualties in the 3rd Army *for the whole of April*, including those of corps cavalry regiments, as 845 of all ranks (fifty-nine officers).

to be destroyed. 'During the next few days a further thirty-nine died or had to be sent away to base.'* Twelve horses of the 4th Machine Gun Squadron of the 2nd Cavalry Division died during the night of 11 April. The squadron's war diary states that: 'the horses seemed just to drop and become unable to get up again. Some few of them were able to get up, and if one could get them on the move in time they seemed to come round. We eventually turned the majority of the poorer-conditioned ones loose, and let them move about as they liked, and I believe had this been done sooner, in spite of the risk of losing horses, that the casualties would have been reduced.'[48]

As for the casualties of the 8th Cavalry Brigade between 9 and 11 April there is no record of the number of horses lost, but the losses of officers and men in the 10th Hussars and the Essex Yeomanry alone numbered 324, including sixty-one killed and missing. The 6th Cavalry Brigade lost a total of 179 of all ranks. The horse casualties in the 12th Lancers (5th Cavalry Brigade), which regiment was hardly engaged at all, (losing only fifty-six of all ranks in the three days), were 'over 100'.[49]† To judge by this proportion, the horse losses of the 10th Hussars and the Essex Yeomanry might well have numbered some 900.§ The leading squadron of the 10th lost *every one* of its horses. The 8th Machine Gun Squadron lost ninety-seven.

There is much evidence that every regiment, except the few which remained in reserve, lost considerable numbers of horses, whether they were directly engaged with the enemy or, as in most cases, only suffering under shell fire from a distance or from exhaustion and death, often as a result of falling off cavalry tracks. The 3rd Dragoon Guards, whose human casualties numbered ninety-seven, including twenty killed, lost 190 horses between

---

*Later in the month, when remounts had arrived, there were still 337 *grey* horses out of the regiment's 534! (Pomeroy: 2D, 111)

†Edmonds, 1917, 1, 272, says that the 5th Cavalry Brigade had 347 horses casualties.

§Preston: *Arras*, 542 says 'about 500'. This is probably well below the real figure.

9 and 11 April.* What is certain is that remounts were amazingly speedily supplied from the base remount depots. The 3rd Dragoon Guards, for example, received 171 remounts on 21 April, while the Essex Yeomanry received 'over 260 horses of a good stamp'[50] at the same time.† It was chiefly because the unhurt cavalry horses were 'perilously near the point of foundering'[51] that Allenby on 12 April ordered the 2nd Cavalry Division, which had lost 274 horses from exhaustion and accident alone, right back to where it had been on 8 April.

* * *

When an officer of the 11th Hussars wrote that 'this gallant occupation and defence of Monchy was something that could at last be put down to the credit of the cavalry',[52] he certainly expressed a view held by many of all ranks in the mounted arm. Byng, who, though an ex-10th Hussar, had by now relinquished any idea of a decisive breakthrough ('We gave up that catchword some time ago'), wrote on 30 May to Chetwode, now in Sinai: 'It seems rather a pity to lose all these chaps who were perfect cavalrymen for the sake of a village which is a complete shell trap for the British side.'

Haig, in sending a congratulatory message, said that 'the action of the cavalry probably saved the many thousands of lives it would have cost to retake Monchy if the Boche had got back there.'[53] The Official Historian believed that the capture of Monchy was 'one of the outstanding feats of the whole battle [of Arras]' and that the village 'might not have been held or even completely cleared' but for the cavalry's aid. It was, of course, lost again in the German

---

*Though in 1963, in *Haig*, 289, John Terraine writes of 'high mounds of dead horses', in 1980, in *Smoke and Fire*, 164, he writes that 'blood-curdling reports of mounds of dead horses and riders should be discounted'. Alas, the 'blood-curdling reports' were correct. Private C.H. Garnett of the 8th Machine Gun Squadron (3rd Cavalry Division) was later told by a man who helped to bury the horses in a corner of the village that 'there were so many that they called it "Dead Horse Corner".' (First-hand, unpublished account supplied to Nicholls).

†109 other rank reinforcements arrived before the end of the month for the Essex Yeomanry from the 5th Dragoon Guards and four yeomanry regiments, 'the first great influx of men having no connection with the county'. (Burrows, 140)

Spring, 1918, offensives. Not until 28 August, 1918, was it finally captured without cavalry help. On that day Haig commented in his diary: 'The enemy knew the value of this position ... and so devoted much labour to strengthening it since he retook it from us.'[54]

* * *

On 20 April the Cavalry Corps moved back to its billets. 'I just hate going back,' wrote Home in his diary. 'One can quite realise the bad effect it has on the men. On the other hand there is no possible use for cavalry just now and we must clear the way for other people until our turn comes once again.'[55]

6

'I am building secure and covered chariots, which are invulnerable, and when they advance with their guns into the midst of the foe, even the largest enemy masses must retreat, and behind them the infantry can follow in safety and without opposition.'
– LEONARDO DA VINCI in 1482

'I discussed with Byng some operations which he proposed . . . and I told him I would give him all the help I could.'
– HAIG in his diary for 16 September, 1917; the genesis of Cambrai

'The Passchendaele offensive had ended in mire and carnage, when suddenly there emerged from the British sector opposite Cambrai a battle totally different in character from any yet fought in the war.'
– CHURCHILL in *The World Crisis, 1916–1918*

'Eventually I decided that, despite the various limiting factors, I could muster enough force to make a first success sufficiently sure to justify undertaking the attack, but that the degree to which this success could be followed up must depend on circumstances.'
– HAIG in his Cambrai Despatch

' "*The Corps Commander intends to seize the Bourlon position as rapidly as possible. . . . It is very important that it should be captured the first day. . . .*" Alas, the distance was impossible without the swift follow through of reserves.'
– ROBERT WOOLLCOOMBE, grandson of IV Corps commander, in *The First Tank Battle*

'Had the Whippet tank, a machine relatively fast compared to the Mark V, existed at this time, Bourlon Hill could have been taken on the first day, for it was only lightly held by the Germans.'
– BREVET-COLONEL J.F.C. FULLER in 1920

'Cambrai . . . was very like the panorama of Waterloo which Papa took me to once. Puffs of smoke, houses burning and fields with broken guns and bits of accoutrements lying about, men looting the German canteens and pathetic stiff dead bodies in unexpected places.'
– CONRAD RUSSELL writing on the eighth anniversary of the battle, 1925

'With no wire and prepared defences to hamper them, it was reasonable to hope that masses of cavalry would find it possible to pass through, whose task would be thoroughly to disorganise the enemy's system of command and inter-communication.'
— HAIG, Despatch, 20 February, 1918

'When news arrived that there was no longer to be what a very distinguished officer of the XIth Hussars called "if not a gallop at least a nice hard canter to Berlin" they all went home.'
— A.J. SMITHERS in *Cambrai*

'On November 21st the bells of London rang out in joyous acclaim of a triumphant success that seemed a foretaste of victory, perhaps at no distant date. And Ludendorff, back at the German Supreme Command, was hurriedly preparing emergency instructions for a general retreat. Both the bells and Ludendorff were premature – although prophetic – by some nine months.'
— B.H. LIDDELL HART in *The Real War, 1914–1918*, 1930

'The Tank Corps proved to be rather too happy to shift the odium once again on to the horsed cavalry.'
— PADDY GRIFFITH in *Battle Tactics of the Western Front*[1]

3rd Ypres – Messines – 1st Cambrai

'To root out the hornets' nests of Ostend and Zeebrugge would itself be a triumph,'[2] writes Cyril Falls of the origins of the great bloody and muddy battles comprising 3rd Ypres, known vulgarly, after the last of them, as 'Passchendaele'. That Haig had been thinking much of such a triumph for at least a year and a half before he could launch his attack is clear.* That it took so long to come to the point of execution was in part due to the diversionary offensive at Arras required by Nivelle. At the time, as has been

---

*Indeed the earliest seed of 3rd Ypres was sown in 1914 by Churchill who urged the freeing of the two ports before they could become U-boat bases. In January, 1916, Haig soon after taking over command, had ordered work to be re-started on launching such an offensive in co-operation with a large-scale amphibious operation, which in the event never materialized.

Messines, 7 June, 1917

shown, Haig saw Arras as a preparation for the season's main campaign in Flanders. Its failure, instead, put that main campaign in considerable peril. A further incentive for the launching and extended continuation of 3rd Ypres was the awful knowledge that much of the French Army was to be, for at least the rest of 1917, more or less, a broken reed.

An essential preliminary was the capture of the Messines Ridge. This was partly achieved by a battle which was preceded by more than a fortnight's bombardment and the explosion of nineteen vast mines under the Germans' front line. It was a brilliant feat, but without an unrelenting exploitation, which, as so often, proved impossible by either infantry or cavalry, was a largely unproductive victory.

* * *

There was now allowed to befall an interval of six weeks of almost perfect summer weather, during which the enemy, given notice by the Messines battle, brought up reinforcements, mostly from the French front. This, if a boon for Pétain, was baleful for Haig.

The chief reason for the disastrous delay was that Haig, believing that General Sir Herbert Charles Onslow Plumer,* who was responsible for the Messines success and was very willing to try to develop his victory, was lacking in enterprise, replaced him in charge of the great offensive by Gough. Gough, new to the area, naturally took time to get to know its problems and to implement the changes to Plumer's plans which he saw as necessary. It was probably Haig's worst bloomer of the war.†

---

*Plumer, an infantryman, had joined the army in 1876. He served with distinction in the Boer War (See Vol. 4, 174 *et seq.*). He commanded successively V Corps (1915), Second Army (1915–17) and became GOC, Italian Expeditionary Force (1917–18) and for the second time commanded Second Army from March to December, 1918. From December, 1918 to April, 1919, he commanded the Army of the Rhine. He was Governor of Malta 1919–24 and High Commissioner, Palestine, 1925–28. In 1919 he was promoted Field-Marshal. He died, aged seventy-five, in 1932.

†This he tacitly acknowledged when for the second period of 3rd Ypres he put Plumer again in charge. This, too, was unfortunate with respect to time loss, since Plumer required three weeks for *his* preparations. These in the event paid off to a large degree. Three step-by-step blows, ending on 4 October, were all as successful as could be hoped for under the deteriorating weather conditions.

Genesis of 1st Cambrai

To make it worse he and Gough had major misunderstandings. Gough became preoccupied with the northern line of attack – that which was intended to remove the U-boat menace from the Ostend and Zeebrugge bases (in fact by late June, but hardly yet realized, a menace rapidly decreasing as a result of the new convoy system). Haig and Plumer, for their part, were more concerned with the other great objective of the coming campaign, namely the capture or domination by artillery of the railway centre of Roulers, ten miles east of Ypres, upon which 'the whole German position in western Flanders largely depended'.[3] As is well known, at a terrible cost in dead, wounded and hellish misery on both sides, neither objective was attained.

Since the cavalry was virtually unemployed throughout the 105 days of 3rd Ypres, a single paragraph would have sufficed in this history to describe what led up to them, had it not been that eight days after Haig closed it down, another, very different kind of battle commenced – in which the cavalry took a controversial part which has never been adequately studied. Without knowing the broad outlines of what went before it, it is impossible to understand why the battle of Cambrai should have been launched as late in the year as 20 November – or, indeed, at all.*

* * *

On the eve of the battle Haig gave his 'final and conclusive reason' for launching the attack. 'Success,' he told the final

---

*The sole advantages of the late date were that the long nights made concentration easier while limiting enemy air observation, and that an offensive was unlikely to be expected.

In a sense Haig's order to Fourth and Fifth Armies in April to prepare plans for an offensive towards Cambrai was the genesis of the battle of seven months later. As a result of that order, indeed, preparations were 'already far advanced in many departments. An excellent system of light railways ... already existed.' (De Pree, 207)

It is interesting to note that Haig's Director of Operations 'with the knowledge we possessed in November of the almost inevitable trial of strength which would take place in the spring, when the Germans would have brought over the heavy reinforcements of divisions released from the Russian front, and before the arrival of the Americans,' believed that the wisest course would have been to 'cancel the Cambrai operations, conserve the tank force and settle down to the necessary and urgent measures to meet the German onslaught'. (Davidson, Maj.-Gen. Sir John, *Haig: Master of the Field*, 1953, 70). He was right, of course – after the event.

conference, 'will greatly help the situation in Italy.'* This, at least, was the impression that Colonel John Charteris, Haig's Chief Intelligence Officer, (known in some circles as 'The Principal Boy'), came away with.[4] Haig's official reason was that since the enemy, so as to 'maintain his defence' on the Ypres front, had been 'obliged to reduce the garrison of certain other parts of his line' a sudden attack 'at a point where he did not expect it might attain a considerable local success'.[5] He was looking, in short, for a comparatively modest operation which would restore British prestige and, as he put it, 'strike a theatrical blow against Germany before winter'.[6] These two reasons do not conflict. Indeed the one reinforced the other. The Italian débâcle at Caporetto at the end of October had been of such a catastrophic nature that troops from the Western Front had had to be rushed to the Italian Front. These included five British divisions, a sacrifice that Haig was loath to make at a time when the manpower shortage was becoming acute.†

Writing to Robertson on 15 November, Haig made it clear that 'the nature of this operation is such that it can be stopped at once if it appears likely to entail greater losses than I can afford'. He told the conference on 19 November that he intended to 'stop short after forty-eight hours, unless by that time the situation is so promising that we can take further risks'. The whole operation, indeed, was full of risks, for there were insufficient reserves with which to follow up a breakthrough. It is interesting to note that Bonar Law, then Chancellor of the Exchequer, in one of the debates in the Commons which followed the battle, said that 'this was nothing like a breakthrough, that it was not intended to be a

---

*Haig claimed in his Cambrai despatch that the battle had diverted hostile reinforcements from Italy. Comparison of the relevant dates proves this to be untrue. The enemy had decided on 10 November to break off serious operations on the Piave front. What is rather more than idle speculation is to assert that the five divisions sent to Italy could have made Cambrai into a battle very different from what it was.

†When in mid-October, Haig eventually approved the operation he said, according to Byng, 'that in spite of having to send troops to Italy, in spite of not getting ahead in the north as much as he wanted, in spite of only being able to give us divisions which had been over the top a great many times, he had determined to carry out the operation.' (Byng's lecture to officers of Canadian Corps: 'Cambrai, 1917', *Canadian Defence Quarterly*, V, 1)

breakthrough and that it was simply an operation which stood more or less by itself.'[7]

Further, Haig had been gravely misled by Charteris. On 12 November he told him that Germany could not 'get divisions from Russia before winter', while in fact by that date twenty-three divisions had already been transferred to the Western front. Indeed as early as 1 November Charteris had received indisputable documentary evidence that a division which had last been located in Russia was actually detraining in the Cambrai area and that other reinforcements were not far behind. The officer responsible for collecting this information has recorded that 'Charteris refused to have these movements shown on the location map of the German order of battle, saying that he did not accept the evidence, and in any case he did not wish to weaken the C-in-C's resolution to carry on with the attack.' At the very moment when Charteris, on the eve of the battle, was writing in his diary: 'We shall have forty-eight hours before the Germans can reinforce,' this new division from Russia was relieving a Landwehr division, exactly opposite IV Corps. Charteris did, however, add that within sixty-four hours the enemy could have 'as many troops as we have'. During the battle's second day four fresh German divisions arrived to reinforce the defence, 'including the 3rd Guard Division' – far in excess of Charteris's forecast.[8]* By the time of the German counter-attack on 30 November sixteen new divisions had been brought to the Cambrai front, while five extra divisions were all that Haig could contribute.†

* * *

Lieutenant-Colonel John Frederick Charles ('Boney') Fuller, one of the more prominent of the begetters of tank warfare, exaggerated, but not excessively, when he wrote that 'by 4 p.m. on 20 November one of the most astonishing battles in all history had been won and, as far as the Tank Corps was concerned, tactically

---

*Between 20 and 29 November thirteen infantry divisions and over 600 smaller units were brought up in 730 trains. (Smithers: *Cambrai*, 104)

†A German infantry division consisted of about 12,000, while a British one consisted of about 18,800. Whether either the German or British divisions were up to establishment is not known. It is unlikely that the British ones were.

10. Cavalry horses waiting for watering, winter, 1915.

11. Horses being treated for mange in gas chambers.

12. The Fort Garry Horse crossing a cavalry track bridge, June, 1916. (See p.43)

13. Part of a taped cavalry track. (see p.227)

finished, for, no reserves [of tanks] existing, it was not possible to do more.'⁹ Though, so far as the future of warfare was concerned, Cambrai, because of the first successful employment of massed tanks there, has few equals for importance in military history, it was the startling innovation in the use of the artillery in conjunction with them that made at least as large a contribution to the enormous success of the battle's first day. To make certain of surprise the hitherto obligatory preliminary bombardment was omitted. Even the usual preparatory registration was excluded, for sophisticated means of surveying and calculation had been developed which made it less necessary. With the infantry following closely in the wake of the wire-smashing tanks, a jumping or lifting barrage could take the place of the customary creeping barrage, for the necessary accuracy of which calibrated guns and registered fire was still required.* In short Cambrai was, in Cyril Falls's words, through the revolutionary methods of infantry, artillery and tank cooperation, 'the type of the battle of the future and its influence on the Second World War was as great as that on the remainder of the First.'¹⁰

It had been the original intention of Brigadier-General (Sir) Hugh Jamieson Elles, a Royal Engineer, who commanded the Tank Corps, and other tank enthusiasts, that the battle should be no more than a large-scale raid, and though it mushroomed into something much bigger, the fact that Haig meant to close it down after forty-eight hours shows that he too half thought of it in that way. With afterthought it is clear that that would have been the right way to think of it. Indeed when John Terraine talks of 'an unclarity of intention, an imprecision of execution' for which the Commander-in-Chief 'must bear a part of the blame' he speaks no more than the truth.¹¹

* * *

*Every one of the 1,003 guns fired a preliminary round of smoke shell, the wind being in the right direction. 432 guns were employed on smoke screens in the course of the day. 'The great curtain of smoke two miles long in front of Flesquières maintained its voluminous and phosphorescent eruption for 2¼ hours. At the far end of the Flesquières ridge, in front of Nine Wood, a 1,000 yard screen of smoke was maintained for four hours.' (Woollcombe, 68)

For the rest of the day there was little artillery fire since the batteries were engaged in moving forward to new positions.

The terrain of the Cambrai area

The Cambrai area was chosen chiefly because, unlike that around Ypres, the ground had not been kneaded and mashed into swampland by shell fire. Being largely hard, gently undulating terrain, it was almost ideal tank – and cavalry – country. The Hindenburg Line here as elsewhere was very formidable. It consisted of two systems between 500 yards and a mile apart, each with its front and support trenches. The barbed-wire 'aprons' in front of them were some fifty yards wide secured by iron stanchions, while the trenches were abnormally wide, mostly fifteen feet at the top and ten feet deep. The tanks would have no difficulty in flattening the wire for the infantry. To get across the trenches, however, they had to carry enormous fascines of tightly chain-bound faggots which they tipped forward into the trenches so as to ease their crossing by crawling over them.*

Elles, his confreres at Tank Corps Headquarters and Brigadier-General (Sir) H. Hugh Tudor (responsible for the new artillery doctrines) were fortunate in that the Cambrai front was held by Third Army, commanded by Byng, who from the moment they broached the project to him and throughout the four weeks of intensive preparation was intelligently enthusiastic. So, in varying degrees, were the commanders of III and IV Corps,† which had the task of breaking through the enemy's line. For this purpose they had between them eight infantry divisions, 1,003 guns, 378 Mark IV fighting tanks and ninety-six supply and other tanks. Fifty-four were supply tanks or gun carriers capable of transporting sixty-pounders; nine were equipped for wireless communication and one for laying telephone cable. For the wire-pulling tanks see p. 115. Each tank was meant to carry two homing pigeons. Whether they all did and whether they were of much use is not clear. The Mark IVs represented a considerable improvement in design (especially with respect to the strength of the armour) compared with the Mark Is which had made their debut at Flers fourteen months earlier. (See p. 61)

* * *

---

*These fascines brought down many of the overhead cables in the rear areas on 19 November. Ground cables were also chewed up by tank tracks. (Moore, 72)

†*III Corps*: Lieut.-Gen. Sir William Pulteney Pulteney.
IV Corps: Lieut.-Gen. Sir Charles Louis Woollcombe.

Cambrai, 20 November, 1917

The necessity for secrecy, surprise and speed was acknowledged as a *sine qua non* by everyone. Except in part, perhaps, for speed, these three requirements were achieved astonishingly well. The overriding importance of securing the Bourlon wood and heights on Z-day, emphasized time and again by Haig, was not as fully recognized as it should have been. Indeed there seems to have been a conflict of purpose between the Commander-in-Chief and the Army Commander. Byng appeared to give priority to exploiting eastwards and trying to get Cambrai. 'I fear', wrote Lieutenant-General Sir Lancelot Edward Kiggell, Haig's Chief of General Staff, after the battle, 'he hankered after that all through.' Haig, on the other hand, was right to lay the chief emphasis on Bourlon. Without the splendid artillery observation which the ridge's possession would provide, the grand aim of the operation, namely the turning of the enemy line, thus causing him to give up his defences for a great distance to the north, could not be achieved. Indeed on 10 November he had pressed for 'specially trained detachments of all arms, lightly equipped ... under one commander' for the task of 'securing Bourlon Wood'. To this Byng, possibly because of lack of time, paid no attention. He believed, moreover, that it would not be possible to get the advanced troops through to Bourlon Ridge on Z-day 'owing to the inevitable exhaustion following on a sleepless night and the subsequent attack'. To this he added the rider: 'I am unable to pass fresh infantry through, as to do so would only delay the cavalry advance.' There *seems* to be some muddled thinking here, since without the taking of the Bourlon position, surely the cavalry could not anyway get through. In any case he was overruled by Haig and the question is largely academic.[12]*

* * *

An essential part in the audacious scheme was allotted to the cavalry. 'The object of the operation,' according to the Third Army Plan, issued on 13 November, was 'to break the enemy's defensive system by a coup de main; with the assistance of tanks to pass the

---

*So is the question of detailed orders for what was to happen after the breakthrough had been made. They did not exist. Third Army's instructions were that 'no precise orders can be issued until the development of the action is known'. Equally the cavalry would receive 'further instructions'. (Woollcombe, 34)

Cavalry Corps through the break thus made: to seize Cambrai,* Bourlon Wood and the passages over the Sensée River.' (See map, p. 109). The battle was to be carried on in three stages: the capture of the enemy's organized lines by the tank-led infantry, the advance of the cavalry (together with the capture of Bourlon Wood by IV Corps), 'the clearing of Cambrai and of the quadrilateral Canal de l'Escaut – Sensée River – Canal du Nord, and the overthrow of the German divisions thus cut off'.[13] Were all three stages to be accomplished the whole of the enemy line west of the Canal du Nord would be in jeopardy.†

In September, at the time when Haig's hopes of 'a speedy advance in front of Ypres were high, he ordered Kavanagh to train cavalry in co-operation with tanks. This was the first time that they had been thought of as other than infantry support weapons. On 10 November Cavalry Corps headquarters issued 'Notes on the Use of Tanks with Cavalry'. Though its precepts had little chance of being followed at Cambrai, it has a certain historical interest:

'1. The sphere of activity and the radius of the tank is limited and the pace of advance is slow. These are the main disadvantages.

'2. On the other hand, the tank can break through wire, move into villages held by Machine Guns and sit on strong points held.

'3. Its use to Cavalry advancing is very great, but in legislating for Cavalry action supported by tanks the following points must be borne in mind.

(a) Tanks work in sections of 3 tanks.

---

*This clearly went against Haig's intentions. He wanted Cambrai not to be entered, but only surrounded and isolated. (Edmonds, *1917*, III, 18)

†The detailed instructions to the Cavalry Corps were as follows:

'[On Z-day] 1st. – To surround and isolate Cambrai, occupying the main points of tactical importance, blocking all exits from the town and destroying means of communication.

'2nd. – To secure the crossings on the River Sensée between Paillencourt and Palluel (inclusive).

'3rd. – To secure the flank of the forces engaged in clearing up the quadrilateral Canal de l'Escaut – Sensée River – Canal du Nord, and the advance North and North-East of V Corps.' (Edmonds, *1917*, III, 309)

(b) They must be given definite objectives, and successive waves of tanks must be used, instead of giving tanks successive objectives.

(c) Cavalry must not wait for tanks, but must push on. On the other hand, if held up, the arrival of tanks will be of the utmost use.

(d) Tanks should be used as pivots for the Cavalry. They are really moving Machine Guns heavily armed, and though they have not the pace of Armoured Motors they should be used on the same principle.

(e) Therefore Cavalry use their mobility to get round the flanks of every village or position held by the enemy, whilst the tanks move straight on it.'

Byng's order of 17 November stated that if surprise was attained 'and we are successful in overrunning the enemy's line of defence, a unique opportunity for the cavalry action becomes possible. This action may have a most far reaching effect, not only on the local situation, but on the course of the war.

'Attacking [infantry] divisions must realize that the boldest action is required during the first two days. Hesitation and waiting for support may enable the enemy to recover from his first surprise and delay the advance of the cavalry. . . . The conduct of the cavalry should be as actively offensive as possible.'[14] To be in a position to carry out its orders the Cavalry Corps would have, in the words of its orders from Third Army, 'to pass its leading divisions through on Z-day *as soon as the infantry have secured the crossings at Masnières and Marcoing** and have ensured the possibility of [its] passage across the Masnières-Beaurevoir line. This may happen at any time after zero plus 4½ hours [i.e. 10.50 a.m.].'[15] Haig, rather more perhaps, than Byng, saw the overriding objective as being 'to break through the enemy's defences by surprise and so permit the Cavalry Corps to pass through and operate in open country'.† He complained that 'this was not . . . fully realised in all the units' which he visited on 13 November.[16] Whether it was ever sufficiently realized by every unit concerned is open to doubt.

* Author's italics.

†Special maps showing what was known of the enemy's rear organization were issued to the cavalry brigades. (Woollcombe, 31)

Cambrai, 20 November, 1917

* * *

From the five divisions of the Cavalry Corps, two extractions were made. First, the 1st Cavalry Division was to come under IV Corps instead of the Cavalry Corps. After the breakthrough it was to turn the villages of the rear Hindenburg Line from behind them and then to attack Bourlon village from the north and east, and, finally, having isolated Cambrai, to join up with the rest of the Cavalry Corps. Second, from the 4th Cavalry Division, the Lucknow Brigade (with part of the corps cavalry regiment, the Northumberlands) was to be attached to III Corps. Its orders were (eventually) to make a raid south-eastward towards Walincourt.* Thus there were left two divisions of the Cavalry Corps, the 2nd and 5th, to make the initial advance on the III Corps front, with the 3rd and two brigades of the 4th in reserve. The 5th's task was to cross the de l'Escaut Canal between Marcoing and Masnières and then to sweep round to the east and the north of Cambrai.

* * *

The task of marching the 27,500 or so cavalrymen and their support troops to their concentration areas was not only a complicated one but it entailed very lengthy and tiring marches.† The Bays for instance had to cover 106 miles in five night marches.[17] Those furthest away started their journeys eleven days before Z-day. The moves, made sometimes by day but for secrecy's sake more often by night, were completed by early on 19 November. The assembly areas (see map p. 109) were mostly around

---

*Towards the end of the day Jacob's Horse, the brigade's leading regiment, kept close up behind the infantry with which it liaised closely, providing patrols which reconnoitred the crossings over the Canal d'Escaut near Crèvecoeur, finding them all held by the enemy. (Maunsell, 129)

In a joint infantry and cavalry attack near Le Quennet Farm, two troops of the Northumberlands, one mounted and the other dismounted, helped in the capture of some field guns. It was a neat operation in which the battery was charged by the mounted troop from a flank, while the infantry and the dismounted troop kept up a heavy fire from the front. (Pease, 159–61)

†One of the chief concerns was the state of the horses' shoes. 'We had been marching,' wrote Furse of King Edward's Horse, 'for five days mostly over wet flints, which wear down iron like a grindstone.' (Furse, 128)

CAMBRAI AREA, 20 NOVEMBER TO 1 DECEMBER, 1917

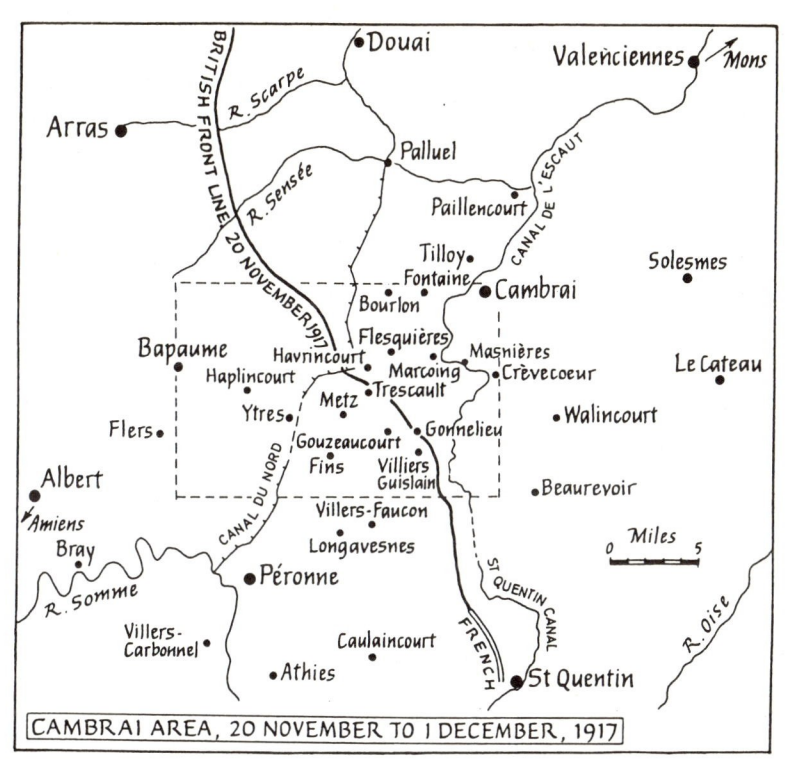

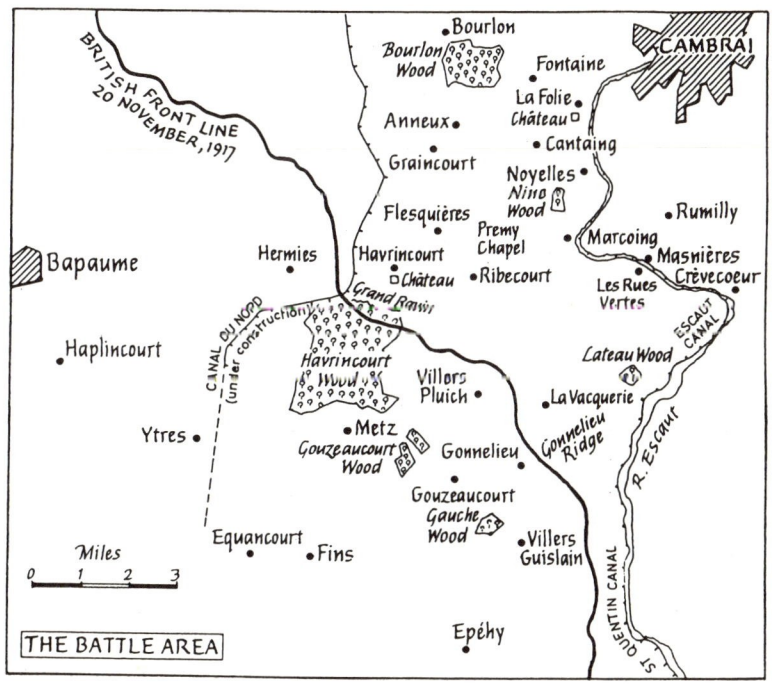

THE BATTLE AREA

Péronne,* with the headquarters of the Corps at Villers-Carbonnel. The nearest to the front line was that of the 5th Brigade about ten miles from Villers-Plouich, while the 3rd was over twenty miles in the rear. For the three leading divisions the concentration areas selected were: 1st and 5th north of Fins and the 2nd in the areas north-west of Villers Faucon. The Lucknow Brigade was concentrated at Longavesnes. These areas were on average some twelve miles from the assembly areas. Elaborate arrangements were made to dump food and forage in the concentration areas. One day's forage supplies for a division came to thirty tons of oats and thirty of hay. In all, 270 tons of oats and hay were dumped in the three areas.[18] The difficulties inherent in concealing so many horses, men and forage dumps were immense. It was almost miraculous that the enemy remained totally unaware of the concentration. Of water except in very limited areas there was no shortage. In Artois there were (and are) numerous Artesian wells, though not of course always in a convenient place. Twenty pounds of oats per horse and three days' iron rations were carried on man and horse and in the regimental wagons.†

* * *

Zero hour for the tanks, infantry and artillery was set at 6.20, at which time a man could just be distinguished at 200 yards. It

* 1 Cavalry Division near   Péronne
  2   "   "   "   Caulincourt
  3   "   "   "   Bray
  4   "   "   "   Atheis
  5   "   "   "   South of Roisel

† The men of King Edward's Horse 'cheered wildly when the troop leaders started to inspect their first field dressings (a package carried by each man for immediate rough bandaging of wounds). They guessed what that foretold. . . . Our main problem was forage. If we got through the trench lines tomorrow,' wrote Furse on 19 November, 'there seemed little prospect of supplies for the next day reaching us. We could not take hay: the regiment had called in all hay-nets, which was a mistake. In the end we carried two days' ration of oats – twenty pounds on each horse – a heavy load but it kept the horses in good condition.' (Furse, 130–1)

was eighty minutes before sunrise.* It was therefore calculated that the cavalry's concentration areas must be reached by zero plus two and a half hours, i.e. at 8.50, for between twenty-six and thirty-five miles would have to be marched from the *assembly* areas (with a short halt for the horses to rest and feed in the *concentration* areas) before the forward objectives were reached. This entailed night marches with little or no sleep for the three divisions and the Lucknow Brigade. Except that the 5th Division was apparently 'blocked on the railway crossings and was over an hour late',[19]† the approach marches were carried out without incident. By zero hour the 1st and 5th Divisions were to be at Fins which was six miles from the nearest point in the front line about twelve miles from Masnières, while the forward objective of the 2nd Division was to be Villers Faucon. The 3rd and two brigades of the 4th were to concentrate at Fins when the 1st and 5th had moved forward.

* * *

Though some Irish prisoners taken on 17 November had revealed that something was afoot for the 20th, the opening of the battle was virtually a complete surprise to the Germans.§ Less than seven hours before zero hour the German general commanding the 2nd Army's Caudry Group wrote in orders: 'Tanks may take part. The four to five hours' artillery bombardment will probably begin between 3 and 4 a.m.' 'This,' as Liddell Hart puts it, 'is

---

*The tanks and infantry on III Corps Front began to move forward at 6.10, and at 6.00 on IV Corps front. ('Y/Z night: Distribution of Tank Brigade', Tank Museum)

†'No mention is made of any level crossings in the 5th Cavalry Division War Diary or in any of its brigade diaries. Furthermore, the whole of these make it clear that the division was saddled up and ready to move at 08.50.' (Maunsell, 132)

§At 10.20 (repeated at 11.15) IV Corps sent the following message to all its formations, including the 1st Cavalry Division: 'Prisoners report that warning of our attack was conveyed to the Germans as the result of a raid by them [that which had captured the Irishmen]. It is therefore possible that opposition may be encountered.' (Woollcombe, 90)

Cambrai, 20 November, 1917

a suggestive example of how habit may contribute to surprise.' The Germans' suspicions had been further aroused when their raids had met with 'the minimum of fighting', and by too much silence on the part of the British artillery in the preceding days.[20]

The more or less fine weather, that had prevailed for some days before the attack, broke in the morning of 20 November. Thick clouds and occasional drizzle, which became heavier as the day progressed, made it almost impossible for aerial observation of the movements of either friend or foe. Some aeroplanes managed to fly very low but little accurate information could be transmitted. This, of course, applied to both sides.

The shock of tanks succeeded by infantry following immediately on the mighty roar of 1,003 guns, many of them hitting with some accuracy the German batteries, was so great that, along the entire six-mile front (from Gonnelieu to Hermies), not only was there no barrage from the Germans' 150 guns in reply, but at many points there was practically no opposition of any kind. By 8.50 the outpost zone and the front system of the Hindenburg Line had been taken 'and the leap-frogging battalions and tanks were passing forward for the attack on the second line'. As, after ten hours of daylight, the early winter evening descended on the battlefield, this, too, had been breached, well over 4,000 prisoners had been taken and the advance had exceeded four miles. Only sixty-five tanks had been put out of action by enemy fire,* though through ditching, mechanical failure and other causes, another 114 were no longer able to take part on that day. As for the infantry they had become, not surprisingly, excessively tired by mid-afternoon. The report of the 1st Tank Brigade on the battle states that 'tanks could have advanced further and taken Bourlon Wood and village on Z-day, but no fresh troops were available and the infantry who had advanced right through to beyond Graincourt were exhausted

---

*It was bad luck that part of the German artillery had been specially trained for anti-tank work and liberally supplied with armour-piercing ammunition. It was doubly unfortunate that, being the only part of the German army thus trained, it should have been on this particular section of the Line. (See Scott: 'Cambrai', 97) Lieutenant-General Freiherr von Watter, an artilleryman, who commanded the division at this point, had studied the problem of countering tanks in some detail. 'He had tested his theories against some French tanks in April 1917 and had specifically trained his artillery to hit moving targets with direct fire from reverse slope positions.' It was from such a position that eleven tanks were picked off at Flesquières. (Farndale, 224)

and informed the tank commanders that they were unable to follow the tanks any further'. Tanks, indeed, according to an officer in 'G' Battalion, entered Bourlon Wood. 'There was little or no opposition: the great wood which was to be the centre of such desperate fighting during the next week appeared to be empty of defenders. It is certain that with a brigade of fresh infantry it could have been occupied and consolidated that evening.... The tanks unsupported could not penetrate far into the gloomy wood, still less attempt to hold it; and after a while they withdrew.'[21]

* * *

Before we look at how the cavalry was faring throughout this startlingly successful tank, infantry and artillery battle, let us look back three weeks to learn about the formation of a special body of twenty British officers and over 500 dismounted Indian NCOs and sowars from the 4th Cavalry Division, most of them recently arrived reinforcements. Commanded by Lieutenant-Colonel R.C. Bell of the Central India Horse, its object was to follow the infantry attack, 'tear away the wire, bridge or level the trenches, fill up the shell-holes, and thus carve a broad track through the German lines to the country where the mounted branch was to come into its own'. This Cavalry Track Battalion, as it was called, (one of three from different units)* practised daily for the three weeks before the battle. Bell records that it

> 'assembled at the aptly named village of Misery, near Chaulnes Junction....
>
> 'I was given aerial photographs of the ground behind the German front line. From these I was able to work out a track from near Gouzeaucourt up to and beyond the Hindenburg Line.... The track would be over five miles in length and would cross twenty-six visible lines of trenches.
>
> 'We then proceeded to construct a replica of the German trench system.... The twenty-six individual trenches and systems of trenches were numbered and squads told off permanently to each particular trench....
>
> 'The bridging work was, of course, the most important,

---

*There were also engaged on general road works, as well as the cavalry tracks, the Pioneer Battalions of the infantry divisions.

and this would have to be accomplished with material found on the ground. "Collecting parties" were told off and they quickly learned what they would require for their particular bridge.

'The general scheme was as follows: a "track leader", a British officer, would go over with the infantry attack. With him would be twenty-six men with notice boards bearing the numbers of the trenches from 1 (our front line) to 26 (the Hindenburg Line). As the leader identified each trench he would place the notice board in position so that the squads [equipped with picks, shovels, sandbags and rammers] could recognize their positions and get on to their work at once.'

On 19 November the battalion was conveyed by lorries to near Gouzeaucourt where it debussed. Bell was taken to see Kavanagh, the Cavalry Corps commander, 'who remarked: "If you don't do your job I can't do mine."' At Gouzeaucourt the battalion was introduced to its vitally important colleagues: twelve wire-pulling tanks which came under Bell's command. As was expected the barbed-wire 'aprons' were found in some places to be as much as 100 yards in depth. Bell's account continues:

'The wire-cutting parties got to work and cut lines through them. The tanks followed hauling anchors [grapnels] behind them and dragging the wire away in great tangled masses.* Meanwhile the bridging parties were hard at work and they had a heavy job on hand. . . . Within a couple of hours practical hands had completed capital bridges fit for artillery to cross. . . .

'One after another came in the reports, "Tracks Ready". By 10.45 a.m. I was able to send the same message, thrice repeated, to Corps HQ. I got no acknowledgment and no cavalry appeared! 12 o'clock, still no sign.'[22]

---

*These wire-cutting tanks worked in groups of three. The letters 'WC' were painted on each tank's rear (see illustration no. 29). When the wire was reached the centre tank 'drove straight across after dropping its grapnel and cut clean through the wire. Once this was done the tanks on each flank dropped their grapnels and gathered up the cut ends before turning right and left to open out the gap. This movement imparted a twisting motion to the wire which increased its strength, thus ensuring that every single strand and picket was cleared.' By this method it only took a few minutes to clear a gap. (Fletcher, D. unpublished MS, Tank Museum)

Cambrai: wire-cutting tanks

The orders for all the wire-cutting tanks were that they should start work 'as soon as the second combined wave of infantry and tanks has moved forward'.[23] They were to clear a gap of sixty yards in each belt of wire 'in succession as the attacking tanks advanced and thus form a track for the passage of the cavalry'. This was undertaken at three points on the front and thirty-six tanks were detailed.* Of these, a proportion failed to

> 'reach the wire in time. . . . The work therefore fell upon the remainder, so that in one case at least the tank functioned seven distinct times, the grapnel† being cut out after each pull with the wire cutter, lifted on to the petrol tank and released again when the next belt was encountered. . . . In no case did the grapnel break or fail to grip the wire.
>
> 'The wire before our own line was of the usual type,' states the 'Report on Wire-Pulling Operations' issued after the battle, 'not a serious obstacle, very straggled and unsatisfactory to pull. In some cases several attempts were needed before the ground was cleared.
>
> 'The strongest belts of wire were constructed of wooden and iron stakes and all were interconnected. This pulled very satisfactorily in every case. . . .
>
> 'After pulling the wire away the ground is absolutely clear of every scrap of wire or obstruction such as posts, etc.' [But see below]

This report states that the wire was pulled back 'in every belt of wire to the final objective, *just after mid-day on 20 November*'.[24]§

---

*Two of these were used to carry up bridging material: 'two rails and about twelve chesses [planks for the flooring on pontoon bridges] per tank.' (Instructions, 2)

†The enormous four-pronged grapnels were carried at the tank's rear, attached by a length of stout, three-inch wire rope. (Fletcher, D. unpublished MS, Tank Museum)

§Author's italics.
   It is interesting to note that should a second *fighting* tank pass through the wire within thirty yards of the first one, 'the original path would spring up again, sometimes in a worse tangle than before' leaving the tank unsupported on the enemy side. (Fletcher, D., unpublished MS, Tank Museum)

However, Major the Hon. Denis Bingham who commanded the wire-pulling tanks, reported to Fuller that on two of the cavalry tracks all the wire had not been pulled until 1.30 p.m. and that on the central one the job had not been completed until 2 p.m., (at which hour 'the tank towing and laying signal cable reached Marcoing safely.')* Their business done, the wire-pulling tanks retired. The two bridging tanks, though, 'went on to the [l'Escaut] canal'. (See p. 127).[25]

One of Bell's officers (from the 2nd Lancers) tells graphically of his experiences:

'I found all sorts of obstacles that the air photo had not shown; and several times the ground looked quite different from my mental picture of it, and I thought I had gone wrong. The wire was ever so much thicker than I expected: I think there were four triple belts and two single belts in front of the Hindenburg line alone; and, of course, I had to climb through it before it was cleared. Of course, the fighting tanks had crushed it enough for us to crawl through: but it was slow and tiring work. Also I had to do a lot of searching right and left to choose the right place for the track to cross the trenches, and in one place I had to alter my plan, and divert the track some distance to avoid obstacles I had not reckoned on.

'Several incidents stand out in my mind. A couple of tanks knocked out in No Man's Land, and the infantry sitting down and looking at them, because the tank man was their guide and they did not know where to go without him. In the Boche front trenches on the firing steps large carriers of hot coffee, untasted, as the Boche had bolted. The Boche hung on in La Vacquerie and enfiladed us from the right; but we had to go on and ignore them. They were cleared out

---

*From north to south the three main cavalry tracks ran thus:- Trescault – Ribécourt – Marcoing; Villers-Plouich – Marcoing, and La Vacquerie – Masnières (known as the Kavanagh track). This track was fit for horses through the German first line at about 8 a.m. At 11.00 it was through 'as far as and including the north-east of Lateau Wood'. The Villers-Plouich track was 'through to a point 3,000 yards east by north of that village at about 11.30'. (Maunsell, 130)

A certain number of wire-pulling tanks on the northern route had orders 'to carry on and advance with the cavalry [1st Cavalry Division] to do further clearing'. None of the others was to proceed beyond Marcoing and Masnières. (Instructions, 2).

afterwards. Shells from nowhere as we were climbing through the Hindenburg wire: everyone swore they were our own. About the Hindenburg line any number of snipers and machine guns lying up hidden; they were brave enough, and they made things rather nasty. I saw one such nest rushed by a party of infantry just after they had shot the subalterns; they hauled them out, held them up, and shot them on the spot. . . .

'I had sent back messages by runner to Col. Bell from each trench system.

'The First Cavalry Brigade did not come over the track for two hours after it was fit to take them.'[26]

* * *

Kavanagh had opened Cavalry Corps advanced headquarters near Fins at 6 a.m., five miles behind the front line. He was in direct communication by telephone and telegraph with all his divisions and with III and IV Corps. On 10 November instructions for the Cavalry Corps had contained these words: 'The order for the forward movement of the cavalry divisions from their forward concentration areas [forward objectives] will be issued by Cavalry Corps. This order will be issued as soon as it appears that the situation is favourable and that there is a possibility of a cavalry advance.'[27] To what degree, after that inhibiting order was given, divisional headquarters were to await further orders from Cavalry Corps HQ is not clear. What is very clear is that communications were far from speedy. IV Corps, for instance, which had taken the 1st Cavalry Division under command in the early morning, was not, almost unbelievably, at any time in direct telephone communication with it. When IV Corps HQ wished to send it a message Cavalry Corps HQ had to be requested to pass it on – and vice versa. The earliest example of this occurs in the Cavalry Corps War Diary. It recorded that at 8.20 '1st Cavalry Division warned by telephone to move its head to Metz. (Transmitted by request of IV Corps).'[28]

The rest of the morning was spent by the 1st Division receiving mostly incorrect information and conflicting orders. Soon after 10.00 it learned that Havrincourt was being 'mopped up', which was correct,* and that Ribécourt had been taken, which was not

*Though in fact the village 'was richly provided with deep dug-outs, and it took considerable time finally to mop it up.' (Anon. 'Cambrai', *Royal Tank Corps Journal*, July, 1936, 71)

BATTLE OF CAMBRAI, 20 NOVEMBER, 1917

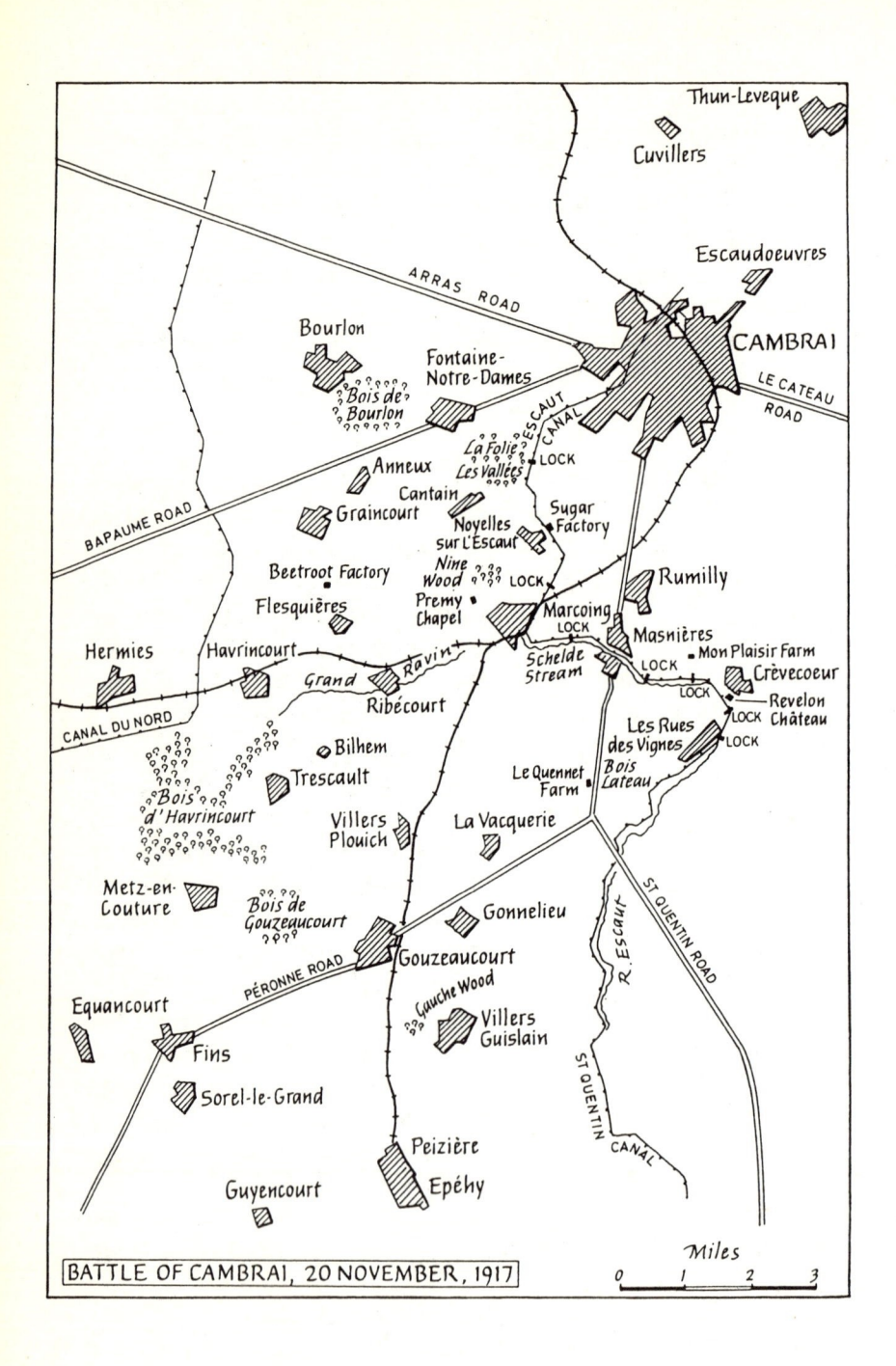

yet more than partially correct. About an hour later Flesquières was reported to have fallen and 'the road from Trescault to that place' was said to be 'fit for cavalry'. Neither statement reflected the true situation. The division's original orders were for it to advance via Ribécourt along the Grand Ravin and not through Flesquières. When the (false) news of Flesquières' capture was confirmed by IV Corps, Mullens, the divisional commander, was ordered by Kavanagh (without, it seems, IV Corps, which after all was still meant to be commanding the division, being informed) to 'advance through Flesquières'.*

Some time after 11.30, by which time 1st Division's headquarters had moved to Metz-en-Couture, with advanced headquarters at Bilhem,† the division was reported to be 'feeling down towards Ribécourt'.[29] The leading regiment of the leading brigade (the 2nd) was the 4th Dragoon Guards, followed by the 5th Dragoon Guards which had been temporarily attached to the 2nd from the 1st Brigade.

---

*Mullens said later that, irrespective of this order, since his information was that 'fighting was still going on in Ribécourt' while 'our troops had overrun Flesquières', the more direct route 'offered a chance, and a more rapid one, of carrying out the spirit of the cavalry instructions.' (Woollcombe, 130)

'At 12 noon IV Corps, unaware of General Mullens' intention, signalled to Third Army what had all the appearance of being a historic message: "Cavalry passed over our old front line 11.15 a.m. Attack progressing satisfactorily".' (Woollcombe, 131)

A more misleading message than this one, even in the welter of misleading messages passing to and fro during the battle, is hard to imagine.

It was reported at some time not long before 12.00 that the cavalry tracks and other roads would be ready for the cavalry to move to both Masnières and Marcoing by that time. (Pitman, 242–3) (See above)

†Furse, of King Edward's Horse, was on the spot at this time. He saw Mullens, commanding the division, standing about 'in the road some fifty yards from me for a very long while, during which nothing much seemed to happen. I took a long cool look at him. He struck me as too soft and fat and old [he was forty-six] for such a venture as this . . .

'A squadron of the 9th Lancers halted on the other side of the road, led by a youthful captain who kept them sitting on their horses. Mullens called out to him: "My dear boy, *do* get your men off their horses".' (Furse, 136–7)

King Edward's Horse, less one squadron which was temporarily allotted to the right brigade of 51st Division, came under the leading infantry brigade of the 62nd Division. By nightfall it was on the point of assisting in an attack upon Anneux. (De Pree, 220) For its functions and actions in the battle see a full account in James, 232–40. The squadron with 51st Division had the duty of maintaining liaison with the 1st Cavalry Division. In *(continued over)*

Cambrai, 20 November, 1917

An officer of King Edward's Horse was sheltering in a captured dug-out when

> 'someone shouted from outside that the cavalry were coming. We all rushed up the steps and saw a long column of horsemen, the 2nd Cavalry Brigade, debouching from Havrincourt Wood and trotting down into the hollow below us. It was a superb sight and I still remember my intense excitement. Had the day really come for which we had been living so long that we had almost given up hope? I could hardly believe my eyes and kept fearing that they would halt. But their advance guard came across the hollow, up the hill to us and on past us over the shoulder of the ridge which hid Ribécourt from our view. The 4th Dragoon Guards were leading. At the head of their main body rode a very fine looking young major on a beautiful horse. He was wearing a pair of dark brown corduroy riding breeches instead of the regulation khaki: what odd details stay in the memory after half a century! I learnt later that he was a Major [Horace Somerville] Sewell who was to win a bar to his D.S.O. for the way he handled his regiment in this battle.'[30]†

---

receiving its orders the brigadier-general commanding the brigade under the direct command of which it came said 'with marked emphasis, "Under no circumstances are you to go off into the blue".' (Furse, 129)

On its way to concentrate before the battle King Edward's Horse passed some of the Highlanders of the 51st Division. An officer of the regiment remembered that

> 'many rushed out and lined the road giving us a tremendous ovation. One of them shouted "We don't want the bloody regular cavalry. We want K.E.H. They're the boys. They came riding their damned great horses over the top of us, looking as big as elephants, when we daren't show an eye above the edge of the shell holes." Our men grinned. [Lieutenant N.G.] Addison remarked drily, "I expect they are dreaming of hanging on to our stirrup leathers in a charge like the Gordons and Greys at Waterloo."' (Furse, 127)

The occasion referred to was during the German withdrawal to the Hindenburg line. The regiment, acting as corps mounted troops, had claimed to be 'the first mounted men to make contact with the enemy during their retirement'. (Furse, 73)

†Sewell joined the regiment in 1900 aged nineteen. As a temporary brigadier-general he commanded the 1st Cavalry Brigade, 1918–19 and he commanded the 7th Hussars, 1919–23. In the Second World War he was attached to the British Information Services, New York. He died, aged seventy-two, in 1953.

As the regiment trotted forward it 'passed hordes of German prisoners being hustled back, and numerous burned-out or ditched tanks, but otherwise they might,' as the regimental historian puts it, 'have been on manoeuvres: there was no sign of enemy resistance.' The resistance which *was* encountered – the difficulties of negotiating the abandoned trenches – was horribly time-consuming. Further, in spite of the claims made by the wire-pulling tanks, it appears that 'the broken coils were hazardous to horses' legs'. Indeed it was 'frequently necessary to dismount and use wire-cutters'.[31]*

The outskirts of Ribécourt were not reached till just before midday. Though the village had been reported taken at least an hour and a half earlier, this meant merely that tanks and infantry had been through it. As so often, the amazing skill, tenacity and the ability to appear when least expected of the German machine gunners and individual snipers made the reports of captures only partially true. There proved to be 'a large number of dug-outs in the village and some of the enemy had evidently remained in these and emerged when the attack had passed on'. 'It appears,' wrote an infantry company commander of the area around Flesquières, 'that many machine-gun posts had escaped the barrage.' When the official account by one of III Corps' divisions complained that the cavalry refused to advance 'owing to the snipers in Ribécourt', it went on to say that 'the village had been in our possession since 10 a.m. and 18th Infantry Brigade had passed through it at 11.30 a.m. and were now two miles beyond it.' The writer of that account was, of course, unaware, as, alas, were nearly all those who have written about the battle since, that from very deep dug-outs which were both numerous and 'regular palaces', men who had cowered in them while the tanks and infantry passed over them, came out, unscathed and fully armed as soon as they thought it safe to do so.† It is also forgotten, all too often, that men on horses present far greater targets for snipers than infantrymen who can at least throw themselves to the ground and make use of

---

*'Even after [the wire-pulling tanks] had cleared a space the denseness of the grass tangled up with odd bits of wire, iron stakes, etc., required a lot of clearing.' (Maunsell, 135)

†It has been asserted that only later on in the battle did the Germans develop the technique of hiding until the tanks had passed on (see Scott: 'Cambrai', 102). There is, however, incontestable evidence that they employed it on 20 November.

minimal cover. At Ribécourt, as elsewhere, there was still some considerable mopping up to be done. This was soon proved when twenty-one year old Lieutenant Lawrence Edward Misa,* at the head of the leading troop, was severely wounded by machine-gun fire, as also were several horses. At about this moment Brigadier-General Beale-Browne, commanding the 2nd Cavalry Brigade, learned from the infantry that 'there was considerable doubt as to whether Flesquières was in our possession'.[32] He therefore ordered the 4th Dragoon Guards 'to push up the valley towards Flesquières and endeavour to clear up the situation'.[33] In short, instead of pressing on towards Marcoing where they would have found twelve tanks (which had rallied on the left of the village in the Grand Ravin) awaiting them, ready to 'co-operate, in accordance with previous arrangements',† the 4th swept westwards towards Flesquières.

When the regiment got as far as the ridge dominated by the village it found the infantry unable to proceed. It, too, found it 'quite impossible' to advance beyond the railway track. Beale-Browne now received a report (at about 12.30) from the regiment saying that Flesquières was held by the enemy and that the Germans were still in action in the northern outskirts of Ribécourt. Beale-Browne consequently gave orders 'to leave Flesquières alone',[34] while Mullens, after the battle, said that 'verbal messages were despatched to the effect that if no progress could be made via Flesquières, the

---

*Misa had joined the Bays on 4 August, 1914 from the Special Reserve and in 1915 he had obtained a regular commission in the 4th Dragoon Guards. He commanded that regiment between 1939 and 1942. He died, aged seventy-two, in 1968.

†These tanks, which had been tentatively placed under the orders of 2nd Cavalry Brigade, remained, waiting for any signs of the brigade, throughout the remaining hours of daylight. 'No word was received, however, of the cavalry until 5 p.m.' Immediately after the capture of the Brown Line (the second objective of the tanks and infantry), these twelve tanks had

> 'advanced on Marcoing, which they reached at 11.30 a.m. Considerable resistance was met, which was quickly silenced by the tanks. One tank arrived just in time to disperse a party of the enemy who were making electric connections to a charge on the bridge [across the Canal de l'Escaut]. One hour elapsed before the infantry arrived to take over the village.' ('Distribution of Tank Brigades: "B" Battalion', Tank Museum).

This seems to prove that Marcoing was more or less clear of the enemy by 12.30 or so.

original scheme was to be carried out'.* Haig writing in his diary two days later, believed that 'the holding up of [the infantry] at Flesquières on the 20th had far-reaching consequences, because the cavalry were also held up and failed in consequence to get through'.[35]

At 1.50 Cavalry Corps sent a message to IV Corps saying: '1st Cavalry Division report infantry have taken Nine Wood. Snipers still in Ribécourt. Cavalry advancing towards Nine Wood.'[36] As a consequence of this, at 2.35, with about two hours of daylight left, IV Corps signalled the division and the infantry (51st (Highland) Division) thus: 'Enemy still hold Flesquières and [German] guns with limbers were seen going into village 12.20 p.m. . . . 1st Cavalry Division will send at least two regiments to endeavour to pass by Ribécourt and Premy Chapel and get round the Flesquières position on the north-east. 51st Division will attack from south.' The importance of this order to an understanding of why the 1st Cavalry Division did not make any attempt to obey it is that it was not received until 3.15, at least *fifty minutes* after it was sent.† At 3 p.m., not surprisingly, III Corps War Diary recorded that the cavalry was 'not yet through'. This, in part, was because there had been encountered from Flesquières persistent machine-gun fire on the crossroads south of Ribécourt.[37]

An air report timed at 1.40 now arrived at IV Corps headquarters, saying that Cantaing was undefended and that the enemy were retiring in 'scattered order'. The impression given by this news was that between Nine Wood and the great objective of Bourlon there was no enemy of consequence. Neither this vital information (which was probably correct when sent, but which, by 3.20 when IV Corps received it, was not, since German infantry is known to have entered Cantaing by then),§ nor IV Corps'

---

*At 'about 1.45' a mounted patrol of King Edward's Horse 'coming from the left brigade of the 51st Division brought word that the division expected to take Flesquières shortly, but were suffering heavy casualties.' (James, 235)

†Edmonds, 1917, III, 81, goes so far as to say that this order did not reach 2nd Cavalry Brigade until 4.30! This seems improbable.

§Just before sunset (which was at 4.03 p.m.) another air report stated ominously: 'Column 1,200 yards long entering Cambrai. Large body of enemy between Bourlon Wood and Fontaine.' (Wires received, 51 Div., Ser. no. 105, quoted in Woollcombe, 135)

order of 2.35 had reached Beale-Browne's 2nd Brigade, let alone the 4th Dragoon Guards. By 3 p.m. the regiment, re-routed from Flesquières, was cautiously approaching Nine Wood, with a distant view of Cantaing through the mist. Almost in despair, at the very moment of sunset, after frantic telephoning between Byng and Woollcombe, orders came on the telephone for the cavalry 'to push on with full strength through Marcoing and carry out the original plan of a breakthrough at that point'.[38]*

The only mounted unit, with the exception of the Fort Garry Horse (see p. 129) that managed to obey those orders and, throughout the battle, actually to make a breakthrough, was 'A' Squadron of the 4th Dragoon Guards. At about 4 o'clock Major Sewell, commanding the 4th, reported that Noyelles, some 4,000 yards from Cambrai, was clear. 'A' Squadron got even closer to Cambrai's outskirts when its head, penetrating the Les Vallées woods, reached La Folie Château, almost at Fontaine-Notre-Dames, having advanced through the 1,000-yard-wide gap between Cantaing to the west and the Canal de l'Escaut to the east, from both of which directions 'heavy fire was brought to bear'. The squadron leader, Captain H. de Gray Warter, took two of his troops, the first led by Lieutenant John Aldam Aizlewood,† the second by Lieutenant L.F. Marson, towards La Folie, while leaving the other two 'to mask Cantaing',[39] from whence machine guns opened fire and where a battery had been sited. 'B' Squadron, which was riding forward in support, got held up by wire, and was 'unable to do more than draw the enemy's fire' from Cantaing.[40] Aizlewood's troop came upon a column of German horsed transport, including four ammunition wagons, which it halted with

---

*It has been argued that, had there been a large force of cavalry available to pass through the infantry to the west of Flesquières, it might have had a good chance of getting through. However, it had been considered during the planning stage that 'the country on the left' was 'too cramped' for massed horsemen. It was decided not to split the 1st Cavalry Division, 'therefore none were diverted towards Graincourt.' (IV Corps Narrative, Woollcombe, 123)

†Aizlewood had joined the regiment aged nineteen in December, 1914. He commanded 3 (Meerut) Cavalry Brigade, 1930–40, 2nd Indian Armoured Brigade, 1940–1, 252 Indian Armoured Brigade Group, 1941–2, 30 Armoured Brigade, 1942 and 42 Armoured Division, 1942–3. He was Colonel of 4/7 Dragoon Guards, 1948–58. He lived well into his eighties.

machine-gun fire before drawing swords and charging it. 'There was no resistance, not a shot was fired: many of the enemy fled, but twenty-odd surrendered at sword point.' Marson's troop meanwhile 'had swung left and galloped a group of German infantrymen who likewise surrendered. The total bag of prisoners now amounted to [about] fifty.'[41]

In view of increasing fire from both sides, Warter now decided to withdraw and join the regiment. As the squadron galloped along the side of the canal enemy machine gunners, lining the bank, fired at it from 300 yards, killing Warter. Three other ranks were also killed, four wounded and six missing. Fifteen horses became casualties, including those of Aizlewood and Marson, who, with some of their men, managed to reach regimental headquarters after dark, bearing with them one machine gun.[42] For the night the regiment took up a position east of Nine Wood strengthening the line of infantry there. One troop, though, which had entered Noyelles, remained in that village.

* * *

Whilst the 1st Cavalry Division had been cautiously moving forward, often, as has been shown, forced to halt for long periods by enemy fire, what had the main body of the Cavalry Corps been doing on the right?

The order from Cavalry Corps to the 5th Cavalry Division to advance from its forward objective areas was received at 11.50. This was in consequence of reports from air reconnaissance that tanks were moving into Marcoing, though there was machine-gun fire from Masnières. With the Canadian Brigade leading, the division set off at 12.05, though the situation between Marcoing and Masnières was still obscure. Patrols were ordered to get in touch with the infantry ahead so as to advance across the Canal de l'Escaut should the situation be favourable.[43]*

At just before 1.40 the advance guard (a squadron of the Fort Garry Horse) reached Les Rues Vertes in the outskirts of

---

*The 2nd Cavalry Division was at this time ordered to move to a position south of and clear of the Gouzeaucourt-Fins road, ready to follow the 5th Division. (Pitman, 243)

Masnières.* It had covered some ten miles in an hour and a half. This was a great tribute to the efficiency of the preparation of the 'Kavanagh track'.

It is perhaps instructive at this point to remember that each cavalry brigade covered about two miles and that when the head of a cavalry division is stated to have reached a certain point, the rear troop of the rear squadron of the rear regiment of the rear brigade will be something like ten miles behind, including the divisional troops such as engineers and ambulances.

* * *

At 1.45 the advance guard of the Secunderabad Brigade (the 7th Dragoon Guards) reached the southern outskirts of Marcoing. 'At that time the village was clear of the enemy but the railway bridge was held by hostile rifle and machine-gun fire.'[44] 'C' Squadron, passing stranded tanks, some stuck in the mud, others out of petrol, reached Marcoing at 1.20[45] and crossed the intact road bridge to the eastern side of the canal to find the infantry 'held up in a cutting near the railway station'. As the squadron came under heavy machine-gun fire it dismounted, extending the right of the infantry.† A second squadron which came up in support was similarly pinned down and also dismounted. When the opposition had been overcome at the railway cutting these two squadrons tried once again to advance mounted. They soon, however, had to withdraw to the canal bank because they came under heavy machine-gun fire from the direction of Masnières.

At 2.15 'D' Squadron under Captain C.W.T. Lane was sent off northwards in an effort to secure, if possible, another crossing over the canal. When he reached Noyelles, Lane led his men at a gallop straight into it, scattering the German infantrymen he found there who fired a few ineffective shots before retiring and leaving twenty-five to be made prisoner, fifteen of whom were captured in

---

*The Canadian Official History states that 'incorrect information led... Seely [the Canadian Cavalry Brigade's commander] to believe that the 88th Brigade had gained its objective east of the canal' which led him to order forward the Fort Garry Horse. (Nicholson, 336; see also Edmonds, *1917*, III, 69)

†'Patrols were sent to find out if the Canadian Cavalry Brigade had succeeded in crossing at Masnières, but could not get in touch with them.' (Scott, 105)

Cambrai, 20 November, 1917

the village street, while ten others were winkled out of hiding places. All were marched back and handed over to the infantry. Then, at about 2.45 p.m. the squadron galloped down the main road towards Cambrai, tarrying only long enough to cut telegraph lines. They soon came upon a blown bridge which was defended by machine gunners. These did not prevent Lane from sending out patrols who found and seized some trestle bridges over the Schelde stream which runs more or less parallel to the canal. They also found another road bridge over the canal. This one, as Lane reported, 'could have been crossed, but the trench line to the north-west of the canal was occupied by the enemy. My patrols were heavily fired on and had to retire.' In all this the squadron did not suffer a single casualty.[46] Though he at once let the Secunderabad Brigade headquarters know of the existence of this bridge, no further cavalry was sent up to take advantage of it. This was no doubt because the light was by then beginning to fail. The squadron remained in touch with the 4th Dragoon Guards near Noyelles throughout the night.

* * *

When, at noon, nine tanks reached Masnières, they found the seventy foot-long iron girder bridge partially blown up. This was the only really sturdy bridge across the canal. None of the others was an iron bridge. There is some evidence that 'efforts were made by fire to assist the infantry, and subsequently some cavalry [a patrol of the Fort Garry Horse]* to cross' it. These met with failure. Only then, it has been suggested, was 'the risk run of sending a tank over' the broken bridge. Under its weight the bridge gave way and the tank fell in. The tank officer on the spot was Major Philip Hamond. He claims that he rushed ahead on foot, almost among the retreating Germans, with one escorting soldier, to try to prevent the bridge from being blown. He further claims that he wanted to make a dash in his tank to save the bridge *from the very start*, but that he was overruled (probably very wisely) by what he called 'The Gunner King'. He goes on to say that his reason for driving the tank 'into the hole in the bridge' (see illustration no. 31) was 'so as to make a solid foundation for the R.E. to build

---

*Alternatively this may have been a patrol of Lord Strathcona's Horse under Lieutenant F.M.W. Harvey, VC (Williams, 156)

upon'.[47] Hamond describes the arrival of the cavalry patrol thus: 'There was a great deal of clattering, galloping and shouting and a lot of our mediaeval horse soldiers came charging down the street; I yelled to them that the bridge was gone but they took no notice of me and went right up to it. One M.G. would have wiped out the lot, and then they turned about and with a very piano air trotted back the way they had come.' It may have been at this moment that a private of the 51st Highland Division saw some cavalry 'riding up under cover of the embankment, the officer commanding asking a lot of questions of him before they all turned about and merely rode away again the way they had come'. Sir Philip Gibbs, the distinguished war correspondent, describes what an onlooker saw of the cavalry at this time: 'They streamed past at a quick trot, and the noise of all the horses' hoofs was a strange rushing sound. The rain slashed down on their steel helmets and all their capes were glistening and the mud was flung up to the horses' flanks, as, in long columns, they went up and down the rolling country. . . . It was a wonderful picture to see and remember.'[48] Witnessing from 150 feet above it the subsiding of the tank on the broken bridge was an AW scout aeroplane. This was one of a number given the job of spotting for the cavalry.* The pilot wound down his signal wire, tapped out his message in morse telling the horsemen to go back, 'when a salvo of shells from some 12" guns nearly dropped him into the canal'. Whether his message was ever picked up is not known.[49]

Hamond, like many other tank officers, scoffing at and scathing about the mounted arm, says that before the Canadians turned about he 'asked for some men to go over the bridge [much of which was just above water] with me but I could get no help from them.' This does not surprise, since Hamond himself thought it 'rather a bad place as . . . only one could get over at a time and the snipers were within eighty yards of us'. He adds that they looked at two other bridges 'passable for cavalry', but complained 'that they couldn't get over because there were machine guns there'. He then sent for a tank which demolished the house from which this fire was coming, blowing 'the snipers out with 6-pdr shells', but 'still

---

*There were 289 aircraft available for the battle. One squadron had been allocated specifically to assist the cavalry.
Due largely to the murky weather, little was achieved by the air element.

these people wouldn't do anything. They had no sense of proportion, of what was too dangerous and what wasn't, in fact they had been living for years in back areas and had no experience of real war.'[50] Major Hamond, one suspects, had never seen what happens when a machine gunner, or indeed a sniper, gets his sights on to men on horseback.

Accounts differ as to the exact sequence of events at this moment. What is clear is that it took a longish time to make a lock, 300 yards south-east of Masnières, over which infantrymen had been trickling for some time, fit for horsemen. Men of the machine-gun squadron, aided by local inhabitants worked feverishly at the job, constructing a bridge with ten inch by ten inch timbers, 'forty inches wide and ten inches thick'. At some point between 3.30 and 4 p.m. 'B' Squadron of the Fort Garry Horse had begun to cross the bridge.*

The Canadian Cavalry Brigade Operation Order of 19 November gave this squadron a 'Special and Independent Mission'. It was to

'(a) Capture the hostile Corps Headquarters reported to be located at Escaudoeuvres, by blocking all exits ... from that place;
(b) Reconnoitre the crossings over the Canal L'Escaut between Eswars and Morenchies, both inclusive.

'The squadron will march immediately in rear of the Advance Guard of the brigade and will be sent through the Advanced Guard immediately after crossing the canal at Masnières.

'The squadron will rejoin the brigade when it reaches the line Tilloy-Cuvillers-Thun Leveque and must be prepared to be detached until dark.

'Reports are required on the following points; (1) Whether bridges at Eswars and Morenchies are intact; (2) The position

---

*Major J.K. ('Tiny') Walker, the officer in command of the machine-gun squadron says that he crossed the bridge which his men had made 'at full gallop' and that it took the squadron 'less than five minutes' by his watch to cross the bridge. (For Strachan's authoritative account of his squadron crossing the bridge, see below.) He also thought that there would have been a good chance of the whole regiment carrying out the whole operation 'on that side of Cambrai' as planned. His view is not supported by other accounts except that of Strachan. (Paterson, 464).

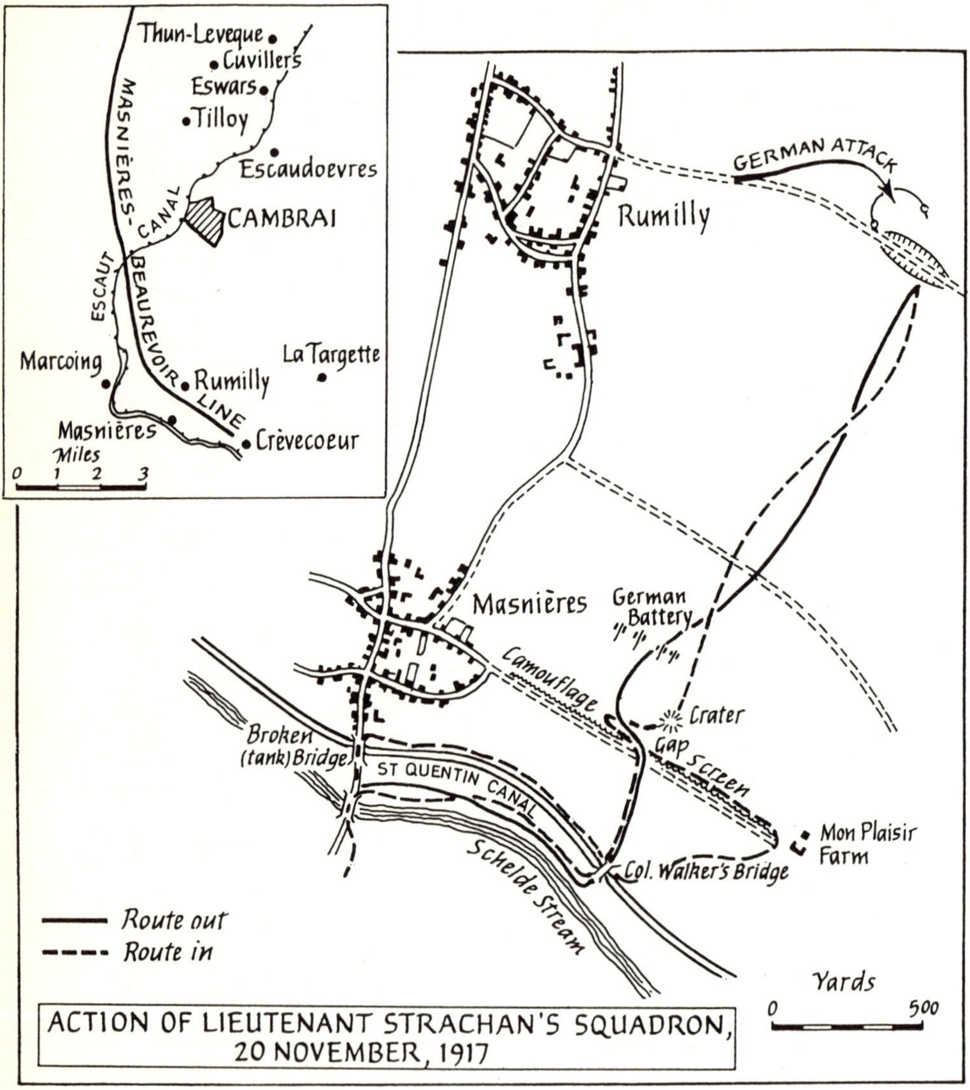

ACTION OF LIEUTENANT STRACHAN'S SQUADRON, 20 NOVEMBER, 1917

and capabilities of any other crossings between those two places.'

A glance at the maps on pages 109 and 130 will show how very optimistic these orders were. They are given in detail to illustrate the type of such orders at this stage of the war.

Lieutenant Henry Strachan, the squadron's second-in-command,* affords a detailed account of what took place. The points made in the special order were

'talked over very carefully with Captain Campbell [commanding the squadron]. I remember that one of my tasks as second in command was to be personally responsible for the German Corps Commander if we captured him. I wonder if he was fat and if he had a red nose!

'Everything went well until we reached the south-west edge of Masnières. Everybody was in high spirits, the squadron being a picture, up to strength with four officers, 129 men and 140 horses, with everything polished and burnished as if for the general's inspection. One might be proud of it.

'At 1.39 p.m. the 88th Infantry Brigade reported that it had reached its objectives and that the tanks were crossing the Masnières bridges. [On this not entirely correct information] General Seely now ordered the advanced guard regiment forward, and it was here that our first casualties occurred from artillery and machine-gun fire round the village.'

As soon as the bridge was made passable:

'Lieutenant-Colonel Paterson gave the order to "carry on", and the squadron, taking horses in single file at a distance, crossed the bridge, which was under fire and very precarious. Several men fell into the canal and a number were drowned, but by the blessing of Providence, we reached the other side and away we went at a gallop at 3.45 p.m.

'We reached the infantry where they had captured the

---

*Strachan, born in 1884 and educated in Edinburgh, had joined the Fort Garry Horse in 1914 as a trooper. He was commissioned in 1916. He retired as a lieut-colonel and died in 1982, aged ninety-eight. He published his account of the action in the *Cavalry Journal* in 1927.

German trenches, but while cutting a [fifteen foot] passage through the old German wire, Captain Campbell [and several men] were killed and the command fell upon me. With a few ground scouts as our only protection, we left the infantry behind and proceeded at a gallop . . .*

'The next obstacle to be encountered was a long camouflage screen running along the side of the Crèvecoeur-Masnières road, which had evidently been erected by the Germans to screen the lateral movements up and down the road. The ground scouts were unable to cope with it by themselves, so a party of men from the nearest troop dismounted and cut a gap. Here the value of previous training was exemplified, for on one word of command each troop passed through the gap in the correct order and reformed "line of troop columns" on the further side without the slightest semblance of confusion or noise.

'The squadron now proceeded up to the high ground, east of Masnières, and on gaining the ridge, came face to face with a German battery of four [77 mm] guns about 300 yards away. Fortunately swords had been drawn before crossing the bridge and the squadron charged the guns, each troop column converging on them. It is interesting to note that one gun continued to fire until the last and those gunners probably escaped owing to the difficulty of reaching them, whereas the remaining gunners, who ran away as soon as we appeared, were satisfactorily accounted for almost to a man. We found out afterwards that the capture of these guns had been a great help to those in the rear as the shell fire round the bridge had been caused by them. Whilst charging the guns we were fired on by machine guns, but these also ceased fire when the guns were taken.

'Up to this point no opposition had been encountered from German infantry. The trenches marked on the map were merely "spit locked" (dummy) and there was practically no wire, but there were a few concrete "pill boxes" completed and machine guns firing from them.

'It will be noted that according to orders we should not have crossed the bridge until after the vanguard squadron

---

*'In section extended to minimise the effect of the flanking fire from machine guns'. (Pitman, 256)

had crossed, but for some reason we were in front and fully expected that not only the remainder of the Brigade, but also the whole Cavalry Corps were close behind. Had we been second squadron we should have escaped the bulk of the casualties, and being on a special mission we should not have been drawn into fighting such as the charging of the guns; as it was, the whole action was forced on us and we suffered a great many casualties which would normally have been shared by the vanguard squadron.

'German infantry* were now observed retiring in great disorder in the direction of Rumilly, and the squadron rode right over them as they discarded arms and equipment right and left. They offered no opposition, but they protected themselves as well as they could by lying down or hiding behind piles of rubbish, etc., where they could not be reached with the sword. Batches of from fifty to a hundred put their hands up, but the squadron could not stop to collect them, as we still thought, as we did on reaching the guns, that they would be "mopped up" by the cavalry following along behind. After passing them, there was no opposition at all; everything was in the wildest confusion and there was every indication of a demoralized retreat on the part of the enemy. We still had quite a long way to go to complete our mission (Escaudoeuvres, six or seven miles) and we were still confident that the remainder of the cavalry would complete the rout.

'The horses were brought down to a walk, small reconnoitring detachments were sent out and the squadron moved in a north-easterly direction, leaving Rumilly on its left flank with the intention of avoiding further action and saving ourselves for our own little "show" at Escaudoeuvres.

'The enemy machine gunners, now in our rear, must have seen that we were not supported, as we now came under fire again. Evidently they had removed their guns from the "pill boxes" in order to fire to their rear. However, they did not have any material success.

'On reaching a sunken road at a point about midway

---

*There was a school of recruits in Rumilly. It is thought possible that most of the enemy's resistance was provided by the school's staff and pupils. (Anon. 'Cambrai', *Royal Tank Corps Journal*, July, 1936, 71)

between L'Epine and Rumilly the squadron was halted for a short rest, and a message was sent back to Brigade stating the point we had reached and that we were proceeding on our mission. Two gallopers [Privates Morell and Vanwilderode] were sent with this message and one got through, but that was the last we heard about it. A hurried inspection was made and the squadron was found to have suffered severely, more so than had been anticipated. Only forty-three men and horses were left, all the pack horses were lost, several men had minor wounds and all the horses but seven were found to be wounded,* many were exhausted and several actually dropped dead while we were going around looking at them.

'Dusk was approaching and although we were on the direct line of advance of the Brigade, no support was anywhere visible. A diversion here occurred by somebody capturing a prisoner. Although the latter appeared to be only too ready to tell us all he knew, he did not appear to know anything useful, so he was not of much use to us.

'The patrols we had sent out returned reporting nothing unusual from the north and west, but from the east, a party of Germans about a company strong was reported advancing along the road, on which we were halted; later on, these Germans attacked us, but after a stiff fight we succeeded in driving them off.

'Two parties were detailed to cut wires, telegraphs and any German communications that could be found. A great deal of this was accomplished and a power line apparently running from Rumilly to La Targette was cut, one of our men, unfortunately, being electrocuted during the operation.

'It now commenced to get dark and no support could be sighted anywhere. In the meantime, two German battalions were observed moving out from Rumilly and taking up a position somewhere about where we had charged the guns earlier in the day. Thus we were now completely cut off. In addition, long columns of motor lorries (which, -

---

*Most of the wounds were from bullets in the horses' bellies and legs. (Woollcombe, 86)

14. Indian cyclists with cavalry, July, 1916.

15. Men of the 20th Deccan Horse, 14 July, 1916.

16. Brigadier-General J.E.B. Seely (*left*), commanding the Canadian Cavalry Brigade, with General Hughes (*centre*) and Sir Max Aitken, Amiens area, August, 1916.

17. The Bays entering the Carnoy Valley, 18 September, 1916.

incidentally, had no tyres and made a terrific din) were moving down the road from Cambrai to Rumilly all loaded with troops.

'A conference of all ranks was called to explain the situation. The German infantry whom we had driven off had established piquets all around us – we were unsupported – and it was nearly dark. Owing to the condition of the horses, several more of which had died, we were reluctantly forced to abandon, as being utterly impossible, any further idea of completing our mission. A few voiced the opinion that to surrender was the only course left, but after considering that everything was really in our favour, i.e., that it was dark – that the Germans were in total ignorance of our whereabouts – that everything was disorganized and that any enemy we might meet would be fresh troops groping in the dark around positions which they had never seen, it was decided to stampede the horses in the direction of the German piquets that were watching us and rejoin the Brigade on foot.* We had inadvertently allowed our prisoner to listen to our deliberations and as he understood English, we had to take him with us.

'The stampeding of the horses was a total failure, as the poor brutes had not even enough life left in them to run. They just roamed off in the darkness, while we started back on foot.

'The return of the squadron, or what was left of it, was of necessity very cautious, as any surprise meeting with Germans had to be in our favour, and above all there was the chance of being shot down by our own troops when nearing their position. It was arranged that any enemy encountered were to be charged vigorously in the hope that resolute action would give them a false impression of our dwindled numbers.

'Quietly giving the German piquets the slip, we moved back in the direction whence we had come; three times before reaching the camouflage screen which we had traversed earlier in the day, parties of Germans in varying strength were

---

*Strachan took a bearing from the church tower of Rumilly the light being just strong enough for it to be seen. (Pitman, 256)

encountered as they were moving apparently into defensive positions. There were no means of ascertaining their numbers in the darkness but they were in every case completely surprised and unprepared for our rushes with the bayonet, and our success was out of all proportion to the numbers engaged. Rather unfortunately several prisoners were captured, all of whom had to be taken with us and this rather hampered our movements.

'On reaching the vicinity of the camouflage screen a large crater was found where the squadron was halted and everybody being totally exhausted was allowed to sleep for an hour. Lieutenant Fleming and myself shared sentry duty. By this time it was raining, making it thoroughly miserable but yet more in our favour for getting away.

'The squadron slept on till about the small hours of the morning. At one period during the watch a working party of Germans came along and commenced putting up barbed wire, only a few yards from the crater. At first we could not tell whether they were Germans or British, so to find out, Lieutenant Fleming crawled up the edge of the crater and talked to them, whereupon they stopped work and listened, then, under the impression that their ears had deceived them, they started to work again only to be interrupted by tentative remarks from Fleming, and the Germans could not make out where the voice was coming from. Fleming told me that at first, by their conversation, he thought they must be Scotchmen, but it was finally decided not to take any more chances.

'Everybody was finally awakened and a fresh start was made. The camouflage screen was reached and a further column of Germans was sighted coming down the road. A fierce fight ensued in which the Germans were finally driven back along the road, but our little force got divided in the darkness and Lieutenant Cowan and the greater part dodged through the hole in the screen taking a number of prisoners with them. This party found the bridge over the canal and got back safely at three o'clock in the morning. The small party, with which I found myself, drifted down the road in an easterly direction along the entire length of the screen. After having another small scrap at Mon Plaisir Farm we made for the canal; there was a light in a house by Walker's

Bridge, so not knowing if it was held by Huns or not, we wound our way along the bank to Masnières, where we commenced to cross at the bridge where the tank had fallen in. There was quite a gap in the structure and the humorous climax came when several including myself fell into the canal in our attempts to jump across in the dark. Once given a lead, all the German prisoners also jumped, many of them falling in, but finally all were over and the regiment was rejoined about five in the morning.

'The total of the squadron which got back was three officers, forty-three other ranks and eighteen prisoners. The casualties in the whole action were undoubtedly severe, but in the opinion of the writer the leading squadron (our squadron in this case, as we were unfortunately the only one) would have taken the bulk of these casualties, and any troops coming in rear would undoubtedly have got off very lightly. It appears that there would have been a remarkable opportunity for a great cavalry success, had the operation in its original form been carried out.'

Strachan, who already wore the Military Cross, was awarded the Victoria Cross for this action. That it was well deserved cannot be doubted.[51]

This first-hand account has been quoted *in extenso* because it is rare throughout the war to find so detailed and authoritative a description of a mounted action by the leading participant.

Captain Wilfrid Miles in the Official History states that half an hour before the Canadian squadron had started to cross, Greenly, commanding the 2nd Cavalry Division,

'which was now drawing near, rode into les Rues Vertes. He conferred with the commanders of the 88th Brigade and the Canadian Cavalry Brigade. The brigade-major of the 88th Brigade, himself a cavalryman, expressed the opinion that it was not practicable for any considerable force of cavalry to pass over the marshy approach or to cross the canal at the lock used by the Canadian squadron; and Major-General Greenly felt constrained to agree. No officer present seemed to know of the bridge, some 1,600 yards south-east of the main bridge, which led to Mon Plaisir Farm. This was a wooden structure, hidden from fire and view and quite suitable for cavalry, but no reconnaissance had discovered it and no French inhabitant had mentioned it.'

Miles adds in a footnote that this bridge was specifically indicated by its map co-ordinates in the order of 18 November governing the infantry's operations in the area, and should therefore have been known to the 88th Brigade. Further, the bridge was very clearly marked on the 1:10,000 map and it showed up well in an aerial photograph taken on 19 November, but this had not been circulated to Cavalry Corps headquarters.[52] In view of the importance of crossing the canal, it does seem extraordinary that no one 'discovered' this bridge.

Greenly and Seely now came to the conclusion that 'there was not sufficient daylight left to enable the cavalry to reach their objectives and so carry out their original plan. In view of this decision and owing to the fact that it would take each squadron from twenty to thirty minutes to cross the temporary bridge, and that it would be therefore impossible to closely support the leading squadron which had set out on its original objective, General Seely sent an order to the C.O. Fort Garry Horse not to cross the canal and to withdraw any of his troops that had already crossed.'[53] It was clear that, since the infantry had not reached the Masnières-Beaurevoir line, 'the necessary preliminary to any large-scale cavalry action was lacking.'[54] The officer commanding the Fort Garry Horse, Lieutenant-Colonel Paterson, did not receive the order not to cross the canal until well after 'B' Squadron had done so. He himself rode forward to recall the squadron, apparently saw no enemy and, having lamed his horse by jumping into the sunken road, failed to catch it up.[55]

* * *

In the area to the right, where the Lucknow Brigade was following up the infantry, that infantry reported that the Bois Lateau had been taken by 11.00. The two officers who had carried forward the cavalry track to this point found everything quiet. Nevertheless, not a man, they reported, except some forward patrols,

Cambrai, 20 November, 1917

appeared before 1 p.m. Both officers 'imagined that the cavalry had gone round by another route.'[56]*

* * *

Due to the difficulty of watering the horses at the canal because of its steep banks, orders were given for the Cavalry Corps divisions to retire during the night. However, slowness in getting orders to their recipients and the increasingly waterlogged state of the cavalry tracks, to say nothing of the appalling congestion of miles of cavalrymen in conflict with the pushing forward for next day's operations of ammunition columns, guns, the 'surplus personnel' of infantry divisions and urgently needed supplies, most of the score or so of cavalry regiments remained more or less where they were till morning. The whole of the 2nd Brigade of the 1st Division remained saddled up all night behind Marcoing. It was a miserable night for it never ceased to rain.

* * *

*Unbelievable though it seems, two troopers of the 3rd Hussars (4th Cavalry Brigade), one the cook and the other the waiter of 'B' Squadron mess, characterized by one of their subalterns as 'an experienced and resourceful couple', not above 'waylaying the general's meat ration after dark if their officers were short of food', actually in the course of the day cycled into Cambrai on the first day of the battle, 20 November, 1917. The subaltern describes the

> 'extraordinary fact that, although they saw plenty of Germans about, it did not enter their heads that they were miles behind the enemy line, nor apparently did the Germans think it strange to see two British soldiers on bicycles – presumably they thought they were prisoners going to the rear.' So Knowles and Gurnham rode 'almost into the centre of the town, and putting their bicycles up against a gateway they went into a building to investigate. The place turned out to be a German soldiers' food store, and they helped themselves to what they wanted and came out again.' [Only then did they realize] 'the awful truth of their situation'; but 'nothing daunted . . . they pedalled the whole of the way back, crossed the canal and rejoined the regiment the same night',

in time to give their officers a 'sumptuous dinner' prepared from the captured food. (Bolitho, 224–5)

Haig decides to continue attacks after 20 November, 1917

It would be tedious to detail the part played by the cavalry in the rest of the battle of Cambrai.* Except for one astonishing, unhappy mounted action (see p. 146 below) it could do little except act as reinforcements to the hard-pressed infantry. This it did to some effect.

* * *

John Terraine gives three reasons for Haig's decision to push forward fresh attacks between 21 and 29 November,

> 'none of which was militarily sound. First he assumed that the ease of the initial assault had been due to the German front being "soft" – not to the novel tactics. Therefore [and in this Charteris bears a grievous responsibility], since the Germans would supposedly be slow to reinforce, the possibility of a breakthrough remained. Secondly, Haig thought that this breakthrough would open the way for a glorious cavalry charge.... Finally, he realised that the initial success was deeply embarrassing to Lloyd George, who had of late been critical of British generals. The possibility of increasing the Prime Minister's embarrassment proved intoxicating. In the end it was Haig who was embarrassed.'[57]

Whether this view of the failure to quit while the Commander-in-Chief was ahead is correct is arguable – and often argued.†

In desperate attempts to augment the splendid success of 20 November, all that was achieved against the swiftly accumulating German reinforcements was the costly and temporary capture of Bourlon Wood but not, except fleetingly, the vital Bourlon Ridge.

---

*Haig, visiting the front in the morning of 22 November, spoke to Mullens. From him he learned that IV Corps had ordered the 1st Cavalry Division back to Metz-en-Couture. The whole division, he said, was 'very disappointed'. In his diary Haig wrote: 'I personally would much have liked to have given him an order to return, but restrained myself because it is impossible to be successful if more than one commander gives orders.' (Blake: *Haig*, 269)

†In the morning of 21 November patrols of King Edward's Horse took prisoners from a German regiment who reported that they had just arrived from the Eastern Front, and that two more new regiments were in or around the Bourlon ridge. (Wyrall, Everard *History of the 62nd (West Riding) Division, 1914-1919*, I, 1924-25, quoted in Moore, 87).

Cambrai: German counter-attack, 30 November, 1917

The wood alone was of minimal value, and there were neither fresh infantry nor tanks with which to consolidate the position within it, let alone achieve the battle's original objectives. With great difficulty certain infantry reserves were tardily brought down from Flanders, but not enough to begin to convert the primary break *in* into a real break *through*. The absence of further help meant that by the 29th there was even greater difficulty in consolidating the ground that had been won nine days before.

* * *

On the 30th the enemy, having successfully concealed much of his now overwhelming force, surprised the British by a major counter-attack. This took the form of a pincer movement against the salient which had been produced on 20 November. Its chief weight fell between Masnières and Epéhy. It was accompanied by low-flying aircraft, numerous gas shells and much use of *minenwerfers*. The result of this major counter-stroke was to cancel out not only most of the territory gained ten days before,* but also the numbers of guns and prisoners taken on that historic day. The cavalry was rushed forward again, and, using its mobility, speedily strengthened the dangerously weak firing line. For instance the Ambala Cavalry Brigade 'trotted eleven miles without stopping to Villers Faucon, followed by the rest of the 5th Cavalry Division', and the 20th Hussars of the 5th Cavalry Brigade virtually saved a company of Royal Engineers which was holding, very thinly, a

---

* 'The Germans had taken a piece of British territory three-quarters the size of the British gains.' (Scott: 'Cambrai', 106)

Not long after the battle there was a series of debates in the Commons during which members tried to get the government to explain why the Germans had been able to achieve such a large success on 30 November. There were held, at the same time, two courts of enquiry, the first in the form of a committee of the Imperial General Staff, plus a committee of the War Cabinet and the War Cabinet itself, and the second instituted by Haig. Both constituted a major cover up, all the senior commanders being absolved of any responsibility for the débâcle. Earlier Byng had given his views. 'I attribute the reason for the local success on the part of the enemy to one cause and one alone, namely – lack of training on the part of junior officers and NCOs and men.' (PRO WO/158/54 (copy of Third Army GS 56/244 or 18-12-17)). There may have been some truth in this, but, as readers of this chapter will understand, it obscured the real culprits, of whom Haig (who specifically took all the blame) was the chief. The whole rather unattractive story, in which incidentally the *(continued over)*

Cambrai, 30 November, 1917

stretch of trenches near Gouzeaucourt. Part of Hodson's Horse, at one point, while crossing 2,000 yards of open ground between Revelon and Gauche Wood at the gallop so as to gain a forward trench line, was subjected to 'a regular inferno of shelling. . . . Diamond formation, with troops about forty yards apart, was taken up and the regiment moved without a waver across the valley. The leading troop was literally blown to pieces.' One who saw this gallop said that the horsemen were 'shot at from both flanks, from ridges at close range. Shot at from the front, much like the valley of death at Balaklava, they never wavered or quickened the pace. The ranks in rear filled up the gaps caused by casualties as if on a ceremonial parade.' Another observer noticed 'an extraordinary feature': how few were the numbers of shells 'that burst between the troops, as distinct from those that hit. Where one hit, four or five men and horses would be knocked out. . . . As it was clear that there was no hope of any further advance the horses were all sent back some three miles.' The regiment lost about fifty men and seventy horses.[58]

Much of the cavalry had been more or less converted into infantry before the great German counter-attack on the 30th, but during it the corps and divisional cavalry did great work as gallopers. All the telephone lines had been cut and messages between infantry units were exclusively carried by gallopers. 'Sometimes,' remembered Furse of King Edward's Horse, 'they were galloping a bare 100 yards behind the firing line, being cheered by the infantry. No message entrusted to them failed to get through. Not a single man

---

cavalry is barely mentioned, is very fully dealt with in Moore, 165–200.

More important than this distasteful cover-up was Lloyd George's and the Cabinet's well-justified belief that Charteris ought to be sacked. Haig, in defending him, disliked his being made a 'whipping-boy for the charge of undue optimism brought against' himself. (9 Dec., 1917, Haig to Derby, quoted in Terraine: *Haig*, 255). He was given another job. He became Director-General of Transportation. In Charteris's place Haig appointed Temporary Lieutenant-General the Hon. (Sir) Herbert Lawrence who had made his name in the South African War as a successful intelligence officer (see Vol. 4, p. 105), and who had been partly responsible for the victory at Romani in Egypt. (See Vol. 5, p. 41, *passim*). Haig's exact contemporary, he had resigned his commission in the 17th Lancers when, in 1903, Haig had been brought in over his head to command the regiment. He was not long in his new post before Kiggell, due to ill health, resigned as Chief of the Staff and Lawrence took over on 24 January, 1918. Colonel Edgar Cox succeeded Lawrence, but it seems that Haig still on occasion consulted Charteris in preference to Cox. (See Marshall-Cornwall, 254–7; Warner, 249–50)

or horse was hit, evidence for my theory that a mounted man can do far more than most people think he can – even in modern war – provided he gallops fast.'[59]

* * *

It will be seen from the map on p. 144 how far on the British right the German counter-attack had advanced on 30 November. Unfortunately it was here that the defences were at their weakest.* At Villers Guislain the artillery had been totally surprised. Indeed it sustained 'the biggest single loss of British guns in one battle ever to date'.[60] The situation on the morning of 1 December was therefore exceptionally threatening. It was a question of panic stations.

The two Indian cavalry divisions, the 4th and 5th, were amongst the troops which had been hurried forward during the 30th. 'At about 11 a.m. the Brigade Major [of the Mhow Cavalry Brigade] rang up the adjutant [of the 2nd Lancers] and gave orders to turn out at once every man available. The colonel, who was just going out for a ride, was only just stoped in time. An hour later the "regiment" marched out. It consisted chiefly in pack horses (those of the Hotchkiss without their guns) . . . farriers, trumpeters. . . . In two General Service wagons were taken all [the regiment's] swords and lances.[61] It was without these weapons because most of the regiment had at daybreak on the 30th been sent forward in a pre-arranged move to take their place in the trenches, equipped, of course, only with rifles. The Hotchkiss guns had gone with them in limbers. The trench party, consisting of most of the regiment with the horseholders, did not join up until about 10 p.m. Both parts of the regiment had been from time to time under fire, including gas shells. 'The reorganization of squadrons took place in the pitch dark. The sword and lance wagons were somewhere in rear and only turned up barely in time for the attack in the morning.' Indeed weapons 'were being thrown to the men of the rear half squadron as they passed the wagons.'[62]

*VII Corps adjoined III Corps. Lieutenant-General Sir Thomas D'Oyly Snow, commanding the VIIth, was convinced that the enemy would attack in his area, which was very thinly defended, especially in artillery. He seems to have warned Haig a number of times, but GHQ had apparently been convinced that the Germans were incapable of mounting a strong attack. This looks as if Charteris had once again miscalculated. (See Edmonds, *1917*, III, 169; Farndale, 249)

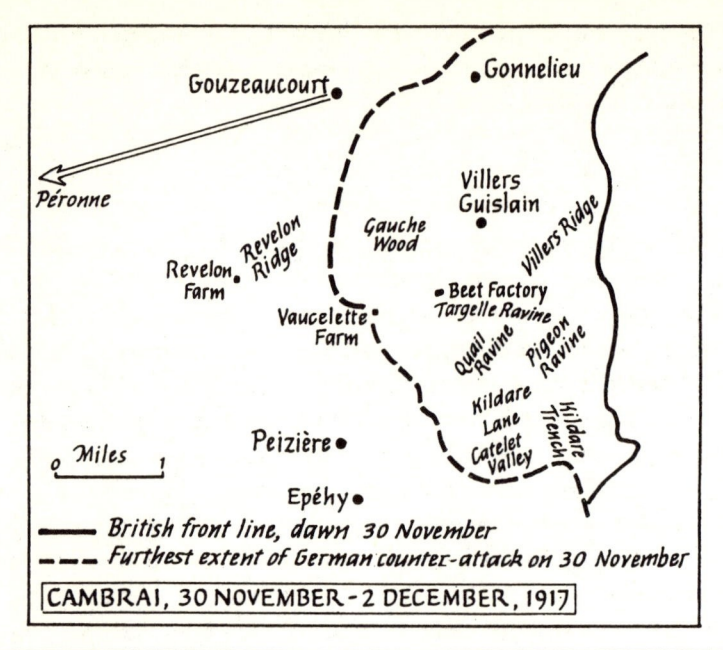

CAMBRAI, 30 NOVEMBER – 2 DECEMBER, 1917

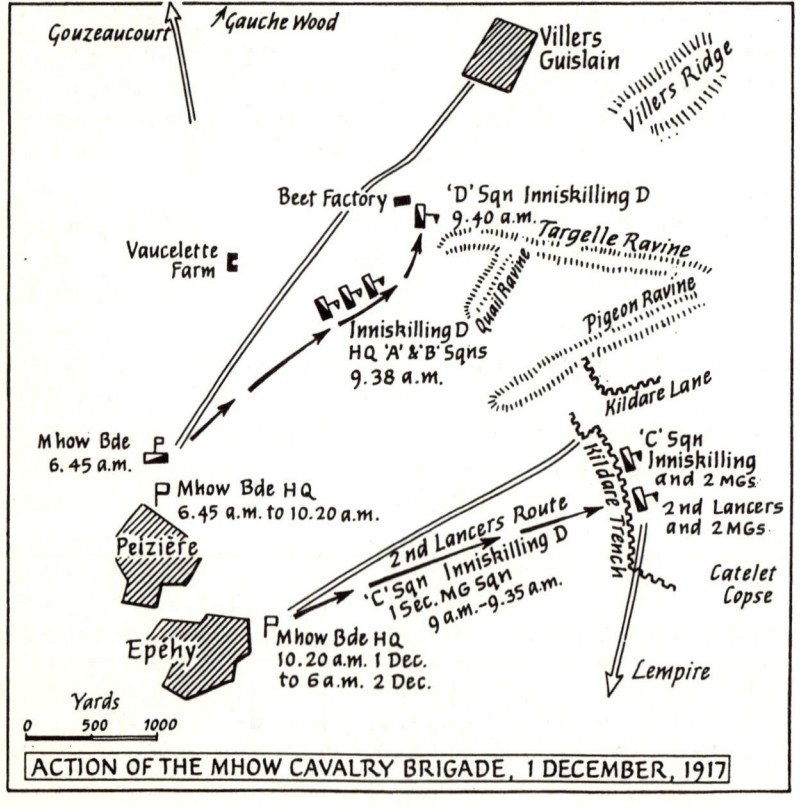

— British front line, dawn 30 November
--- Furthest extent of German counter-attack on 30 November

ACTION OF THE MHOW CAVALRY BRIGADE, 1 DECEMBER, 1917

The Cavalry Corps' orders for a considerable counter-stroke against the enemy who had successfully resisted the British counter-strokes of 30 November were issued at 6.40 p.m. on that day. The 5th Cavalry Division with the Lucknow Cavalry Brigade attached was to attack Gauche Wood and Villers Guislain, 'co-operating with fourteen tanks, eight of which will be directed on Gauche Wood and six on Villers Guislain'.[63] As they were to follow tanks, these attacks were, of course, to be on foot. The 4th Cavalry Division, less the Lucknow Brigade, was ordered to 'assemble west of Peizière with the object of taking advantage of the advance of the tanks and seizing Villers Ridge' and to 'keep close liaison with the tank attack.'[64] This order the Mhow Cavalry Brigade received at 2.50 a.m. In this case 'mounted action was insisted upon by Lieutenant-General Kavanagh.'[65]

By 6.30 a.m. the whole brigade was massed in the low ground north and north-west of Peizière. An observer of the scene recorded that when daylight came (by about 6.50) he

> 'could see the Mhow Cavalry Brigade . . . standing quietly in mass. . . . There were probably good reasons for so dense a formation. The German guns [chiefly 77 mm, firing high explosive, 'timed' high explosive and shrapnel][66] were soon on to so excellent a target. For a long time I watched shell after shell fall into those closely packed ranks. Save for occasional flying fragments of man or horse there appeared no movement or unsteadiness whatever. I was profoundly impressed by the total unconcern exhibited by those three regiments. At about 8 a.m. they filed away and were lost to sight beyond the railway embankment.'[67]

Half an hour before that, patrols had established that there were sufficient exits through the wire on the Peizière – Villers-Guislain road and on that from Épéhy to the derelict buildings of a beet factory.

The tank liaison officers at the Mhow Brigade headquarters heard at 8.10 a.m. that none of the tanks had arrived at their rendezvous because it had proved impossible to get them serviceable in time. In consequence the attack by the Lucknow Brigade leading the 5th Cavalry Division against Gauche Wood and Villers-Guislain Ridge would not now be carried out. Instead that brigade would be 'supporting infantry in Vaucelette Farm'.[68]

When this news reached Brigadier-General N.M. Haig, commanding the Mhow Cavalry Brigade, he naturally assumed that there was now no chance of his brigade being required to carry out the task which it had been given. Its attack was to have been 'made on a suitable opportunity presenting itself on the advance of the tanks' which could not now occur.[69] It could hardly now 'keep close liaison with the tank attack', since there was to be no attack and there were no tanks.

Meanwhile Major-General Alfred Alexander Kennedy, commanding the 4th Cavalry Division, was called to the telephone by Kavanagh who wanted to know how the attack of the Mhow Brigade was progressing. Kennedy explained that since the Lucknow Brigade's attack, preceded by tanks, was not to go ahead, the Mhow Brigade's attack had not started. The Official Historian states that 'the corps commander, though made fully aware of the difficulties of the situation, would not tolerate further delay'. Kennedy therefore at 8.15 ordered the Mhow Brigade to go ahead.

> 'He could only hope,' as the Official Historian puts it, 'that the mounted attack would gain some ground and help the Lucknow Brigade forward. Brigadier-General Haig was convinced that the enterprise was a desperate one and said as much when questioned by a divisional staff officer as to the chances of success. The only artillery support was that afforded by the brigaded R.H.A. batteries of the division*.... There was no time to make any arrangements with the 55th Division artillery which was shelling Villers Guislain.'[70]

Orders for the 2nd Lancers accompanied by one squadron of the 6th Inniskilling Dragoons and four machine guns were to seize Targelle, Quail and Pigeon Ravines. These were about 3,000 yards from their starting point. As soon as the three remaining squadrons of the Inniskillings saw the Lancers approaching Targelle Ravine, they had orders to advance by the Peizière – Villers-Guislain road and the valley between the beet factory and Quail Ravine.

Soon after 9 a.m. the 2nd Lancers, 'about 440 of all ranks, including ten British batmen', still under shell fire, set off in open

---

*The Chestnut Troop, 'Q' and 'U' Batteries.

column of line of troop columns extended. 'Just forward of the level crossing [out of Epéhy]', remembered Captain Whitworth, the adjutant of the regiment, 'we passed through the trenches of our own very astonished infantry.'[71] At the fork in the road about 250 yards from the level crossing, Major G. Knowles commanding the leading squadron, took the right-hand road leading to the Catelet Valley. When Whitworth pointed this out to the commanding officer, Lieutenant-Colonel H.H.F. Turner, the latter said, 'Let him go. We will get more cover that way,' which, though true, did not mean that the cover was very effective, though infinitely more so than on the route taken by the Inniskillings (see below). Knowles's intention seems to have been to turn north and gain Targelle Ravine from the east instead of going straight for it.

Knowles's squadron, according to Whitworth,

'seemed to have barely started down the valley when there was a tremendous outburst of machine-gun fire from both sides, and the pace was increased to a gallop. The apparently deserted landscape became alive with running grey figures, but that all had not run was obvious from the intensity of the fire which was now brought to bear on the regiment. Although the air seemed to be full of bullets, and the flying turf showed that not all were going over our heads, very few casualties were noticeable; in fact, there was no apparent diminution in the strength of the regiment when we dismounted for action two miles further on. Except for the shell holes, the going was splendid, and the pace must have been at least fifteen miles an hour. The number of German machine guns in action is uncertain, but there must at least have been half-a-dozen. Firing from both sides of a narrow valley, according to all the then known laws of musketry they should have annihilated a regiment of cavalry coming down it, at whatever pace. As it was, the effects of their fire were tactically negligible, a fact which must be ascribed to badly shaken nerves on the part of the enemy machine gunners.'[72]

This astonishing gallop of some 3,000 yards avoided what ought to have been the regiment's fate, not only through its speed but also because there happened to be nothing in the way of wire obstacles. The Germans' shocked bewilderment at so unaccustomed a sight must also have had something to do with it. The gallop was checked when the two leading squadrons came to a fortified sunken road, known as Kildare Trench. Here there were three parallel lines of wire only about eighteen inches in height which had been put up the previous night by the Germans.[73] In this wire there were two gaps. Through these the horsemen managed to clamber down into the sunken road. 'Risaldar Mukand Singh was sent round to the right at the same time to outflank the enemy. In doing so he found a single apron of wire between him and the retreating Germans. This he and his troop jumped, and went in with the lance.'[74] A few men, led by Lieutenant N.H. Broadway, scrambled up the opposite bank and 'went in pursuit of the Germans. Eyewitnesses say that Lieutenant Broadway [who had already killed two Germans] was approaching a German officer who was holding up one hand and apparently wished to surrender, when the latter, drawing the other hand, in which was a pistol, from behind his back, fired, killing Lieutenant Broadway instantaneously. A moment later, Acting Lance Dafadar Sahib Singh killed the German with a hogspear.'[75] The Commanding Officer who, with regimental headquarters, had followed the second squadron was killed instantly by machine-gun fire the moment he had passed through the wire. 'His orderly Hidayat Ali and Trumpet Major Ganga Ram remained with his body throughout the day, lying in a shallow shell hole, the former being wounded while doing so. Woordi Major Dhara Singh, who had been shot through the ankle, also remained there for some time.'[76] Knowles now assumed command. It seems that fifteen Germans were killed by lance and sword and twenty or so 'knocked over by rifle and machine-gun fire' as they fled from the sunken road, leaving three light machine guns and two prisoners behind them.[77]

In the sunken road there was just room for the men and 169 horses of the two leading squadrons and the Inniskilling squadron. The rest of the horses had to be led back by the same route as they had come. They started off only a quarter of an hour after the regiment had reached Kildare Trench. Their casualties, especially in horses, since they were obviously unable to go at speed (and as any earlier surprise felt by the enemy had now evaporated) were very much heavier than had been those inflicted during the great gallop.* Those men who remained defended their position throughout the rest of the day, using their machine guns, rifles and captured German bombs to good effect. They even attempted to move on foot northwards into Pigeon and Quail Ravines, but were always frustrated by intense machine-gun fire from all directions.[78] Messages were sent back telling of the regiment's position and plight by galloping sowar volunteers, one of whom, Gobind Singh, for going back and forth time and again was awarded the Victoria Cross.† The first message arrived about two hours after the

---

*'Of the men of the led horses, Kote Dafadar Nihal Chand, of "B" Squadron, was dismounted by having his horse shot and was himself shot through both thighs. Some Germans from a post to the right rear of Kildare Lane now came out and took some of these men prisoners. (By a coincidence, one of the Germans in this post was taken prisoner by the regiment at Beisan ten months later (see Vol. 5, p. 287)). They stripped Nihal Chand of his haversack, waterbottle, and accoutrements, and began to carry him towards their post. At this moment other Germans, who were attacking [Kildare Trench] from the same post, were counter-attacked by "B" squadron under Major Salkeld. The men carrying Nihal Chand, then dropped him and ran back to their trenches, whereupon Nihal Chand dragged himself by his hands to the shelter of a shell hole. Here he remained all day, and that night he dragged himself in the same way towards Epéhy. Daybreak found him half way there, and again he had to lie up till dark, being without food or water. Early next morning he reached the wire of the British trenches, where he managed to attract attention, and was taken in. In dragging himself he had worn out the toes of his boots, and his lacerated toes had become frostbitten, necessitating afterwards the amputation of both feet.' (Whitworth, 108)

†Though under intense machine-gun fire, this remarkable man 'covered over a quarter of a mile before his horse was killed.' He was unhurt. For a time he lay low 'until he judged that the attention of the Germans had been attracted elsewhere. Then, alternatively wriggling and running, he worked his way on. Occasionally, when things became too hot he toppled over and shammed dead again.' He covered two miles before he reached brigade headquarters. At once volunteering to take back the brigadier's reply he was furnished with a new horse. This was soon killed but he got the message through. An hour later a second message had to be got through to brigade. Gobind Singh again volunteered. 'He said that he now knew where the German post lay and that he knew a safer route . . .' His horse this time was 'cut literally in two', but its rider again escaped unscathed. 'This time it was a long range for the enemy machine guns and he got up at once and ran for his life.' On reaching brigade headquarters he volunteered to make yet another trip. 'He was told that he had done enough.' (Anon. 'Second Lancers at Epéhy', *Cav. Jnl*, Oct., 1928, 566–7).

regiment had started. Brigade headquarters meanwhile had thought it totally lost.

Whitworth managed somehow to get in touch with the infantry brigade on the right whose commander gave him orders for the cavalry's immediate retirement. Whitworth then reconnoitred a route for this and when darkness set in at 5 p.m. and before the moon rose at about 6 p.m. in a clear sky it was carried out.* By 5.40, indeed, all unfit horses having been shot and a bridge over a trench constructed and covered with earth to deaden the sound of the horses' hoofs, the withdrawal due south towards Lempire had been accomplished without a single casualty. All the unwounded horses, the commanding officer's body and all the wounded men were got safely in. In the course of the day the Brigade Commander sent forward dismounted squadrons of the Central India Horse to try to extricate the 2nd Lancers. Not surprisingly, they got only a short distance before suffering fifty-seven casualties and being forced to retire.

The casualties of the five squadrons and the machine-gun section amounted to forty-eight killed or died in hospital, fifty-three wounded and twelve who became prisoners of war, totalling 113.[79]

* * *

In the meantime how had the main body of the Inniskillings fared on the left? Their route from Peizière to the beet factory was over terrain which provided for its first 1,500 yards perfect going for cavalry. It was virtually clear of obstacles and very open. Nothing, therefore, could have been more obviously perilous when overlooked by a numerous well armed enemy. There was not a shred of cover. Every single movement could be seen from the beet factory area, which was known to be and certainly was well supplied with machine guns.

When 'at 9.35 a.m. the 2nd Lancers were seen moving forward,' the Inniskillings' leading squadron, with four machine guns, moved off 'rather prematurely' at a gallop.[80] The remaining two

---

*Before leaving, a red light was sent up from a captured Very pistol. This was the signal for 'This is a German position: raise your barrage.' It had the desired effect. (Whitworth, 111).

squadrons and the Field Troop, RE followed 'in column of squadrons in line of troop columns, widely extended, at a distance of about 600 yards'.[81] They were immediately assailed by intensive, continuous machine-gun fire from front and flank. With extraordinary gallantry, the leading squadron, together with the machine gunners, losing men and horses rapidly all the while, pressed on, the survivors of this ghastly gallop actually reaching the beet factory, some 3,000 yards from their starting point. There they were greeted by 'a tremendous burst of artillery fire' and 'a large force of the enemy were seen to come in from all sides and surround them'. Very few managed to escape the net and return whence they had come. Those who had survived the gallop were for the most part made prisoners. As soon as Lieutenant-Colonel Ewing Paterson* saw what was happening, realizing that his whole regiment would be lost were he to continue, he at once turned round the two following squadrons and the Field Troop, RE and galloped back to Peizière. 'Many acts of devotion and gallantry were carried out during this retirement.'[82]

The losses sustained in this hideous fiasco were horrific. It had lasted, (as also had the 2nd Lancers' gallop), but ten minutes (see below) during which it lost six officers, 108 other ranks and 187 horses. The machine-gun section was a total loss: beside the four guns, two officers, fifty-three other ranks and eighty-four horses were squandered.

* * *

It is ironical that the Germans had not intended any fresh advance in this part of the field. They had had eighteen hours in which to 'consolidate a defensive flank' which relied upon their machine gunners and a fairly powerful artillery.[83] In short, had the cavalry moved forward not a single inch, the situation at the end of 1 December would have been exactly the same as it had been at nightfall on 30 November. This could not, of course, have been known to Kavanagh or anyone else on the British side. Had this not been the case, the hollowness of the following statement by Captain Whitworth would have been cruelly obvious: 'It is

---

*Paterson took command of the 6th Cavalry Brigade in 1918 till the end of the war and became Commandant of the Cavalry School from 1920 to 1922. He had joined the regiment in 1893. He died in 1950, aged seventy-seven.

undoubted that the sacrifices of the regiment in this action were entirely justified by results. On the morning of December 1st, a German attack on Epéhy was imminent, and there was only a weak and disorganised force of British infantry to meet it. The regiment's swift attack broke right into the German attacking troops, and caused such confusion that no attack on Epéhy could be made that day, and it is probably not an overstatement to say that a breakthrough of the British line was avoided.'[84] Even the horrifying, suicidal gallop of the leading squadron of the Inniskillings might have lost some of its futility had there been a real as opposed to an imaginary enemy threat. As it was, there was nothing, except a display of extravagantly courageous valour, second to none in the whole history of the cavalry, to show for the sacrifice of lives. It is to be fervently hoped that the survivors went to their graves in ignorance of the truth.

It is hardly necessary to point to the truth of the verdict given by Colonel E.B. Maunsell in an authoritative article in the *Cavalry Journal*, nearly nine years after the battle: 'In the case of the Inniskillings, not a single element that has conduced to success in mounted attacks since, and including, the days of Napoleon was present.'[85] The enemy was in strength and completely unshaken. The ingredient of surprise was wholly absent, as was any scrap of cover. The fire support was derisory and, above all, what were the mounted men to do when eventually they came up against the enemy's wire and trenches? As an attack designed to hold the enemy back so as to give other troops more time to contain an enemy onslaught, neither the Inniskillings' nor the 2nd Lancers' mad, oblatory gallops had, as has been shown any worth whatsoever. It seems almost incredible but the official timing of both, before they were held up, was 09.35 to 09.45 – a mere ten minutes.[86]* It is worth noting, perhaps, how much greater than they actually were, the casualties might have been. Discounting the leading Inniskilling squadron, the rest, according to their Commanding Officer, were under machine-gun and rifle fire, going to within 1,000 yards of the beet factory and returning therefrom,

---

*The Brigade's 'Summary of Operations' reads as follows: '9.35 a.m. – 2nd Lancers seen moving forward. . . . At the same moment the leading squadron of the Inniskilling Dragoons moved off. . . . 9.40 a.m. – Headquarters and two squadrons Inniskilling Dragoons returned.' (Whitworth, 186). This fits in with a ten-minute overall timing.

for about 2,000 yards in absolutely open ground. Yet the whole regiment lost little more than 30 per cent of its strength, while the 2nd Lancers' casualties were not very great until they reached the sunken road and the wire in front of it. There can be no question about the efficiency and numbers of the German machine gunners. They were organized in considerable depth and were well wired in. The quality of the enemy's infantry, however, was not great. Large numbers bolted on seeing the galloping horsemen.

To sum up the cavalry's part in what came to be known as the 2nd battle of Cambrai, what ought to have stood out as the chief reason for not launching the two attacks was that the enemy was known to be in entrenched, wired positions. The fact that neither attack reached these positions does not alter this. It was no good throwing mounted men at an enemy who could not *actually be got at* by them. This seems to be so elementary that the reasons why Kavanagh should have insisted upon the mounted attacks and his state of mind at the time must be surmised. There probably existed a real sense of imminent doom, even panic. Not only did it look as if the enemy was going to regain all the ground he had lost on 20 and 21 November, but that he was actually going to break through the original British line. Any sacrifice to avoid this might have been thought to be justified. Further, after what in retrospect was the wise restraint shown by him on 20 November, but which was making the cavalry even more despised and ridiculed than before, Kavanagh may well have thought that here was an opportunity for his men to show their mettle and if necessary fulfil the classic role of sacrificing itself to save the infantry.*

* * *

In considering the battles which succeeded the initial attack on 20 November, it is of interest in retrospect to note that on 27 November Haig had believed that the German troops were 'very thin on this front except at Bourlon. In fact,' he wrote, 'the situation is most favourable for us, but unfortunately I have not got the necessary number of troops to exploit our success. Two fresh

---

*Kavanagh ordered further attacks by the 4th and 5th Cavalry Divisions for the afternoon of 1 December. These were not in fact carried out. Brigadier-General Haig reported to Kennedy that 'he had too few troops in hand for another attack'. (Edmonds, *1917*, III, 236). In horses alone the Mhow Brigade had lost 933 – 386 killed and 547 wounded, of which 101 were evacuated.

divisions would make all the difference and would enable us to break out in the neighbourhood of Marcoing north-eastwards.' Even before that he had given serious thought to withdrawing to a line which did not form a salient. Ironically, it so happened that at about the same time the Germans had decided to halt all offensive operations on the Cambrai front and to consolidate with nothing more than a 'maintenance of activity'.[87]

* * *

During the night of 4 December the whole of the Third Army retired undetected to a line more or less on the Hindenburg support trenches. By 7 December both sides had consolidated and the battle of Cambrai came to an end. The total losses of both sides added up to some 90,000, shared more or less equally.

* * *

To understand why the present work delves so deeply into the actions of 20 November, during which so little of any use was performed by the mounted arm, it is necessary to look at what historians and commentators have said about the causes of that inaction on the cavalry's part.

The views of the tank fanatics, such as Fuller, should not be disregarded out of hand, though they did not spend much time or effort in studying the actual practicality of the cavalry breaking through. After all, among other misconceptions, they wrongly believed that the tanks had totally cleared the way for the cavalry to pour through the gaps provided, and that there were sufficient canal crossings available. Fuller falls back on blaming 'the leadership': that is Kavanagh. At Byng's conference on 8 November he states that

> 'in spite of the obvious necessity for a free hand, the Cavalry Corps Commander, strange to say, tied his command down in such a way that in any conceivable set of circumstances [a manifest inaccuracy] it would have been impossible for it to develop its mobility. . . . In place of moving as close up to the front as possible, Cavalry Corps Headquarters remained at Fins, six miles in rear of the nearest point of the front line and some twelve miles from Masnières, and no action was to be

taken except by order of these headquarters. This meant that opportunity would be lost, because all information would have to go back to headquarters and from there be transmitted to cavalry divisions, and by them to brigades and thence to regiments and squadrons. This is what I believe actually delayed the advance of the cavalry on the 20th; yet at the time General Byng never once criticised the Cavalry Corps Commander's proposals, neither did General Kiggell, who, throughout this conference, scarcely uttered a word.... Occultly though it may be, November 8, 1917, was the end of an epoch; for the fateful dice were then cast, not by the enemy, but by [the cavalry's] own leader, which brought them to an inglorious and bloodless ruin twelve days after this conference was held.'[88]

Hobart, another distinguished tank officer, agreed with Fuller as to the reasons for the cavalry's inactivity, but showed how little importance could be attached to them by adding, 'It is only fair to say that cavalry at this time possessed mobility only off the battlefield and when unopposed: that it had no longer the means to overcome opposition: and that there was no real opportunity at all for horsemen so that cavalry HQ were wise in refusing an activity that would have meant merely incurring heavy losses and achieving nothing.'[89]

Churchill put the truth of the matter succinctly: 'The cavalry who scampered forward [perhaps an exaggeration!] were naturally soon held up by snipers and machine-guns.'[90] The latest chronicler of the battle, A.J. Smithers, goes further. 'Kavanagh,' he says, 'is not always numbered among the Great Captains. Nevertheless, he deserves to have his name written in letters of gold for, by masterly inactivity, he saved four divisions of cavalry from massacre.'[91] There is something in that, yet it is just as likely that Byng was responsible for the cautious approach and that both corps commanders were almost certainly not against it.

The most influential and in some respects the best of all modern historians of the war, John Terraine, declares in his life of Haig that 'once again the complete ineffectiveness of horse soldiers on a modern battlefield was demonstrated'. He added what is a novel aspect of the matter: 'Their complete failure gave the Germans the opportunity they needed to rally and regroup.' He does go on to say, however, 'Cavalry were effective in 1918, against Germans who were demoralized.' (see pp. 265).[92] Elsewhere he writes: 'The advancing infantry and tanks, aware of wonderful opportunities of a kind rarely seen during the war, looked in vain over their shoulders for the mass of horsemen who should have been exploiting them.' For what he calls this 'lamentable failure', he suggested three explanations: 'First, the normal difficulty of quick communication which haunted every battle of the First World War; second, staleness – long waiting for a big event does not improve efficiency or morale . . .; third, the quality of the commander of the Cavalry Corps. . . . It is difficult to detect, on the part of General Kavanagh at Cambrai, any of that thrusting leadership which one associates with cavalry commanders.'[93] This surely was exactly why it was a very real blessing that Kavanagh was in command and not, for example, a thruster like Gough. It is only necessary to look at the numerous and useless casualties incurred by those small units that did thrust forwards to be satisfied that the firm restraining hand was a godsend. It is very understandable that the unsuccessful part of so seminally important a battle as that fought on 20 November should not have been gone into by most historians sufficiently thoroughly for a proper assessment of it to be made. Typical of the oft repeated view, handed down from historian to historian, biographer to biographer, is the statement in John Colville's life of Lord Gort (who was wounded in the battle): 'By fatal hesitation, the cavalry lost the one great opportunity . . . during the whole war. . . . For a few brief hours the men on horseback could have taken over the advance from the men in machines.' C.R.M.F. Cruttwell, in his excellent, neglected 1935 history of the war, for instance, says that 'the inaction of the . . . cavalry divisions has never yet been intelligibly explained.'[94] The present author believes and hopes to have proved that it is easily explained – and was fully justified.

* * *

It is worth looking at the factors which influenced the cavalry leaders at all levels on 20 November. First and most important were their orders (see p. 106). For the Cavalry Corps and the 1st Cavalry Division to surround Cambrai and secure the Sensée crossings as well as the Third Army's flanks, the orders made it an absolute *sine qua non* that the infantry must have wrested the Masnières and Marcoing canal crossings and the Masnières–Beaurevoir line from the enemy, while the 1st Division under IV Corps, was (rather less unequivocally) ordered, to 'pass through along the Trescault–Ribécourt road as soon as it is clear'.[95] As night fell both Masnières and the Masnières–Beaurevoir line were still held by the enemy, the main bridges over the canal were broken, the crossing that had been made was narrow and had only just been made passable by horses and all the crossings were still under enemy fire. It is probably true that there was a period when the Masnières–Beaurevoir line was so lightly held that it would have afforded little obstacle to a cavalry force, but the crossings situation, of course, ensured that it could not be assailed before enemy reinforcements came to its defence. As to whether the Trescault–Ribécourt road could be classified as 'clear' by nightfall there must be great scepticism.

It has been argued that had the Canadian Cavalry Brigade 'been at hand when Bois Lateau fell' the canal crossings might have been rushed and the bridges saved.[96] The evidence already deployed in this chapter shows that that would not have been possible (see p. 127, especially). Further it has been suggested that the leaders at regimental, squadron and even troop levels ought to have disregarded their orders and, wherever possible, pushed on regardless, displaying the cavalry spirit. The chief occasion on which this happened – the Fort Garry Horse squadron's ill-fated breakthrough – shows too well how lucky it was that there were not more thrusters in command!

There were, of course, numerous 'excuses' made by the cavalry, none of which would have had any value when weighed against the cavalry spirit, *had there been only a demoralized enemy ahead.* Imperfect passages through the wire, marshy ground near the canal, cavalry tracks much cut up by hooves and made muddy by rain, with wire-pulling tanks drawing fire on the parties making and repairing them: most of these difficulties could have proved surmountable. The only ones which proved not to be were the machine gunners and snipers who, even where for a time gaps were more or less clear, never failed to appear in time to impose an insuperable obstacle to a mounted advance.

Had the part assigned to the cavalry *ever* been possible – that is to say, had communications been swift, had roads and tracks been sufficient and completely cleared for horsemen early on, had all the crossings over the de l'Escaut Canal been taken intact, had all the villages been completely cleared of snipers and machine gunners, had there been more hours of daylight and had there been both tank and infantry reserves, still the cavalry would have been met in open country by the arrival of the enemy's rapidly assembling reinforcements. The saying of an American observer on another occasion that 'you can't have a cavalry charge until you have captured the enemy's last machine gun' would then have been proved tragically right.[97]

There can be little point in stressing the number of 'mistakes' made on 20 November by the cavalry commanders, especially by Mullens on the left and Kavanagh on the right, since they all, in effect, contributed to the saving of the arm from virtual annihilation. However, it is worth stating that there seems to have been no excuse for Mullens not insisting on his units using the sheltered route along the Grand Ravin to outflank Flesquières. Yet even there it is impossible to be sure that the route was as sheltered as most authorities declare it to have been. Certainly, Byng put down 'the tardiness of the cavalry' to 'the deadlock at Flesquières'.*

On the right, as Captain Miles says in the Official History: 'The neglect of the canal crossings east of Masnières is difficult to understand when it is remembered that the gap in the German position was, in any case, to be widened as far as Crèvecoeur and beyond in the next stage of the British advance.† The Commander-in-Chief had emphasized the need to expedite

---

*He might well have added that the 'tardiness' of the *infantry* and the *tanks* was considerably increased by their looting, 'which went on all through the battle'. Hobart

'saw many cases of infantry going off on expeditions of this nature, and to give you one example, I met a sergeant of the Argyll and Sutherland Highlanders who had collected eighteen watches and twenty-four gold rings by the time he had got as far as the Gran Ravin. The tanks, too, indulged in a fair amount of looting at this point and a very brisk trade was done in Mauser revolvers, Zeiss field glasses and breakfasts. This all tended to disorganise the forward movement . . .

'On reaching the Hindenburg Support Line the infantry and tank crews were standing about smoking German cigars, talking and laughing. . . . One prisoner, a cobbler from Coblentz . . . handed me a very useful 12-bore shot gun and a canvas bag of cartridges. During the next two hours I got 3½ brace of partridges on my way down to Marcoing.' (Hobart, 51, 62)

†But see p. 157.

such action.'⁹⁸ This aspect of the battle has not hitherto been referred to as it was a III Corps matter, not a Cavalry Corps one. Yet it is of some interest to speculate as to whether, with more viable canal crossings, more cavalry might not have got over the canal.

A major 'excuse' for the cavalry's inability to perform at Cambrai was that most of the regiments' officers and men had never taken part in mounted action and that three years had passed since virtually *any* had. Nearly all, though, to the detriment of their cavalry spirit, had become efficient infantrymen and were adept at trench (i.e. static) warfare. All of this was of course true. So also was the fact that the numerous occasions on which the cavalry had been led to believe that they were on the point of breaking through the 'gap', invariably followed by frustration, did little for morale. Further there is much evidence that, particularly in officers, the best men had left the arm for more active service. Though the Official History cannot bring itself to admit the undoubted fact that the cavalry's caution on 20 November saved it for the battles of 1918 and the expected eventual pursuit of a demoralized enemy, it does say, referring to 1914, that 'a number of the senior officers remembered how vulnerable were bodies of horse to the fire of even a few machine guns and, with some reason, were more fearful of wire than ever they had been in the hunting field.'⁹⁹*

'People are daily more annoyed with our cavalry. . . . The Anzac School at Aveluy have sent a message to 'G' [General Staff branch, GHQ] offering to ride straight for Cambrai if only the cavalry's horses could be given to them.' Thus a sapper staff officer at Third Army Headquarters. Against this understandable but pitifully ignorant utterance should be set Smithers' summing up: 'The effect of bombing and machine-gunning upon acres of terrified and uncontrollable horseflesh is not pleasant to dwell upon without even considering such refinements as phosgene and mustard gases. On this occasion at least everybody would have been better off had the cavalry remained in their stables.'¹⁰⁰ On Christmas Day, at Cavalry Corps headquarters, Home, who eleven days earlier had written in his diary: 'Depression reigns everywhere – I do not know what has come over people,' now wrote, 'As regards the cavalry –

---

*For a full account of the actions of the cavalry machine-gun squadrons in the battle, see Preston: 'MG', 288–99.

Cambrai: post-mortem

people at home ask, "They had a great chance at Cambrai – is it any use keeping them? They will never have such a chance again." That is the crux of the whole matter – on this they may do anything – make the cavalry into latrine caretakers.'[101] For what 'they' did, see p. 163 below.

As regards the battle as a whole, Liddell Hart may have the last word: 'For military history the lesson of Cambrai is that the welcome renaissance of the essential principle of surprise was offset by a fundamental breach of the principle of economy of force – both in adjusting the end to the means and in appreciating the capacity and limits of human endurance.'[102]

* * *

Cambrai was certainly the most interesting and the most original of the battles of the First World War on the Western Front. It reinstated the art of surprise which had been almost entirely forgotten.

* * *

As the fateful year of 1918 loomed ahead, '1917,' in Churchill's words, 'closed on the allied fronts . . . in a gloom relieved only by Allenby's sword-flash at Jerusalem.'[103] Repington, the *Times* correspondent, wrote in his diary on New Year's Eve: 'The end of a dramatic year. The crumbling of Russia, the Italian defeats, the U-boat successes and the slow advent of the Americans have all been serious for us.'[104]

7

'On 20 March [the day before the Germans launched the great Spring Offensive] 1st Cavalry Division's routine orders included an appeal by Lieutenant Brown of the 16th Lancers: "LOST. A red lurcher greyhound.... Broken tail, orange eyes, large scar between eyes. Answers to 'Jack'. Last seen Péronne on 17 March. Reward – 50 francs."'

'It need not be anticipated that the French will run themselves off their legs and hurry at once to help their Entente comrades. They will first wait and see if their own front is not being attacked also.'
— Letter received by LT-COL WETZELL on 16 January, 1918, from the German Eighteenth Army.

'26 January [1918] . . . We are confronted with:-
(1) A longer front to hold.
(2) Reduced establishment to hold it.
(3) No hope of reinforcements.
(4) A German attack in greater strength than anything we have yet experienced. Not a cheerful prospect. The only bright point is that D[ouglas] H[aig] – who saw Pétain and Pershing last week – says that both of them realize the situation and will help when the crisis comes.'
— BRIG.-GEN. JOHN CHARTERIS in *At G.H.Q.*

'We must beat the British.'
— LUDENDORFF, November, 1917

'From 7 a.m. on 22 March the movements of the regiment were kaleidoscopic, split up, merged and split again. They were sent here to fill a gap, there to cover a retirement or hold a bridge and even to do troop drill between the enemy's line and our own, "pour encourager les autres".'
— MAJOR G. MICHOLLS, historian of the 17th Lancers

'The mounted detachment of the Royals had an experience which few cavalrymen on the Western Front had enjoyed, they actually took part in a charge and got right in among hostile infantry with the *arme blanche*.'
— C.T. ATKINSON in *History of the Royal Dragoons* on the action at Collézy, 24 March, 1918

'It appears that [Gough] took every measure, both before and during the battle, which experience and energy could devise and of which his utterly inadequate resources admitted; that his composure never faltered, that his activity was inexhaustible, that his main decisions were prudent and resolute, and that no episode in his career was more honourable than the disaster which entailed his fall.'
– CHURCHILL in 1927

'It was more interesting than any phase in the war since 1914.'
– CAPTAIN A.W. KEITH-FALCONER, Oxfordshire Hussars on 28 March, 1918

'The story of what occurred reads like a brilliant page by Alexander Dumas. Both sides fought with extraordinary courage. The wood was taken little by little after complicated movements and the bitterest of bitter fighting, in which squadrons commanded by Nordheimer, Newcomen, Timmis and Flowerdew suffered heavily and won a fame not to be forgotten.'
– W.S. SPARROW in *The Fifth Army in March, 1918*, on the engagement at Moreuil Wood, 30 March, 1918[1]

Reduction and re-organization of the cavalry – the German spring offensives – Falvy – Collézy – Gough sacked – Moreuil Wood

In December, 1917, Lloyd George, chairing the War Cabinet Manpower Committee, gave it as his view that 'cavalry would never be used in France'. He took up an idea of Churchill's that it should be disbanded and its personnel transferred to the Royal Flying Corps, the Tank Corps or to armoured cars.* With this notion the Prime Minister said that Robertson, the CIGS, was 'in substantial agreement', since he was no longer able to support Haig's

---

* 'Are we really to keep in being at a time when every man is precious ... 30,000 to 40,000 cavalry with their horses, when these admirable cavalrymen would supply the personnel for the greatest development of mechanical warfare both for offence and defence in tanks, in armoured cars ... that has yet been conceived?' (Dec., 1917 Churchill, 'Memorandum on Man Power' for War Cabinet)

Haig fights for retention of cavalry

contention that the 188 squadrons in France in the summer of 1917 were justified. When Haig appeared before the War Cabinet on 7 January, 1918, he once again maintained that 'the value and importance of cavalry [was] very great not only in offensive but also in defensive operations. This was due,' he added, 'to their superior mobility and the ease with which cavalry could be moved from one sector to another and then be dismounted. He pointed out that British cavalry resembled highly trained mobile infantry rather than the old cavalry arm.' With this Curzon, particularly, did not agree. 'It would appear,' he said, that 'the character of warfare during the ensuing few months would present few opportunities for the use of cavalry.' To this Haig rejoined 'that once the cavalry had been disbanded it would be difficult to build up again so highly trained and technical an arm, and it would be many months before the cavalry, once dissipated, could be re-created.'[2]

The result was an unfortunate compromise which ended in there being only two extra cavalry regiments in Palestine and twenty less on the Western front. Further, though Robertson gave his consent to the two Indian cavalry divisions being sent to Palestine, he was well aware that this would not save in shipping (see p. 38). Indeed six times the quantity of shipping was required to supply troops under Allenby's command from home as was needed to supply those in the BEF. What appeared, falsely, to be the saving effected in France was the supplying of forage to the eleven Indian cavalry regiments – less than 2 per cent of the quantity of oats consumed daily by the horses of all arms in France, but this saving was more than compensated for by the extra shipping cost involved in the moves. These were complicated. The Yeomanry Division (and the separate brigades in Palestine) were broken up and used to reform the 4th Indian Division when it arrived there. This was necessary because the British regiments which formed part of these divisions, as well as the three Household Cavalry and two corps cavalry regiments, which remained in being in France, were intended to become cyclist or machine-gun units. The nine yeomanry regiments in Palestine left over from this process *were to be sent to France*, where they did not in fact arrive until May, 1918. They, too, were to be converted into machine-gun battalions. In the event, however, the four British regiments released from the Indian divisions, with the exception of the King's

Dragoon Guards,* went to the other cavalry divisions in exchange for the three Household Cavalry regiments and the yeomanry regiments (except the Oxfords which remained in the 4th Cavalry Brigade, 2nd Cavalry Division).† These, together with the two RHA brigades ('A', 'Q', 'N' and 'X' Batteries) belonging to the Indian Divisions, were then allotted as Army troops to the Fifth Army. The four yeomanry regiments (Leicestershire, Bedford, North Somerset and Essex), which had successfully resisted being made into cyclists and were about to become machine gunners, were, soon after the offensive started, urgently re-formed as mounted cavalry. This measure was taken as the need for mobile 'fire brigade' troops became obvious.§ These complex arrangements are here detailed to illustrate the sort of intricate, expensive, positively harmful, adjustments which emerged from the running battle between the Prime Minister and the Commander-in-Chief on the subject of the cavalry.[3]††

*The KDG had left the 4th Cavalry Division on 7 October, 1917, for India. It was not replaced in the division, which was reformed when it reached Egypt. The regiment took part in suppressing a rising in Peshawar, May, 1919, and in the minor war with Afghanistan of that year. On 16 May it made a mounted charge near Jalalabad 'checking the enemy's advance sufficiently to enable our infantry to retire on to fresh positions, and bringing back on their horses many wounded sepoys'. (Anon *A Short History of 1st King's Dragoon Guards . . . 1685 to 1929*, 1929, 40–1)

†The British regiments which were left behind from the Indian divisions were immediately reorganized on the three squadron basis of the British establishment instead of the Indian four squadron basis. This did not lessen their total strength, for one squadron was broken up and absorbed in the other three.

§Complete squadrons from these four yeomanry regiments were in some cases attached to regular cavalry regiments. Other squadrons were employed to make good casualties in the cavalry divisions. For instance, the Leicesters sent a squadron to each of the regiments of the 3rd Cavalry Division. (Preston: '1918', VII, 501). All four regiments, even if not as complete units, finished the war as mounted troops. The Northumberlands, III Corps cavalry regiment, which had been converted into cyclists just before the March offensive, were remounted in the summer, though one squadron had been hastily mounted on 24 March. King Edward's Horse (XI Corps regiment) also avoided becoming bicyclists just in time and remained mounted until the war's end. (Furse, 161). The Northamptonshires remained with XIV Corps and did good service in Italy (Preston: '1918', (2), IV, 9)

††It is of interest to note that, when the Americans arrived in force, they had to ask for 25,000 transport horses from Haig. (23 June, 1918, and 23 Oct., 1918, Haig Diaries, Acc. 3155.132)

The net result was that Haig now had three cavalry divisions instead of five, just in time for the great German spring offensive.* 'The change,' wrote Home in his diary, 'has been forced on D.H. by the War Cabinet who in turn are ruled by the Northcliffe press. They are trying,' he added, 'to blame the cavalry for the non-success of the Cambrai show because ten days afterwards the infantry were driven in at Villers-Guislain and we lost 160 guns! It is very disheartening to a soldier and must have a bad effect on the cavalry.'[4] The removal of the two cavalry divisions from the scene meant that instead of about 27,000 cavalrymen in the BEF only some 16,200, at the very most, were available at the moment of greatest crisis. Though these figures are very rough, they are sufficiently accurate to illustrate how successful had been Lloyd George's campaign to cut down the number of Haig's only mobile troops.†

At the very moment when the storm broke, the two Indian divisions were embarking at Marseilles, and the Household Cavalry and yeomanry regiments had just surrendered their horses. As Gough, whose Fifth Army was to bear the brunt of the offensive, later wrote, 'a more convincing assertion of the imminence of the

---

*Thus the composition of the three divisions was:-
1st: 1st Brigade: Bays, 5th Dragoon Guards, 11th Hussars;
2nd Brigade: 4th Dragoon Guards, 9th Lancers, 18th Hussars;
9th Brigade: 8th Hussars, 15th Hussars, 19th Hussars.
2nd: 3rd Brigade: 4th Hussars, 16th Lancers, 5th Lancers.
4th Brigade: Carabiniers, 3rd Hussars, Oxfordshires. (This was the only yeomanry regiment left in the Cavalry Corps. It had been the first yeomanry to arrive in France.
5th Brigade: Greys, 12th Lancers, 20th Hussars.
3rd: 6th Brigade: 3rd Dragoon Guards, Royals, 10th Hussars.
7th Brigade: 7th Dragoon Guards, 6th Inniskilling Dragoons, 17th Lancers.
Canadian Brigade: Royal Canadian Dragoons, Lord Strathcona's Horse, Fort Garry Horse.
(Each brigade had a Vickers machine-gun squadron of twelve guns.)
In due course two new divisions bearing the names of 4th and 5th Cavalry Divisions were formed in Palestine. They consisted of thirteen Indian and five yeomanry regiments.

†In January, Haig and Kavanagh, concerned that promotion was being blocked in the Cavalry Corps, replaced a few of the older senior officers, chiefly at brigade level. Two days before the battle commenced, Haig also considered removing Kavanagh, but, probably wisely, decided to retain him. (15, 20, 27 Jan., 19 Mar., 1918, Haig Diaries, 3155. 123 & 124, quoted in Badsey, 335)

storm [on GHQ's part] might have retained these two [Indian] divisions for a few weeks longer at the spot where the great decision was being fought out. They would have been a valuable reinforcement.'[5] The yeomanry regiments, (with the exception of the Oxfords), at once reclaimed their mounts (see above). The three Household Cavalry regiments took no part in the coming battle. Instead they underwent intensive training as machine gunners.* Their horses were mostly sent as remounts for Palestine.

* * *

Nine days before Cambrai and exactly one year before the Armistice was signed, Ludendorff held a staff conference to discuss the wonderful opportunity afforded by the Russian collapse in the east to bring overwhelming force against the allies on the Western Front, in time to forestall the eventual Allied superiority which the arrival of the Americans would ensure. This conference in due course led to the decision to launch two great offensives against the front held by the British, a chief object of the first being to destroy the BEF. The second, in April, was the one more feared by Haig for it threatened his vital northern sector (see below)[6]. Ludendorff's plan was designed to induce the British to retire north-westwards, while the French were to be persuaded to fall back on Paris.† As Churchill has put it, what in fact happened was that 'Ludendorff, reintroducing the Great Battle period and consuming the German strength in desperate offensives without the necessary mechanical weapons§ and vehicles, was destined to bring about the Allied "general battle on a 300 km front" which

---

*The reason given for this seems to have been that their horses were 'too heavy to mount'. The Blues' Commanding Officer (Lord Tweedmouth) was told that well-disciplined men were required 'to travel quickly from one part of the line to another in lorries, Ford cars and [on] motor-cycles, to be stuffed into any gap that had to be held at all costs and that each squadron was to have sixty-four machine guns.' (Buckmaster, 183)

†See also Ironside, Sir E. 'Ludendorff's Last Great Bid for Victory', *Journal of the Royal Artillery*, LV, 1928–9, 297–311. This is one of the best appreciations of the Germans' intentions for the offensives of March and April.

§Though he employed his air force with skill. Nevertheless, when the fogs of the first two days dispersed, the RFC held its own.

18. Cavalry crossing the Yser to enter the battle zone.

19. Cavalry crossing a log bridge over a communication trench, 7 May, 1917.

20. Horses of the 3rd Cavalry Division waiting in the snow behind Arras, April, 1917. (See p.76)

21. Cavalry waiting to go forward near Arras, 1917. (See p.76)

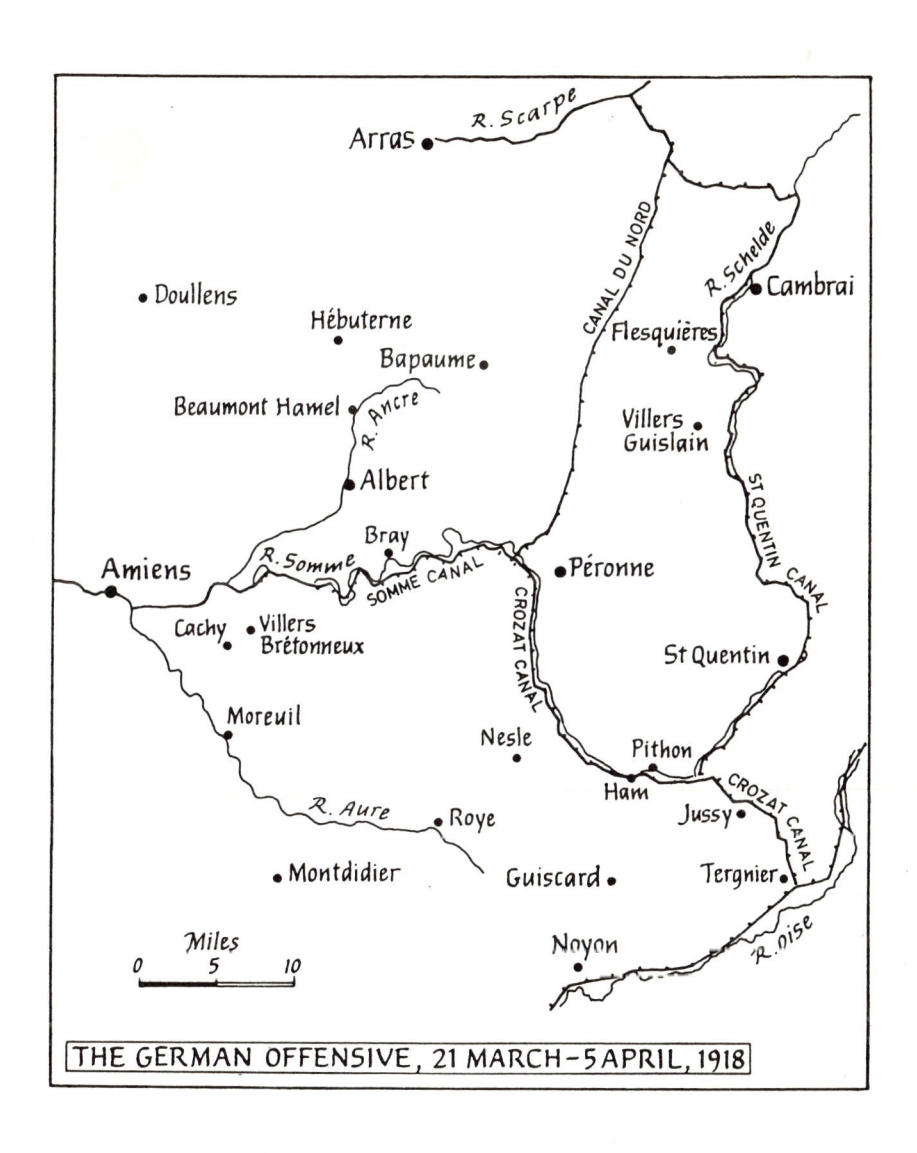

THE GERMAN OFFENSIVE, 21 MARCH – 5 APRIL, 1918

ended the war; and to bring it about after periods of awful peril one year earlier than our best plans could have achieved.'[7]

The 'periods of awful peril' started on 21 March when the largest scale battle the world had ever seen was begun in an early morning fog. A five-hour bombardment of unparalleled ferocity and devastating skill by some 8,000 guns, howitzers and trench mortars* preceded a mass infantry attack along a fifty to sixty mile front spearheaded by some 10,000 picked 'storm troops' with orders to by-pass centres of determined resistance and press on regardless. The chief surprise was the overwhelming scale, weight and above all speed of this first offensive.† Its date and locality were known to the Allies well beforehand. Unfortunately, in spite of some evidence against it, Haig felt quite sure that it would take much the form that his own offensives had taken, allowing time for measured counter-attacks and, where necessary, the introduction of reinforcements.

His intention was to retire slowly, fighting, from the southern end of his line where Byng's Third and Gough's Fifth Armies were to take the main force of the storm. There he could afford to lose ground while in the north, where he rightly assumed that the Germans would before long attack, any considerable retirement would bring the enemy to within striking force of the Channel Ports. Indeed, the great communications centre of Amiens, one of Ludendorff's major objectives, is only thirty miles from the Channel. Haig's plan seems to have depended upon the French coming to his aid from the south, (much as Wellington at Waterloo had depended on Blücher), and there is no doubt that Pétain gave him what seemed to be sufficient assurances. It was for these reasons

---

*Edmonds, *1918*, 460, says that the total intended was 10,000. The actual number employed is in doubt.

†More than a month before the tempest burst it was known that the British reduced divisions were facing eighty-one chiefly fresh, reinforced German divisions and that each week more and more were closing up behind, arriving in hundreds of trains from the Eastern Front. Four further divisions were arriving from the Italian front.

Fifty German divisions were identified on the first day alone. On 24 March, sixty-two, of which forty-eight were fresh from reserve, were identified in the battle. Behind these were a further twenty-five of which about half were on the Third and Fifth Armies' fronts.

The British artillery numbered 1,212, not including trench mortars. (Farndale: *WF*, 261)

that Haig was unhappily prepared to allow both Byng's and especially Gough's armies to face immensely poor odds in men. These in the event turned out to be for Gough initially four, rising to eight to one, and for Byng considerably smaller but nonetheless formidable.

At no time during the war, it has been asserted, was the BEF so low in numbers compared with those of the Germans opposite it. The five more or less idle divisions in Italy, others in Salonika and Allenby's enlarged army in Palestine were not the chief reasons for this weakness. Due partly to Lloyd George's determination to deprive Haig of manpower so as to prevent him embarking on further 'Passchendaeles', there were supposed to be some 600,000 trained soldiers available for general service sitting inactive at home.* The equivalent of 141 BEF battalions had had to be disbanded on account of the supposed chronic manpower shortage.†

Yet Haig was more or less unhappily ordered by the War Cabinet earlier in the year to take over twenty-eight miles of the front from the French along the Somme, the trench system of which was found to be primitive compared with the British, largely, perhaps, because the swampy nature of the ground in front of it was thought to be more or less impassable. This, however, because of an unusually prolonged winter drought, offered little opposition to the Teutonic hordes, though GHQ refused to take seriously the evidence presented to it on this head. Gough's line was now forty-two miles in length manned by the equivalent of twelve divisions.

---

*Typical perhaps of these was Sergeant D. Brunton of the 19th Hussars, who had gone home wounded in May, 1917. He had reported fit again in early July and was posted to Aldershot. There he had 'a rotten time as regards soldiering. I have practically nothing to do. Any amount of Warrant Officers and N.C.O.s spare. Pass time away by having plenty of leave.' (20 May, 1917 – 14 Jan., 1918, Brunton)

It was observed by another that there were 'a lot of troops in Norfolk'! (Terraine: *Haig*, 393)

†Though, due to complicated rearrangements, this did not represent so serious a reduction of total numbers as the bare statement suggests. What is certain is that the infantry's *effective* strength on 1 March was only 36% of *total* strength as compared with 45% in September 1917. (Gray, 24)

Each battalion of four rifle companies, nevertheless, was short in numbers of about one company, while other arms were about 20% below establishment. (Farrar-Hockley, 243)

The BEF's lack of defence in depth

In immediately available reserve he had, beside the three cavalry divisions, equivalent in rifle power to at most three weak infantry brigades, two GHQ-controlled infantry divisions, one of them fifty miles behind the front, neither of which, of course, was exclusively his to direct. The enemy opposed to him possessed an initial total, including reserves close at hand, of forty-two. Opposed to Byng's eight divisions, covering only twenty-eight miles of front, were fifteen of the enemy.

* * *

Since 1914 the BEF had had no experience of any substantial withdrawal. Now, all ranks having been intensively trained to take part in static warfare and annual offensives, they were to be called upon to conduct an extensive retreat. Neither morally nor technically were they prepared or trained for so different and specialized a mode of warfare. The chief physical weakness from which they suffered was the lack of well built defences in depth. Indeed the construction of rear lines, upon which to fall back, was hindered partly by what was considerable but in many accounts probably exaggerated lack of labour. In places nothing more than cut turf indicated where trenches were to be dug.*

* * *

In the fog of 21 March, which was densest on the 5th Army's front, the British could see at most twenty yards ahead, which appears to have given the Germans some immediate advantage, though normally it was apt to favour the defence. Concealed by it, the storm troops were initially enabled to pass round and envelop the machine-gun 'keeps' which were a vital part of the defence on so thinly held a front line.† By evening the forward

---

*Between January and mid-March the labour available is supposed to have doubled. Most of it was engaged on making roads and tracks, parks, depots, dumps, railways and hospitals in the rear areas devastated by the German withdrawal to the Hindenburg Line. Thus too few were free 'to assist the fighting troops in the construction of the battle zone' (Farrar-Hockley, 258), and even the zone immediately behind it.

†In spite of orders, it seems, there was 'a distinct tendency' on the enemy's part 'to attack old style, and *not by infiltration*, especially after the initial breakthrough'. (Travers, 86–7)

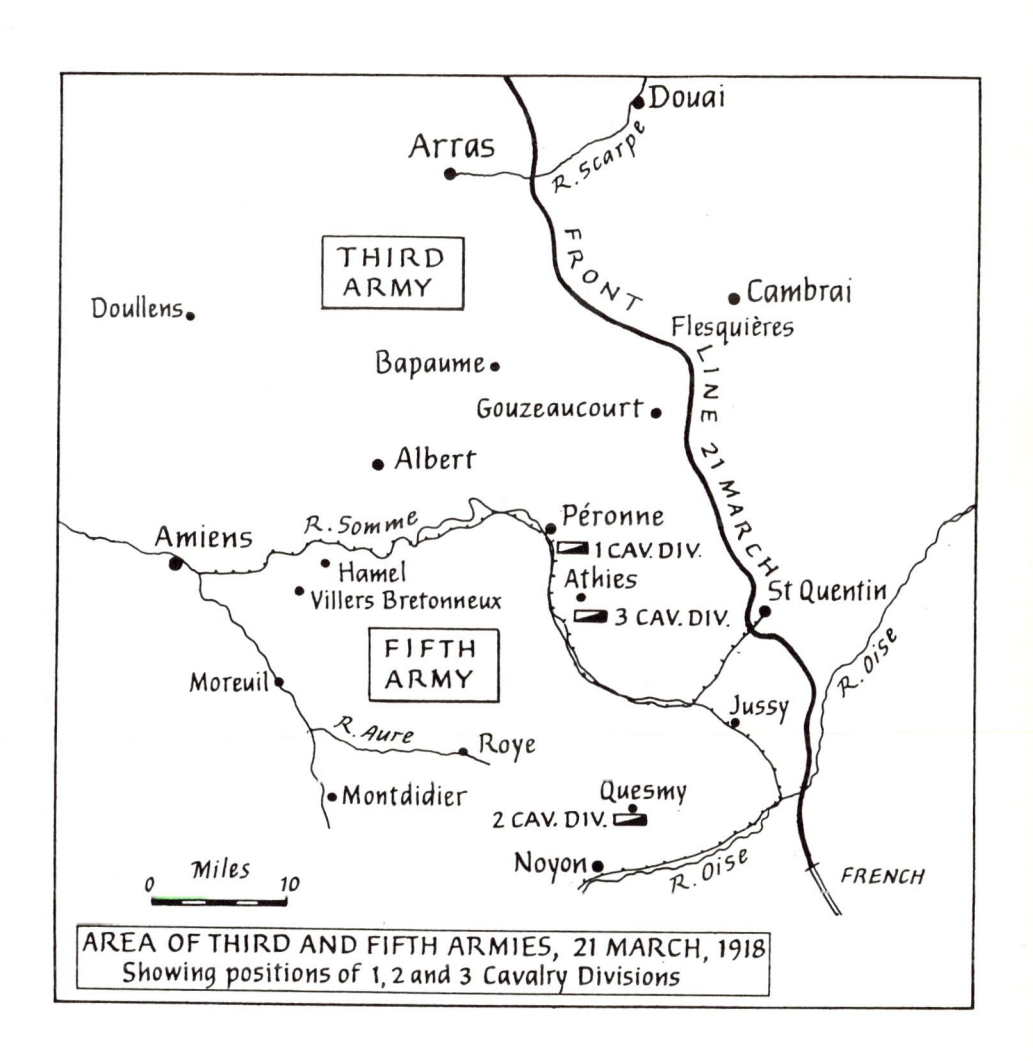

AREA OF THIRD AND FIFTH ARMIES, 21 MARCH, 1918
Showing positions of 1, 2 and 3 Cavalry Divisions

defence zone had been overrun and in sections of the 'battle zone' severe fighting did not cease till dark. During the afternoon Haig released the four reserve divisions, two to each Army, and the three cavalry divisions, mostly dismounted (see below), were brought forward, partly by lorries and buses. Gough pulled back to behind the Crozat Canal, thus linking the Rivers Somme and Oise.

The second day also opened with fog, as did to a lesser degree the next two days. Incorrectly informed that the enemy had penetrated behind his right flank, Gough ordered a retirement to the Somme. This meant that he temporarily lost contact with the French on his right. Had the Germans exploited this gap they would probably have found themselves free to march on Paris. That they did not do so was one of Ludendorff's worst blunders. Before nightfall the whole of the Fifth Army's 'battle zone' was lost, while the Third Army held on in the Flesquières salient, the legacy of Cambrai. There 'it remained too long . . . and,' in Cyril Falls's words, 'was to pay for it. Individual acts of heroism in the defence were numberless, but they influenced the German tide only as a high patch of sand remains unsubmerged longer than the rest of the beach.'*[8]

On the third day the Germans seized the Crozat Canal. On the fourth day they reached the outskirts of Péronne and the line of the Somme down to that point. John Terraine describes the agonies of 24 March, the critical day of the battle: 'It emerged, out of all the confusion of contradictory reports, that the momentum of the German advance was, if anything, increasing. French intervention had not had the expected result. All their commanders faced grim problems of adjustment to the fluid conditions of the fight. On the Third Army front the Germans entered Bapaume. Haig's problems were acute. He sent Lawrence to the southern sector, to meet Gough and General Fayolle, under whose orders the Fifth

---

*On this day the 19th Hussars and part of the 8th Hussars made a dismounted counter-attack in conjunction with three tanks which were speedily incapacitated. (Edmonds, *1918*, I, 285, which says that there were six tanks engaged; Murray, 623, which states incorrectly that the 15th Hussars were present.)

In the evening of this day the exhausted commander of the 14th Division, which by now was near extinction, was relieved by Greenly, who handed over the 2nd Cavalry Division to Brigadier-General Pitman from the 4th Cavalry Brigade. Greenly, in his turn, had, after only five days, to be invalided home. According to Gough, 'he went off his head with the strain.' (29 March, 1918, Haig diaries, Blake: *Haig*, 299; Edmonds, *1918*, I, 270)

The Doullens conference, 26 March, 1918

Army now came. He himself concentrated on the Third Army area; he told Byng "to hold on to his left at all costs to the right of the First Army near Arras.".⁹

In the first four days the advance had covered fourteen miles. On the fifth day Gough was compelled to retreat a further four. To keep touch with him Byng eventually followed suit.

At this point it is worth looking at the much debated question of the origins of the famous Doullens conference on 26 March. The official and conventional view is that the half-hearted French aid was not unintentionally so. Indeed, it is alleged that Pétain made no bones about allowing a gap to develop between the Allies. Despairing of the British, he is supposed to have intended to leave Haig in the lurch – and to have told him so. He would retire on Paris. As a result, run Haig's and the Official History's accounts, the British Commander-in-Chief at once sent for Wilson, (CIGS since the sacking of Robertson (a Lloyd George victory!) in February), accompanied by Milner, (Minister without Portfolio, soon to become Secretary of State for War), representing the Prime Minister, to come over and try to reverse this decision. On 26 March, in consequence, the historic conference was held at Doullens.* To it came the French President, Poincaré, Clemenceau, 'the Tiger', recently appointed Premier, and all but one of the Army Commanders (known to Haig's staff as 'the Robber Barons'¹⁰), including Byng. Gough, pointedly, was not invited or indeed even informed that the conference was to take place.† At it, with Haig's concurrence, it was agreed that Foch, who, since its formation in 1917, had been president of the ineffective Inter-Allied Council at Versailles, should co-ordinate the action of the two allied armies. 'We must fight in front of Amiens,' Foch is thought to have declared. 'We must stop where we are now.'

This until recently generally accepted version of what happened has now been challenged. There are said to be differences

---

*'So uncertain was the outlook that tanks were stationed at the eastern exits, lest hostile cavalry might break in.' (Cruttwell, 510). In fact the Germans had so little cavalry that, even had there been a truly dramatic breakthrough, the possibility of it reaching Doullens, twenty-five miles from the furthest point reached on 26 March, would hardly have existed. For the lack of German cavalry see p. 213 below.

†This may have been because his Army was wrongly given up as virtually *hors de combat*, but also because he had now come under French command.

Meetings between Haig and Pétain, 23 and 24 March, 1918

between Haig's *hand-written* diary entries and his later *type-written* versions. Further there seems to be some evidence that at the seldom-mentioned meeting on 23 March between Haig and Pétain, the latter had made it clear that his main concern was that the Allied armies should keep closely in touch. He undoubtedly promised (and later arranged) that his reserve divisions in the Somme valley should be employed to this end.* He was understandably unable at once to provide twenty divisions behind Amiens, as Haig requested. When the two men met next day, the 24th, it is now maintained that Pétain pointed out that whereas he had large territories to retire into, the BEF was in the opposite situation. Were the BEF therefore to retreat to the Channel ports, and *only then*, would he be compelled to withdraw southwards to cover Paris. It is asserted that Haig, in a panic, did in fact intend to retreat northwards. The new version holds therefore that it was Pétain who was threatened by Haig's desertion rather than vice versa, and that consequently Haig called the Doullens conference because he was desperately alarmed at the German offensive succeeding so well beyond anything that he had expected, and *not* because Pétain threatened to leave him in the lurch.†

Pétain and Haig from now on came under Foch, the dynamic

---

*On 22 March one French division was sent; on 23, 24 and 25 March three more were provided on each day and on 26 March two more and parts of another two, (Edmonds, *1918*, I, 549 and II, 475). By 1 April thirty-two divisions had been committed. (Edmonds, *1918*, II, 486). Nearly all of the first twelve (three of which were dismounted cavalry) arrived without their 'artillery, ammunition supply or field kitchens and other transport, even without officers' chargers'. (Edmonds, *1918*, II, 485)

†The above is of necessity much over-simplified since its effect on the cavalry's actions is minimal. Cooper, 254–6, accepts only with some reluctance the authorized account. Travers, 66–9, gives chapter and verse in great detail for the revised record and Winter, though generally unreliable, 183–8, summarises it. The Official History goes along with Haig's story but it appears (see Travers above) that Edmonds was unhappy about allowing it to.

The temptation to produce, with a veneer of scholarship, conspiracies and scandals where the high command is concerned is too seldom resisted. Such works, alas, reach a wide readership. Occasionally of course they do bring to light new, convincing versions of what happened, but generally it is wise to treat them with caution. For instance it is hard, impossible in this case, to establish whether the supposed alteration of Haig's diaries would stand up *(continued over)*

optimist. Seventeen days later Foch assumed full command 'des Armées Alliées en France', which included the Americans. In this supreme position he remained until the Armistice six months later. It would be wrong, though, to suppose that he often had much more than a very considerable advisory role. Both Haig and Pershing, the American Commander-in-Chief, and also to a lesser degree Pétain had to be persuaded rather than ordered.

On that sixth day, 26 March,* Albert and Noyon fell to the Germans, but on the seventh day, the tide temporarily slowed down to a ripple, except to the south where the French lost Montdidier. By the evening of the eighth day the Fifth Army had been reduced to one corps, holding about nine and a half miles of line. Its northern corps had earlier been placed under Third Army and the French had been gradually taking over the other two corps. On this eighth day, too, while the first offensive was losing its impetus, the second was launched, again on a wide front, to the north and south of the Scarpe against the Third and the First Armies at Arras. It failed. But though Ludendorff's bewildering switch meant that the momentum of the advance against the Fifth Army (now commanded by Rawlinson (see below)) was greatly lessened,

---

to expert examination of handwriting and paper. This has never been applied to the 750,000 words of those diaries. Until it has been, it would be rash to pontificate.

Included here alongside the official one is a rough outline of the case put forward by Travers and Winter. It will be for serious historians of the future to try to uncover the truth. There are of course good reasons for criticizing some of Haig's actions. It would be amazing were there not. Indeed Winter admits that 'it is the number of important decisions Haig got right rather than his errors of judgement which stand out'. (p 177)

It is perhaps significant that the official version of Haig's reason for calling the Doullens conference has never, to the present author's knowledge, been challenged by any French historians.

*On this day too started large scale indiscipline by the survivors of the original German assault divisions. They 'did not spend time resting when they were left behind in reserve but in looting, eating and drinking' (Farrar-Hockley, 307). They were confronted everywhere by evidence of the superior living conditions and rations of the British troops. Their own had been reduced as a result of the increasingly successful blockade of the German ports.

By the seventh day the enemy's progress lay across the wilderness of the old Somme battlefield and the loss of so many of the picked storm troopers was beginning to be felt. Further, difficulties in moving guns forward and transporting ammunition caused the infantry to outrun its artillery support.

Haig's 'backs to the wall' proclamation

between the Somme and the Avre the enemy reached Hamel. Next day that town was taken.*

Severe fighting of an inconclusive nature continued until 9 April† when Ludendorff launched his offensive in Flanders, confirming Haig's fears for the Channel Ports and prompting on the 13th his famous 'backs to the wall' proclamation.§ Part of this offensive hit the Allied line where there were demoralized Portuguese troops about to be relieved. It broke through (see p. 216 below). Eventually, however, this assault also lost momentum, but not before considerable gains had been made.

One of the only tank-versus-tank engagements of the war – thirteen on each side including, for the first time, seven British 'Whippet' light tanks – took place on 24 April at Villers-Bretonneux. It put an end to all serious anxiety north of the Somme. On 25 April the Germans regained the Kemmel heights lost by the French. On the 29th they gave up the struggle on the Lys. In the third battle of the Aisne, which started on 27 May, no cavalry was present. Three tired British divisions supporting the French were smashed and there followed

---

*On this, the ninth day, the Germans ratified the horrifyingly draconian Treaty of Brest-Litovsk against the Bolshevicks. Its appallingly harsh terms (which, of course, were never consummated) acted as a warning of what the Allies would have faced had the German offensives led to their winning the war. They go far to refuting the view that the war was, unlike the Second World War, totally unnecessary.

Further evidence of this came on 7 May when the Romanians were forced to sign the Treaty of Bucharest which was not one jot less cruelly rigorous than that of Brest-Litovsk.

It is often forgotten that when in 1914 the Kaiser ordered his army to 'walk over General French's contemptible [*verächtlich*] little army', he prefaced that injunction with the words 'exterminate the treacherous England'. It is quite possible to believe that the terms of a treaty imposed on Britain and France would not have been much more lenient than those inflicted on Russia and Romania.

†On the 2nd, the Americans for the first time agreed to brigade certain of their troops with the British and the French. They had no cavalry at any time. Virtually all their heavy equipment, including most of their artillery, was provided by the French and the British.

§The full text of this, drafted in Haig's own hand with only three corrections, is: 'To all ranks of the British Forces in France.

'Three weeks ago today the enemy began his terrific attacks against us on a fifty-mile front. His objects are to separate us from the French, to take the Channel ports and destroy the British Army. *(continued over)*

176

Ludendorff's gamble fails

what was arguably the most complete breakthrough of the war. The enemy's exhausted divisions could not take full advantage of it. They got to within fifty-six miles (by road) of Paris before grinding to a halt on the Marne a week after the battle had started.

Ludendorff now possessed a larger salient than that from which he had withdrawn some fourteen months earlier. He had nearly fifty extra miles of front to hold, none of which would ever be as strong or defensible as the Hindenburg Line from which the offensives had started. His gamble had failed – at a fearful price. The Allies suffered approximately the same number of casualties as the Germans: some 350,000 each, but there were a good deal more Allied than German prisoners.

A further offensive was launched by the Germans on 9 June. In the first battle of Lassigny they attacked towards Compiègne, reached the Forest of Villers-Cotterets and failed to advance further. American troops supported the French in this battle (as they had in the Aisne battle). It ended on 13 June. On 4 July an Australian division with sixty British tanks captured Hamel and Vaire Woods with very few casualties. This gem of an engagement restored the Australians' belief in tanks. This had been shaken by an unhappy action in 1917. It also made Rawlinson reflect upon

---

'In spite of throwing already 106 divisions into the battle and enduring the most reckless sacrifice of human life, he has as yet made little progress towards his goals.

'We owe this to the determined fighting and self-sacrifice of our troops. Words fail me to express the admiration which I feel for the splendid resistance offered by all ranks of our army under the most trying circumstances.

'Many amongst us now are tired. To those I would say that victory will belong to the side which holds out longest. The French Army is moving rapidly and in great force to our support.

'There is no other course open to us but to fight it out! Every position must be held to the last man: there must be no retirement. With our backs to the wall, and believing in the justice of our cause, each one of us must fight on to the end. The safety of our homes and the freedom of mankind alike depend on the conduct of each one of us at this critical moment.

'D. Haig. F.M.' (Terraine: *Haig*, 432-3)

It is difficult to say what effect this order of the day had. Whether it encouraged the enemy more than the British troops is an open question. An infantryman on reading it is reputed to have asked 'What bloody wall?'! (Pitt, 125)

the chances of a much greater battle on similar lines – namely the battle of Amiens on 8 August (see next chapter).

* * *

In mid-March Mullens' 1st Cavalry Division was near Péronne and at the disposal of XIX Corps. For much of the time it was operating twenty or more miles north of the other two divisions. Greenly's (later Pitman's) 2nd Cavalry Division, at the disposal of III Corps, had two brigades near Guiscard and the third at Jussy, while Harman's 3rd Cavalry Division (in Army reserve) was posted near Athies behind XVIII Corps (see map, p. 171). From each of these divisions, for the purposes of assisting the inadequate labour forces engaged on preparing the 'battle zone' (from half a mile to three miles from the front line) and the 'defensive zone' behind it, one brigade had at the beginning of the year been extracted to provide 'pioneer battalions', each about 400 strong. Late on 21 March, as the massive offensive developed, a dismounted 'division' was hastily formed from each cavalry division, each brigade providing a battalion, between 400 and 550 strong, of four companies, one from each regiment with a machine-gun company. These 'dismounted battalions' absorbed the pioneer battalions. The Royal Horse Artillery brigades were at first dispatched as reinforcements for the infantry divisions in the line. 'Thus,' as the Official Historian puts it, 'the divisional commanders were left with their staffs, two brigadiers and the led horses.'[11] This dismounted force almost at once lost any cohesion that it was intended to possess and parts of it were employed separately as urgently needed.

* * *

The figures cannot be precise, but on 21 March only about one-third of the three divisions of the Cavalry Corps was mounted: perhaps 5,000. Many of the rest – the hastily formed 'dismounted divisions' (see above) – from next day onwards were thrown into the battle as weak infantry.* Initially their horses were sent ten to fifteen miles to the rear. The origin of this dismounting order is not known. It probably came from Fifth Army headquarters. It was a

---

*'On no single occasion during these operations were the cavalry driven back by a frontal attack: they only vacated a position when ordered to do so in consequence of withdrawals by people on their flanks.' (Preston: '1918', VII, 506)

grave mistake. The cavalrymen became involved in a fast-moving retreat. They were not equipped for constant marching on foot. Neither their equipment nor their transport, especially for machine guns and ammunition, were designed for it. The result was that much of both had to be abandoned. Further, as will be seen, the real and urgent need was for mobile reserves to fill gaps in the infantry's line and to collect information as to enemy and friendly units' locations and strengths. When the men had to be remounted (see below) much time was lost in doing so. None of the senior commanders had made any preparations for the famous and much-trained-for 'Gap' being made by the enemy and not by their own troops. That there would be a situation in which more than helping the infantry to hold their trenches was required had hardly occurred to them. In consequence, for the first few days most of the cavalry was rendered immobile when the real need was for maximum mobility.*

During the course of 25 March the 2nd Cavalry Division, then perhaps 1,100 strong, was more or less completely remounted, while, except for the 6th Cavalry Brigade (which did not rejoin the division till the 27th), the 3rd Cavalry Division was also mostly remounted on that day. These feats of organization entailed withdrawing from the line all dismounted cavalrymen. III Corps' commander had begged the French general who had taken over Fifth Army's right to accede to this operation and he had agreed.[12] Though many of the men were reunited with their own led horses, others were hastily placed on any that became available,† making

---

*There is evidence that on 22 March two dismounted cavalry brigades consisted in total of only 875 men.

The Canadian Cavalry Brigade's Machine Gun Squadron was the only one to retain its pack horses when ordered to dismount. In the others the machine guns had to be carried by the men, who soon became exhausted. On one occasion, when a machine-gun squadron was required to get forward into three groups of four guns each, it took two hours to get them into position over a distance of two miles. It would have taken less than half an hour had the squadron been mounted. (Preston: '1918' I, 180–1)

†For example

'the dismounted company of the Carabiniers [6th Dragoon Guards] took the horses of the 5th Lancers which they found somewhere along the Oise and then became a squadron in [Cook's Detachment (see below)]. The number threes, who would be holding the horses, would either *(continued over)*

them into very effective mounted infantry. Many of those employed in digging parties were caught by the Germans' onrush and were either made prisoner or could not join their units for some days.* As in 1914, especially during First Ypres, the cavalry proved to be widely useful as 'putty' with which to fill the breaches in the defence, employing their mobility in so doing. An excellent example of this was afforded by the action of parts of the 1st Cavalry Division on 27 March. That morning four squadrons of the 4th and 5th Dragoon Guards were holding the village of Sailly Lorette when heavy attacks from three directions were launched against them. They refused to be dislodged, but in the course of the day the division received orders to go to the help of XIX Corps south of the Somme. At 5.30 p.m., under cover of a counter-attack, the beleaguered squadrons, with others near by, were relieved by Australian infantry. They quickly regained their led horses, crossed the river and rejoined the rest of the division ready to carry out their new orders.[13]

There were occasions, even, when mounted troops under rifle fire brought their horses right up to the point at which the men were to dismount so as to fill a gap, particularly if it were on a ridge, the horses being speedily trotted back under cover. A good illustration of this occurred when, on 29 March near Hamel, a squadron of the 11th Hussars 'rode up to within 300 yards of the enemy, dismounted, fixed bayonets and walked up the slope. The Germans did not wait, but scurried off, and the line was restored.' This was an operation often practised in training, but rarely in trench warfare circumstances. Most experience hitherto had been confined to trench parties leaving their mounts several miles behind the line.[14]

Mounted troops, when brought up to fill a gap, had one

---

accompany the regiment which requisitioned them, or else be taken under the command of some strange officer who had been ordered to plug a gap somewhere. In spite of all this the regiments naturally tended to hang together as far as possible, and it is interesting to note that even when mixed parties had to mount someone else's horses, an effort was always made to sort them out by regiments before closing with the enemy.' (Oatts: *3DG/6DG*, 231)

*Not only was there a shortage of men. A very considerable amount of equipment had also to be abandoned. The 15th Hussars, for instance, was 'short of many indispensable articles, and the whole of the 4th April was spent in drawing stores and refitting.' On 21 March the regiment's band instruments had been among the loot left for the enemy. (Carnock, 164, 179)

'Harman's', 'Bonham's' and 'Cook's' Detachments

considerable advantage over the infantry. When nearly surrounded they were able to mount and gallop clear. This happened, typically, to the Carabiniers on 25 March. Older officers were reminded of similar actions in the South African War. The infantry in corresponding circumstances would have had either to surrender or fight to the bitter end.[15]

From 22 March and on succeeding days numbers of composite mounted formations were formed. They were very much ad hoc. Chief of these was 'Harman's Detachment' (see p. 189). Typical of other smaller ones was 'Bonham's Detachment', formed on the 22nd, which consisted of the 'brigade details' of the 4th and 5th Cavalry Brigades and a troop of about thirty men each from four regiments under a captain of the Greys. Another was 'Cook's Detachment', formed on the 25th, comprising six squadrons from various brigades under the 20th Hussars' Commanding Officer.

The regimental diary of the Oxfordshire Hussars gives an idea of how its mounted squadron in Cook's detachment employed its mobility:

'*25 March.* 5.30 p.m. Ordered to ride to aerodrome at Catigny. . . . Dug a line with right on Catigny road, left in touch with 5th Brigade. Sent a patrol to canal. . . .

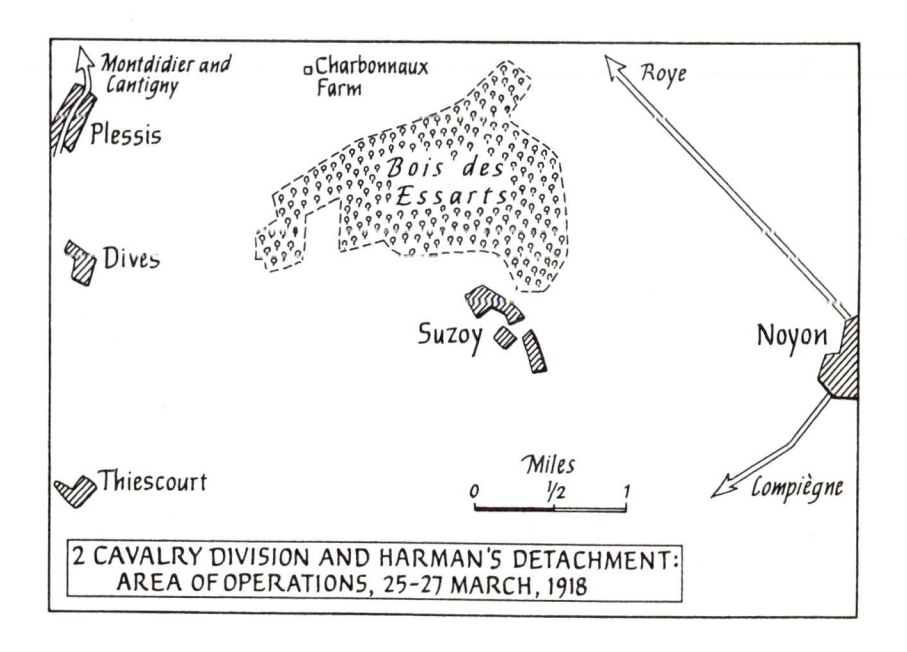

2 CAVALRY DIVISION AND HARMAN'S DETACHMENT: AREA OF OPERATIONS, 25-27 MARCH, 1918

'Fane's Composite Regiment'

'11 p.m. Ordered to take up a new line on Roye–Noyon road. On arrival there sent a patrol to get touch with Canadian Brigade.... Horses left about 1,000 yards behind.

'*Midnight 25–26 March*. Ordered to return to horses and march to Lassigny–Dives road ...

'10.30 a.m. Ordered to seize and hold Charbonnaux Farm.... Dug in.... Whole line under fire. Led horses of brigade also heavily shelled.

'4.30 p.m. Owing to left flank being turned, ordered to retire.... Successfully accomplished with few casualties.... Mounted and retired through belt of fire. Took up new position facing Plessis. Heavily shelled whilst mounting....

'6 p.m. Ordered to retire. Mounted and marched through Dives under heavy shell fire to Thiescourt.'[16]

Yet another scratch force was 'Fane's Composite Regiment', formed from parts of the 5th Cavalry Brigade. The 12th Lancers' squadron was commanded by Major Charrington who recounts what happened when, on 26 March, it was advance guard trying to make good some high ground overlooking Suzoy.

'We bumped into a proper hornets' nest at Suzoy, and it would have been most awkward if a most providential road hadn't lain at right angles to our path, into which we dropped. It was grand cover and we hung on there for some time with both flanks in the air and got some good shooting; but eventually ... the Boche got round and was proceeding to enfilade us and would have made an awful mess of our horses jammed up there, so we had to move. There was one way out, a stretch of 300 yards, without an inch of cover and with about 15-20 machine guns trained on it.... I made the men go singly, about fifty yards apart. You never would believe the old horses could go so fast.... Our French interpreter ... didn't pull up till the next village two miles on! The rest all pulled up quite coolly directly they had covered the open space and wanted to know where to come into action next. I came across last expecting to find the path strewn with men and horses, but there wasn't *one*. A good many horses were hit but only two or three killed and only six men hit out of the whole 120 odd and none badly.'[17]

'Brooke's Detachment'

An excellent example of the cavalry's mobility now that the line of trenches had been left well ahead was provided by the action of 'Brooke's Detachment' formed from parts of the three regiments of the 3rd Cavalry Brigade on 25 March. The following day, near Noyon, it was ordered to seize

> 'a dominant wooded feature. . . . Colonel Brooke [16th Lancers]* soon had his men in the saddle, and riding "hell for leather" for the ridge in a few minutes, but they found that the Germans . . . were already in possession of the greater part of it; but the highest part of it was still "No Man's Land", and the troopers, galloping furiously up the steep southern slope, reached it first, formed a line and held the enemy, cutting them off from the Bois des Essarts. I am told,' writes the 5th Lancers' historian, 'that there has been no more splendid sight in war than this wild rush of cavalry across fields and through villages to gain the coveted ground. The French were on the left, but echeloned back; so the composite regiment went through the French, with the 16th Lancers [perhaps seventy-five men] acting as advanced guard to protect the left flank. Two farms were seized . . . and the Germans driven out. Then an attack was made through the wood by the 4th Hussars, in conjunction with the Canadian Cavalry Brigade on the right. [When it became necessary to retire] being in a salient, both the Canadians and French withdrew, being heavily attacked upon both flanks.'

The 4th, the 5th and the 16th suffered much from machine-gun fire as they retreated. The 5th's historian states, though, that 'they came back slowly, almost leisurely, in order not to dishearten the troops, and they halted repeatedly to check little rushes of the enemy and to keep down their fire'.[18]

---

*(Later Major-General) Geoffrey Brooke, an Irishman of legendary bravery, had been Brigade Major of the Canadian Cavalry Brigade before taking command of the 16th Lancers. (For his part in the action at Moreuil Wood on 30 March, see p. 199). He commanded the Cavalry Brigade, Egypt, 1930–34 and became Inspector General of Cavalry, India, 1935–39. He was a prolific writer, chiefly on equine and equestrian subjects. His books include *Horse Sense and Horsemanship of To-day*, 1924; *The Way of a Man with a Horse*, 1929; *The Foxhunter's England*, 1937 and *Riding and Stablecraft*, 1955. He died, aged eighty-two, in 1966.

For the activities of his wife in saving army horses in Cairo after the war, see Vol. 5, p. 343.

An immediate and urgent problem was how to get the led horses of regiments back to safety. This persisting dilemma was aggravated by the constant removal of horseholders to produce these composite units. On at least one occasion led horses were sent to the rear tied to wagons. The led horse party of the Oxfords on 27 March were so short of horseholders that their charges had to be 'roped together like beasts going to market, with about two men per troop, one at each end, to control them'. During the southwards march on the Compiègne road, this column, as an officer wrote,

> 'overtook a crowd of infantry stragglers.... A brilliant idea struck [the commanding officer]. 'Any of you fellows like a ride?' he said, and in a few minutes they had all clambered up safely on the backs of the many riderless horses. One man in particular climbed on a horse behind the saddle which was piled up with blankets and, finding no chance of sitting on top of the bundle, seated himself on the horse's quarters, but this was disallowed. After continuing at a walking pace for some time, the Colonel thought he would try a trot, but this was too much for our infantry friends and the rest of the march was completed at a walk.... One Lancashire lad, after dismounting stiffly and standing well back from his charger, gazed at him with a look of deep admiration and said: "Well, when aa gets back to battalion, aa's for the traanspoort."'[19]

On Easter Sunday, 31 March, for the first time since the 21st, all three cavalry divisions were more or less concentrated. They came on that date under XIX Corps.

* * *

Except for the action at Moreuil Wood five days earlier (see p. 199), the most telling example of cavalry as a mobile reserve holding the line until the infantry could be brought up to take it over took place on 4 April, the day on which the Germans made a final effort to destabilize the Allied line. Early that morning they launched a massive attack on Villers-Bretonneux which was the key to Amiens. An exhausted infantry division had only that night taken over the section of the line attacked. The enemy soon broke through and was advancing with speed when, as the historian of the 6th Cavalry Brigade puts it, 'the way to Villers-Bretonneux lay open. . . . It was not a question even of an hour or two. It was a question of minutes. The only roads by which infantry in lorries could have been rushed up were under concentrated shell fire. None but mounted troops moving quickly over open country could have saved the situation.'[20]

Both flanks of an infantry brigade were uncovered, leaving gaps to north and south of it. The 10th Hussars with four machine guns galloped up to fill the northern gap, losing in the process fifty horses from machine-gun fire.[21] Almost simultaneously, the 3rd Dragoon Guards, followed on their right by the Royals, each with four machine guns, galloped up to fill the other gap, and join up with the Australian brigade to the south. 'B' Squadron of the Royals 'had dismounted and the led horses were galloping back to cover,' according to the Royals' historian, 'before the Germans could get their range. The enemy were coming on hard and the Royals were only just in time. However, 'B' Squadron shot straight and steadily.' As the rest of the regiment came into action 'every rifle the regiment could put into line was busily employed'. The worst moment of that critical day came when, due to a misunderstanding, the Australians at about 5.30 p.m. began to retire. Fortunately the 7th and the Canadian Cavalry Brigades had earlier been ordered up as reinforcements. While the Brigade-Major of the 6th galloped across to the Australians and persuaded them to resume their former positions, from the 7th Brigade there galloped up a squadron of the 17th Lancers to form a temporary defensive flank.[22]*

The line held and the enemy, discouraged and heavily shelled, ceased to press. The rest of the 7th and Canadian Cavalry Brigades and fresh infantry took the line over during the night. For the time

---

*In mid-afternoon great assistance was afforded the over-strained cavalry by five Canadian motor machine-gun batteries with six armoured cars. (Edmonds, *1918*, II, 126) These, from the early days of the German offensives, had played an important part, using their mobility skilfully, though, unlike the cavalry, mostly restricted to roads. Their original orders had been 'to get in touch with the enemy, kill as many as possible and delay his advance'. They had been trained 'to fight on their own initiative – training which bore good results when orders could not reach them and headquarters of divisions and brigades, continually on the move, could not be found'. ('Summary of Operations and appx 14 to War Diary, 1st Canadian Motor Machine Gun Brigade,' quoted in Nicholson, 372)

Falvy, 23 March, 1918

being Villers-Bretonneux was safe. But for the cavalry's use of its mobility, it is extremely likely that it would have fallen on 4 April. In fact it did fall twenty days later, only to be recaptured by a chiefly Australian counter-attack after nightfall.

* * *

Reverting to 21 March, the first day of the battle, the 1st Cavalry Division had then found itself consisting of the 9th Brigade only. The other two were speedily scattered amongst the nearest or most threatened infantry units. Sometimes they rode to the danger points, but early on as often as not they marched or were transported by motor vehicles. The 1st Cavalry Brigade, for example, lost the 11th Hussars to the 24th Division and the Bays and 5th Dragoon Guards to one of that division's switch lines, 'where their timely arrival about 5 p.m. was most valuable'.[23]

In mid-afternoon Gough ordered the 3rd Cavalry Division to move southwards to support III Corps. By 10 p.m. it had arrived after a very tiring march.[24] A measure of how the cavalry, both mounted and unmounted, was employed at this time is indicated by the 3rd Dragoon Guards being split up between five distinct infantry formations. One of these parties which held a part of the line consisted of the regiment's 'orderly room clerks, signallers, cooks and mess waiters'.[25]

* * *

The first mounted action of any consequence took place on 23 March near Falvy on the Somme. (See map, p. 187). Sergeant Brunton of the 19th Hussars (9th Cavalry Brigade, 1st Cavalry Division) wrote in his diary: 'Up early and soon into action. Very hot time. Have many casualties of officers, men and horses. During early part of the afternoon we had taken shelter in old stone quarry.'[26] There, according to the Official History, the regiment, 'waiting mounted for an opportunity to make a counter-attack,' was spotted by an enemy aeroplane which directed artillery and trench mortars on to it.[27] This caused a stampede of the horses. The historian of the 8th Hussars, which had been ordered to join the 19th, states that an officer of that regiment 'galloped up and told [Major Andrew Cotterill Curell, the 8th's second-in-command] to advance as quickly as possible. While advancing up the hill the 8th was met by thirty of the 19th's stampeded horses.'[28]

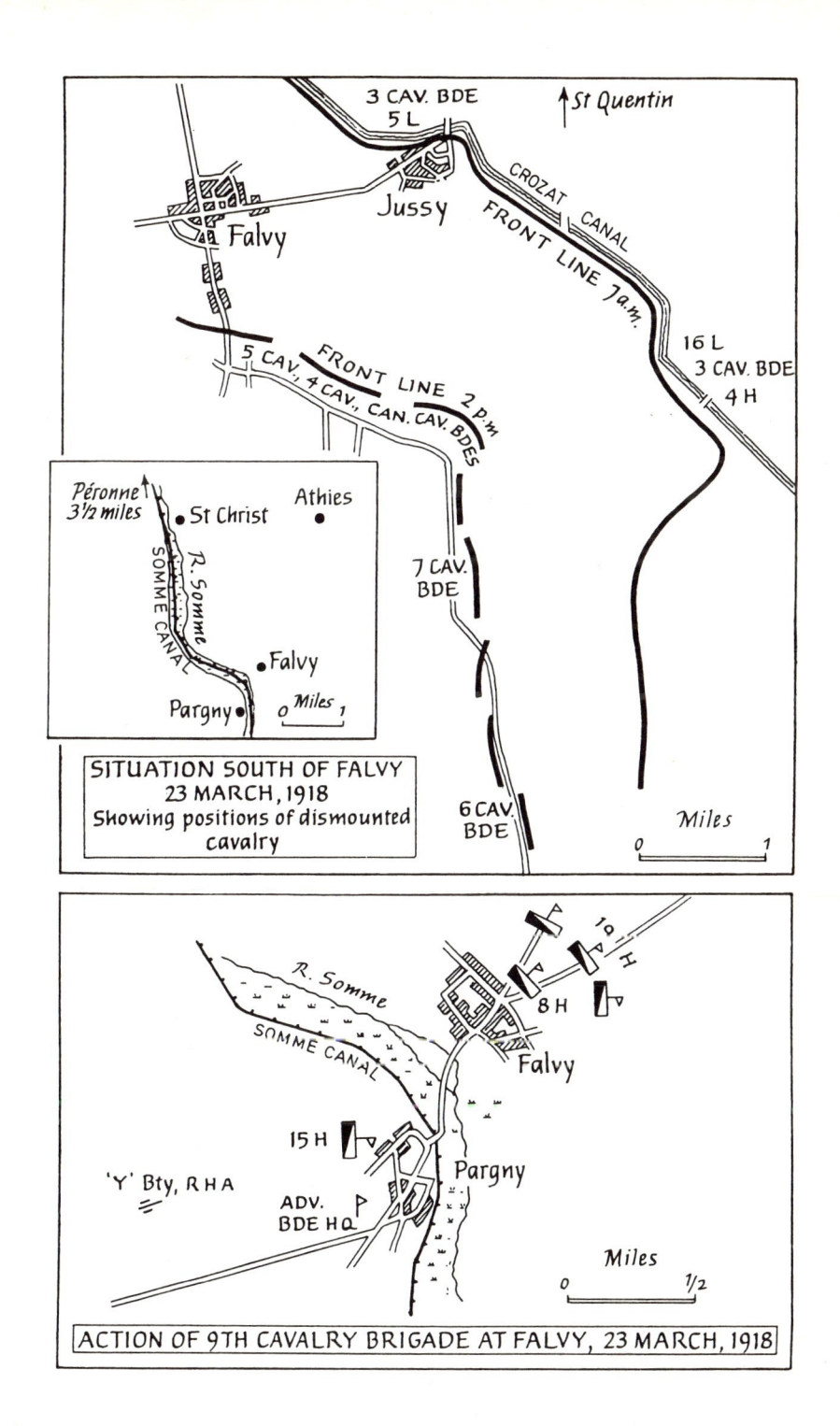

SITUATION SOUTH OF FALVY
23 MARCH, 1918
Showing positions of dismounted cavalry

ACTION OF 9TH CAVALRY BRIGADE AT FALVY, 23 MARCH, 1918

The predicament now faced by the two regiments was not an enviable one. 'With ever-increasing enemies to their front, broken bridges and an unfordable river in their rear, their retirement now became absolutely imperative if they were to avoid annihilation.'[29] Though the villages of Falvy and St Christ

> 'were being heavily shelled, in order to cover the retirement of the remainder of [the 8th Hussars], Major Curell took one squadron across the river. When the remainder tried to follow, the [Falvy] bridge had been blown up by German shell fire. The horses were consequently sent to cross at St Christ. On their way they were met by a party of the 19th, who reported that the bridge at St Christ had also been blown up [but not entirely demolished; horses in single file could be persuaded to cross it]. Attempts were made to repair the [Falvy] bridge with the material found in the village and also to swim the horses over. The bank was so boggy that horses stuck the moment they got to it, and swimming had to be abandoned.
>
> 'Machine-gun and rifle fire was being brought to bear on the village. As it was impossible to repair the bridge with the material available, the planks being too short, a few horses were brought over singly. As direct fire was being brought to bear on the village, and as no men were available to guard the approaches to it – for all of them were required to assist the horses over the river – and as the horses were continually being hit and fast becoming unmanageable, it was decided to get all the men over on planks and to abandon the horses not already taken over. This was done and the regiment rallied dismounted at Pargny.'[30]

The 19th Hussars found it 'impossible to cross at this spot [the Falvy bridge] and, in order to shake off the enemy, they mounted and, drawing swords, moved forward towards the hostile infantry.'[31] Sergeant Brunton records what happened next:

> 'Formed up for the charge under heavy machine-gun fire. Charge successful and dispersed enemy infantry. We now received orders to retire over the Falvy bridge. [Lieutenant-] Colonel [George Despard] Franks [who was killed in October (see p. 260)] with "A" and "C" Squadrons galloped in a northerly direction to cross St Christ bridge. I received orders to take control of "B" Squadron and get into dismounted

action to hold the enemy. Later, when ordered to join HQ west of the river, I found the bridge had been destroyed by our own engineers. Had to leave horses behind. . . . Enemy planes very active during the above stunt.'[32]

Whether in fact there had been a charge in a proper sense is doubtful. One account – not first-hand – says that the 19th's 'threat of a mounted charge had the desired effect, for, on the appearance of the cavalry, the Germans hurriedly abandoned their positions, and thus allowed [the regiment] to gallop for the bridge at St Christ, where they were able to cross the Somme.'[33] Unfortunately, except for Sergeant Brunton's cryptic narrative there appear to be no first-hand accounts.

* * *

On this eventful day, 23 March, a German dawn attack forced the passage of the Somme at Ham and at Pithon, driving a wedge between two divisions of XVIII Corps and threatening the left flank of III Corps and its communications. So as to watch this flank, III Corps commander ordered the small mounted parts of the 2nd and 3rd Cavalry Divisions 'to form such combined mounted force as they could from their scattered commands'.[34] Possibly as many as 700 cavalrymen were thus brought together under the command of Major-General Harman,* commanding the 3rd Cavalry Division. Thus was born 'Harman's Detachment'†. This, coming under the 14th Division, was concentrated at Berlancourt (see map, p. 192) by 4.30 p.m. Typical of the contributions made to this detachment by the cavalry brigades was that of the

---

*Harman had commanded the 6th Cavalry Brigade since May, 1916, and took over the 3rd Cavalry Division in February, 1918. After the war he became Commandant, Cavalry School, Netheravon and from 1920 until 1924 he commanded the 1st Cavalry Brigade at Aldershot and, between 1930 and 1934, the 1st Infantry Division there. From 1930 for fifteen years he was Colonel of the Bays. He died, aged eighty-nine, in 1961.

†Included in the detachment were some 600 infantry, 'a scratch lot and rather shaky' (Atkinson, 453), and eight Lewis guns from No. 3 Balloon Company, 'O' Battery, R.H.A. and 'one lorry and one tender'. (Bickersteth, 83). None of the cavalry's own machine guns were with the detachment, as all were with the dismounted brigades. (Preston: '1918', II, 333).

The mounted men of Harman's Detachment equalled only about a regiment and a half, the dismounted men about four infantry battalions. *(continued over)*

Collézy, 24 March, 1918

6th: twelve officers and 150 men raised chiefly from the horseholders, each of the three regiments finding about fifty men.*

Next day, the 24th, the mounted parts of these three regiments – the 3rd Dragoon Guards, the Royals and the 10th Hussars, commanded by Major Evelyn Hugh Watkin Williams of the 10th – took part in the second mounted action of what came to be known as the battle of St Quentin.

* * *

'The remainder of the 2nd and 3rd Divisions had so many led horses to look after that their fighting value was practically nil.' (Preston: '1918' II, 338).

During 25 March the detachment was added to by about 600 mounted men from the 4th and 5th Cavalry Brigades, including some from the 5th Lancers and the Northumberlands from the 3rd Cavalry Brigade. (Edmonds, *1918*, I, 457). Included was 'Reynolds' Force' formed during the night of 24 March by Lieutenant-Colonel Alan Boyd Reynolds, a 12th Lancer, commanding the Northumberlands. He 'drew 120 horses from the led horses of the 3rd Cavalry Division and with 120 men of his regiment thus mounted joined Harman's detachment at 8 a.m. on the 25th.' (Bickersteth, 871; Preston, '1918', III, 483–4)

*Vital help to III Corps was given by mounted patrols from Harman's Detachment.

'It was the practice from 23 to 26 March to keep four officer's patrols – strength one officer and ten other ranks – at General Harman's headquarters, for employment as required. These patrols started out before dawn each day and were drawn in after dark. They supplied reliable information, not only of the position of the enemy's advancing troops, but also of our own infantry or of the French troops. Reports were submitted every two hours, on an average, by mounted dispatch riders. . . . [These patrols sent] a continuous stream of information of the situation on a front of five or seven miles, which proved invaluable to the Higher Command. No casualties to patrols were reported, although they worked often in front of our infantry in close touch with the enemy. The utmost self-reliance and bravery were shown.' ('Personal experiences written by a distinguished officer of the 3rd Cavalry Division', Sparrow, 216). 'Never in the whole course of the war,' wrote Major Preston, and it is hard to disagree with him, 'was it more clearly proved that, under such conditions, the mounted man was the best and quickest method of transmitting information.' (Preston: '1918', II, 335).

When the offensive started a squadron of the 17th Lancers was on duty in the rear areas dealing with prisoners of war. Until 30 March it was therefore an independent unit. Gough personally on the 25th ordered it to act as his 'eyes'. This it did by means of mounted patrols from dawn to dusk day after day. (The exploits of this squadron are very fully told in Preston: '1918', 339–41.)

Collézy, 24 March, 1918

A German account of the action at Collézy (sometimes referred to as that of Villeselve) runs thus: 'Five English squadrons, followed by infantry, rode an audacious charge from Villeselve. Part of the Guard fell back a bit, but soon recovered themselves and drove the Englishmen back whence they had come.'[35] In outline this tells the story correctly, though 'five squadrons' is a gross exaggeration, as will be shown. In detail this is what happened. In the early morning of 24 March Watkin Williams' 150 or so mounted men, so as to protect the left flank of the 14th Division, took up a position north-east of Villeselve in touch with the infantry portion of Harman's Detachment. This was sited south-west of the little red-brick village, blocking its exits.* During the early afternoon, the two German divisions, which had been driving two weakened British divisions south and south-westward since early morning, were converging on the Villeselve-Collézy locality at considerable speed. The dispirited British infantry were retiring before them in some confusion. The situation was clearly critical. Though on the right a few infantrymen were 'still hanging on', a further German advance must have outflanked them.[36]

Lieutenant-Colonel Paterson (Fort Garry Horse) (see p. 48), in overall command of the 3rd Cavalry Division's mounted detachment, gave Major Watkin Williams the order to move his three troops to Collézy, which it could approach unseen by a sunken road in a shallow valley and 'to charge through the Germans in front and then swing right-handed along the enemy line, using the sword only'.[37] It was to attack the enemy infantry, protected by machine guns, which had reached a position to the immediate south of two small copses and to drive them northwards towards Hill 81. The object was to regain ground and to give the weakened infantry much-needed reassurance. As the detachment, equal in numbers to a squadron, approached Collézy at a steady trot, it came under machine-gun fire from near Golancourt. The worst effects of this it managed to escape by taking cover in the large farm at the south-eastern exit of that village from which the officers then made 'a hasty reconnaissance'.[38] In this position the three detachments found themselves between the scattered infantry in action to the east of the farm and a few French infantry who were

---

*At about 6 a.m. mounted patrols were sent out northwards from Berlancourt. One of these of the 3rd Dragoon Guards ran into the enemy near Cugny and had 'several men killed'. (Parry, 78)

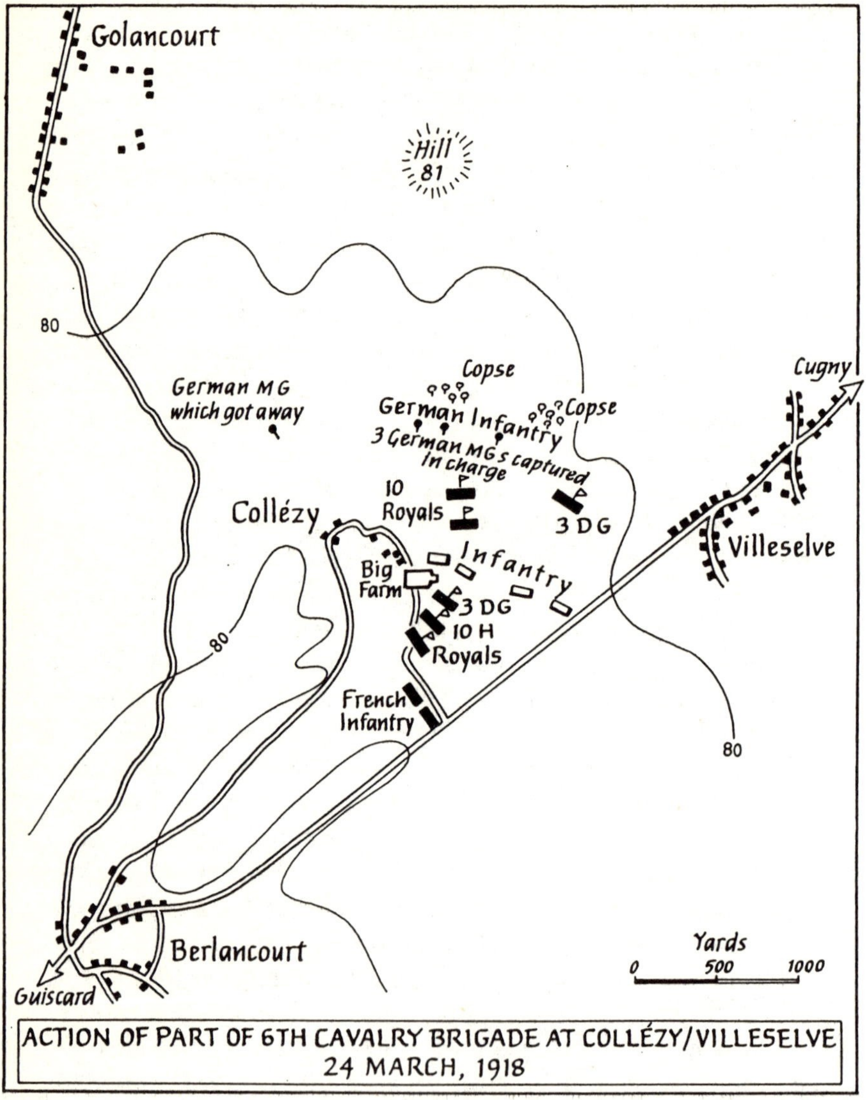

ACTION OF PART OF 6TH CAVALRY BRIGADE AT COLLÉZY/VILLESELVE
24 MARCH, 1918

lining the sunken road in rear. The plan of attack for the three detachments (each equivalent to a strong troop) was given out on the march. They at once set off, passing through the infantry, galloping towards the two copses 'with troops in line', crossing 600 yards of 'heavy' ground, the last 200 of which were ploughed.[39]

The 3rd Dragoon Guards made for the right-hand copse, so as to distract the enemy from the main attack, while a little later the 10th Hussars rode for the left-hand one, going straight for the infantry and machine guns. The Royals followed 150 yards behind them, 'in sections, covering the flanks' of the 3rd and 10th. 'When the charge started the men were knee to knee, but owing to the machine-gun fire and the fast pace' they opened out and were soon well extended. The 3rd came under fire almost at once – fire which was kept up until the troop was some 200 yards from the enemy. Parties of German infantry were soon met, 'some of whom ran into the copse where they were followed on foot [being chased through the trees]. Many were shot at point blank range as they ran away. Twelve prisoners were handed over to the infantry and the right flank was secured.'[40]

The troop of the 10th, meanwhile, galloped 'straight through the enemy lines' towards the left-hand copse. The moral effect of this charge on the Germans was great. 'The moment the men cheered and the swords came down to the "sword in line" they either put their hands up or else bolted into the copse. This did not save them, for once cavalry had been launched,' as the historian of the 3rd puts it, 'it was always far too late for the enemy either to run or to make placatory gestures. They were ridden down and 100 sabred.'[41] The Royals as they followed on mopped up 'small parties who had run together'.[42]

There is nowhere in the accounts of this action any mention of supporting fire from machine guns or the Royal Horse Artillery. It must be assumed that there was none.* This being the case, it is surprising that the casualties were so low. These, it seems, amounted to seventy-three, about half the troops engaged. Out of this total 'only one officer and a few men', according to the historian of the 3rd Dragoon Guards, 'were killed and the wounds of the majority were slight, so that in most cases they were able to continue at duty. Had the [British] infantry attempted to cross the

---

*There *may* have been machine-gun support. It is almost certain that no artillery was present. (See Preston, '1918', II, 341).

600 yards of ground they would have been decimated to no purpose.'[43] This was undoubtedly true, for there were four or five machine guns enfilading the advance and about 500 German riflemen to its front. Only cavalry moving at maximum speed could have got away with it so lightly. Yet such a success could not have been achieved had the element of surprise been absent. The enemy infantry had been marching and fighting furiously for four days with little respite. The last thing that these tired but triumphant soldiers expected was 'the sight of cavalry swooping down on them, sword in hand'.[44] The three troops had been entirely concealed from view by the sunken road until their sudden emergence from it. No wonder that those Germans who stayed to shoot did so wildly and that the rest decided to fly.

The estimate of those cut down by the sword is between seventy and 100, while 107 prisoners were handed over to the infantry. Others 'kept giving themselves up to the infantry who followed up the charge'.[45] Of the four (some say five) German machine guns, only one managed to escape across the ploughed field just in time. Of the remainder one was taken intact, another was presented to the French infantry and one (or two) were put out of action.[46]

The most immediate effect of this example of shock action – one of the best of the whole war on the western front – was to invigorate the previously down-hearted infantry. It temporarily exhilarated them to such a degree that men who before the cavalry action would not have dreamed of advancing did so. They even got well beyond the furthest limits of the charge, almost to Cugny, allowing the remnants of two hard-pressed battalions which had been virtually surrounded to extricate themselves and reform, thus securing the 14th Division's flank. Indeed the charge, though on so very small a scale, can be truly characterized as a model of what cavalrymen were so often taught to believe was an essential duty, namely to sacrifice themselves for the infantry. The historian of the 6th Cavalry Brigade sums up what was certainly felt by the men of the mounted arm at the time: 'Demoralisation of the enemy, encouragement of our own tired troops, the immediate capture of important ground – these are solid advantages which the expert soldier has always realised cavalry could give. But,' he added, 'the opportunities have been few.'[47] There can be no doubt that the charge at Collézy temporarily delayed a major breakthrough at what was an important but shaky part of the line. Any hold-up during a retreat is always acceptable, however fleeting. The fact that this one was on a scale microscopic compared with what was going on elsewhere does not belittle what was, once it became generally known, a morale booster for the whole of the cavalry. 'The cavalry barometer,' wrote Home at Cavalry Corps headquarters in his diary, 'stands very high again. It was very low a month ago.'[48]

It was not until 4.55 p.m., some three hours after the three troops had received their orders, that Harman's Detachment was ordered to retire to Guiscard, the mounted men covering the retirement of all the infantry in the area. These then, until next day, took up 'a good rear line prepared by the French'.[49]

* * *

When recovering from an operation in England, Home, Chief Staff Officer at Cavalry Corps headquarters, heard on 22 March that Kavanagh, the Corps Commander, was going to be sent home (see above, p. 165). When he returned to duty he 'found that Goughie had evidently reported badly on the C[orps] C[ommander] – this was the result. Luckily the CC was in a strong position and the result is that Goughie has gone home and that Henry Rawlinson succeeds him. Everyone is thankful. Poor little Goughie has not stood the strain – it is a great pity with all his ability but quite unforgiveable.'[50]

Though studies of the known facts show that what was more unforgiveable than Gough's supposed and not, in all respects, completely non-existent inadequacies, was his sacking in the middle of the battle. Home's peculiar explanation of part of the background to it, given above, is both revealing and unique. Gough's criticism of Kavanagh's performance at Cambrai (and perhaps since the beginning of the German offensive), sounds like the truth, for Gough was still believed, probably rightly, to be enamoured of the possibility of successfully thrusting the cavalry through gaps and generally sacrificing itself for glory's sake. Yet it is certain that this criticism was at most only a minor contributory factor in the sorry tale of Gough's dismissal. That tale has been exhaustively dealt with by numerous historians, but since it closely involved the BEF's two most prominent surviving cavalry generals, its salient elements are worth reiterating here.

For three months there had been a tendency at the highest political and military levels to find fault with Gough. On 14 December,

1917, Haig had mentioned to him 'how many divisions had hoped that they would not be sent to the Fifth Army to fight. This feeling I put down to his Staff. . . . It was, of course, a surprise to Gough to learn this, but from the facts which I gave him, he realized that there were cases bearing out what I told him.' Churchill refers to a conviction that in the Fifth Army 'supplies were awkward and attacks not sufficiently studied'.[51] As long ago as 23 December, 1917, the Earl of Derby, the Secretary of State for War, had written to Haig saying that he had heard in London, presumably from officers on leave, numerous criticisms connected with Gough's supposed responsibility for some of the 'Passchendaele' failures.* On 5 March Derby had reiterated his criticisms, giving Haig 'a loophole' should he wish to replace Gough before the battle.[52] What is likely to be true is that Gough had made enemies by sacking inefficient officers and by asking too much of others.† He was not the only senior commander in such a position, but there is evidence that he often refused to listen to advice§ and

---

*Gough had, in fact, repeatedly begged Haig to bring the operations to an end in the summer and again in the autumn. There is evidence that jealousy of Gough's speedy promotion informed the attitude of a number of his contemporary officers. (Farrar-Hockley, A. 'Sir H. Gough and the German Breakthrough', Bond, B. (ed.) *Fallen Stars*, 1991, 78, see also, 83.)

There is evidence, too, that Gough was always determined if he possibly could to carry out his offensives with a view to a thorough breakthrough, rather than as wearing down operations which entailed not advancing beyond the artillery's range. In his diary for 3 July, 1917, Rawlinson wrote that he had urged Haig 'to make Goughie undertake deliberate offensives without the wild "hurooch" he is so fond of and leads to so much disappointment.' That Haig did not do so is clear. He, too, after all, half wanted to believe that a breakthrough was on the cards at Passchendaele.

His orders were therefore sufficiently ambiguous to allow Gough his head. (Rawlinson diary, 3 July, 1918, quoted in Travers, 15)

†Haig wrote in his diary on 5 October, 1917, that 'the Canadians do not work kindly' with Gough. 'The idea seems to be prevalent that he drove them too much in the Somme fighting last year. I think that Gough's Staff Officer [Malcolm] is partly the cause of this feeling'. (Blake: *Haig*, 257). Major-General Sir Neill Malcolm and another member of Gough's senior staff were given other jobs by Haig in December, 1917. (Blake: *Haig*, 272)

§Ironside, for instance, found that Gough 'was supercritical of orders from above and sneered at GHQ and so ignored GHQ's orders'. (Ironside diary, 11 and 29 Nov., 1936, Vol. I, quoted in Travers, 63)

Haig's offer to resign refused

that he had enemies from the days of the Curragh 'mutiny', including of course members of the Cabinet.

Further, Wilson was anxious to relieve Rawlinson of his new job as British military representative on the Executive War Board of the Supreme War Council at Versailles which he had taken up in late February. This had been set up chiefly at Lloyd George's instigation, to try to circumvent Robertson's and Haig's authority. Haig had proposed Rawlinson for the post when Wilson, its first holder, had succeeded Robertson as CIGS. Wilson, when he was at Versailles, had been anxious to build up the Council's importance. Now he 'was concerned to downgrade it.'[53] Particularly was this so as Rawlinson soon came into conflict with Foch, Wilson's special 'blue-eyed boy'. This made it easy for the CIGS to agree with Lloyd George's determination to make Gough a scapegoat, and to replace such 'a strong man' as Rawlinson at Versailles.[54]

Because the Prime Minister's responsibility for the débâcle was, if not undivided, at least considerable, since it was he who had withheld the men necessary to prevent it,* his incentive to fix the blame for it elsewhere was imperative. Though Haig offered to resign, his position was impregnable since there was no one, either militarily or politically, obviously capable of taking his place. Thus Gough and his staff had to go, to be replaced on 28 March by Rawlinson and the Fourth Army staff. 'I am to reconstruct the

---

*Between 21 March (that is immediately after the first German offensive) and 31 August a grand total of 544,005 men were sent to France from the United Kingdom. These included 418,000 Category 'A' men. Between 1 January and 21 March only 129,357 Category 'A' men had been sent. (A further 100,000 or so men were returned to Haig soon after 21 March from Italy, Palestine and Salonika). As John Terraine puts it controversially: 'Much suffering and much loss, to say nothing of the reputation of their luckless commander, might have been spared the Fifth Army, if Lloyd George and his Government had taken a different view of their responsibilities.' (Terraine: *Haig*, 436; but see Travers, 36, where it is argued that it is likely that a figure of '70,000 fewer combatant men at the beginning of 1918 than in 1917' was accurate. This was only about 7 per cent of the million or so men in the BEF.) This argument is academic so far as the cavalry is concerned. Reinforcements for the mounted regiments were forthcoming without a suspicion of difficulty.

Haig put much of the blame for the débâcle on lack of troops, yet on the eve of the offensive he had allowed 88,000 men to go on leave! (Travers, 89). There is much evidence that he was greatly over-optimistic about the strength of the assault, and the BEF's capacity for meeting it.

remnants of the Fifth Army as the Fourth Army,' wrote Rawlinson in his diary.[55]

On 26 March Haig had met Milner and Wilson when he was out riding. 'They spoke to me about Gough. I said that whatever the opinions at home might be, and no matter what Foch might have said, I considered that he (Gough) had dealt with a most difficult situation very well. He had never lost his head, was always cheery and fought hard.'[56]*

Though Haig offered him a job connected with the defences of Amiens, London ordered his immediate return home. He was told that he would have an opportunity to defend himself before a promised court of enquiry. Shockingly, this never took place and Gough was denied not only that but all the honours, including a peerage, a field-marshal's baton and the £30,000 given to his fellow Army commanders. When after the war others, including Churchill, when Secretary of State for War, exculpated him, these fruits were still denied him. 'Democracy,' wrote Duff Cooper, 'demands its victims.'[57] Even Lloyd George in the end admitted that he had been wrong. In 1936 he wrote to Gough saying that, now that he knew 'the facts', he had 'completely changed his mind as to the responsibility' for the defeat. 'You were completely let down,' he added, 'and no general could have won that battle under the conditions in which you were placed.'[58] Throughout the rest of his long life Gough behaved impeccably, defending the reputation of his Fifth Army considerably more than himself in a number of books. He died in 1963, aged ninety-three.

* * *

On 30 March Rawlinson wrote in his diary: 'The Boche attacked all along the line this morning and again in the afternoon. He penetrated in two places, but counter-attacks by the 2nd Cavalry Division and Seely's Canadian [Cavalry] Brigade

---

*In February, 1919, Haig apparently told Beddington that he agreed that Gough's treatment had been 'harsh and undeserved', but that he had 'decided that public opinion at home, whether right or wrong, demanded a scapegoat and that the only possible ones were Hubert or me. I was conceited enough to think that the army could not spare me.' (Beddington, 173–4). Though Haig's final despatch did Gough some justice, its author does not seem to have tried very hard to get him properly rewarded after the war, which, since he had agreed to Gough's dismissal, is perhaps understandable.

22. Cavalry crossing a trench on their way to Monchy, April, 1917. (See p.81)

23. The scene after the action at Monchy, April, 1917. (See p.94)

24. (*above left*) Brigadier-General Sir Archibald ('Sally') Home, early 1915.

25. (*above*) General Byng.

26. (*left*) General Rawlinson.

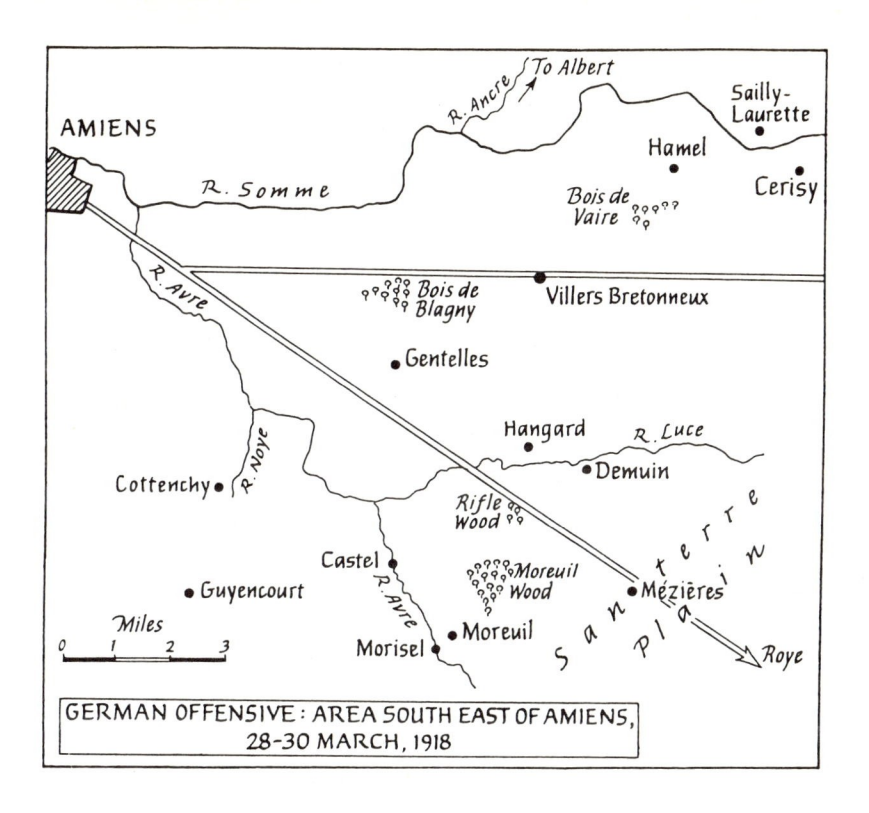

GERMAN OFFENSIVE: AREA SOUTH EAST OF AMIENS, 28–30 MARCH, 1918

re-established the line again.' Four days later he wrote to Wilson: 'The 2nd Cavalry Division and Seely's brigade have done exceedingly well. Seely has on two occasions commanded a mixed force in two counter-attacks. He handled his men with great skill and determination and brought off a considerable and most valuable success on both occasions.'[59] Thus Gough's successor described the actions of Moreuil and Rifle Woods on 30 March and 1 April, the first mounted and the second on foot. These were perhaps the most important cavalry engagements to be fought on the Western Front since 1914. His praise of Seely, whose nickname was 'Galloper Jack', is perhaps too fulsome, but it was not entirely unjustified. It was he without doubt who carried out 'the coup' which, according to Liddell Hart, seemed 'to have extinguished the now flickering flame of German energy'.[60] Though he was a great self-publicist, whose delightful memoirs, entitled *Adventure*, contain some half-truths, Seely's account of the two engagements, mostly corroborated by other accounts, is worth quoting from.

Early in the morning of 30 March, Pitman (see p. 172), (now, since Greenly's transfer (see p. 137), commanding the 2nd Cavalry

Division, under which the Canadian Cavalry Brigade had temporarily found itself),

> 'came to see me [at 8.30]. He told me,' says Seely, 'that the German advance continued, and that the situation was grave in the extreme; we must do what we could to delay the continued onslaught; the German advance guard had already captured the Moreuil Ridge, and were pouring troops into the Bois de Moreuil on the Amiens side of the ridge. Villers-Bretonneux, on the ridge further north, was still held by us, but was being very heavily attacked. I remember his final words, "Go to the support of the infantry just beyond Castel, this side of the Moreuil Ridge. Don't get too heavily involved – you will be needed later."* Pitman was a cool hand if ever there was one. From the way he spoke I knew that things were pretty desperate.
>
> 'We were soon on our way. The roads were blocked with men and vehicles of all kinds, but the country was open, and we moved straight across it at a trot. I galloped forward on my faithful Warrior to the village of Castel, leaving my brigade more than two miles behind. As I rode down the main street the road was spattered with bullets. I had with me only my brigade major – Major Connolly, now commanding Lord Strathcona's Horse Royal Canadians – and my well-beloved aide-de-camp, Captain Prince Antoine of Orléans.†
>
> 'At a crossroads we found the French General, commanding the division on our right. Our front line was spread out before us, some six hundred yards away, just across the River Luce. Enemy fire came from the lower part of the Bois de Moreuil, some fourteen hundred yards away, but as we

---

*Connolly gives Pitman's actual order as 'The Germans have captured Mézières and are rapidly advancing on Amiens. The brigade is to cross the Noye and the Avre rivers as quickly as possible and engage and delay the enemy.' (Connolly, 10). The brigade was some six miles behind Moreuil at the time.

†James Lunt describes the Prince as 'a sort of Aramis to Seely's D'Artagnan'. President Poincaré refused to let him join the French army, but George V allowed him into the British, without a specific rank. He served both as Seely's ADC and as intelligence officer to the brigade. He was killed shortly after Moreuil, having received the MC and having been appointed Chevalier of the Legion of Honour by Foch. 'He was a born soldier, completely fearless, and the finest type of aristocrat.' (Lunt, 227–8).

turned the corner behind the little house where the French General stood we were in complete security.

'I saw at once,' concluded Seely, 'that the position was desperate, if not fatal.'[61]

The Moreuil Wood was unquestionably of vital tactical importance to the Germans. It stood at the western extremity of the ridge, which is the southern border of the Santerre plain (See map, p. 202). It was, as the map shows, pear-shaped, about a mile and a quarter from north to south and about a mile wide in the north. From the village of Moreuil, to which it tapered southwards, it was separated by half a mile of sloping ground. Composed chiefly of ash saplings not yet in leaf and a great deal of rough undergrowth, it was not easily ridden through.[62] It was the point of juncture between the British and French and commanded the Avre and Luce river crossings where the Allies joined.* Its capture would mean that the excellent means of observation that the ridge provided would make the lightly held line along the River Luce untenable and the encirclement of Amiens almost a certainty. Further, the chances of the British and French diverging to the north and south respectively would be considerably increased once the whole of the ridge had been firmly secured. The urgency was all the greater because in the afternoon of 29 March most of the Moreuil sector, including of course the wood, had been, unknown to the British, abandoned by the French. Parts of it were now only very thinly held by the British infantry in hastily dug trenches. Indeed, at 4.30 a.m. the infantry reported that 'under cover of a slight mist the enemy was dribbling men into the wood from the south-east'. XIX Corps therefore ordered the two closest infantry divisions to move up so as to 'safeguard the point of juncture of the Allies'. At 7.15 a.m. Pitman had been ordered by the corps commander, Lieutenant-General Sir Herbert Edward Watts, to employ his division 'to clear up the situation in the wood and secure the line as far as the village of Moreuil without delay.'[63]†

---

*On the night of 29 March the infantry was holding a line from Moreuil village along the southern edge of the wood to Demuin.

†Pitman's headquarters moved at this time to Gentelles. The 4th and 5th Cavalry Brigades were to be in reserve in the Blangy Wood.
At 6 a.m. XIX Corps had telephoned Pitman 'to concentrate ready for mounted action'. (Pitman: 'Amiens', 362).

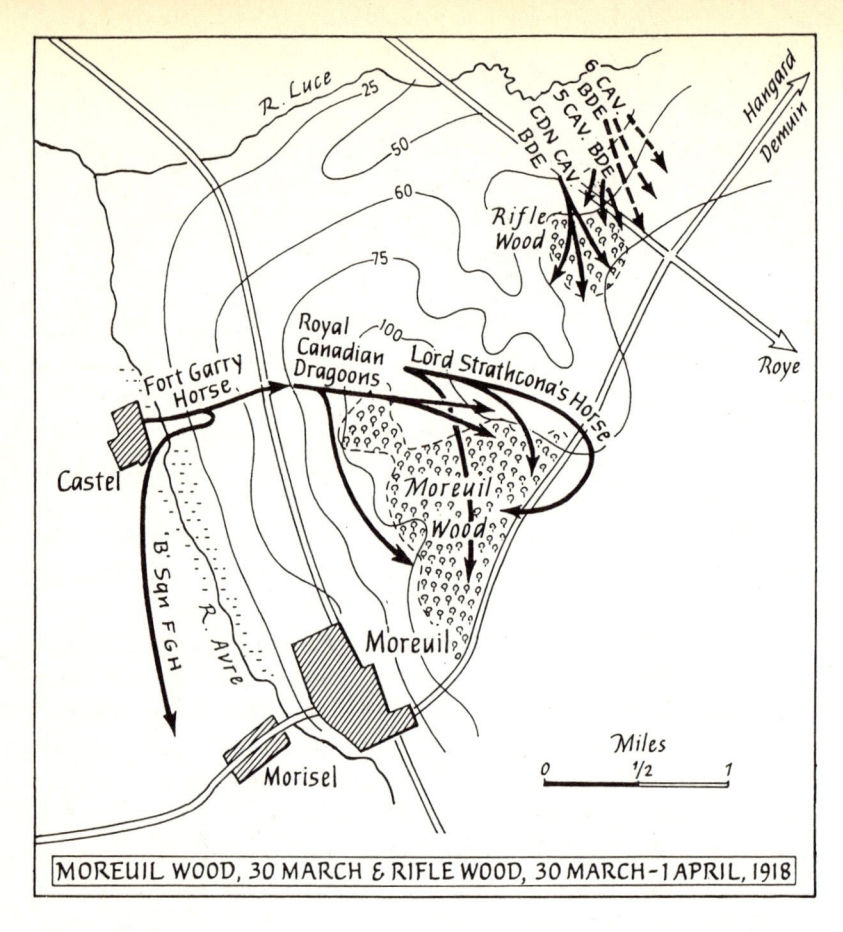

MOREUIL WOOD, 30 MARCH & RIFLE WOOD, 30 MARCH – 1 APRIL, 1918

Pitman's visit to Seely at Guyencourt in his motor car had been preceded by another at 7.30 to Brigadier-General John Ambard Bell-Smyth's 3rd Cavalry Brigade at Cottenchy. This he ordered 'to cross the River Avre as rapidly as possible and, moving by the shortest route, to seize the high ground north of Moreuil Wood, then, in conjunction with the Canadian Cavalry Brigade, to restore the situation up to the line of the Moreuil–Demuin road'.[64] The Canadians had been ordered at 2.00 a.m. to be ready to move at dawn. By 6.30 they had saddled up. They were the nearer brigade to the wood. They therefore moved first. They were to go via Castel. Seely's account continues:

'I asked the French General what the position was. He said ... that strong detachments were already on the outskirts of the village of Moreuil, some two miles to our right; that his flank was unprotected and that he had already sent orders to his troops to fall back ... I knew that moment to be the supreme moment of my life. . . .

202

> 'I said to the French General: "We must retake the Moreuil Ridge," He replied: "Yes, if we do not, all is lost, but it cannot be done." I said: "I have ample troops and will send orders now. Will you send orders to stand fast in Moreuil?" He saw from my badges of rank that I was only a brigadier, and said: "But your poor little force cannot do it. The Germans have a whole division in the wood this side of the ridge." I answered: "I have the whole of the British cavalry coming to support me, and following me 'le grand push' Foch." ... I do not think the French general believed me, but he saw that I was in deadly earnest. He said: "Very well, let us send our orders."'[65]*

Seely was relieved to see the French general send off his orderly 'with precise orders to hold on to Moreuil at all costs'.[66] He established his headquarters at the northern edge of the small wood which adjoined the larger one. It had not yet been entered by the enemy. Connolly, his Brigade-Major, at about 9.15 ordered the Royal Canadian Dragoons, the advance regiment of the brigade, to send its leading squadron, led by Captain Nordheimer, to clear the north-eastern corner of the wood at the gallop and to try to make contact with the French in Moreuil village. Covered by Vickers machine guns, the squadron, according to Connolly, 'though exposed to heavy rifle and machine-gun fire, succeeded in getting into the wood and engaging the enemy in hand to hand combat. Many of the enemy were killed, all refusing to surrender, but a large party, estimated at about 300, retired from the wood south of the point where the squadron had entered it.'[67]

A few minutes later the dragoons' second squadron, led by Captain Newcomen, was sent mounted to the south-west face of the wood

> 'with the object, if possible, of gaining touch with the third squadron [under Major Reginald Symonds Timmis] which had been ordered to gallop round the north-east corner of the wood down to the southern corner. The second [Newcomen's] squadron penetrated about half way up the south-west face of the wood, where they found heavy machine-gun fire directed on them from the enemy, between

---

*Seely's initial orders were 'Advanced guard squadron [of the Royal Canadian Dragoons] to clear N.W. corner of wood. One squadron to gallop to N.E. corner and endeavour to join up with second squadron.' (Pitman: 'Amiens', 363)

Morisel and Moreuil. [Forced to dismount] they turned into the wood and established themselves there. The third [Timmis's] squadron met with considerable opposition.'[68]

The remainder of this squadron was forced to wheel to the north where it retired to a hollow north-east of the wood.[69] The three dragoon squadrons, though they had got a footing on either side of the wood, had not been able to get round its southern side which the enemy was therefore still able to reinforce.

Before all this happened Seely, with his ADC, an orderly 'with a little red pennant', and his signal troop, had

> 'galloped down the hill, across the bridge over the Luce, through a field of young wheat and over a road to our front line. A few bullets flew about, but not many, for we were in dead ground, except to the enemy at the point of the wood.
>
> 'As I rode through our front line, who were lying down and firing, I said to a young captain: "We are going to retake the ridge. Fire on both sides of us, as close as you can, while the rest of us go up." He knelt up and shouted: "Good luck to you, sir." Our infantry opened a glorious fire on both sides of us as we galloped on. Five out of about twelve of my signal troop were shot by the enemy, but the remaining seven reached the wood, jumped off and opened fire. My orderly jammed the red flag into the ground at the point of the wood, and I looked back to see my gallant brigade galloping forward by the way I had come.'[70]

Connolly carries the story forward: 'Lord Strathcona's Horse [supported by four machine guns, which were to fire from the unoccupied detached part of the wood][71] were now ordered to send one squadron to pass round the north-east corner of the wood at a gallop, to support the first [Nordheimer's] squadron of dragoons, while the remaining two squadrons of the regiment advanced to follow up the main attack south-eastward through the wood.'[72] The first squadron, as has been shown, was to make a mounted attack. When it had dispersed the German reinforcements which were entering the wood, it was to occupy its eastern face. The second and third squadrons, under Lieutenants Trotter and Morgan, were to leave their horses near brigade headquarters and to enter the wood and 'fight their way through and join their

Moreuil Wood, 30 March, 1918

comrades on the eastern side of the wood'. The Fort Garry Horse was kept back as brigade reserve, 'ready to occupy the high ground between Moreuil and Hangard, and thus get in touch with our troops still holding Villers'.[73]

As Seely saw the dragoons and Strathcona's Horse come up to him, he remarked how curious it was that 'galloping horses seem to magnify in power and number; it looked like a great host sweeping forward over the open country. I galloped up to [Lieutenant Gordon Muriel] Flowerdew, who commanded the leading squadron of Strathcona's, and as we rode along together I told him that his was the most adventurous task of all, but that I was confident he would succeed. With his gentle smile he turned to me and said: "I know, sir, I know, it is a splendid moment. I will try not to fail you." '[74]

Nordheimer's dragoon squadron, meanwhile, had suffered severe casualties in the course of its gallop and had failed to reach the north-east corner of the wood. Instead it had turned into it 'and engaged the enemy. The air,' says Seely, 'was alive with bullets, but nobody minded a bit. It was strange to see the horses roll over like rabbits, and the men, when unwounded, jump up and run forward, sometimes catching the stirrups of their still mounted comrades.'[75]

Flowerdew's squadron of the Strathcona's now came up against a steep bank. When it reached its top it was confronted by

> 'two lines of enemy, each about sixty strong, with machine guns in the centre and flanks; one line being about two hundred yards behind the other.* Realizing the critical nature of the operation and how much depended on it, Lieut. Flowerdew ordered a troop under Lieut. Harvey, V.C. [see p. 73 above], to dismount and carry out a special movement, while he led the remaining three troops to the charge [riding 100 yards ahead of them]. The squadron (less one troop) passed over both lines, killing many of the enemy with the sword; and wheeling about galloped on them again. Although the squadron had then lost about 70 per cent. of its members, killed and wounded from rifle and machine-gun fire directed

---

*The first was formed from the Germans who had been forced out of the wood by Newcomen's dragoon squadron and the second by another column marching towards the wood from the open country to the south-east.

on it from the front and both flanks, the enemy broke and retired. The survivors of the squadron then established themselves in a position [about the centre of the wood's eastern side]* where they were joined, after much hand-to-hand fighting, by Lieut. Harvey's party. Lieut. Flowerdew was dangerously wounded through [his chest and] both thighs during the operation, but continued to cheer his men. There can be no doubt that this officer's great valour was the prime factor in the capture of the position.'[76]

Thus reads the citation for Flowerdew's posthumous Victoria Cross. He died soon after the charge, but not before loudly shouting, 'Carry on boys. We have won'.[77] An infantryman, Frank Rees, watched this astonishing charge. He saw 'stumbling, falling, screaming horses. Men sprawled on the ground, some running, some trying to turn to hold their horses . . . [He] could see only confusion, horses galloping free as the troopers tried to catch them.' Rees dared not fire his rifle. A Cockney comrade shouted to one of the troopers: 'Oo are you?' 'Strathcona's Horse,' came the reply. 'Strathcona's Orse! You'll be bloody bully beef if yer don't get art the way!'[78]

The survivors of Flowerdew's charge were later joined by Trotter's and Morgan's dismounted squadrons. These, meanwhile, were taking a terrible beating. They might well have been cut off and surrounded had not the Germans themselves, who could hear the firing going on from the remnants of Flowerdew's squadron in their rear, been fearful of the same fate. At this point Seely ordered up the Fort Garry Horse. One squadron was ordered to help out Newcomen's and Nordheimer's squadrons which were unable to move either forwards or backwards, while a second squadron crossed the Avre near Castel to enfilade the enemy from high ground to the west of Morisel. This was a critical moment for the Canadians. They were in real danger of being surrounded or driven back to their start line. Their losses had been horrendous, especially in horses. The enemy was not only holding on to the southern end of the wood, but was being slowly reinforced. It seemed that the time for a German counter-attack had come.

*From there they kept up machine-gun fire, employing captured German guns.

Before this alarming moment arrived, Seely had ridden to the eastern side of the wood to find Flowerdew's survivors

'securely ensconced in a little ditch, which bordered the wood, in twos and threes, each with a German machine-gun and with three or four Germans lying dead by their side. It was recorded that seventy Germans were killed by sword thrust alone outside the wood. I saw perhaps another two or three hundred lying there, who had been killed by machine-gun fire. In those brief moments we lost over eight hundred horses, but only three hundred men killed and wounded. The fanatical valour of my men on this strange day was equalled by the Bavarian defenders now surrounded in the wood. Hundreds of them were shot while they ran to their left to join their comrades still holding on to the south-east corner. Hundreds more stood their ground and were shot at point-blank range or were killed with the bayonet. Not one single man surrendered. As I rode through the wood on Warrior with the dismounted squadrons of Strathcona's I saw a handsome young Bavarian twenty yards in front of me miss an approaching Strathcona, and, as a consequence, receive a bayonet thrust right through the neck. He sank down with his back against a tree, the blood pouring from his throat. As I came close up to him I shouted out in German, "Lie still, a stretcher bearer will look after you." His eyes in his ashen-grey face seemed to blaze fire as he snatched up his rifle and fired his last shot at me, saying loudly: "Nein, nein. Ich will ungefangen sterben." [Literally, "I will uncaught die"]. Then he collapsed in a heap.'[79]

Throughout this morning's activities the RFC*, which had been alerted early on to the seriousness of the situation and ordered to pursue 'a vigorous offensive action with bombs and machine-gun fire at ground targets', was, in cooperation with the French air force, according to the history of the German regiment which was chiefly engaged at Moreuil, circling over the wood and attacking every target that it could discern. 'A pair of British aviators,' reads the account, 'pass at such low height over the wood that one

*Two days later the Royal Flying Corps became the Royal Air Force

expects them to hit the tree-tops. They have dropped their bombs and used their machine guns, and now, flying at the speed of arrows, attack our batteries. . . . One bomb dropped from a negligible height places the whole staff of the 1st Battalion *hors de combat*. Moreuil Wood is a hell.'[80]

The 3rd Cavalry Brigade's guns – 'D' Battery of the RHA – had been active too. They had come into action at about 9.30 with six guns 'just east of the windmill on high ground north of the wood', firing at 'selected points on the far edge of the wood on information supplied by the Canadian Cavalry Brigade'. They found, though, much difficulty in 'maintaining communication'. An hour later the battery position was moved as the enemy was 'observed advancing down the valley of the Luce. . . . Observation was impeded by mist and rain. Towards evening fire was concentrated on the eastern edge of the wood, where the enemy had penetrated'.[81] The Canadians' two batteries of the Royal Canadian Horse Artillery were also active throughout the engagement. Their commander 'had his forward observers with their telephones up in the front line,' wrote Seely. 'They, at any moment, could and did direct a fierce fire on any point.'[82]

Seely, after seeing the position at the eastern side of the wood, galloped back to his headquarters, which had been moved about a third of the way along its northern face.

'I sent messages to Pitman and to the French Divisional Commander at Castel, telling them of our success. It was necessary too to get a message to Villers-Bretonneux, a few miles to our left on the same ridge which we had captured. Villers-Bretonneux was completely hidden by a dense cloud of black smoke illumined each second by the bright flashes of the bursts of the German big shells. In all my experience I had never seen such an intense concentrated bombardment. I gave identical written messages to Antoine d'Orléans and to Colonel Young of the Dragoons, also on my staff, telling them to gallop by different routes into Villers-Bretonneux, find the commander, describe our position and assure him that I was confident of being able to hold on to our portion of the ridge for the rest of the day. Young was to go to the west of Hangard, Antoine, on his very fast horse, was to try and get through direct. Antoine had only gone 300 yards when his horse was shot dead. He jumped up unhurt, waving his hand for another horse. My orderly, Corporal King, galloped up to him and gave him his horse, also a very fast animal. It was wonderful to see Antoine swing himself into the saddle completely unconcerned and gallop off again. This time he got through, and gave the message to both the Australian and British commanders in Villers-Bretonneux....

'Both commanders replied to my message that they could hold on to their place and would be obliged if we could hold on to ours. I like to think that our recapture of Moreuil Ridge helped the heroic defenders of Villers-Bretonneux; certainly, but for them, we should have been surrounded and destroyed.'[83]

At about the time that 'D' Battery was opening fire Bell-Smyth's 3rd Cavalry Brigade, which had crossed the river soon after the Canadians, came up to their aid. 'A' Squadron of the 4th Hussars

'got a footing on a ridge between the wood and Moreuil village and sent patrols south-westwards to make contact with the French beyond Moreuil.... The squadron then,' according to the regimental historian, 'came under heavy machine-gun fire from positions in the south-west corner of the wood and eventually had to retire, covered by "B" Squadron on another ridge half a mile to the north. Meanwhile "C" Squadron was working north along the western edge of the wood and in spite of heavy fire they made contact with the right of the Canadians.'[84]

The situation by 11 a.m was that the centre and southern parts of the wood were still in the Germans' hands, while the Canadians and the 3rd Cavalry Brigade had established themselves on three sides of it. Half an hour later a squadron of the 16th Lancers was sent to reinforce the 4th Hussars. At about 1 p.m. another squadron of the 16th was sent to reinforce the Canadians. It 'proceeded mounted into the wood along the track running north and south through the centre of the wood. On the advance posts reaching the centre of the wood,' writes Pitman, 'they were fired on with machine guns and rifles by the enemy still in the wood.'

The squadron retired a short distance and dismounted, then advanced supported by two machine guns.[85]*

The 16th's commanding officer was Geoffrey Brooke (see p. 183). He preceded his men. 'I knew,' says Seely, 'he would come at such a moment wherever he might be. Together we rode through the wood towards the south-east corner.... We saw a line of men two hundred yards away. I said to Geoffrey: "They look like Germans. They should not be here." As he took out his field glasses they opened fire. "Drive them out," I said to Geoffrey, "while I go to the eastern face of the wood."'[86]† A second squadron of the 16th, accompanied by eighty men of an infantry battalion, now arrived on the scene and Seely and Brooke, according to Pitman, 'organized a line which drove through the wood, and after heavy fighting got in touch with the 4th Hussars'. This line was reinforced by two squadrons and later by a third of the 5th Lancers at about 3 p.m. A general advance, dismounted of course, was then made along the whole line. This freed the eastern side of the wood, but at about 4.15 p.m. a slight withdrawal had to be made from the south-west corner, which was only thinly held, a consolidated line being organized facing south and east.[87]

As night fell the enemy's shelling increased. It included a large proportion of gas shells. This showed, to the relief of everyone, that an immediate counter-attack was not contemplated, since gas hangs about in a wood for a long time. Nevertheless, minor German attacks were made, and these had to be held off.

---

*At about 10 a.m. two guns of the 3rd Machine Gun Squadron supported the 4th Hussars 'on the western slopes of the hill above Moreuil. These two guns had no good targets, but fired on the southern corner of the wood and the ridge at that corner. The two remaining guns went forward into the wood with the 16th Lancers and took up a position on the main north and south track through the centre of the wood,' but they too had no good targets to fire on. They employed what Pitman calls 'grazing fire'. (Pitman: 'Amiens', 366)

†A few years before he died, Brooke told James Lunt that he had

> 'just passed the word down the line to advance, when a soldier, who had temporarily lost his nerve, started to run back. I had a large pair of wire-cutters which I hurled at him and hit him on the knee. This may have restored his equanimity as he then carried on – or it more likely may have been due to the remark of an old soldier seeing the German machine guns ripping up the grass in front of us. "God," he said, "it reminds me of old Nobby cutting up the billiard table!"' (28 Nov., 1959, Letter to Lunt, Lunt, 234)

Moreuil Wood, 31 March and Rifle Wood, 1 April, 1918

By the early hours of 31 March the cavalry in the wood were relieved by the infantry. Both Moreuil and Rifle woods were retaken by the enemy on that day, but vital time had been gained for French and Australian reinforcements to be summoned in time to save Amiens. Further, the village of Moreuil remained in Allied hands.

It is tempting to describe how on 1 April the cavalry of the 2nd Cavalry Division and the Canadians in a brilliant operation commanded by Seely captured Rifle Wood near Hangard, but since, because a narrow bridge could not take horses, the operation had to be undertaken dismounted, the temptation must be resisted.*

In the two actions the 2nd Cavalry Division, including the Canadian Brigade, suffered 1,079 casualties. The Canadians lost 488, nearly half of this number: three officers and seventy-two other ranks killed, eighteen officers and 319 other ranks wounded and one officer and seventy-five other ranks missing.† It is impossible to state with certainty whether these enormous casualties were justified by the results.

Weygand, Foch's Chief of Staff, later told Seely, 'While you held on to that ridge I got ninety-five batteries of seventy-fives into position, and during the ensuing thirty-six hours they fired one million, three hundred thousand shells.'[88] This, which has the ring of truth about it, seems to warrant a good measure of vindication of Galloper Jack's remarkable yet perhaps excessively expensive fight.§

---

*'Perhaps one of the finest sights of the day,' wrote Pitman, 2nd Cavalry Division's commander, 'was to see the Inniskillings go forward at a gallop. They had to move for the best part of a mile over the open before they disappeared into the hollow ground, and then their led horses came back at a gallop, while at the same time you could see the dismounted troops filing slowly up the hollow to the wood.' (Quoted in Preston: '1918', 343)

†The 4th Hussars lost their commanding officer, two other officers and fourteen other ranks killed and two officers and forty-four other ranks wounded. (Daniell, 272) The Bays lost one officer killed, two wounded and twenty-three other ranks wounded and two missing. The 8th Hussars lost eleven killed and twenty-two wounded. (Preston: '1918', 338, 339). The other regiments may have suffered similarly: the figures are not obtainable.

§Foch later wrote to Seely a letter which was to be read to the survivors of the brigade. It included the following: 'En grande partie, grâce à elle, la situation, angoissante au début de la bataille, était rétablie.' (Edmonds, 1918, II, 91)

Post-mortem, Moreuil Wood

Major-General James Lunt, writing in 1960, has this to say about the engagement at Moreuil Wood:

'Theoretically Seely's plan was doomed from the moment of its inception, for he was pitting men on horseback, armed with swords, against men in trenches,* armed with machine guns. But the theory of war is often a very different thing from its practice because the human factor, which plays such a dominant part in battle, is an uncertain and ever-varying quantity. The Seelys and the Flowerdews of this world have proved this time after time, and we should honour them for having done so.'[89]

With that it is hard to disagree, yet in cold, unglamorous terms, it is legitimate to ask (in spite, in one sense, of the 'odiousness' of the comparison) whether Kavanagh's extreme discretion at Cambrai is not almost as worthy of honour.†

* * *

With the engagement at Moreuil came the end of mounted actions of any significance, though the cavalry continued to use, effectively, its capacity for getting with speed from crisis point to crisis point, right up to the end of the battle of the Lys.§ Acting thus, as mounted infantry, it proved Haig's point that a cavalry force was worth preserving. There can be little doubt that a larger one would have been a considerable boon to Gough and Byng.

* * *

---

*Though, of course, most of the trenches must have been vestigial.

†Edmonds, *1918*, II, 91, states that there is a lengthy account of the fighting in the two woods in Zimmermann's *Die Englische Kavallerie in Frankreich in März und April 1918*. Since Edmonds says that 'it agrees with the British account', it has not been consulted.

§There is much evidence that the cavalry did exceptionally well in the dismounted fighting of these hectic days. Unlike the infantry, which was getting increasingly war-weary after suffering enormous casualties in the offensive battles of the last three years, the cavalry had spent much of that period training – training, indeed, to a large extent, in open warfare. Further, a respectable number of officers and non-commissioned officers were still pre-war men. In the absence of divisional cavalry or cyclists, the shepherding of *(continued over)*

In the following chapters it will be shown that the mounted arm had its uses in the advance as well as in retreat and this raises the question as to whether the Germans would or would not have benefitted had they employed any respectable number of cavalrymen in their spring offensives and indeed earlier in the war. It is a fact that they employed no mobile arm for exploitation whatsoever: less indeed than had been employed in August, 1914. Since the idea was to break through into open country and to set no limit to the advance this does seem surprising. It is no surprise, though, that Haig, in his final despatch, wrote, respecting the March offensives, 'The absence of hostile cavalry at this period was a marked feature of the battle. Had the German command had at their disposal even two or three well-trained cavalry divisions, a wedge might have been driven between the French and British Armies. Their presence could not have failed to have added greatly to the difficulties of our task.'[90] The Official Historian hardly liked to 'contemplate what might have happened had the Germans pushed up masses of cavalry or mechanized forces to exploit their early success.'[91]* Gough, not unexpectedly, believed that 'had the Germans been able to make use of cavalry of the same calibre [as the British cavalry], it is more than probable that the whole course of the battle would have been altered'.[92] An infantry officer thought it 'a crowning mercy that [the Germans] had no cavalry. How many times during the retreat did we thank heaven for this! The sight of a few mounted men in the distance would at once start a

---

routed infantrymen ought to have been undertaken by battalion staffs mounted. In fact very few of these staffs took to their mounts not only to guide bewildered and frightened foot soldiers and rally them but also to gallop back so as to reconnoitre the next positions and to stop the troops on them. Adjutants and other battalion headquarter officers and NCOs could only perform these functions satisfactorily mounted, yet they were seen on horses very seldom indeed. No doubt many of them knew not how to ride after years of static warfare. German officers, on the other hand, such as company commanders, were often seen riding about. (Preston '1918', VII, 507).

*A German historian thought that the attack on 21 March was

'on too wide a front: there should have been one Army, wedge-shaped, to break in; two Armies to roll up the British line right and left of the break-in; two Armies to attack right and left and push for the enemy's communications; and a sixth Army, the strongest of all, with a large force of mobile artillery followed (not preceded) by cavalry, to "leapfrog" the front Army and reach a strong strategic position to deal with enemy reinforcements.' (Hentig, H. von *Psychologische Strategie des 'Grossen Krieges'* 1927, quoted in Edmonds, *1918*, II, 462)

ripple of anxiety.... Cavalry was the one factor which would have smashed the morale of the defence in a twinkling.'[93] Indeed it is said that a battalion at Nesle was sufficiently alarmed by a false report of enemy cavalry attacking to retreat prematurely.[94] An infantry brigadier on the Fifth Army's left reported that he was immensely relieved when on 24 March he realized that the horsemen he saw 'coming over a ridge some two miles away were only German gunners coming into action'.[95]

It is not quite accurate to say that the Germans employed no cavalry. In principle each division had attached to it one squadron, used as much for escort as for scouting duties. It seems unlikely that in practice all of these squadrons were present. However many there were, these 'penny packets' played so minor a part that their effect on operations was scarcely perceptible.* British prisoners taken on 21 March recorded that the few cavalry mounts they came across looked like 'a collection of old cab-horses' and that those corpses they saw had clearly died from exhaustion or under-feeding and not from any British action.[96] On 24 March, according to Philip Gibbs, some enemy cavalry were seen 'in small bodies acting as scouts. Our own cavalry patrols have met them and turned them back.'[97]

The bulk of the enemy cavalry, as has been shown (see p. 64), had long ago been dismounted. Others, about three divisions in strength, had been sent to the Eastern Front, most of them to the Ukraine, 'supporting', as Terraine puts it, 'grandiose and senseless dreams of power'. Some of them played a useful part against the

---

*The 'penny packets' system had been deplored by Haig when criticizing the German use of cavalry in 1870. There should have been, he wrote in 1907, an independent cavalry body or reserve such as Napoleon always retained under his own command for special purposes. (Haig, Maj.–Gen. D. *Cavalry Studies...*, 1907, 101–02).

An 'isolated' squadron, early in the March retreat, was engaged by dismounted 12th Lancers (Croft, 217). On 23 March the 9th Cavalry Brigade reported: '2.30 p.m. Three squadrons enemy cavalry reported advancing from east.' An officer of the 19th Hussars saw some cavalry at Falvy and infantry reported 'German cavalry coming down to village'. On the same day an officer of the 7th Cavalry Brigade observed elsewhere 'a German cavalry squadron, halted and drawn up in line, near Tergnier'. (Preston: '1918', IV, 21).

During the three weeks of intensive training undertaken by the German assault formations, the difficult task of keeping as close as possible behind the creeping artillery barrage was practised by men with lances held aloft being stationed at 300 metre intervals. The pace of advance was timed at four minutes between lances. (Gray, 17)

27. Cavalry horses tethered behind a line of dugouts in a dip in the ground in front of Zillebeke, September, 1917.

28. 4th Dragoon Guards on the way up to Cambrai, November, 1917. Note the man, seated right, with a pigeon basket on his back.

29. A disabled Mark IV female tank, marked WC for Wire Cutter, being used as a vantage point, photographed near Ribécourt, 23 November, 1917. (See p.114)

30. A grapnel as used by wire-cutting tanks at Cambrai. (See p.114)

31. 'Flying Fox', a Mark IV male tank which broke the bridge at Masnières, falling into the canal, photographed by German troops. (See p.127)

32. 'Flying Fox' helping to support a replacement bridge built by the Germans over the canal at Masnières.

33. Lieutenant Harcus Strachan, VC, Fort Garry Horse. (See p.131)

34. After Cambrai, 'B' Squadron, Fort Garry Horse, led by Lieutenant Harcus Strachan, who won the VC in the battle, passing through Epéhy, 30 November, 1917.

Russians. There is evidence that not many of these were among the troops transferred to France on the Russian collapse, though some, dismounted, were identified in the later stages of the spring offensives as having been moved from the Russian front. A major reason for the dismounting on an increasing scale since 1915 seems to have been a chronic forage shortage, though even had that not been the case Ludendorff's fixed disbelief in the utility of cavalry would almost certainly have ensured that he did not employ it. Further, the Germans' development of mechanical transport had not been great: not, certainly, on as large a scale as that of the British. The number of horses needed for the transport of the enormous quantity of troops from railhead and for making the artillery as mobile as possible for the great offensives was so vast as to necessitate nearly all fit horses being thus employed. That no tanks were employed has sometimes been put down to the German industrial capacity not being up to producing them. This has been proved to be nonsense. The truth is that Ludendorff, the infantryman, unlike Haig, the cavalryman, had little faith in them. Indeed General von Kuhl, Prince Rupprecht's Chief of Staff, is on record as saying that the German 'industries were capable of producing them' and 'that if 600 tanks had paved the way for our infantry' they would have made all the difference to the final issue.[98]

There were certainly moments when gaps were created in the British line, some of them of considerable extent, followed by various degrees of demoralization. No doubt enterprising cavalry could have exploited these with at least temporary good results. The first large gap occurred on 24 March at Longueval. It was some 4,000 yards wide. The 1st Cavalry Division was largely responsible for filling it, but of course only very thinly.* Probably the most extensive gap occurred on 27 March before Montdidier when the French general on Fifth Army's right cried in despair, 'There is a gap of fifteen kilometres between our two armies, in which there is nobody at all'. It is not improbable that, had there

---

*An artillery officer describing the scenes that met his eyes on this day wrote: 'While it would be wrong to say there was a panic, the retreat resembled more of a rout than had been previously the case. Everyone seemed anxious to get away as quickly as possible and regardless of anyone else.... A few military policemen dashed up and down on horseback trying to enforce some kind of order, but no one took much notice; had the Germans been able to break through with cavalry or armoured cars the war would have ended for most of us.' (Quoted in Terraine: *Impacts*, 132).

been a large, fresh cavalry force available, the enemy might have employed it to considerable, at least local, effect, especially as by that date the German infantry was exhibiting clear signs of weariness. It is hard to say how demoralized the British infantry opposed to it was – probably not sufficiently to guarantee more than a temporary cavalry exploitation. On 4 April a dangerous gap developed between Beaumont Hamel and Hébuterne. Thirteen miles to the south were the very first, newly arrived Whippet tanks. These, unsupported by any other arm, entered the gap and 'drove the Germans out of it just', in the words of Fuller, 'as cavalry might have done 100 years ago'.[99]*

Another possible opportunity for a successful use of German cavalry arose when, on 9 April, the three weak Portuguese brigades gave way when attacked by four German divisions at Neuve Chapelle (see p. 176). Yet a complete breakthrough was not achieved even at that critical moment. It was largely prevented by part of King Edward's Horse (274 strong) and the 11th Cyclist Battalion (516 strong) which, in a classic gap-filling operation, sacrificed themselves so that the British infantry might have time to arrive on the scene and stop the rot.†

Three days later (the day before Haig's famous Order of the Day), at what came to be known as the battle of Hazebrouck, there was, according to Furse of King Edward's Horse, 'an opening for the enemy if a large body of German horse had been at hand. For three hours – say 7 a.m. to 10 a.m . . . there was a gap of nearly three miles in the British front. . . . What a chance for enterprising cavalry! I ought to know. I was there from 7.30 a.m. onwards and for a short time was nominally in command of that dangerous

---

*At Cachy on 24 April seven Whippets, sent forward to reconnoitre, passed through the infantry, topped a rise 'to see, a few hundred yards below them, a German regiment . . . preparing to advance. Rapidly forming in line, with all guns firing, they charged through the enemy, scattering him in every direction.' Only when returning from this 'charge' did any casualties occur: one tank put out of action. This, as Fuller puts it, was 'the first mechanical cavalry charge in the history of warfare'. (Fuller, 316).

†The Germans brought up tanks on this day, but the ground was too soft for the few heavy German machines, while the ten captured British ones somehow failed to come into action. (Edmonds, *1918*, II, 189).

The enemy 'never in all the war used more than thirteen tanks on a single occasion.' (Terraine: *Impacts*, 131).

gap.'¹⁰⁰ Fortunately, as the Official Historian puts it, the enemy's success 'was not pressed in any way, either by cyclists, cavalry or tanks, as it might have been.'¹⁰¹*

It is the present author's view, knowing as the reader and he do, the difficulties of massing far enough forward large mounted forces at the right place at the right moment behind the assaulting infantry, that, conjecture as one will, the results of the spring offensives could not have been radically different had large enemy cavalry formations been included in Ludendorff's forces. Indeed, as for the British at Cambrai and on other occasions, the clogging up of roads by their concentration might well have made the offensives less successful, not more, than they were.

* * *

Speaking in 1921, Haig, referring to the spring offensives, said, 'On our own side we had then no more than three divisions of cavalry in an army of sixty divisions, but ... those three divisions did work that was invaluable ... because it was work that only cavalry could do. ... Cavalry is a special arm, and it is not every occasion on which it can be used; but when it is wanted, it is wanted very badly.' One authority exaggerated only slightly when he declared that 'the British cavalry rendered the best service to their country and Empire that can be recorded in all their annals'.¹⁰²

On 10 April Home wrote in his diary: 'The Chief told the Corps Commander that he was going to keep the Cavalry Corps as his reserve and at midnight we got these orders. ... We are now fairly concentrated and ready to move in any direction. ... All our people are full of heart and ready to take the Boche on anywhere.'¹⁰³ Thus, in spite of something like 4,300 casualties,¹⁰⁴† at the conclusion of the great German spring offensives the mounted arm's self-confidence was probably higher than at any time since the end

---

*The gaps referred to above are only a few examples of the many which opened up, some for only a short time and of no great width, others nearly as extensive and of as long duration as those mentioned.

†The Cavalry Corps, between 21 March and 7 April, lost: *officers*: 54 killed and missing, 188 wounded; *other ranks*: 1,220 killed and missing, 2,680 wounded: a total of 4,142. By an extraordinary coincidence the 1st and 3rd Cavalry Divisions each suffered exactly the same number of casualties: 1,349. The 2nd's losses numbered 1,444. (Preston: '1918', VII, 500) The divisional cavalry's casualties are not included.

of 1914. It had performed, though on a much smaller scale, at least as well as in that year. In less than four months it was in some degree to further justify its restored morale.*

* * *

The great German offensives of the spring of 1918 failed either to divide the British from the French or to destroy the former. They failed, too, to capture a single important centre such as Amiens, or even Hazebrouck. Further there was a marked lowering of morale in the German army from early April onwards, though not enough, as the next chapter will show, to produce anything like a general rout. In the British cavalry there was, in Lieutenant Alan Lascelles' words, 'no longer the uneasy feeling which one had for so long, that we were, perhaps, only cumberers of the ground. Everybody, I think, be he gunner, infantryman or aviator, admits now that in those touch-and-go days in March, the cavalry proved itself not only invaluable, but indispensable. The thorny question "Is the cavalry worthwhile?" was answered once and for all in our favour; and this has quieted many troubled consciences, mine included.'[105]

* * *

'We have a curious epidemic – called PUO (Pyrexia Unknown Origin),' wrote Home in his diary on 20 June. 'You go down with a temperature of 103°F for two or three days and then you are alright. It is very catching and whole regiments go down with it. It is a curious malady, the result of war.' This influenza epidemic raged throughout Europe and killed more people than had died in the whole of the war. It was infinitely worse in the enemy countries, especially in Germany, where food shortages due to the Allied blockade lessened resistance. By the end of July it had mostly subsided in the BEF. During June there were nearly 500 cases in the 6 Cavalry Brigade alone. The epidemic continued

---

*The French cavalry – five divisions, two of them completely dismounted – also performed particularly effectively in the later stages of the offensives.

The best brief account of the German spring offensives is in Gray. The fullest account from the cavalry's point of view is to be found in Preston: '1918'.

on and off for many months. In the last weeks of October, for instance, the Greys were 'visited with a severe "go"' of 'flu. This reduced the regiment to only one strong squadron. For some unknown reason one troop entirely escaped the scourge.[106]

8

'Yesterday I said to you: Obstinacy, Patience, your American comrades are coming. Today I say to you: Tenacity, Boldness and Victory must be yours.'
— FOCH's Order of the Day, 7 August, 1918

'On the German side, in spite of sensational triumphs, all was "disillusionment". Behind the Allied front, with all their bitter experiences, the foundation of confidence was solid.'
— CHURCHILL in *The World Crisis, 1916–1918*

'At the battle of Amiens, though tanks and infantry had created a gap of no less than 20,000 yards in width and the ground was practically free from wire and trenches, no pursuit was developed, the ubiquitous machine gun and the scarcity of water completely preventing this. This state of affairs existed right up to the end of the war; there was no cavalry pursuit in the correct sense of the term; further, there were no infantry advances either against any type of opposition unless the infantry were preceded by tanks or heavily supported by artillery.'
— FULLER in 'The Influence of Tanks on Cavalry Tactics', 1920

'Another determined attack is being made by our friends at home on the cavalry. The proposal is to abolish the corps, turn one division into corps cavalry and keep one division mounted. If we make peace with the Boche on the Hindenburg line, then we don't want any cavalry; but if we are going to beat him, we shall want every bus, car, horse, mule and donkey we can raise.'
— HOME, 3 August, 1918

'The Germans were surprised. In all their discussions about possible attacks this front had not been mentioned.'
— CYRIL FALLS in *The First World War*

'Not a derelict machine gun but had its group of silent grey-clad figures who had fought their gun to a finish. . . . Brave fighters, those German gunners.'
— LIEUTENANT-COLONEL W.T. WILLCOX, Commanding Officer, 3rd Hussars

> 'We [the cavalry] are no longer anachronisms. From the unpleasant doubt that we might be only fashionable claret, likely to be poured down the sink at any moment, we have passed to the certainty that we are '34 port, very precious on great occasions. That the great occasions only come rarely, and that in the meantime our cellar is cool and secure, are accidents not of our making.'
> – CAPTAIN ALAN LASCELLES, Bedfordshire Yeomanry, 30 July, 1918

> 'The 8th of August will always be remembered ... as the day on which the cavalry, after so many years of waiting, had at last come into its own.'
> – LIEUTENANT [THE REV.] HAROLD GIBB, 4th Dragoon Guards[1]

The advent of the Americans – Amiens

The advent of the Americans – by 2 July over a million had embarked for France* – compensated to a gradually increasing degree for the very heavy Allied losses incurred since 21 March. Further, by the end of July, the BEF was able to reconstitute the ten divisions which had been temporarily broken up. The Germans, on the other hand, who had lost about 800,000, enjoyed no such comfort. Nevertheless, Ludendorff, wrongly discounting the readiness for battle of the Americans, still conceived that the initiative was his. His comparatively modest offensive of 9 June had failed even tactically, yet he intended, nevertheless, to hurl his still considerable forces against the British in Flanders. Before this, though, so as to attract the Allied reserves southwards, on 15 July he launched, on a fifty-mile front east and west of Reims, what was to prove to be his final offensive. As in the case of his 9 June offensive the French had advance intelligence and the considerable territorial gains made were halted on the second line of defence. Two days later he brought what many of his troops believed to be the final *Friedenssturm* to an inglorious end. Even now, he persuaded himself that the time had come for his Flanders offensive.

---

*Pershing was a cavalryman and he made demands for cavalry to be included in his forces. These were resisted by his Chief of Staff because he 'knew that the British and French each had for a long time, in rear of the lines, large bodies of cavalry in reserve, simply eating their heads off and serving no useful purpose.' (Gen. Peyton March, quoted in Liddell Hart: *Outline*, 226). Another reason was the shortage of horses in France for mounting further cavalry units.

Foch's first counter-offensive begins, 18 July, 1918

Though he was slow to perceive it, there was emerging an appreciable drop in the morale of his men and this was quickened by the influenza outbreak over the previous few weeks which undermined them physically. The very next day Foch's first counter-offensive began. The French and Americans, employing tanks with infantry and achieving a high degree of surprise, drove the Germans out of their Marne salient. They managed, however, to recross that river and form a strong line on the Vesle. They lost 20,000 men and 400 guns and by 4 August the battle was over. 'From this moment onwards,' wrote Churchill, 'to the end of the war, without exception, the Allies continued to advance and the Germans to retreat.'[2] Pershing had now succeeded in forming the First American Army and on 6 August Foch was promoted to the rank of Marshal of France. Two days later there started the great Allied assault known to history as the second battle of Amiens and to Ludendorff as the 'black day of the German army', with which this chapter is chiefly concerned.

Eighty-three days before that great battle opened Haig had told Rawlinson, commanding Fourth Army, 'to begin studying in conjunction with General Marie Eugène Debeney [French First Army] the question of an attack eastwards from Villers Bretonneux in combination with an attack from the French front south of Roye. 'I gave him,' he wrote in his diary, 'details of the scheme.'[3]* That scheme, as will be shown, was to involve the whole of what remained in being of the British cavalry, which had been resting and training for four months. On 17 July Rawlinson sent Haig his proposals for the attack. On the 24th both Foch and Haig approved them and the supreme commander placed the French First Army under the British Commander-in-Chief.† On 26 July, at Foch's insistence, Z-Day was brought forward from 10 August by two days. Haig did not see the battle in the same light as the

---

*Travers, 115, believes, with some justice, that the idea was 'basically' Rawlinson's.

†On this day there took place the only conference ever attended by Foch, Pétain, Haig and Pershing together. There Foch propounded his strategy: attacks would be made with only short intervals between them, 'so as to upset the enemy's arrangements for the use of reserves.... At all costs they must achieve surprises. Recent fighting has shown this to be an indispensable condition of success.' (Edmonds: *1918*, III, 369).

Preliminaries to the battle of Amiens

Cabinet, Wilson and the War Office did. For them it was to be merely the final counter-attack of the year – purely preparatory to the great tank offensive which was already being planned for 1 July, 1919! Haig was a great deal more optimistic.

The terrain to the east of Amiens and south of the Somme was well suited to cavalry and tanks, open and undulating with comparatively few shell craters – much as it had been at Cambrai, though the soil was hard since there had been little rain in the preceding months. Except for the little River Luce and small villages and woods there were few important obstacles. The general lie of the land favoured a surprise attack since it afforded a number of lines of approach. If ever the mounted arm was to enjoy success and be of large scale use to the other arms before the moment when a complete breakdown of enemy morale occurred, it seemed to be now. In some degree it was.

Other advantages included the fact that the enemy did not expect an offensive in this area. His front line, in consequence, was weak: primitive entrenchments, few dug-outs and minimal communication trenches. Next came the 'Old [or 'Outer'] Amiens Defence Line' which was the final objective for the first day's attack. Dug by the French over two years ago, these defences comprised front and support lines with a thick belt of wire on the far side. These were nearly eight miles east of the British front line. Beyond them were between three and four miles virtually without obstacles. When these had been crossed the real difficulties started, for the seven or so miles of the loathsome wastelands of the 1916 Somme battlefields, completely covered with shell-holes and masses of old wire, overgrown with thistles and rank grass, practically put an end to the passage of cavalry or even of tanks. The final objective was laid down as the Roye-Chaulnes line consisting of the largely decayed British entrenchments of early 1917, nearly fourteen miles from the start point.

The seven German divisions on this front were known to be debilitated. None was believed to possess more than about 3,000 effectives[4] and the eight available reserve divisions were thought to be unable to arrive on the scene much before late on 11 August – over-sanguinely as it turned out. Rawlinson's Fourth Army, with most formations and units well up to establishment, numbered fifteen infantry divisions, the three cavalry divisions of the Cavalry Corps and 530 tanks, fifty-eight more than at Cambrai. 342 were Mark Vs and V*s (the latter employed as troop carriers),

BATTLE OF AMIENS, 8 AUGUST, 1918

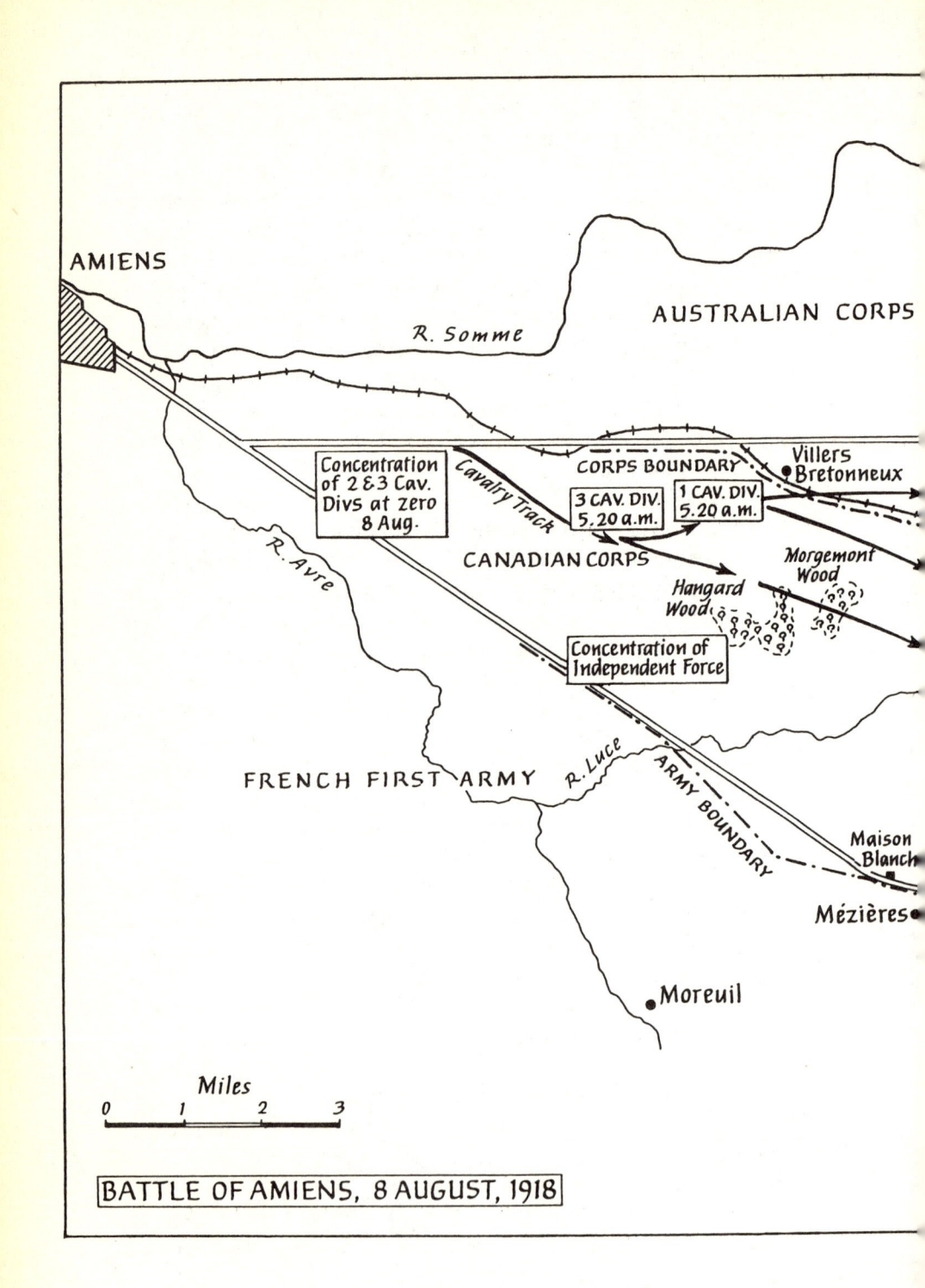

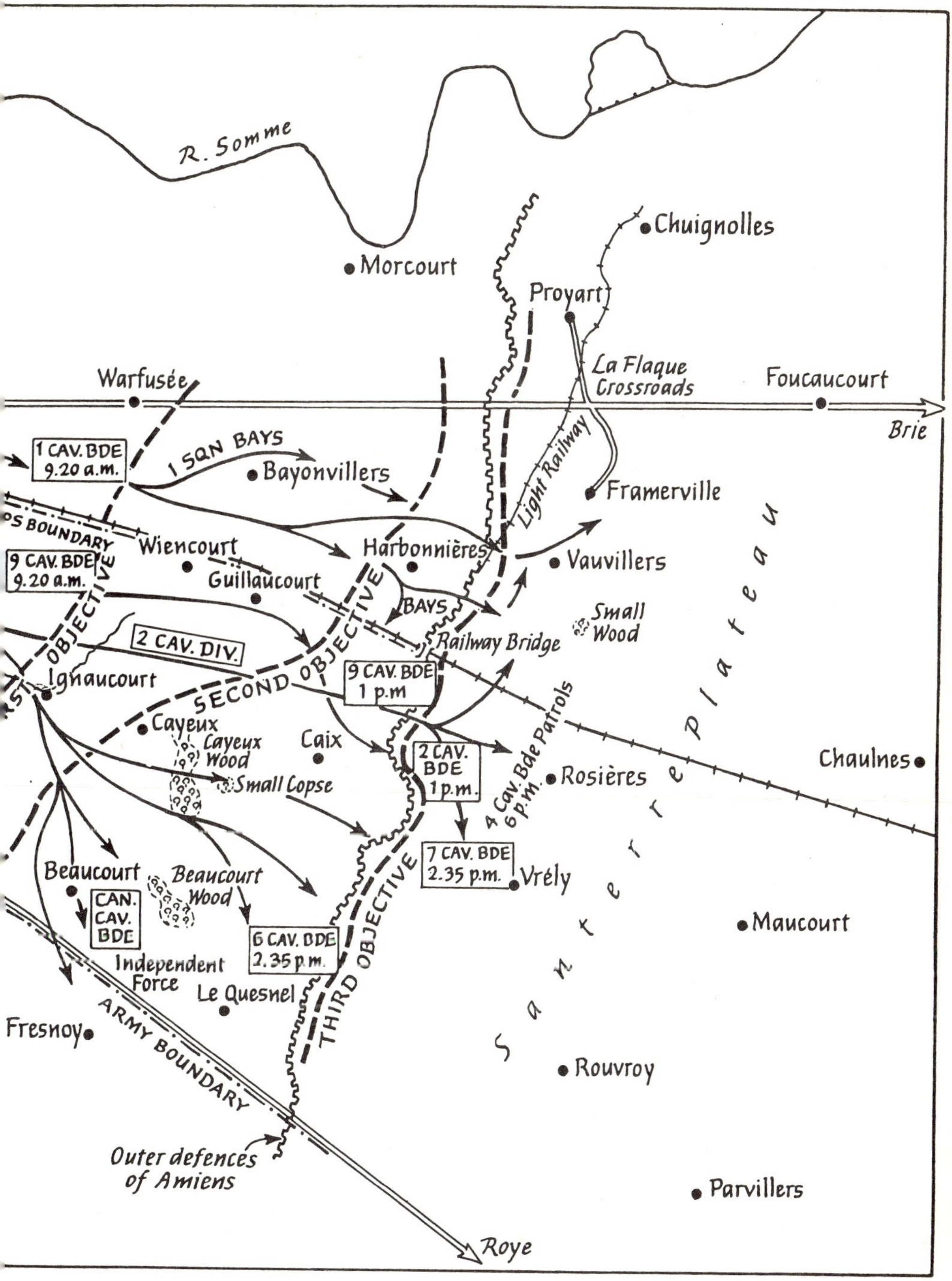
R. Somme
Morcourt
Chuignolles
Proyart
La Flaque Crossroads
Warfusée
Foucaucourt
Brie
1 CAV. BDE 9.20 a.m.
1 SQN BAYS
Bayonvillers
Light Railway
Framerville
S BOUNDARY
Wiencourt
Harbonnières
Vauvillers
9 CAV. BDE 9.20 a.m.
Guillaucourt
BAYS
Small Wood
Railway Bridge
2 CAV. DIV.
FIRST OBJECTIVE
SECOND OBJECTIVE
9 CAV. BDE 1 p.m.
Ignaucourt
Cayeux
Cayeux Wood
Caix
2 CAV. BDE 1 p.m.
4 Cav. Bde Patrols 6 p.m.
Rosières
Chaulnes
Small Copse
Santerre plateau
7 CAV. BDE 2.35 p.m.
Vrély
Beaucourt
Beaucourt Wood
CAN. CAV. BDE
THIRD OBJECTIVE
Maucourt
6 CAV. BDE 2.35 p.m.
Independent Force
Le Quesnel
Fresnoy
ARMY BOUNDARY
Rouvroy
Outer defences of Amiens
Parvillers
Roye

seventy-two were Whippets and 120 were supply tanks. There were also about twenty-four armoured cars. Close at hand were four reserve infantry divisions. The artillery numbered 2,070 guns, including howitzers. In the air 1,904 Allied aeroplanes faced only 365 of the enemy. The RAF possessed a local superiority of seven to one. A squadron was allotted to the Cavalry Corps* of which a part was detailed to drop ammunition to the machine-gun squadrons by small parachutes.[5]

On Fourth Army's left was the Australian Corps and beyond it to the north came III Corps, acting as 'virtually a gigantic flank guard'.[6] On the Australians' right came the Canadian Corps. An American division was in reserve. The French First Army was on the right.

* * *

On 1 August Haig impressed on Kavanagh that 'the training of the troop under its leader' as the basic tactical unit was vital from now onwards. So was direction from the front in the attack. Two days later Home wrote in his diary: 'The cavalry are about to go to war again, this time under the 4th Army.... If the Boche does not reinforce this front, all will be well.' Two days later he added: 'Provided a surprise is effected, we shall have a real good gallop. Secrecy is the main thing nowadays.'[7] Indeed, the lengths to which precautions were taken to deceive the enemy were prodigious. To detect the hand of Fourth Army's 'wily' commander is not difficult.[8] The chief ploy was to convince the enemy that an offensive was to be opened in Flanders. The Canadian Corps, which had not been much employed during the heavy fighting of the year and was actually over establishment, was to come under Fourth Army, and to share with the heavy tanks the brunt of the attack.†

---

*The machines of this squadron were to carry 'two streamers on both inside struts' as identification. (Fourth Army GS Instructions, 4 Aug., 1918, Edmonds: *1918*, IV, 558).

---

†To dupe the Germans into believing that this first-rate formation was about to be used to take Kemmel Hill, the key position of the northern front, was a major object. Two Canadian battalions were therefore put into the line opposite the hill, complete with a wireless station and casualty clearing stations. The whole of the corps was embussed northwards, but in the middle of the night the buses turned round and made for Amiens! (Anon: 'E.P.', 398) These ruses worked perfectly, as did many another intriguing stratagem.

Preparation of a cavalry track

One of the most difficult tasks was to conceal the assembling of the three cavalry divisions. As with all arms, movement was only allowed after dark. On the nights of 5 and 6 August all twenty-seven regiments, with their multitude of attendant divisional troops,* which had been stationed between Amiens and Flixécourt, moved into billets and bivouacs just west of Amiens. At dusk on the 7th they marched through the city, 'dark and silent', except for 'the continuous clatter of hoofs in the streets, deadened somewhat by a lavish sprinkling of sand'. They moved in 'one long column of sections, closed up nose to croup',[9] and assembled on open ground in the fork between the Villers Bretonneux and Roye roads, where the horses were watered. 'Eighteen miles of cavalry,' according to Home, 'passed one point between 10.00 p.m. and 6.00 a.m.,'[10] The Whippets joined the horsemen en route. The most careful timings and the strictest march discipline had to be achieved, for there was only one road out of Amiens and the regiments had to reach their positions by zero hour, 4.20 a.m. on 8 August. This target, in spite of 'much delay caused by numerous tanks',[11] was just about met.

At 7 p.m. on 7 August the Cavalry Corps engineers, with the help of an American engineer battalion, 'which had never been under fire before', continued in earnest the construction of a cavalry track up to and forward of the assembly positions (see map, p. 224). This had been begun the previous night by detachments from the cavalry regiments. The exact route of this track was painstakingly worked out so that the infantry through whose reserves the cavalry would have to pass were not interfered with and so as not to mask the massed artillery, much of which was only now getting into prepared positions. Work on the track continued through the front line as soon as the tanks and infantry attack had started. The track was so well made that wheeled vehicles and

---

*Each division was accompanied by its horse artillery brigade and its engineer and signal squadrons, RASC, motor transport and 'Auxiliary (Horse)' companies, field ambulances and veterinary sections.

Each regiment carried three days' iron rations and 20 lbs of oats per horse 'on man, horse and A2 Echelon'. To provide these there was an army reserve of 48,000 iron rations and as GHQ reserve 480,000 lbs of oats. For drinking water Cavalry Corps had twenty lorries. (Fourth Army Admin. Arrangements, 6 Aug., 1918, Edmonds, *1918*, IV, 564).

The Chestnut Troop, 'Q' and 'U' Batteries, RHA were brigaded separately under army and were put under the Australian Corps.

Rawlinson's Cavalry Corps HQ conference, 4 August, 1918

armoured cars had no difficulty in using it next morning. 'The mounted troops were quick to realize this and several of them gave the working parties thanks and cheers as they rode past them.'[12]

* * *

On 4 August Rawlinson, at Cavalry Corps headquarters, had explained to the cavalry divisional and brigade commanders what was expected of them. For the first time they were made aware both of the fact and also of the object of the offensive, which was to disengage Amiens and the Paris–Amiens railway. As at Cambrai there was to be no bombardment before zero hour. Again as at Cambrai the heavy tanks were to precede the infantry. So as to be in closest touch with the infantry the 3rd Cavalry Division with a battalion of Whippets was to be under the Canadian Corps,*

*To each of the three brigades of 3rd Cavalry Division sixteen Whippets (maximum speed seven mph.) were to be attached. (For how they fared see p. 234).

So as to avoid the Cambrai situation, the leading cavalry, instead of waiting for orders from the rear, was given a timetable for its advance from point to point. In many instances this timetable was in fact beaten. (Lumley, 366).

So as to indicate that 'advanced troops of cavalry are here' a 'white star turning to red on a parachute' was to be fired 'from a 1½ in. Very pistol'. (Fourth Army GS Instructions, 4 Aug., 1918, Edmonds: *1918*, IV, 554).

A Whippet Tank.

The battle of Amiens opens, 8 August, 1918

while more Whippets were to come under the Australian Corps on the left. As soon as they passed through the infantry, as opportunity offered, all these were to revert to Kavanagh's command. On 5 August final orders were issued. Once the cavalry had pushed through the infantry it was to hasten to the old Amiens Defence Line and hold it until relieved by the infantry. It was then, if so ordered, but not otherwise (but see p. 243), to press on south-eastwards at all speed towards the Roye–Chaulnes line and cut the enemy's communications, thus easing the situation in front of the French.* This second task, as will appear, it was unable to fulfil.

* * *

At 4.20 a.m., just before sunrise, the artillery opened a shattering rolling bombardment over a twelve-mile front and the tanks and infantry advanced – in a thick ground mist that did not entirely disperse until about 10 a.m. It was followed by day-long brilliant sunshine. The surprise was so complete that numbers of the enemy guns never came into action at all. The mist, indeed, enabled many of the tanks to overrun the batteries without a shot being fired at them. By 11.00 a.m. both the Australians and the Canadians were more or less on their second objectives.

'By this time... the whole Santerre plateau,' writes the Official Historian, 'seen from the air was dotted with parties of infantry, field artillery, cavalry and tanks moving forward. Staff officers were galloping about, many riding horses in battle for the first time, prisoners in formed companies marching back with hardly more escort than the Canadian wounded whom they were carrying, whilst overhead the planes of the R.A.F. were flying noisily to work. Indeed, at this stage there was more noise of movement than of firing, as the heavy batteries, almost wheel to wheel, with their muzzles cocked up to the highest elevation, were no longer in

---

*Since the French, as soon as they had taken the German lines, intended to put a heavy bombardment on all the villages in rear of their area, 'the British cavalry were ordered not to go south of the Amiens–Roye road.' (Fourth Army GS Instructions, 4 Aug., 1918, Edmonds, *1918*, IV, 559).

action; for the infantry had gone so far that it was no longer possible for them to shoot.'[13]*

He might have added that some of the cavalry were even further ahead.

* * *

At the conference on 4 August Rawlinson had told Harman, commanding 3rd Cavalry Division: 'I have decided that, if the bridges at Ignaucourt [three miles from the start line] are reported intact by your patrols, you will cross there and move south of the River Luce.'[14] A glance at the map on p. 224 will show how important these crossings were. If they had been destroyed, the division would have had to go round by Caix, four and a half miles further on.[15] Consequently, a patrol of the Fort Garry Horse was ordered to follow closely behind the infantry line 'with instructions to slip through at the earliest opportunity and report on the state of the bridges' direct to Harman. This it did, with admirable promptitude, at 9.15: 'one of them passable for Whippet tanks and both of them passable for cavalry'. It also reported that the tank and infantry attack had been a complete success and that the Germans were in full retreat.[16]

At 7.45 the Canadian Cavalry Brigade, closely followed by the 7th,† made its first bound towards Ignaucourt. As it came up immediately behind the infantry it found that the southern end of the Bois-de-Hangard was still being fought for as the leading troop arrived at its northern end. By 8.30 both it and the Bois-de-Morgement were clear. The two brigades advanced just to the east of the latter, where the Fort Garry Horse gave them the good news. Harman, on the spot, at once ordered a speedy further advance. At 9.20 Lord Strathcona's Horse began to cross the river. As they passed through the leading infantry they took forty-five prisoners

---

*The speed with which the thousands of horses needed to drag the field guns forward to new positions as each of the objectives was gained had never before been equalled. (Farndale: WF, 287)

†Temporarily commanded by Lieutenant-Colonel Ewing Paterson of the Inniskillings, not to be confused with Brigadier-General R.W. Paterson, commanding the Canadian Cavalry Brigade.

35. Field-Marshal Erich von Falkenhayn. (See p.36)

36. General Henri Pétain.

37. General Sir Hubert Gough, in 1932.

38. Field-Marshal Sir Henry Wilson.

39. Brigadier-General A.E.W. Harman. (See p.77)

40. Brigadier-General Ewing Paterson. (See p.151)

41. Haig inspecting a guard of honour with the King of Montenegro, 1916.

42. Haig talking to a French resident at a Horse Show near Arras, May, 1917.

43. Haig with Dominion journalists, September, 1918. Note his hand holding a journalist's arm in friendly embrace.

and a field gun. The 7th Brigade followed on and both brigades, together with their horse artillery and all their Whippets, were formed up ready to make for the second objective. From then on to the final objective brigades were to advance without further orders from division. Initial instructions to all units had made it clear that where opposition was encountered that front had to be 'picquetted lightly', while the remainder of the unit was to 'sideslip' until it found an opening.[17] The ground to be crossed was undulating and unfenced, with steep rises 'having small narrow crests on top. . . . As [the troops] topped the rises they could easily be seen by the Germans on the main crest from Beaucourt Wood to Cayeux Wood, who opened up on them with bursts of artillery and machine-gun fire; but owing to the rapid pace of the horsemen and the short time it took them to cross the exposed ridges, very few were hit.'[18] This is another instance of the speed of cavalry limiting casualties.

The Strathconas with eight Whippets pushed on well ahead to the extreme right and by 10.35 reached the Amiens–Roye road, near Maison Blanche, without difficulty. Here they made contact with an 'Independent Force', made up of Canadian motor machine guns, cyclists and trench mortars mounted on lorries, operating along the road 'to form a flank to the Candian Corps' attack, and if possible help the cavalry'.[19] They then crossed the Fourth Army boundary with the French and took 125 prisoners near Fresnoyen-Chaussée, two and a half miles due south of Ignaucourt. On their way there they took another forty-five prisoners. The Strathcona's historian of the regiment tells what happened next:

> 'Two troops moved on the wood 1,500 yards east of Beaucourt which position was found to be strongly held by machine guns. The latter two troops located the enemy line, which was in small pits extending from 1,000 yards west of Le Quesnel. This party lost most of their horses from machine-gun fire and suffered heavy casualties.
>
> 'At once, the tanks advanced against this position followed by a patrol of the second squadron. Heavy fire was concentrated upon the tanks which were forced to retire, the patrol in turn all becoming casualties.
>
> 'Enemy artillery fire was then opened upon the Strathcona's from the south and German infantry were seen advancing from the southeast.

'A battery of the Royal Canadian Horse Artillery was then put into position close to the Roye Road northeast of Mezières and the position organized for defence in the valley. Small parties were sent out to round up prisoners between Mezières and Fresnoy. These parties brought in 70 of the enemy. A large number of machine guns were put out of action and left on the ground.

'Later touch was obtained with the Royal Canadian Dragoons on the left and the position held until taken over by the 4th Canadian Infantry Division, their advance guard reaching our position at 3.00 p.m.

'Instructions were sent to Lord Strathcona's Horse to concentrate in the valley northeast of Beaucourt as soon as they were satisfied that the infantry line was safe, and they withdrew at about 5.00 p.m., the French 322nd Infantry Regiment having in the meantime taken over our portion of the position that was south of the Roye road.

'During this period the enemy made two endeavours to force the position from the direction of Fresnoy, but with the assistance of the Independent Force they were prevented from advancing.'[20]

This account is given in full as it so graphically illustrates the type of action the cavalry was engaged in on this eventful day.

Elsewhere on the 3rd Cavalry Division's lines of advance, things were less easy. The Royal Canadian Dragoons, with eight whippets, were held up north-west of Beaucourt Wood by Germans in a line of rifle pits. When the Whippets tried to reach the wood artillery fire drove them back. At about midday the dragoons made a gallant but futile attempt to gallop the wood. An officer of the Royal Canadian Horse Artillery witnessed this. 'I now know,' he wrote in his diary that evening, 'what it is like to gallop through machine-gun fire and it's not pleasant.' Beaucourt itself, with the help of the machine-gun squadron, was taken just as the enemy was trying to leave it. Nearly 300 prisoners were captured there.[21] However, as the Official Historian puts it: 'any attempt to approach le Quesnel [just before the third objective], the ground in front of which was level and devoid of any sort of cover, encountered very strong resistance and came under fire from Fresnoy, which the French had not yet occupied. Beaucourt Wood was not taken until infantry came up later; Fresnoy not until 9.30, and Le

Quesnel remained at the close of the day in the enemy's hands.'[22]

To the Canadians' left the 7th Brigade had advanced with the Inniskillings on the right, the 7th Dragoon Guards on the left (each regiment with a sub-section of machine guns) and the 17th Lancers behind them, with 'K' Battery, RHA, the remainder of the machine-gun squadron and twelve Whippets. The Inniskillings almost at once found themselves under artillery and long-range machine-gun fire. They increased their pace and soon found themselves near Beaucourt Wood and in touch with the Canadians who, as has been shown, were held up there. They were fortunate in finding a steep bank behind which to take cover. Beside several prisoners, they captured an anti-tank gun.[23]

Seeing the fire to which the Inniskillings had been subjected Paterson, the brigade commander, ordered the 7th Dragoon Guards 'to change direction half left'; this brought the regiment 'facing nearly due east, towards the stretch of open ground between Beaucourt and Cayeux Woods.' Paterson describes what happened next:

> 'The two leading squadrons had become echeloned, the leading squadron some 150 yards in front of the second squadron, and on rising over the last crest its squadron leader grasping that the small copse south of Bois-de-Cayeux was the key of the position, without a moment's hesitation gave the order to charge, and with one loud yell the squadron were down the hill, across the open space, up the rise and into the copse, capturing the key to the position, some dozen maxims, a couple of guns and some fifty prisoners.
>
> 'O.C. 7th Dragoon Guards almost simultaneously directed the second squadron on to the open crest line between the copse already captured and the Bois-de-Cayeux, and they, in the same gallant manner as the first squadron, charged straight for the position, which they successfully captured, and had at one time a large number of maxims and close on a hundred prisoners; they, however, owing to the heavy cross fire from Bois-de-Beaucourt, had to retire below the crest line and many of the prisoners escaped.
>
> 'The 3rd Squadron was now directed by the O.C. Regiment on to the south-western edge of the Bois-de-Cayeux, which they occupied in spite of the heavy fire of the enemy, and captured a battery of guns, some half-dozen maxims, and

a number of prisoners, and also found the complete equipment of some two hundred men, who had evidently bolted when they saw the rapid movement of the horse soldiers.'

It seems almost superfluous to say that the 7th suffered a considerable number of casualties in both men and horses during these charges. Seven officers were wounded, five other ranks killed and thirty-six wounded. They were heroic examples of cavalry using its initiative, yet, as in so many cases since 1914, it is hard to believe that in the face of stubborn machine-gunners either the charges or the casualties were really justified.[24]*

It was at this point of the battle that the cooperation between the cavalry and the Whippets broke down. Those Whippets that were attached to the 7th Brigade failed entirely to keep up with its speedy movements. Across undulating country their speed was not more than half its nominal seven mph. Had they been on hand they might well have provided effective covering fire and have put at least some of the machine guns out of action. There seems to have been 'a certain amount of mutual recrimination'[25] resulting from this lack of cooperation. The 7th's dilatory Whippets, in fact, drove southwards and gave substantial aid to the Canadian Brigade's attacks on Beaucourt and Beaucourt Wood, losing seven tanks. Thus, acting on their own, they proved themselves. It seems foolish to have placed the Whippets under the Cavalry Corps. When not under fire the cavalry would always be too fast for the Whippets and when under fire it would be unable to follow them. Of course, the Whippets were a very new weapon. They had only been twice in action before Amiens and there had been virtually no cooperative training between the two, because there was not enough time. As early as January, though, a number of cavalry officers had been transferred to the Whippet units, precisely so as to promote co-operation. Fuller suggests that had the Whippets been on their own, and especially had they been given their head from zero hour and not held back until the cavalry started off, they could have advanced through the gap made by the heavy tanks and infantry 'and taken the whole of the German forces opposing the French' by moving south-eastward towards Roye. 'Chaos,' he says, 'would have resulted . . . and quite possibly the German

---

*For many years after the war 8 August was observed as a regimental holiday. (Brereton, 339).

armies in France would have bled to death before the month was out.' Though this is clearly far too extreme a prophecy, it does seem that the Whippets, acting independently, might have been of very much greater use than they were as attached to the cavalry.* Nevertheless, it appears that it was Fuller himself who proposed to Rawlinson in a letter of 23 July that his light tanks should be used 'in conjunction with the cavalry to speed the advance ... and thwart any attempted German retirement'![26]

Paterson now ordered up the 17th Lancers, his brigade's reserve regiment. It at once broke into a gallop, 'squadrons in echelon from the right' on the 7th's left, and took possession of the remainder of Cayeux Wood. So as to exploit these two regiments' success from their 'favourable position on the high ground',[27] Paterson sent two officers to recall the Inniskillings from the right flank. One had his horse shot under him and was rendered unconscious. The other was killed. When it was clear that the message had not got through, the brigade-major galloped off and got through to the Canadian brigadier (the other Paterson), who had earlier asked the Inniskillings to cover his left flank. He at once released the regiment, which speedily rejoined the 7th Brigade. Before this happened, 'K' Battery, RHA, had taken up a position about 700 yards behind the 7th Dragoon Guards. This regiment, 'notwithstanding the stiff fight they had just been through, had remounted their horses and formed up for moving on.'[28] It had hardly done so when there developed a strong German counter-attack from Beaucourt Wood. This was beaten off with the help of 'K' Battery and the 7th Machine Gun Squadron, whose guns had been in reserve with the 17th Lancers.

That regiment at this moment reported the whole of the Cayeux Wood clear. Paterson therefore ordered it to picquet the northeastern edge of the wood with a small detachment and to advance with the rest of the regiment in place of the 7th Dragoon Guards who were now almost a spent force. Advancing as far as a small copse half a mile beyond the wood, the leading troop of the 17th almost immediately found itself under local machine-gun fire and, worse, heavy artillery fire from the direction of Caix. Both troop

---

*Fuller based his extravagant prognostication above on the operation of a single Whippet's amazing adventure. This tank *did* cause chaos a long way behind the enemy lines: a thrilling story, but one based largely on good luck and unlikely to be often repeated. (Fuller, 316–19).

officers were killed and their men 'practically wiped out'. Paterson, making a personal reconnaissance, had his and his orderly's horses killed.[29] Until the German machine guns between Caix and Cayeux could be silenced, no advance in that direction was possible. Consequently a squadron of the 17th was ordered to outflank them from the north. This side-slip was entirely successful and made it possible for the remainder of the regiment, followed by the rest of the brigade, to move south of Caix on to the final objective. This was reached at about 2.30 p.m. En route thirty-eight prisoners were taken, as well as two field guns, three machine guns, two complete field hospitals and a large amount of stores.

The officers of a Canadian infantry battalion which came up in the afternoon, stated 'that since capturing the enemy's front line at daybreak they had not set eyes on a German and thought that they had all gone for good. It was only as they went further and came upon the dead horses . . . that they realized what had happened.'[30] Indeed, as Paterson recorded: 'the lines of horses lay dead as though they had been pulled out, dressed in line and shot with a revolver.' Each of the 7th Brigade's squadrons that had charged had done so at the swiftest possible gallop, the majority of the casualties occurring when they were within fifty or sixty yards of the enemy's machine guns. These had no time to change their elevation and therefore fired too high until their last bursts reached the charging horsemen. 'Once the men were on top of the enemy,' says Paterson, 'they put up no fight and appeared completely demoralized.' He adds that a German officer, when asked why he and his men had surrendered, said, 'Look, look! Wherever you look you see British cavalry.'[31]

The 6th Cavalry Brigade came up to assist in holding the line of the final objective, all of which, except for the extreme southern portion of it around Le Quesnil, was now occupied. The Canadian Brigade's section of the trenches was taken over by infantry. Numerous mounted patrols which were sent eastwards 'could see nothing and were not fired on'.[32]

The casualties of the 7th Cavalry Brigade were not as numerous as might have been expected, except in horses. These numbered 303 killed and wounded, while only two officers were killed and thirteen wounded. Thirteen other ranks were also killed, ninety-six wounded and, surprisingly, twenty-six missing.[33] The Canadian Cavalry Brigade's losses for the day are not known.

The 3rd Cavalry Division, since crossing the start line, had advanced nearly eight miles as the crow flies. Since the open warfare of 1914, such progress had never been made in a single day. For the next day's operations the division was brought back into reserve.

* * *

When Mullens' 1st Cavalry Division, working with the Australian infantry, set off it knew that its task would be easier than that of the 3rd on its right. It had no river to cross. It could therefore advance with two of its brigades abreast. Further, the double-line railway from Amiens to Chaulnes lay nearly parallel to its line of advance which assisted it in keeping direction even in the thick mist. The 9th Brigade was on the right, the 1st on the left and the 2nd in reserve behind the 9th. The leading units crossed the front-line trenches at about 7.30 a.m. after wasting some time disposing of uncleared wire.[34] Each regiment was accompanied by four Vickers machine guns. At 9.20 the tanks and infantry reached Guillaucourt, four miles from the front-line trenches and one and a half miles from the first objective. The 9th Brigade (19th Hussars on the right and the 15th on the left, touching the railway) now passed through them, heartily cheered on their way by the Australians. The 8th Hussars, in reserve, followed on.

The 19th Hussars, at about 11.15, came under machine-gun fire just east of Guillaucourt but successfully side-stepped first northwards and then to the east and found shelter in a small valley. There they awaited the arrival of the Whippets which in due course put the enemy machine guns out of action. This enabled the regiment to carry on. Sergeant Brunton recorded in his diary that evening: 'The last mile of ground was taken at the charge, our officers cheering and the men shouting war cries. We had fought and rode hard all day and this last charge under heavy machine-gun fire was a fitting climax to a great and glorious cavalryman's day. A day we had all been praying for.'[35]

Meanwhile the advance squadron of the 15th Hussars arrived at Wiencourt to discover that the road between that village and Guillaucourt was under machine-gun fire. Undismayed, it crossed the 1,000 yards between the two villages 'at full gallop' and the following squadrons 'going as hard as they could swept into Guillaucourt.... There were practically no casualties and the men were able to reform behind the ruins of the village.' As the leading squadron pressed on it sent back reports that the enemy was in retreat and that the infantry were about to reach their second objective. The commanding officer now ordered the regiment to gallop on to the final objective. The regimental historian takes up the story:

' "B" and "C" Squadrons formed line of half squadrons, "B" Squadron on the left, and "C" Squadron on the right, with "A" Squadron in reserve. This formation was rapidly taken up, and the 15th Hussars, breaking into a fast gallop, dashed forward. There is little doubt many felt that this moment was worth all the years of waiting. As the 15th swept past the position just captured by the Canadians, these latter leapt to their feet, and loudly cheered the Regiment as it passed by.

'The distance to be covered was about two thousand yards, and almost at once the 15th came under machine-gun fire, a few men and horses fell, but the momentum was gained, the forward rush continued, and in a remarkably short time all squadrons reached their objectives, dismounted and occupied the old trenches [of Amiens' Outer Defences]. "C" Squadron came under heavy fire from the right in the valley of Guillaucourt, and the men were forced to dismount and reach their objective on foot, after having exchanged a few shots with the enemy, and with the help of the covering fire of the machine guns. "B" Squadron, whose objective was the railway bridge, found it to be held by the enemy; by a gallant charge they succeeded in obtaining a foothold on the bridge. For a time they had some difficulty in holding on, but finally the enemy was driven off and the position secured.

'Both squadrons reached the final objective by 11.30 a.m.'[36]

'C' Squadron had the double satisfaction of knocking out a German staff car and of capturing 'a complete motor-pigeon-loft, crowded with carrier pigeons. These pigeons were promptly killed and eaten by the troops who relieved the squadron in the evening.'[37]

The whole of the 9th Cavalry Brigade was firmly established on the final objective by 1 p.m. It had covered nearly eight miles as the pigeon flies in five and a half hours. The men were set to work improving the trenches of the old outer Amiens defences.* An hour earlier an aeroplane had landed at 9th Brigade's headquarters just east of Wiencourt.† Its wounded pilot reported that the enemy was on the run at least as far east as Rosières two miles east of the final objective. It is clear that, except for the stubborn bravery of the German machine gunners, the enemy's resistance to the cavalry, as also to the heavy tanks, had not been 'of a very desperate nature'.[38] In the course of the afternoon the 15th Hussars watched 'the less brave of the enemy leaving the battlefield in large numbers and the efforts of their officers to rally them could be clearly seen and caused some amusement to all ranks'.[39] The 1st Cavalry Division's reserve brigade, the 2nd, was now brought forward to fill a gap which had occurred east of Caix between the 7th and 9th Brigades. In the evening at about 6 p.m. its patrols were pushed out towards Rosières, which by then was firmly held by the enemy.

* * *

As the 15th Hussars occupied the final objective,§ it found the 3rd Cavalry Division already established to its right. The infantry and tanks had by then cleared most of the ground up to the second objective west of Harbonnières. To the south of that village the leading squadron of the Bays (2nd Dragoon Guards) of the 1st Cavalry Brigade was fired on by 'a party of the enemy. . . . Two troops immediately charged the Germans, who evidently had not much fight left in them, for they were driven off, leaving a score of dead on the ground.'[40] They took twenty-six prisoners and two machine guns. Earlier they had captured thirty prisoners and two trench mortars. The squadron then turned south towards a tunnel under the railway. Here a troop killed seven men, took two prisoners and two machine guns. Another troop nearby killed eight Germans and captured nine prisoners. The squadron was now

---

*'The 15th Hussars held a long line. . . . What with horse-holders and casualties none of the squadrons could muster more than twenty-five rifles.' (Carnock, 188)

†Each Whippet battalion had an aeroplane attached to it. This was one of them. (Edmonds: *1918*, IV, 55)

§At 5 p.m. the regiment was relieved by Canadian infantry and it concentrated south of Guillaucourt. (Carnock, 188)

joined by two Whippets whose commander said that he was about to attack the enemy between Harbonnières and Rosières. Two squadrons of the Bays agreed to co-operate, 'with a Whippet going forward right and left of them. But one of the tanks broke down and the other was knocked out by a direct hit with a shell.' A third which now came on the scene also broke down,[41] further evidence, perhaps, that Fuller's forecast (see p. 234) was too optimistic. The two squadrons immediately came under intense fire, three officers being among the wounded.

One of the squadrons, facing south, now held a line along the railway, 'with a patrol pushed forward to a bridge further down the railway'. From there, dismounted, some of the troops brought 'an effective rifle and Hotchkiss fire to bear upon the bodies of the enemy which were retiring towards Rosières'. Others, mounted, made 'a successful dash at two wagons that came within fairly easy reach of the position. Their escort was cut up and the wagons were captured, with the officer in charge of them.' Meanwhile the Australians threw the enemy out of Harbonnières and 'hoisted their Dominion flag on its church tower'. It was now coming up to 10 a.m. The reserve squadron of the Bays was then brought up and on the way 'captured a lorry loaded with officers' kits' emerging from Harbonnières. A tank's report that a counter-attack was about to be launched proved false, but patrols that tried to advance were instantly shot at. These two squadrons therefore remained where they were, in touch with the 15th Hussars, south of the railway.[42]

The squadron on the left meanwhile had advanced to the north of Bayonvillers and later dismounted to drive off a minor local counter-attack 'whilst the Australian infantry were digging themselves in behind'.[43] Before that, however, a patrol under Lieutenant Cockerill managed at about 11 a.m. to get behind the enemy, a good mile and a half beyond Harbonnières, striking the road between Vauvillers and Framerville.* The regimental historian states that it rounded up seventy-two stragglers, whom it passed back to the nearest Australians. Unfortunately, though, as it was reconnoitring Framerville, which it found to be held by the enemy, it was fired on by two armoured cars which were also well ahead

---

*Here it came into contact with the 5th Dragoon Guards and seems to have assisted that regiment in its remarkable exploit against a train (see below). (Preston: '1918' (2) II, 342)

The 5th Dragoon Guards at Harbonnières, 8 August, 1918

along the main road (see p. 240). 'After this experience, it was decided that it was time to turn back. The little party had to find their way back through the enemy.' This it eventually did.[44]

* * *

The first of all the cavalry to reach the final objective were the 5th Dragoon Guards. At 10 a.m. they moved off in 'double echelon of squadrons'[45] and rode through the Australians, reaching a point 1,000 yards beyond the second objective without the slightest opposition. There it came across Cockerill's patrol to the south of Harbonnières (see p. 240). 'C' Squadron was on the right, 'A' Squadron in the centre and 'B' Squadron in advance on the left. According to Captain Henry Ormsby Wiley, commanding 'C' Squadron, who witnessed what took place, 'A' Squadron, though fired on by machine guns, ignored them and rode on to the final objective which it found unoccupied. It crossed the trenches and was shot at from a train on a light railway which ran south westwards from Proyart. At about 10.30, according to the official RAF historian, two Sopwith 'Camel' pilots, 'flying in search of targets east of Harbonnières, saw three trains near the village. . . . Each pilot dropped four 25-lb bombs from a height of 100 feet' and set one of them on fire. The two other trains apparently began to steam away but the third, carrying mostly men who had just returned from leave, was brought to a halt. It is not clear whether 'A' Squadron managed to stop and do damage to the two moving trains. What is certain is that they overran the halted one and managed to kill, wound or capture all its occupants as they tried to escape towards Framerville.[46] The squadron at once continued its advance, braved further machine-gun fire and reached the Vauvillers–Framerville road, beyond which, it seems, it was not authorized to advance. Here it dismounted and brought heavy fire to bear on the retreating enemy, capturing, beside numerous prisoners, a 5.9 in. howitzer, two field guns, two anti-aircraft guns, two lorries, as well as the staff (including some female nurses) and patients of a casualty clearing station numbering about 180 men in all. Captain Wiley's account continues:

' "B" Squadron . . ., having helped to round up the Germans escaping from the train, advanced over the Vauvillers– Framerville road and then swung south towards the small wood 1,300 yards S.S.E. of Vauvillers, killing many of the retiring enemy and capturing some transport. However, the wood was wired and full of machine guns, its defence being – so it was said – organized by a divisional general who was thought to be Austrian. The squadron, therefore... wheeled round and joined "A" Squadron.

'Turning now to "C" Squadron – which moved on the right with regimental headquarters – they captured a light engine and some trucks before reaching the Amiens Outer Defence line which they crossed. Heavy enfilade machine-gun and rifle fire was now turned upon them from the right flank and they were thereupon ordered to swing left-handed and occupy the trench line. This proved to be a difficult operation owing to the heavy fire, under which the led horses had to recross the trench, and a number of men were hit.

'The defence of the trench was then organized, some more Germans found in it being captured, whilst a message was sent back to 1st Cavalry Brigade headquarters asking for reinforcements; meanwhile a heavy machine-gun fire was kept up on the trench on the right. Several small parties of the enemy just in front of the trench were attacked and taken prisoner.

'Just about an hour had now elapsed since the regiment had passed through the infantry. At 11 a.m. the Australians came up and took over the trench from "C" Squadron which withdrew, joining up with the other two squadrons and concentrating north-west of Harbonnières.'[47]

All three squadrons were much depleted by this time. Their casualties amounted in all to the remarkably small number of sixty-two, including one officer and six other ranks killed. Of their horses 122 were killed, wounded or missing. 'A' Squadron, which started the day ninety strong, suffered only five casualties. Considerable numbers of men 'had to be detached for prisoner escort duty, destroying material, searching headquarters for important documents and so forth.' The extent of the regiment's success can be gauged by the fact that it captured and brought back, or obtained signatures for, twenty officer and 740 other rank prisoners, fifty horses and five wagons. It had covered a good six and a half miles in five hours, forty minutes. The honours and awards that were showered upon it were perhaps, even by the generous standards of the war, excessive: two DSOs, five MCs for the officers and five DCMs and seventeen MMs for the other ranks.[48]

* * *

Hearing that the 1st Cavalry Brigade was now short of men and that there was strong enemy resistance east and south of Vauvillers, Mullens, with Kavanagh's approval, decided soon after noon to commit his reserve division, the 2nd. He ordered it to 'prolong the right of the 9th Cavalry Brigade and get in touch with the left of the 3rd Cavalry Division'. It therefore rode to the north of Caix and at about 1.45 crossed the final objective. Soon after 4 p.m., with the 3rd Hussars leading, the 4th Cavalry Brigade pushed out patrols towards Rosières and as far south as Vrély. At Rosières they found enemy infantry reinforcements arriving in numbers by bus. Both villages were clearly strongly held. It was probably at this point, while the men of the 2nd Division were manning the trenches, that a pilot of a damaged Sopwith 'Camel' landed in front of their outposts, joined them 'and, shouldering a rifle, took part in the fighting'.[49]

Here there seems to have been an unfortunate series of misunderstandings and accidents. The Fourth Army orders of 6 August clearly stated that 'Cavalry Corps, as soon as they have accomplished their first mission, will push forward in the direction of the line Roye–Chaulnes with the least possible delay.' Yet, according to the Official Historian, Cavalry Corps gave no orders 'to go farther'. At 12.30 Rawlinson told Kavanagh that the cavalry was to push on at once to the Roye–Chaulnes line. The historian of the 11th Hussars says that 'so rapid had been the cavalry advance that the headquarters of the cavalry divisions had outstripped cable communications [and] that this message did not reach [them] until 4.15', by which time, of course, the stiffening enemy opposition had been going on apace for some hours. It appears that Kavanagh may have thought it wise to ignore Fourth Army's order and to keep control of the further advance in his own hands, or, alternatively, that Rawlinson had verbally modified his order of 6 August. Whatever the truth, it is likely that there never was a real hope of the cavalry alone making progress much beyond the trench system of the final objective. There is considerable evidence that quite early on in the day enemy reinforcements were arriving on the scene in numbers.[50] The inadequacy of communications on

8 August well illustrates how in this respect as in many others the staffs were not yet thinking in terms of fast-moving warfare. 'The limit of speaking on cable had been reached and passed.' Wireless, though employed more than hitherto, was still pretty primitive and unreliable. Motor-cycle despatch riders, motor cars and officers on horseback were the sole reliable means of communication between leading formations and headquarters.[50]*

At 2.15 Kavanagh, who until now, by design, had taken little part in directing the day's operations, gave the 4th Cavalry Brigade verbal orders to 'seize the high ground beyond Caix' and shortly before 6 p.m. the 3rd Hussars joined the other regiments of the division in trying to get forward towards Rosières and Vrély, but, of course, without success. For the night, the 2nd Cavalry Division took over from the 3rd which came into Corps reserve. The horses had mostly been without water all day. Now, until late in the night, when water carrying lorries arrived, they had had to depend on inadequate wells and ponds in the villages. Neither they nor the men had much rest that night.[51]

The exploits of the 17th Armoured Car Battalion are worth noticing. There were twelve cars. (Some sources say sixteen). Each was equipped with Hotchkiss guns, one in each of two turrets. The 'tourist chassis' and engine were protected by thin steel plates. They were capable of a maximum speed of 20 mph both forwards and backwards. Allotted to the 5th Australian Division, their orders were to race along the Roman road from Amiens towards Brie and to try to disrupt enemy communications. In this they were remarkably successful. By 7.40 a.m. they had reached Warfusée, 'towed [in some cases] by tanks over the broken roads'. After being shot at by British artillery, which seems to have done no damage, they soon got ahead of the infantry in the valley south of Morcourt. There they 'obtained splendid targets on the German troops massing in it, causing confused movements amongst them which called to mind,' as the Official Historian puts it, 'the disturbance of an ant heap'.[52]

Near the La Flaque crossroads they put a train out of action and fired on large dumps. They then drove on as far as Foucaucourt, over 4,000 yards beyond the final objective, where they had a fight

---

*In the Australian sector mounted orderlies of the 13th Australian Light Horse 'were constantly used as despatch riders'. (Bean, C.E.W. *The Australian Imperial Force in France*, VI, 545).

with some guns, sent back some prisoners and lost one car. En route they divided into two sections since the road was blocked 'by press of vehicles trying to escape'. One motored on northwards to Chuignolles where it threw long transport columns, 'moving without any precautions', into confusion before returning to the road. Another section went south to Framerville and surprised the advanced headquarters of the German LI Corps, where plans of the up-to-date Hindenburg Line were seized. The importance of these is hard to exaggerate. They showed all the trenches, wire, battery positions, barrage lines, headquarters, and even machine gun emplacements, as well as much else. Lieutenant-Colonel E.J. Carter, commanding the battalion, tells what happened next: 'They found all the Boche horse transport and many lorries drawn up in the main road ready to move off. Head of column tried to bolt in one direction and other vehicles in another. Complete confusion. Our men killed the lot (using 3,000 rounds) and left them there; four staff officers on horseback shot also. The cars then ran down to the east side of Harbonnières . . . and met there a number of steam wagons; fired into their boilers causing an impassable block.' By the day's end nine of the cars were out of action, eight requiring only slight repairs. Carter's was towed home across the final objective 'by prisoners he had taken'.[53] This exciting example of a 'gap' being exploited is recited here to show what lightly armoured vehicles could do in the way of pursuit. It is interesting to consider whether, had they been more numerous and had they possessed wide pneumatic tyres and lower reduction gears, they might not have been able under modern fire conditions to perform nearly all the functions of cavalry.

* * *

Haig felt sure 'that without the rapid advance of the cavalry the effect of the surprise attack on the 8th would have been much less'. Though from his diary there is evidence that he and Rawlinson on 5 August had an argument as to the scale and value of the role intended for them, even Rawlinson believed after the battle that the cavalry had done 'splendid work'. Nevertheless neither Byng nor Rawlinson, whose armies were to be employed in the coming offensives, right up to the war's end, gave the cavalry, as will be shown, much of a part in them.[54] At Cavalry Corps headquarters Home summed up the day's work, in which only four of the nine cavalry brigades had been seriously engaged, thus, 'The prisoners came in in fifties and hundreds with two men guarding them. They had no real heart; some of our men told me that they put up their hands at once. It has been a great day. We might have done better of course, but in war decisions are made with eyes blindfolded.'[55]

The Canadians and the Australians between them took prisoner 297 officers and 12,661 other ranks as well as 334 guns and many hundreds of smaller trophies. Their losses were under 3,000. The cavalry's losses for the day are not specified, but for 8, 9 and 10 August, at which last date it was withdrawn (see below), they amounted to 1,052, of whom 117 were killed. These losses were serious, for there was little prospect of their being made good. The horse casualties were 521 in the 7th and 9th Cavalry Brigades alone. The total therefore is likely to have been not much less than 800. Over 2,800 horses had been lost in March and April. By 19 August the Corps was still 1,100 short and, according to Home, 'not likely to get them!!!' Something like 3,000 prisoners were taken, the 1st Cavalry Division alone obtaining receipts from the infantry* for 1,361 on the 8th and 9th. The total number of Germans killed and wounded is not certain, but that it was very large is not doubted. The official German estimate puts it at about 27,000, of which two-thirds were prisoners. The short-term objects of the battle, the freeing of Amiens and the vital Paris railway from artillery fire were both fully achieved and were to be made even more sure in following days. Nevertheless, a genuine breakthrough was not attained, nor was it to be, right up to the end. Yet, as Liddell Hart put it in 1930: 'The 8th of August is a date which grows ever larger on the horizon of the historian . . . [It is] a proof that the moral element dominates warfare.'[56]

* * *

At a conference on 11 August, Kavanagh tackled Wilson 'on the question of doing away with the Cavalry Corps and [H]enry [W]ilson said that he intended doing so. Home's comment was: 'They will regret it.'[57]

---

*An order specifying that 'infantry divisions will take over prisoners captured by the cavalry and give receipts for the numbers' was issued on 6 August. In the stress of battle, these receipts were not, of course, by any means always given. (Fourth Army Admin. Arrangements, Edmonds: *1918*, IV, 571).

9

'On more than one critical occasion Haig by strenuous insistence deflected the plans of the Supreme Commander with results which were glorious.'
– CHURCHILL in *The World Crisis, 1916–1918*

'We are engaged in a "wearing out" battle and are outlasting and beating the enemy. If we allow the enemy a period of quiet, he will recover, and the "wearing out" process must be recommenced.'
– HAIG in his diary, 21 August, 1918

'The Cavalry Corps was now so weak in proportion to the total size of the army that it could hardly be counted on as a really formidable offensive weapon.'
– LIEUTENANT-COLONEL T. PRESTON in the *Cavalry Journal*, 1935

'Our shortage of cavalry is daily becoming more noticeable, and there is no doubt that your predecessor committed a serious error in sending off to Palestine two cavalry divisions last February. I hear that they are doing little or nothing there.'
– HAIG to Wilson, 1 September, 1918

'If we act with energy now, a decision can be obtained in *the very near future*.'
– HAIG in his diary on 10 September, 1918

'[Haig] showed me the order he had just given for three British armies to attack simultaneously and pointing to the German lines, Siegfried, Wotan, Brunhilde, Hindenburg, etc., with which the map was scored, he said: "Now you will see what all these fortifications are worth when troops are no longer resolved to defend them."'
– CHURCHILL in late August, 1918

'The discipline of the German Army is quickly going.... *It seems to me to be the beginning of the end.*'
– HAIG's account of his meeting with Milner on 10 September, 1918[1]

End of battle of Amiens – 2nd Cambrai and 2nd Le Cateau

The 8th of August was the last day with the exception, possibly, of 9 October (see p. 263), on which the British Cavalry was able to play any truly significant part in the great Allied advance to victory. This is why so much space has been devoted to it in Chapter 8. As will be seen there were moments, especially in the very last days of the war, when splendid but minor mounted attacks were made with some success. Otherwise from 9 August onwards the mounted arm's chief use was for occasional patrolling and reconnaissance. Of the few exceptions an action on 10 August is of interest. On that day a most unrealistic order reached the 4th Cavalry Brigade. It was to ride from Vrély and 'proceed to seize and hold Nesle' which was eleven miles to the east! 'C' Squadron of the 3rd Hussars led the way through the maze of old trenches and barbed wire. It encountered little opposition till just past Rouvroy (see map p. 225) where 'a perfect hell arose'. The squadron was caught in an ambush. 'Machine-gun bullets,' according to Hector Bolitho in his excellent history of the regiment, 'tore at them from the front and flanks and a tornado of shrapnel burst overhead. Stout wire fences bounded each side of the narrow road, so all they could do was to turn about and retire, which they did "in perfect order".' The few minutes on the Parvillers road cost the squadron thirty-four casualties and the loss of thirty-three horses. It seems that the regiment had been told, as so often before, that the villages they were to pass through were in British hands![2] On the 9th a squadron of the 16th Lancers also made a fruitless and costly charge. Next day a squadron of the 9th Lancers did the same. The Fort Garry Horse tried on this day to get on but with the same fate, losing forty-five of all ranks and 112 horses.[3]

It was on 10 August that a German regiment 'moving up through troops in flight was shouted at thus, "We thought that we had set the thing going; now you asses are corking up the hole again." The history of the crack Alpine Corps says: "All ranks in large parties were wandering wildly about, but soon for the most part finding their way to the rear." This was . . . at a detraining station seven miles from the front, but under air attack.' It is little wonder that four days later the Kaiser said 'that a suitable time must be chosen to come to an understanding with the enemy'.[4]

* * *

Though the Cavalry Corps was so small a part of the BEF, Haig, if not most of his army commanders, believed that the time would still come when it would be able to carry out its chief object: the pursuit of a demoralized enemy and the disruption of his communications. There are grounds for supposing that, had the war been carried on well beyond the Armistice, when it is reasonable to conclude that the German army would have undergone a near total collapse, there might have come a moment when this would have been possible. Of course, with only three cavalry divisions at a time when, from September onwards, over ninety divisions on both sides were sometimes actively engaged on the same day, it is doubtful whether the Corps could have caused much damage except on a very limited front. Yet, it should be remembered that there was in being no other fast-moving mobile force anywhere available except for the tiny, road-bound armoured car battalions. That Haig was right to retain his small body of horsemen has often been contested, but chiefly by historians who knew that in the event there was to be no important role for them. To say that they would have been better employed as machine gunners or infantry or in the Tank Corps is not only to be wise after the event, but also to overlook the fact that so small a number could hardly have made more than a trivial contribution to the manpower problem – a problem which was becoming daily less pressing. Further, as earlier on, units' mobility on a number of occasions produced extra rifle strength at critical moments and in crucial places, when and where infantry could not arrive in time.

* * *

The map on p. 250 shows how much further the British advanced during the rest of the battle of Amiens, which was brought to an effective close on 12 August. Since the opposition was stiffening day by day this was a wise decision. Before he could make it, Haig had his worst struggle with Foch, who wanted the continuation of the battle. That Haig got his way is a tribute to the generalissimo's good sense. It heralded the so-called strategy* which was perhaps more forced on Foch than initiated by him

---

*In his diary Haig described Foch's initial strategy as 'a simple straightforward advance by all troops on the western front and to keep the enemy on the move'. (Aug., 1918, quoted in Cooper, II, 354)

THE ALLIED ADVANCE, 1918

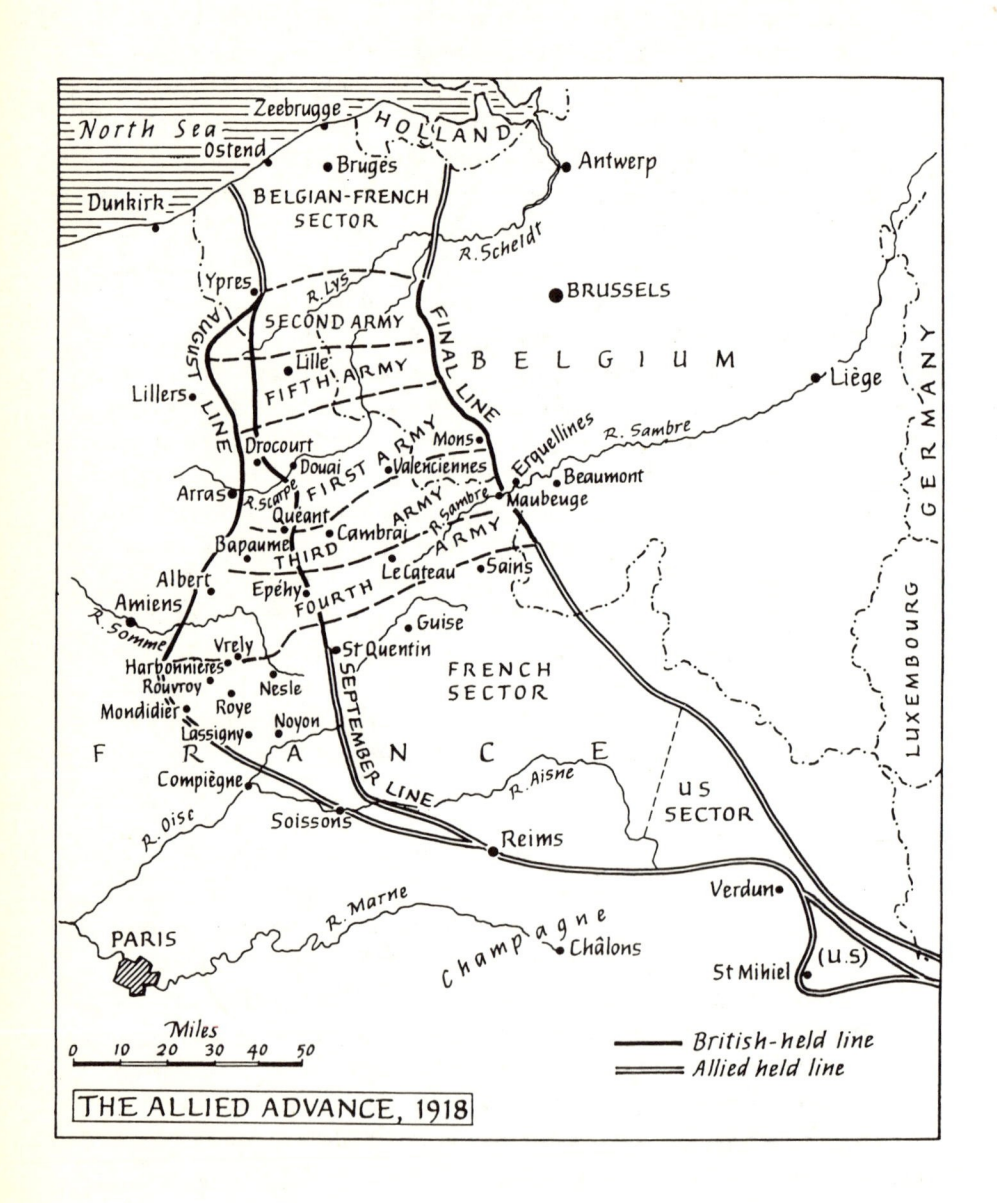

(though this is a much debated question). In fact this strategy was already beginning to be put into effect. (See below). The idea, as first mooted at the conference on 24 July (see p. 222), was to launch surprise offensives in as quick succession as possible at as many different points as possible and to close them down as soon as enemy reserves had been brought to bear, thus ensuring that the German ability to move divisions around effectively was tested to breaking point. It was similar, on a vast strategic scale, to the side-stepping tactics impressed and acted upon by the British cavalry on 8 August.

* * *

The realization of the new strategy was started by the French with the 2nd battle of Lassigny on 9 August which was broken off five days later. On 21 August Haig launched the battle of Bapaume and brought it to an end ten days later. In the course of it the First Army on 25 August advanced four miles down the Cambrai road over the old Arras battlefield. The battle of the Scarpe started on 26 August and ended on 1 September. Nine days later the six-day battle of Epéhy began. By its end the Germans were back to the strong defences of the Hindenburg Line. The American two-day offensive to pinch out the St Mihiel salient in the south was launched on 12 September. It was the first important achievement of the Americans as an independent army. On 18 September the BEF advanced on a sixteen-mile front north-west of St Quentin. On 26 September the great French-American offensive in Champagne was launched on a forty-mile front. It went on until 12 October. On 27 September the French battle of St Quentin and the British second battle of Cambrai commenced, both ending on 5 October. The six-day second battle of Le Cateau (see below) was halted on 12 October.* On 14 October the great Allied offensive in Flanders, under the King of the Belgians, was initiated, the BEF taking Lille and entering Douai. The Belgians, having occupied Zeebrugge, stormed Bruges. (See endpaper map). On 26 October Ludendorff resigned. His armies had suffered defeat after defeat. Yet even by the advent of what Haig in his despatch categorized as the open country phase starting on 8 October they were still a long way from being sufficiently broken to be cut

*2nd Cambrai and 2nd Le Cateau were really two parts of the one offensive.

Amiens, 8–12 August, 1918: cavalry's last actions

down by sabre and lance, even had the supply situation been favourable for such an operation, which, as will be seen, it emphatically was not.

* * *

The part played by the British cavalry between the second week of August and the first week of October was not great. It is nevertheless worth looking at, since it has never before been seriously considered.[5]

Patrols sent out by the 1st Cavalry Division on 9 August were invariably met with machine-gun fire. It was therefore decided that morning that all the cavalry should from now onwards follow, not precede, the tanks and infantry, hoping that it might find opportunities to pass through them. A patrol of the 8th Hussars managed to get as far as Vauvillers, 2,000 yards east of Harbonnières. The fact that it was fired on 'all the time it was out'[6] well illustrates how hopeless the cavalry's task was. Another attempt to get forward in front of the infantry was made by the 9th Lancers of the 2nd Cavalry Brigade but with the same fruitless result. From now onwards the virtually impassable terrain of the 1916 and 1917 battles had been reached. On the 10th the Fort Garry Horse made a mounted charge straight down the road to Roye, with the inevitable result that many horses and a number of men became casualties. This was the last spurt made by the cavalry in the battle of Amiens. (See map, p. 225). A GHQ order for the Cavalry Corps to advance on the 11th was only cancelled when Home motored to Fourth Army headquarters 'and pointed out that, apart from the increased enemy resistance, the ground was quite impassable for large bodies of cavalry: the order was therefore cancelled.'[7] When, soon after midday on 12 August, orders for the withdrawal of the cavalry were received, its part in the battle of Amiens was over. Had the ground been perfect, it is just possible that on the 9th and 10th the horsemen could have manoeuvred to avoid and outflank the machine gunners, but these indomitable men were probably by then becoming much too numerous and ubiquitous. As it was the tanks and infantry too were finding it hard to cope with the appalling terrain.

* * *

The battle of Bapaume, 21–22 August, 1918

Because of the total unsuitability of the terrain, minimum use of the mounted arm was made in the coming battles – until the second week in October. The shifting of Haig's attacks to the north and to the Third Army sector resulted on 21 August in the battle of Bapaume. Before the offensive started, he warned Byng, rather unfairly, against 'a repetition of the loss of opportunity which had occurred in the Fourth Army' in the battle of Amiens. He was dismayed, too, to learn that Byng 'had only arranged to use about a brigade of cavalry. I told him,' he wrote in his diary on 19 August, 'that the Cavalry Corps is now 100% better than it was at Cambrai. *He must use the cavalry to the fullest extent possible.* . . . I ordered him to detail a cavalry regiment to each corps . . ., because the enemy's *line of resistance* may have been withdrawn some distances from our front trenches, and it will be necessary to push forward *Advance Guards* of all arms to reconnoitre.'[8]

Once the battle had started he issued on 22 August a directive to his army commanders and to Kavanagh. This entreated every division to press on even if its flank 'is thereby exposed for the time being' (as both flanks had been on 8 August by the tardiness of the French on the right and by III Corps (due to special difficulties) on the left). He further made it clear that 'risks which a month ago would have been criminal to incur ought now to be taken as a duty'.[9] Neither he nor Foch took into full account that the Germans, owing to the reserves at their disposal and by thinning unattacked fronts, were able to attain actual numerical superiority in divisions over the Third and Fourth Armies and that, though these enemy divisions were weaker in men and often greatly so in morale than the British divisions, their superiority in machine guns, though not in artillery, was considerable.

In the Bapaume battle, though the 1st Cavalry Division was employed initially, by about 4.30 on its first day it was manifest that its withdrawal was in every way desirable. It could only advance at a slow walk through the endless trench, wire and shellhole obstacles and was proving therefore more of a hindrance than a help. Moreover, the question of moving the supply columns forward was becoming acute. It was a problem that was to get worse as time went on. The enemy's destruction of roads, railways, bridges and pollution of water supplies as they withdrew was systematic and almost total. For the cavalry lack of water was a crucial factor from now until well into October and to some degree beyond.

The Northumberlands' charge near the 'Happy Valley', 22 August, 1918

On 21 August the 4th Dragoon Guards and the 8th Hussars alone, in sending out patrols, lost ninety-eight men and 163 horses 'without', as the Official Historian puts it, with considerable inaccuracy, as the patrols were of real service to the infantry, 'having had an opportunity of effecting anything'.[10] Next day III Corps, on the left of Fourth Army, joined the battle and managed to take Albert, where the leaning statue of the Virgin atop the much-shelled church at last fell to the ground. It had been said that when it did so the war would be about to end. This news, spreading everywhere, was a boost to morale.

Parts of two squadrons of the III Corps cavalry regiment, the Northumberlands, on the orders of corps headquarters, wildly misinformed as to which villages had been taken by its infantry, made a dashing, foolhardy and unsupported charge near the inappropriately named 'Happy Valley'. In this they managed to achieve the appallingly high number of sixty casualties to no good end whatsoever. Six Whippets which came under the regiment's command never appeared due to breakdowns and the wounding of their commanding officer. It seems that the hussars' commanding officer must bear responsibility for allowing the charge to go ahead without them against totally unbroken infantry and under both artillery and machine-gun fire. An Australian officer, who witnessed the charge, was moved to send to the *Daily Mail* some verses poking fun at the rule about not mentioning regiments' names or numbers, and parodying Tennyson:

> '*The Charge of a Body of Mounted Troops.*
>
> Forward a certain cavalry unit!
> Was there a man dismay'd?
> Not tho' the soldier knew
> Someone had blundered.
> Theirs not to make reply,
> Theirs not to reason why,
> Theirs but to do and die;
> Into the Valley of Death
> Rode the certain number of mounted
>   troops from nowhere in particular.
> When can their glory fade?
> Oh! The wild charge they made;

The 3rd Hussars' patrols, 3 September, 1918

All the world wondered.
Honour the charge they made,
Honour the unmentionables,
Noble indefinite number!'[11]

There were a few occasions in the battle when patrols managed to bring in valuable information, not chiefly about enemy positions, but more often about where the infantry had got to – information that adjoining battalions and headquarters were anxious to have. Since it was becoming palpably impracticable to use cavalry *en masse*, at any rate for the present, it was decided on 4 September to split up one cavalry division, the 2nd, so as to provide infantry formations with their own cavalry regiments. These twenty-seven squadrons, (not including those of the Northumberlands, King Edward's Horse, the Canadian Light Horse and the 13th Australian Light Horse, all of which remained with their corps), were nearly always split up: squadrons to divisions (of which there were fifty-nine at this time), troops to brigades and even officers' patrols to battalions. Very occasionally the cavalry brigades worked as complete formations.*

During the battle of the Scarpe in the first week of September when the First Army captured the notorious Drocourt–Quéant 'switch' (see map, p. 250), an offshoot of the Hindenburg Line, individual regiments – even squadrons and troops – served their infantry formations well, especially in determining battalions' flanks. There are a number of examples of these small bodies rendering profitable service, both mounted and unmounted. The commander of the 13th Infantry Division reported one such on 3 September:

'One troop of "B" Squadron, 3rd Hussars, was divided into three patrols in front of the 112th Brigade, advanced guard to the division. The centre patrol, under 2nd Lieutenant

---

*It is interesting to note that the 20th Hussars were sent to the II American Corps in mid-October. (Darling, 122).

It will be remembered that in 1914 the first six infantry divisions each had a squadron of the 15th or 19th Hussars as divisional cavalry. These were replaced by yeomanry in April, 1915. The Dominion and Indian infantry divisions had squadrons of light horse and Indian cavalry. All other infantry divisions, both in the BEF and in other theatres, (if they had any) had yeomanry squadrons from the outset.

J.W. Sutherland, was stopped at the Canal du Nord by machine-gun fire from Havrincourt Wood. The patrol dismounted and the officer, with Lance-Corporal T.H. Hawkins, climbed down into the dry bed of the canal and ran up it to a bend just north of the wood, where they saw a slag heap on the east bank. Climbing cautiously up, they found themselves within 200 yards of a German machine-gun post and some riflemen, who were in action against our infantry and holding them up. Leaving the corporal in observation, the officer went back to the nearest infantry and brought up a Lewis gun, with which he knocked out the German post, and the infantry were able to continue the advance.'[12]

When not engaged in patrols like these, the individual units were constantly employed as dispatch riders, orderlies, military policemen and prisoners' escorts, in all cases using their mobility to the benefit of the infantry.[13] In the thirty-six hours which ended at 9 p.m. on 3 September a squadron of the Oxfordshires covered eighty-four miles 'and many officers' horses and those of patrols' as much as 110 miles.[14] This was not untypical of the strain placed on the cavalry at this time.

* * *

On 1 September the Cavalry Corps, numbering at this time less than 14,000 – not more than 60 per cent of its nominal strength – was completely pulled out. In the middle of the month, whilst making his plans for the final assault on the Hindenburg Line, Haig wrote in his diary:

'Kavanagh with our Cavalry Corps will be ready to pursue. . . . I am holding an exercise for the Cavalry Corps against a marked enemy, in order to practise all ranks in the pursuit. . . . Troops started at 8.30 a.m. . . . I motored about looking at the operations till 10.30. . . . Reports from the various umpires came in by wire and dispatch riders. The enemy was represented by detachments of infantry with machine gunners. The latter fired their machine guns into holes dug in the ground, and pointed a big arrow (wooden and painted white) in the direction in which they were firing. This seemed to answer well. Some of the bridges over the rivers were

Staff Sergeant (instructing): 'Stop whisperin' to 'im in public! D'you think it's a bloomin' secret that you're a beginner!'

purposely unguarded, so that the cavalry patrols should be given an opportunity of scouting and reporting what passages were open. Thus it was possible to see how far the leader on the spot took advantage of a favourable situation to press on.

'At about 11 a.m. we reached Villeroy-sur-Authie. Here the bridge was destroyed because there was a ford in the vicinity. This latter was well found by the contact squadron of the 4th D.G. and the village was quickly captured. I got on my horse here and rode about amongst the troops. Although the village was captured about 11, it was not for 1½ hours that the brigadier [2nd Cavalry Brigade] (Algy Lawson) heard of it and took advantage of the success to cross the river in force. I found that the signals were not in touch with the brigade headquarters. . . . Soon after 4 p.m. I then had a conference . . . which was attended by all commanders and staff officers down to officers commanding regiments. I commented on the lack of method in reconnoitring and the thoughtless riding of horses in many cases, etc. Much useful work was done and Kavanagh stated that they had all learnt a very great deal.'[15]

With hindsight it is too easy to laugh at such an exercise taking place at this time, yet it served two purposes: it showed to the Commander-in-Chief that communications, amongst other more minor points, needed drastic improvement and it possibly gave the cavalry a boost to morale and certainly something active to do whilst sitting in the rear. Further, of course, if the sole mobile force was ever to be used, it was right to try to ensure that it was efficient.

A few days after this training operation Haig was urging Wilson in London to send him 'yeomanry, cyclists, motor machine-guns, motor lorries, etc. In fact anything to add to our mobility. The resources of the French and of ourselves here are being strained to the utmost for the coming effort. Anything you can spare should be sent to us *at once*.' The CIGS received this urgent plea at a time when there was a railway strike in Britain! He could do little to help. Haig was also anxious, if an assault on the Hindenburg Line were to be launched, to have support for the cavalry 'with large numbers of low-flying [RAF] machines'. Major-General (later Air Chief Marshal Sir) Geoffrey Salmond, commanding the RAF, assured him of 300 at once.[16]

The second battle of Cambrai starts, 27 September, 1918

* * *

Since the best German divisions were massed behind the Hindenburg Line, Haig was very much aware that if a great offensive against them failed with high casualties, the Cabinet and the War Office would be bound to insist on no more being done in 1918 and that all efforts should be concentrated on a great largely mechanized summer offensive in 1919. This is what Wilson and Churchill, among others, thought to be the only realistic course. On 18 September at the end of the battle of Epéhy, after the Third and Fourth Armies got to within striking distance of the main Hindenburg defences Rawlinson, on whose advice Haig was now much reliant, agreed that the risk of a major offensive was worth accepting. The courageous decision therefore was taken and preparations were continued at an accelerated rate.

The 2nd battle of Cambrai was the result. This immense nine-day onslaught, in which thirty BEF divisions, the equivalent of one and a half cavalry divisions and two American divisions, engaged thirty-nine German divisions, started on 27 September. It carried the two armies right through the furthest east of the formidable trench systems. As Haig put it in his penultimate despatch: 'The effect of the victory . . . was decisive. The threat to the enemy's communications was now direct and instant, for nothing but the natural obstacles of a wooded and well-watered countryside lay between our armies and Maubeuge. . . . Great as were the material losses the enemy had suffered, the effect of so overwhelming a defeat upon a moral already deteriorated was of even larger importance.'

There were, waiting in the wings, seven cavalry brigades, ready and willing to operate in 'the wooded and well-watered countryside'. Before it was reached, though numerous orders from on high, based on totally inaccurate information, poured down on the cavalry brigadiers between 27 September and 8 October, telling them to go through the infantry, they were all wisely resisted. It is important to understand that GHQ believed in the evening of 4 October that, since, 'in the country ahead no lines of defence could be seen, at least none had been reported; [and that as] no signs of devastation were visible . . ., the ground, open and undulating, devoid of hedges and wire,' must be 'well suited for the employment of cavalry'.[18] When the two armies launched, on 8 October, their attack on a 12,000-yard front the infantry gained all their objectives and took over 4,000 prisoners and fifty-six guns. By

2 p.m., though, in the words of one cavalry officer who witnessed the fight, it 'had developed into a regular infantry battle . . . and although efforts were continuously made by the leading cavalry troops to pass through to their objectives, it was always found impossible to advance far in the face of machine-gun and artillery opposition, without incurring heavy losses.'[19]

Haig had issued particular directions to Kavanagh, who alone was to be responsible for orders to the 1st and 3rd Cavalry Divisions, that heavy losses were to be avoided. Kavanagh therefore committed only the 1st, whose commander, Mullens, the moment his leading brigade (the 9th) came up against opposition, tried to work his other two brigades round the flanks. Three wonderfully gallant, desperate mounted charges, two by parts of the 19th Hussars and the third by a troop of the 20th Hussars, took place on this day. All were totally fruitless and resulted in unnecessary casualties, including the 19th's commanding officer, Lieutenant-Colonel Franks (see p. 188). At the start, according to Sergeant Brunton, Franks had told the senior NCOs, 'I am the man to drop the flag and off we go to *Death or Glory*. If it is successful it will be a bigger thing than the Palestine affair.' Two troops of the regiment actually reached some field guns and were able to cut down a few gunners with the sword before being virtually destroyed by machine gunners who had appeared from dugouts in their rear. The regiment's casualties were 111, including four officers killed and 120 horses. 'The cavalry,' comments the 20th's historian, 'were out to justify their existence at last.'[20] Thus had deep frustration resulted in what was nothing short of a criminal dereliction of duty.

When it was clear that no headway could be made both divisions were withdrawn. In a few cases it can be said that patrols, aided by the machine-gun squadrons and the horse artillery, did afford the infantry some genuine assistance. The split-up 5th Cavalry Brigade, under XI Corps, also failed to get on. It too was withdrawn. The total casualties for the day in that brigade and in the nine regiments, three machine-gun squadrons and horse artillery of the 1st Division, numbered about 220: not perhaps too high, but nonetheless regrettable, considering the little progress made and help given.

Though Haig said that the area was 'well-watered', in fact there seemed to be hardly any streams or ponds. The 9th Cavalry Brigade were without water from 1 p.m. on the 7th to 7.45 p.m on the 8th – nearly thirty hours. To reach proper supplies the regiments had to retire a good deal further than the tactical situation required, adding largely to the fatigue of men and horses.*

The 2nd battle of Le Cateau continued on 9 October with a massive attack by the Fourth Army in conjunction with the First French and the Third British Armies on either flank. The American II Corps was placed between the IX and XIII Corps. The Cavalry Corps was in rear of the XIIIth. Its objectives were to secure the Le Cateau and Busigny railway junctions and then to 'cut the enemy's communications about Valenciennes'.[21] The 3rd Cavalry Division was put in the lead. The 1st remained in close reserve. As the by now customary mist cleared soon after 8.30 a.m. it was established that the infantry had progressed to a line to the north-east of Maretz. Kavanagh and Harman decided to advance on a two-brigade front: the 6th on the right of the Roman road with three armoured cars and the Canadian with two armoured cars on the left of it (see map, p. 262). The 7th with four armoured cars was to be in reserve.

The Royals led the 6th Brigade, followed by the 10th Hussars, one squadron of which as right flank guard was fired on by machine guns from a wood on its right as soon as it reached the infantry's line. At the same time the Royals and the 3rd Dragoon Guards were fired on from both Honnechy in front and Escaufourt on the right. As they advanced they became aware that the local inhabitants in the villages through which they were to advance had hung out large white sheets hoping thereby to avoid being shelled. This was indeed evidence that un-fought-over country had at last been entered. The leading squadron of the Royals reached a quarry near the railway west of Honnechy. A few of the regiment's scouts managed to get a house in the railway fork south-west of the village.

At about 11.30 Paterson, the brigadier, in the course of a personal reconnaissance, came across the brigade major of an infantry brigade which was held up in front of Honnechy. He told him that the strength of the German resistance and the tiredness

---

*Because after dark there was considerable enemy night bombing, which did surprisingly little damage, in spite of much frightening of the horses, the cavalrymen were denied any form of fires after dark, thus depriving them of 'hot meals either when starting before dawn or on arrival in bivouac after sundown. Infantry "cookers",' as officers of the Royals lamented, 'would have been invaluable.' (Bickersteth, 111).

SECOND BATTLE OF LE CATEAU, 9 OCTOBER, 1918

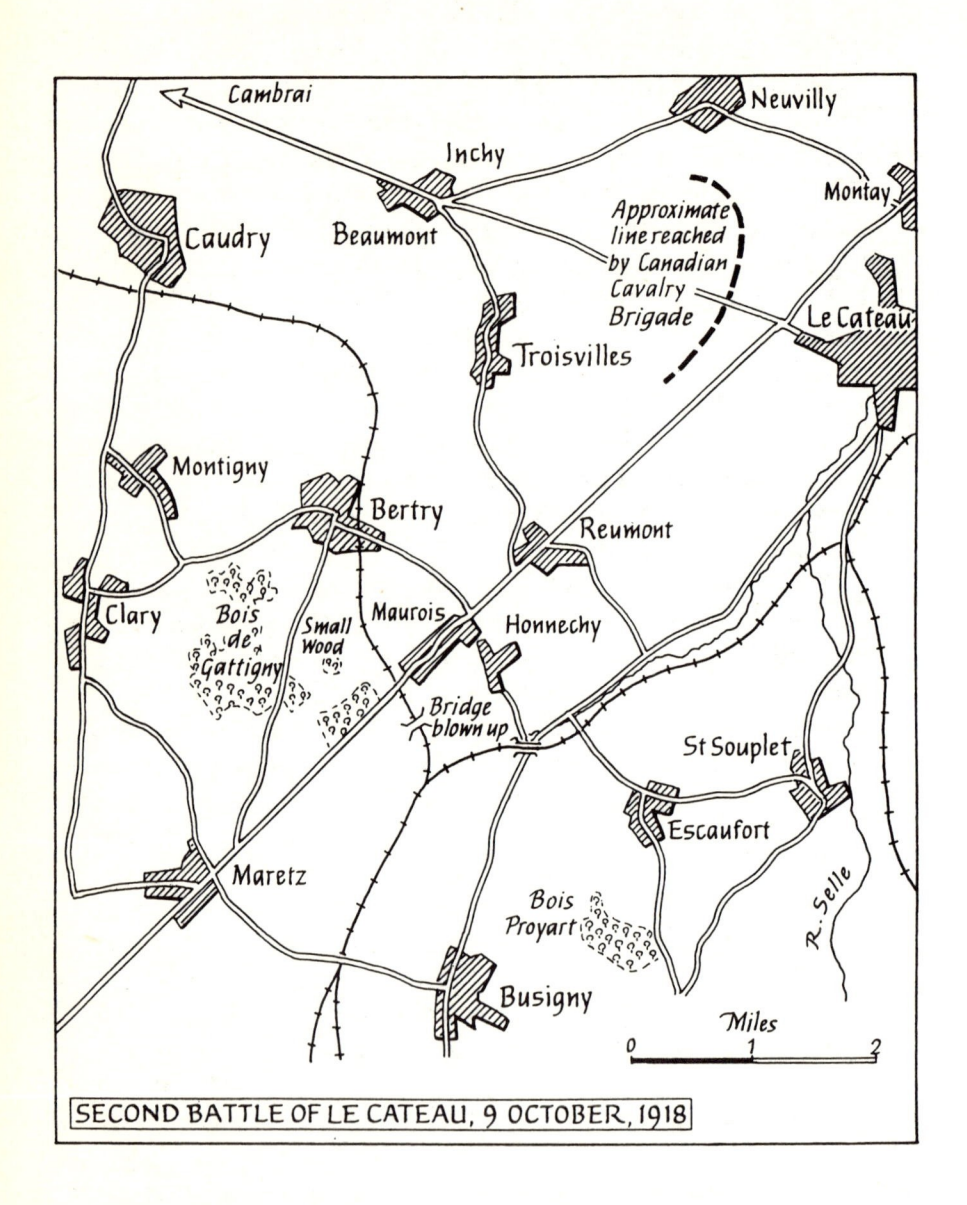

44. Cavalry waiting to advance near Trescault, battle of Cambrai, 20 November, 1917.

45. No. 4 Remount Depot, near Boulogne, February, 1918.

46. The aftermath of the charge of the Canadians at Moreuil Wood, 30 March, 1918. Photograph taken on 3 April. (See p.206)

47. The Scots Greys behind the line, May, 1918.

Honnechy, 9 October, 1918

of his regiments meant that it was not intended to advance further that day. A message also came from the Canadian Brigade stating that it could not get on until Honnechy and Reumont were captured. There followed a conference between the divisional and his two brigade commanders. They decided that 'the whole advance would peter out'[22] were the two villages to remain untaken. The 6th Brigade was therefore ordered to take them by means of mounted attacks and then to push on to the ridge west of Le Cateau.* To reinforce it the Inniskillings were moved from the 7th Brigade. An artillery barrage was arranged and the attack started at 2 p.m.

The Royals, with the 10th Hussars 'wide on the right as flank guard', and the 3rd Dragoon Guards followed by the Inniskillings rode forward simultaneously. 'C' Battery, RHA, shelled the south-western outskirts of Honnechy and the 6th Machine Gun Squadron covered the advance. On the other side of the road the Canadian Brigade cooperated by moving parallel to the 6th and aiming for the high ground north of Reumont (see below). 'As each squadron rode forward it was met by heavy H.E. shell and machine-gun fire, and to make matters worse a number of enemy aeroplanes suddenly appeared and, flying low, followed the advancing cavalrymen with machine-gun bullets and bombs.'[23] The Royals, avoiding a deep railway cutting, crossed the railway and the Roman road and galloped to a farm midway between the two villages. From Reumont German machine guns, firing down the road at 400 yards' range, caused some casualties to the leading squadron as it crossed the road. The rest of the regiment therefore crossed it further back and reached the ridge south-east of Reumont. Thus, having swept down 'a little dip into Maurois', the Royals outflanked Honnechy, 'the Germans clearing out just as the 3rd Dragoon Guards were coming round the village to the south-west and south.' (see below).[24] Lieutenant Bickersteth of the Royals, acting as Brigade Intelligence Officer, found that 'the bursting H.E., the rattle of machine-gun fire, both from the ground and from the air, the explosion of the bombs dropped by the aeroplanes – all contributed to make the noise absolutely deafening.'[25]

---

*Edmonds: *1918*, V, 217 says that Rawlinson sent Kavanagh an order, received at 11.30, to push on and that it was the latter, after consulting Harman, and not Harman himself who made the decision to launch mounted attacks. No other authority mentions this.

Honnechy, 9 October, 1918

'Seeing the Royals,' as the regimental historian puts it, 'threatening their retreat the German infantry [helped on their way by the Canadians and the 3rd Dragoon Guards] cleared out of Reumont,' only three miles from Le Cateau.[26]

Meanwhile Honnechy had been taken by the 3rd Dragoon Guards. Their leading squadron had galloped forward from its start-point north of Busigny 'in squadron column, extended'. It covered about two miles, most of the way under enfilade artillery and machine-gun fire from Proyart Wood and Escaufourt and led by their commanding officer, temporary Lieutenant-Colonel Charles Leslie Rome*, an Australian, who was wounded later on in the battle, followed by his trumpeter in good old-fashioned style. Coming to a brook with 'a bad take-off', which not a single horse refused, they passed through the infantry who 'rose with a cheer and followed in support'. A staff officer who witnessed this advance described it as the finest thing he had seen in the war.[27] It is clear that at Honnechy, as also in several cases during the March retreat (see especially p. 194), the élan of the galloping horsemen inspired the flagging infantrymen.

Now the speed and wide intervals so far employed by the dragoons, which had spared them many casualties, were temporarily curtailed. As each squadron came up to the railway embankment it had to close in to pass under a railway bridge. 'This was a trying moment, since they were under heavy machine-gun fire, and mines were plainly visible under the bridge.' It was here that most of the regiment's casualties occurred, including most of the ninety horses it lost on this day.[28] Opening out again, the squadrons galloped into Honnechy, 'immediately seizing the orchards to the east of the village'. The place was under heavy shell fire which caused 'many casualties to men and horses. ... A German battery and a line of machine guns were plainly visible' to the south-east 'and the position was extremely uncomfortable'. One squadron assisted

---

*Rome had joined the 11th Hussars in 1898, served with the Imperial Yeomanry in the Boer War, and as Military Secretary to the Australian Governor-General, 1908–11. He had only recently taken over the 3rd Dragoon Guards. Between 1924 and 1928 he commanded the Cavalry Brigade in Egypt and became Assistant Director of Remounts, 1929–33. He died, aged fifty-eight, in 1936.

in the taking of Reumont. Throughout these operations the 'seven armoured cars were on the flanks.'[29]*

The 6th Brigade, mostly dismounted, having established rifle and machine-gun posts along the line St Souplet–Reumont, now came under severe and continuous shelling from the ridge which just hid Le Cateau from view. A little after 5 p.m. Harman had decided to withdraw the 6th and substitute the 7th Brigade (returning the Inniskillings to it). This reached a position just north-east of Reumont a little before 6 p.m. As dusk was now falling, nothing more could be done that day. Le Cateau had not been taken, but the two armoured cars actually went into the town, which they soon established was still in German hands.[30]

* * *

There can be no doubt that the 6th Brigade's actions made it possible for the Canadian Brigade to play their part in the advance. The indomitable Fort Garry Horse with four horse artillery guns (RCHA)† and four machine guns attached, led the advance. Lord Strathcona's Horse was given the task of protecting the left flank and reconnoitring out to the line Montigny–Inchy–Neuvilly.[31] Soon after 9.30, as the Canadians reached the front line east of Maretz, the infantry told them that without the machine gunners in Gattigny Wood and Clary being knocked out they were unable to advance. The four guns at once came into action. Under their fire the Strathconas made a spirited charge which cleared out the German rearguard near Clary. They had driven thirty prisoners into the infantry's hands. At 12.25 they had got a squadron into

---

*Early on in the battle the armoured cars accompanying the 6th Brigade drove up the Roman road a mile beyond Maretz and scattered about thirty Germans, killing four of them and capturing ten machine guns. Pushing on to Maurois, the leading car had just crossed the bridge across the railway when it was blown up behind it, leaving the others behind. This car went on to disperse a demolition party thus preventing it from blowing up the bridge near Honnechy railway station. This lone car, which fired 2,500 rounds, cruised around shooting up small enemy parties before rejoining its companions, having given useful reports as to the situation. The cars also served as conveyors forward of staff officers anxious to ascertain what was going on. (Preston: '1918', V, 178)

†The RCHA had two four-gun batteries unlike the single six-gun battery of the RHA

Mont-aux-Villes Wood and were trying to outflank a factory and farm about 1,000 yards east of Clary. This squadron reported that the infantry was marching into the village.[32]

Meanwhile, shortly after 11.00, five troops of the Fort Garry Horse had made a dashing attack on the western and north-western edges of Gattigny Wood. They charged mounted, supported by the horse artillery and by the Vickers guns of the machine-gun squadron firing at 800 yards' range. One troop charged the machine guns in the southern half of the wood, putting them out of action. It lost more than half its men in doing so. The other troops 'galloped through a gap between the northern and southern halves of the wood to take the same objective in flank. With the assistance of the infantry of the South African Brigade in mopping up, the Gattigny Wood was cleared.' Some 200 prisoners were taken here as well as a 5.9-inch howitzer, an anti-tank rifle, a trench mortar and as many as forty machine guns. Further, a large number of Germans were killed by the sword and by bullets: a real triumph.[33] At about 11.40 the regiment had reached a small wood 1,500 yards south of Bertry. Here they were held up by machine-gun fire from Honnechy.

At the same time as the 6th Brigade was attacking Honnechy, one squadron of the Fort Garry Horse charged a party of the enemy to the west and north of Maurois, taking a number of prisoners and three machine guns. Meanwhile the Strathconas had entered the western outskirts of Bertry a mile and a half further west, capturing forty-two prisoners and five machine guns. The German machine gunners in Reumont now held up the advance of two Fort Garry Horse squadrons at about the same time as they were holding up the 6th Brigade's.

The brigadier therefore ordered the regiment's reserve squadron to try to approach Reumont from the north-west, while the other two squadrons, dismounted, attempted to enter the village along the Roman road. The Strathconas were to provide flank protection by pushing north-east from Bertry to Troisvilles. Simultaneously Major Newcomen's Squadron of the Royal Canadian Dragoons (which had not yet been engaged) was to swing further to the left and, gaining touch with the Strathconas, to seize the high ground north of Reumont. For this well-planned operation all eight horse artillery guns, acting with a battery of 4.5 inch howitzers and as many machine guns as could be brought to bear, were grouped in a valley 1,000 yards west of Maurois to give covering fire. Two armoured cars were in attendance.[34] Newcomen's squadron charged the enemy who were retiring from Reumont, 'killing several with the sword and capturing an officer and twenty-nine other ranks, with three machine guns'.[35] The dismounted Fort Garrys were now able to march into Reumont, while at about 4 p.m. the Strathconas rode past Troisvilles. About half an hour earlier the brigadier learned that enemy guns and transport had been seen moving along the Inchy–Le Cateau road, which crossed the path of the Canadians about a mile beyond Troisvilles. While the Fort Garry Horse retired into reserve the dragoons and the Strathconas were ordered to cut this line of retirement as soon as possible. This manoeuvre they carried out just as it was getting dark. The two regiments then took up an outpost line with their right on the Roman road above Montay, less than a mile from Le Cateau.

During the night patrols of the dragoons worked along the west bank of the Selle.[36] The Strathconas' patrols found Inchy clear of the enemy, but Neuvilly, east of the river, strongly held. 'In the meantime,' according to the brigade diary, 'the relief of the 6th Cavalry Brigade by a cyclist battalion [soon after dark] had left the Canadian right flank open from Reumont to Le Cateau until two squadrons of the Fort Garry Horse were brought forward to fill the gap.'[37] They got in touch with the 3rd Dragoon Guards on the right and on the left with the Royal Canadian Dragoons near Montay. These various posts were held throughout the night under considerable shell fire which caused a number of casualties among the Canadians.

Thus came to an end the final action of the Canadian Cavalry Brigade in the war. It had advanced some eight miles, cleared a strip of country about three miles wide, killed numbers of Germans, taken over 400 prisoners, several guns, two motor cars and nearly 100 machine guns. More important, by its speed of advance – and the same applies to the 6th Cavalry Brigade – all attempts by the enemy to demolish the villages through which it swept were frustrated. The Official Historian, missing this important point, expresses the view that the Cavalry Corps, which lost 604 of all ranks on 8, 9 and 10 October, and had taken over 500 prisoners, ten guns and about 150 machine guns,* 'had done

---

*Edmonds, V, 235, says that the Corps' total was sixty, but most evidence puts the number far higher.

nothing that the infantry, with artillery support and cyclists, could not have done for itself at less cost'. A detailed study of what admittedly is sometimes *parti pris* evidence, refutes this opinion. Further, he neglects the undeniable evidence that the infantry as early as 11.30 had decided that no further advance could be made that day and that it was Harman's brave decision which made it possible for it to do so. However, he goes on to add, without giving chapter and verse, that 'the sending up ammunition and the rations for the other arms' was 'gravely interfered with' by the need to supply forage and water for the horses. This may well have been the case.[38]* The Canadian Cavalry Brigade lost 158 of all ranks and 171 horses; the 6th Cavalry Brigade lost ninety and 255 horses, both including the horse artillery and the machine-gun squadron.

Though the village had been liberated on the 9th almost intact, numbers of the inhabitants were killed or wounded during the fighting: far fewer almost certainly than had the task been left to the slow-moving infantry. The 6th Cavalry Field Ambulance set up a large dressing station in Maretz where the unfortunate wounded civilians mingled with those of the cavalry and infantry.†

* * *

*'The watering of the cavalry had presented great difficulties, but these had been overcome by the Chief Engineer ... by the use of "canvas belt elevators" carried on [the water] wagons, which drew water from deep wells. The elevator consisted of an endless canvas belt which, on revolving sufficiently fast, brought up water clinging to its surface. A heavier device of the same nature was the "châine helice".' (Edmonds, *1918*, V, 235)

†On 18 October a shed in which the horses of a squadron of the 3rd Hussars were stabled received a direct hit from a shell. 'The shed, a perfect shambles, was soon besieged by a large crowd of townsfolk – men, women and children – piteously asking for the dead horses, as they had not tasted meat "for very many days", poor devils!' (Willcox, 306)

'One of the strangest features of the fighting at this period,' states the Greys' historian, 'was the large number of civilians that turned up directly there was any firing. Their object was horse-flesh and they did not seem to mind whether they were hit or not. It was most unusual to come across a dead horse from which all the best joints had not already been cut away.' (Pomeroy: 2D, 167–8)

Le Cateau taken, 10 October, 1918

First thing in the morning of 10 October the 6th Brigade concentrated between Reumont and Troisvilles – the battlefield of Beaumont, where both the Royals and the 3rd Dragoon Guards had fought 124 years before. (See Vol. 1, 45, 46). It was also where Smith-Dorrien, against orders, made his splendid stand more than four years before at the 1st battle of Le Cateau. (See Vol. 7, p. 134). The 7th Cavalry Brigade on the 10th lost the alarming number of ninety-three of all ranks as well as 131 horses in reconnaissances which only established what had anyway become clear, namely that the enemy resistance had greatly hardened overnight. In the afternoon all the cavalry was withdrawn, except the 18th Hussars which was detailed to stay in the forward area to keep in touch with two infantry divisions. On the 12th Le Cateau was eventually taken after a major artillery barrage and infantry assault.*

Though in the battle of the Selle which began on 17 October, and in which twenty-four British and two American divisions defeated thirty-one German divisions, the Cavalry Corps took no part, the split-up 5th Cavalry Brigade and the three infantry corps cavalry regiments continued to be of some use in reconnaissances. These became less effective as soon as the terrain beyond the Selle was reached. The slopes became steeper and the woods more frequent, while thick hedges enclosed the fields.

---

*The regiments of the 5th Cavalry Brigade under IX Corps and the three regiments with VI, XIII and XVII Corps (Oxfords, Northumberlands and the Carabiniers, respectively) all seem to have accomplished serviceable reconnaissances during the battle, without suffering too many casualties. (Preston: '1918', V, 181–6)

10

'When Haig visited Foch on 6 October he found the Generalissimo sitting with a Paris morning paper open on the table in front of him. In large type was printed a note from Germany, Austria and Turkey asking for an armistice. "Here," said Foch, pointing to the paper, "you have the immediate result of the British piercing the Hindenburg Line." It was nobly and generously said.'
— DUFF COOPER in his life of Haig.

'I just hate moving back, but it is a question of roads and food. Until we get the railways on, there is not much chance of getting a move on.'
— HOME in his diary, 12 October, 1918

'From the recesses of his martial spirit the German soldier summoned up reserves of courage and determination exceeding that of his leaders.'
— JOHN TERRAINE in his life of Haig

' "An officer sent to look for a suitable bivouac ... tried to billet in a village full of Germans." Open warfare had indeed come into its own again.'
— CAPTAIN KEITH-FALCONER, historian of the Oxfordshire Hussars, 25 October, 1918

'Yesterday the main [railway] of the army went up in three places with delay-action mines and the result was chaos – neither food nor reinforcements could be taken up.'
— HOME in his diary, 5 November, 1918

'[The enemy's] policy appears to be to continue withdrawing until he forces us to a standstill through the impossibility of maintaining our communications, and so gain sufficient time to reorganize his defeated troops.'
— XXII Corps War Diary, 8 November, 1918

'To the end the machine gun was the hard core of the [German] resistance.'
— THE OFFICIAL HISTORIAN

'11 November dawned bright and sunny, a glorious morning with a sharp frost.'
— CAPTAIN KEITH-FALCONER, Oxfordshire Hussars.[1]

Last days on the Western Front – administrative chaos – the Armistice

On 20 October Home spoke to Lawrence, Haig's Chief of General Staff, about 'the future prospects of the cavalry. At present there does not appear to be a possible use of the cavalry mass as the Boche has his rearguards in very great depth. But should he take a big jump back, then we ought to be pushed forward to harass his rearguards and push them in. It is not going to be an easy job, as there are no flanks in this sort of warfare. The Boche sees to *that* and keeps his line very straight unless it is covered by a pretty good obstacle.'[2] The Boche did not 'take a big jump back'. Ludendorff had early decided instead to give 'not a foot's breadth of ground . . . without stubborn fighting'. Had he taken the swift withdrawal option and had there been no revolution in his rear (which just conceivably might then have been avoided) the end of the war could well have been relegated to 1919. With his complex reasons for the course he took this work is not concerned. It is perhaps enough to sum up the chief of them in Foch's words: 'The man could still get away if he did not worry about his baggage.'[3]*

As for the cavalry, there were a number of reasons, resulting partly from Ludendorff's decision, why the long-cherished hope of a pursuit of a demoralized German army never materialized. It was not given time to become demoralized; even if it had been, there was not enough cavalry for the task. Beside the three British there were three French and one Belgian cavalry divisions available. Above all the Allies' supply situation had become so chaotic that even an inadequate cavalry force could not have been effectively provisioned. So desperately chaotic was it that the Army commanders, Rawlinson and Byng, from mid-October, had no realistic alternative to giving precedence to the infantry and artillery when it came to transport in their rear areas.

It is not surprising that after nearly four years of static warfare, insufficient attention had been given to the question of moving forward 200 and more Allied divisions at a rate hitherto quite unheard of over rapidly elongating communication lines. For all supplies each division required about two standard trains *per diem*. For every set-piece battle numerous extra daily trains were

---

*By far the most telling of all the comments on the German dilemma is made by Churchill. (Churchill, *'16–'18*, 510–12)

needed to carry artillery shells alone. These would have been sufficiently daunting administrative problems even had the railways been plenteous enough and in excellent order. The opposite was in fact the case. Throughout the war the French railway system had been strained to the utmost. Though enormous efforts had been made to improve and extend the lines, they were not enough when the moment for speedy advances arrived. Over 1,200 locomtives and 52,000 railway wagons had been carried over the Channel to supplement the French rolling stock, while British engineers had built or reconstructed 3,688 miles of railway in northern France alone. 'The needs of the armies were always growing faster than were the resources of the railways.' This could be accepted when an advance of eight miles in a day was a very rare occurrence. It no longer could be. Beside the conventional blowing up of rails, culverts, bridges, workshops and turntables, the Germans had developed time fuses which could be set to retard explosions not only for days but actually for many months. They made much use of them. On 24 October, for instance, the level crossing at Roisel was blown up 'about forty days after the Boche left'.[4] A visiting senior officer was told in late October by an Army commander that owing 'to the constant explosions of mines behind his front . . . his railhead was retreating faster than his troops were advancing.'[5] Completely new lines of rail were the only answer to this massive wrecking. It was therefore calculated that to reach the German frontier would not be possible for the railways before, at the earliest, February, 1919. As for roads, the mining of every junction and the use of delayed explosions were just as devastating. Horses were particularly vulnerable. 'We have had many accidents lately,' reported Home on 1 November, 'through horses striking unexploded shells.' There were numerous occasions during the last weeks of the war when the cavalry patrols provided by the units of the split-up 2nd Cavalry Division were immobilized because the rations could not be got up. One such befell a squadron of the 20th Hussars on 20 October. Even their iron rations had been exhausted on the previous day.[6] The limited resources in motor transport,* even when the widespread destruction had been remedied, could only provide a very restricted solution to the problem. The heavy artillery particularly

---

*On 11 November more than half Fourth Army's lorries had broken down. (Maurice, 231).

needed roads, especially as winter came on. It is not surprising therefore that even the Official Historian, who could never quite make up his mind with respect to the use of cavalry, blamed the 'severely felt absence of mounted troops' in the last days of the war on the supply situation.[6]

* * *

A week after Ludendorff sent in his resignation, the battle of the Sambre started. On 4 November Austria–Hungary ceased to be at war with the Allies. The same day the last great Allied offensive was launched. In conjunction with the French the First, Third and Fourth Armies attacked on a thirty-mile front from the east of the Scheldt at Valenciennes to Guise on the Oise, the Belgians on their left advancing towards Ghent. On 6 November the German armistice delegation left Berlin for the western front. Two days later Foch told its members that the Allies' terms must be accepted or refused by 11 a.m. on 11 November. On 8 November, too, the BEF entered Maubeuge and on the 11th captured Mons. (See below.) The Armistice was signed at 5 a.m. that morning and came into effect at the stipulated hour.

* * *

From the last week of October until the Armistice the various units of the 2nd Cavalry Division, split up between formations and units of the First, Third and Fourth (and eventually the Second) Armies, did useful work in reconnaissance. They acted mostly as mounted, but occasionally also as dismounted, patrols. There is much evidence that these small detachments using to the full their mobility were made considerable use of by their infantry commanders. Had there been a much larger mounted force this would have been the best way to employ it throughout the war's final months. That these squadrons and troops managed to operate with few casualties is especially remarkable considering that the terrain soon after the Selle was crossed was a veritable 'machine-gunners' paradise' – a well-populated paradise – 'more like England than the open land between Amiens and Cambrai ... with grass meadows intersected by wire and hedges'.[8] It is clear that the art of reconnaissance under modern fire-power conditions had been well learned. Furse of King Edward's Horse gives a good idea of how his squadron did the job:

> '[The enemy's] positions were usually well concealed. But once these had been located a swift turning movement, when the country permitted it, invariably forced him to retire, sometimes with precipitation. The vital thing was to gallop fast. The comparative immunity of horsemen moving at speed, even when under MG fire at close range, was strikingly shewn by the fact that in a running fight of ten miles [on 9 November] against an enemy who admittedly was only fighting a delaying action but who was in superior numbers we lost one man killed and one wounded together with five horses....
>
> 'MGs behind wire are fatal to cavalry; MGs in the open are not.... It is the man behind the MG or the rifle that matters. Rattle his nerves and you upset his aim.... To rattle his nerves your attack must threaten him directly or must endanger his line of retreat.'[9]

There were moments near the end when touch with the enemy was totally lost for a time. Cavalry patrols were much employed in regaining it, particularly on 9 November. On that day many of the patrols advanced unopposed for distances of up to ten miles, reaching most inconveniently the eastern edge of their maps.

The regimental histories are very short on first-hand accounts of actual combats during these last three days of the war. Furse, though, in his unpublished memoirs, recounts two episodes of interest. '[Probably on 9 or 10 November] Lance-Corporal Fishlock with two men charged six Germans with the sword and took four prisoners. A little later he alone charged three Germans. These stood firm and blew his helmet off at ten yards range. He was nearly unseated but his horse carried him into cover. He then threw himself off his horse and engaged the enemy with his rifle.' On the same date the squadron was working with some Belgian cavalry. It seized ten machine guns and fourteen motor-cycles.

> 'By the time we had started back it was dark. Quite possibly we were behind German troops. So I sent my points a few hundred yards ahead and kept galloping to and fro between them and our main body myself, to keep touch. The Belgian officer after a while said: "I see your difficulty. Let my dog [a trained Alsatian war-dog] do the work for you." He said something to that sagacious animal. From then till we rejoined the main guard he galloped from me to my points

and back to me, his little bell tinkling in the night and telling me where everybody was.'[10]

When on the 9th the Greys reached Sains they found the inhabitants all in their best clothes and the village decorated with Allied flags. One of their patrols picked up a message dropped by an aeroplane which read: 'Enemy in great quantity and confusion trying to cross bridge three miles on. Impossible drop bombs owing to large number of civilians waving flags.' The 20th Hussars rode some miles with both flanks in the air and without seeing any enemy until they reached the Belgian frontier, the regiment spending the night five miles ahead of the nearest infantry!* In the course of the day the Oxfords were the first regiment to enter Maubeuge.

The 12th Lancers, making its 'first successful mounted advance' since 1914, rode for eight miles on a four-mile front with, like the 20th Hussars, both flanks exposed, making 'large captures of men and material'.† In one small country town, where the regiment was greeted enthusiastically by the 3,000 inhabitants, it found that the enemy had left in a hurry. A field gun, a fully loaded ammunition train, a large shell dump and hundreds of transport wagons were abandoned. Some of the regiment's troops rode with their saddles stripped of all unwanted impediments, so as to save weight on their horses.[11] These everywhere by this time were suffering from chronic under-feeding due to the difficulty of getting forage forward.

The supply situation had now become so anarchic that on the Fourth Army front a halt was called. A small mobile force under Major-General (Sir) Keppel Bethell§ was swiftly organized for keeping in touch with the retreating enemy. It included the

---

*The only other night during which the regiment had been entirely isolated was in October, 1914. (Darling, 126)

†General Sir Richard Loudon McCreery, then a twenty-year-old lieutenant, commanded one of the 12th Lancers' troops in this advance. His distinguished career in the Second World War ended by his commanding the Eighth Army in Italy, 1944–5. In 1923 and 1928 he had won the Grand Military Gold Cup at Sandown Park. He died in 1967, aged sixty-nine.

§Bethell, an ex-7th Hussar, commanded during the war successively an infantry regiment, a brigade, and finally a division. From 1919 to 1923 he was Military Attaché in Washington and died, aged sixty-five, in 1947.

9, 10 and 11 November, 1918

5th Cavalry Brigade, the South African Brigade, an armoured car battalion, two squadrons of the RAF and detachments of other arms. Before long it found the German rearguards well established with plenteous artillery and machine guns. There was no sign of anything approaching a demoralized enemy! By the time of the Armistice Bethell's Force had reached the most easterly point arrived at by any troops of the BEF.[12]

On 9 and 10 November those parts of the Greys which were not in its one influenza-free squadron, including a newly arrived draft of some sixty men, performed a spectacular forced march. They covered seventy-four miles in a day and a half. To what purpose is not now clear, but it shows that the cavalry spirit was not entirely dead![13]

* * *

Captain Wellesley of the Oxfords describes how he and his squadron spent the last hour before the Armistice:

'On reaching the outskirts of [Erquellines] I was met by a cheering mass of inhabitants, some of whom sang, others wept and others begged me to be careful as German machine guns were in position round the corner. (To these civilians, of course, it was complete news that an Armistice was at hand.) So great was the crush that, having sent back for the squadron to come on, it was with the greatest difficulty that I got down to the market-place on foot, only to find that the last of the enemy had just gone.

'On returning to my pony I found her bestraddled by a huge fat Belgian who was addressing the crowd from her back. Having kicked him off I went to investigate, charged through the mobs of wildly excited inhabitants and finally got through the town on to the main road beyond. Here I met a patrol who had come round the outskirts and we established a Hotchkiss post on the road and sent back for the squadron.

'Meanwhile I tried to round up some escaping Boches, who finally jumped into the river Sambre. . . . I sent a patrol down the road to Solre, only 600 yards away, but found the village full of Germans. . . .

'We began to take stock of the situation. At 11.15 it was

THE AREA OF MONS/MAUBEUGE
11 NOVEMBER, 1918

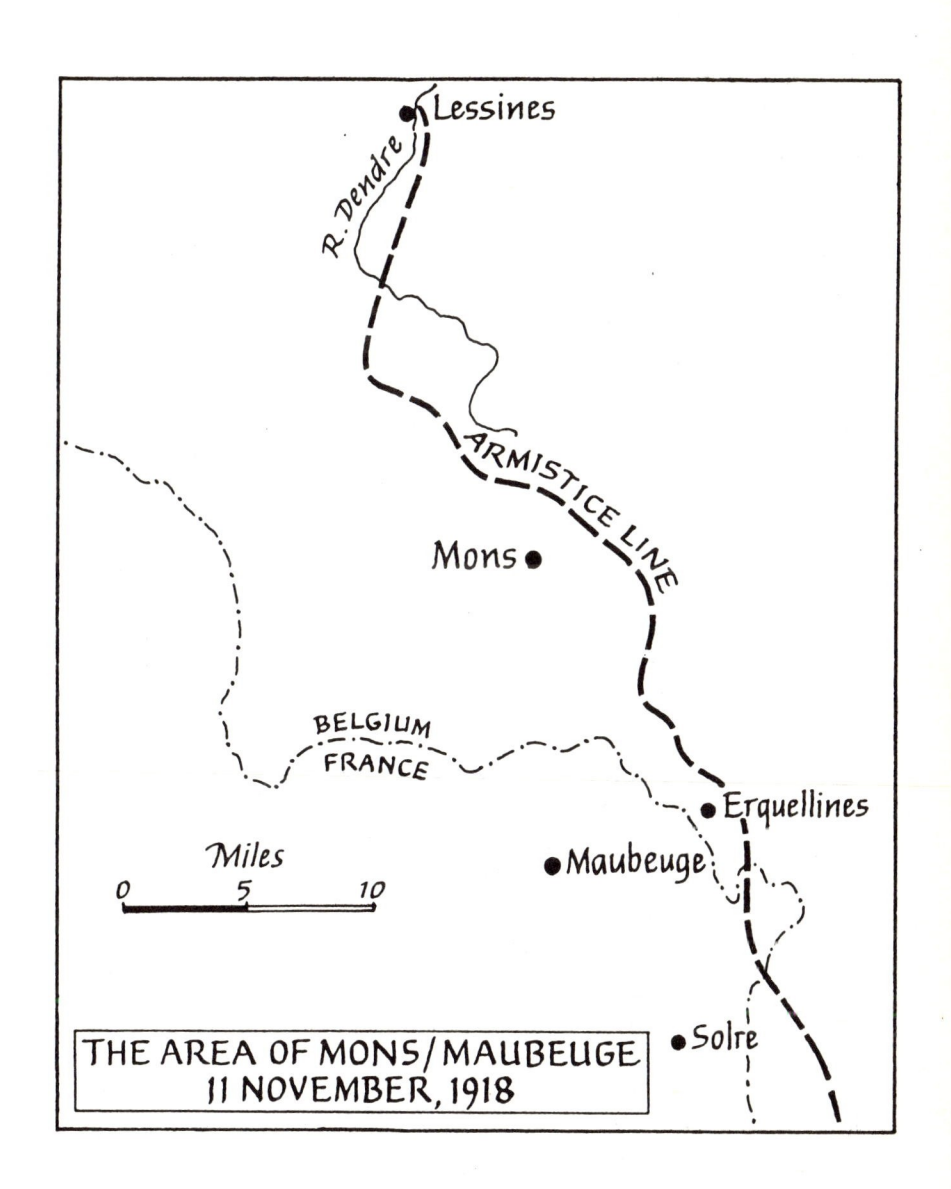

found necessary to end the days of a Hun machine-gunner on our front but there was no alternative. Perhaps his watch was wrong, but he probably was the last German killed in the war – a most unlucky individual.'[14]

Even beyond the eleventh hour the machine-gunners were not bereft of their morale! Had the end not come there can be little doubt that a successful cavalry pursuit would have been out of the question. Further evidence of this is provided by the action of a patrol of the 16th Lancers. At about 10 a.m. it made 'a daring mounted attack' against some machine-gunners. These 'kept their heads and engaged the charging lancers at point-blank range; every horse was brought down.' Amazingly, only the patrol commander and four other ranks were wounded: the sole casualties of what must have been the last formal mounted charge made in the course of the war.[15]

* * *

On 6 November, after the battle of the Sambre had been in progress for a few days, Haig decided that the Cavalry Corps which, since the middle of October, had been held back in GHQ Reserve should be allocated to General (later Field-Marshal Lord) Birdwood's Fifth Army. He hoped, as ever, that a final great mounted chase of a broken enemy was now feasible. He was once again to be disillusioned. Birdwood, wisely, diluted the cavalry force at his disposal by placing each of the three regiments of the 9th Brigade under his three corps as 'advanced guards'. He kept to himself the issue of orders for an advance by the remainder of the Cavalry Corps, ordering its brigades to be 'ready to operate . . . if the necessary conditions occur'.[16] However, a little later, the 7th Brigade was sent to Second Army. Thus the First, Second, Third and Fourth Armies now had a cavalry brigade each. Kavanagh complained that his much-reduced corps was a great deal too far to the west to be of much use. He was, of course, right, but the congestion on the roads made it quite impossible to bring it forward. Throughout 10 November it was between six and eight miles from the front line. The congestion was daily getting worse. This was partly because the BEF's front had contracted from ninety-eight miles in the beginning of August to about sixty-five miles three months later. All five armies had been obliged, therefore, to dispose their troops in much greater depth as their frontages became less.

Of the rump of the Cavalry Corps only one regiment, the 7th Dragoon Guards of the 7th Cavalry Brigade of the 3rd Cavalry Division, was able to come into any sort of useful action. The commander of the 88th Infantry Brigade, twenty-nine-year-old Bernard Freyburg,* told the dragoons' commanding officer that the Armistice was to come into force at 11 a.m., but that 'he particularly wished to seize Lessines [and the adjacent river crossings] before that hour.' He therefore ordered part of one squadron 'to saddle up and push on at once'. He himself, with his groom, led the way, conscious that there were only an hour and a half to go. Freyburg's biographer recounts what happened next:

'It was a wild ride, and at the outskirts of the town the German outposts began firing [from five machine guns]; but the hard-riding advance party swept past them without casualties and thundered down into the main street of Lessines. There was firing from some of the windows and a bullet lodged in Freyburg's saddle. But the headlong advent of the British forces roused the inhabitants of Lessines against the Germans; men and women stoned and beat the German soldiers, driving them from the houses and cellars. Round the bend of the road swept the Brigadier and nine of his party (some horses had been hit), and reached the main [steel-girder] bridge across the Dendre a few seconds before 11.00 hours – just in time to save the demolition from taking place.'

The regimental historian takes up the story:

'The Squadron had galloped ten miles, captured the bridge and village of Lessines, and taken three officers and 103 other ranks prisoners.

'The German officers started to argue in the middle of the village that they had been taken after the time of the Armistice. While this argument was going on, a German appeared at a window, with a rifle, and took a shot at the Squadron, killing a horse. The inhabitants, who were very

---

*General Lord Freyburg, VC, the famous New Zealander, who commanded the New Zealand Forces, 1939–45 and died in 1963, aged seventy-four.

short of food, skinned and cooked the carcase before the Squadron left.

'Soon afterwards a senior German officer and forty other ranks appeared on the scene. They were very much frightened of the inhabitants, so, as it was now after eleven o'clock, they were escorted out of the village and sent back to their own lines.'

The importance of this squadron's action lies in its saving of 'the very important road bridge over the Dendre from being destroyed', as was handsomely acknowledged by the infantry divisional commander.[17]

* * *

The 5th Lancers had the honour of being the first troops into Mons. The Canadian Corps followed them and in the afternoon the formal entry took place. Lieutenant-General Sir Arthur William Currie, the Corps Commander, made 'Second-Lieutenant Allison of the 5th stand beside him on the steps of the Hotel de Ville, introduced him to the Maire and afterwards directed that the escort [of thirty-four other ranks 'with pennons on their lances'] should march off the parade first, as they were representatives of the old British Army that had fought at Mons in 1914.'[18]

The 17th Lancers, which almost exactly four years before had detrained near Lillers, found themselves almost forty miles due east of that place on 11 November. 'As in the days of Caesar,' comments the regiment's historian, 'it was done *quam celerrime* – as quickly as possible.'[19]

It is interesting to note how the officers and men of the various regiments reacted to the 'silence of the guns' made so impressive in 'the calm windless weather' of the day.[20] The trumpeters of the 15th Hussars 'sounded the regimental call and then the "Cease Fire". The men gave a loud cheer. The call to stables was sounded and all then proceeded prosaically to groom and look after the horses.' In the 4th Hussars 'there was nothing in the way of cheering or any demonstration; men merely dismounted and sat on the side of the road, and pulling out a cigarette proceeded to light it, and the only remark was: "Well, thank God that's over".' In the 11th Hussars 'the officers ran round their men, shaking them by the hand and everybody congratulated each other on being alive

Armistice Day, 11 November, 1918

to see this day.' At Erquellines the men of the Oxfords in the hour before 11 a.m. 'experienced considerable difficulty owing to the pressing attentions of the civilians, who besieged all our posts with presents and souvenirs of every kind, while they were trying to keep their eyes skinned for the enemy.' When the 19th Hussars entered a newly liberated village on the 10th the villagers gave them 'a great reception: fruit, flowers, etc., church bells ringing. People awfully excited,' wrote Sergeant-Major Brunton in his diary. When next day news that the Armistice had been signed arrived, there was 'wild cheering by our fellows and hats thrown in the air. . . . Band play as we pass through and altogether a jolly time.'[21]

The Official Historian says that 'after dark all gave way to rejoicing, searchlights wobbled in the sky, coloured lights of every description and S.O.S. signals illuminated the front lines, rockets went whizzing into the air, and field batteries fired their star shells. Some adventurous spirits lit bonfires, exploded small ammunition dumps and laid trails of guncotton and explosives which ran spluttering over the countryside like huge fiery serpents.'[22]

* * *

Had the revolution not broken out* and had Germany's leaders, including Ludendorff, emulated the staying power of the majority of their army, there can be little doubt that the bulk of it could have retired behind the Rhine pretty well intact. To have speedily followed it up in any numbers would have been quite beyond the powers of the Allied armies. As it was, the supply situation dictated a stand-still, even for small bodies of mounted men. Neither food nor forage could be got up to them. Five days elapsed before the BEF could manage to begin its move to the German frontier. It took another twelve days before it was reached,

---

*The revolution was the clinching factor in Germany's speedy collapse. It was not, though, the cause of it. The end of the Empire had been brought about entirely by the superiority of the Allied armies.

By 9 November eleven cities and all the main railway centres had been taken over by revolutionaries. In the navy and in parts of the army behind the front, even at Spa where the Kaiser was facing up to abdication, Bolshevik councils were being set up. That day a Socialist Republic was proclaimed in Berlin.

cavalry patrols crossing it at Behu.* Throughout this long period the broken but not destroyed German armies withdrew to behind the Rhine, the men keeping their personal arms. This had been allowed chiefly because of the need to keep order. As the cavalry advanced, 'everywhere,' wrote Sergeant-Major Brunton of the 19th Hussars, 'we were received by the Germans with welcome. Owing to internal conditions . . . riots had spread. This explained why the civil population were pleased to see us, as it meant for them protection.'[23] On 6 December mounted troops began the occupation of a bridgehead east of Cologne.

Except for peace-keeping duties during the occupation, the British cavalry as an active force had virtually reached the end of its useful life.†

* * *

Churchill, who, though a cavalryman himself, had been sceptical before the war about the arm's value, in 1920 summed up very fairly the part it had played on the Western Front:

---

*By the time Haig wrote his final despatch in March, 1919, he must have forgotten all about the realities of the situation. 'On the morning of the Armistice,' he wrote, 'two British cavalry divisions were on the march east of the Scheldt, and before the orders to stop reached them they had already gained a line ten miles in front of our infantry outposts. There is no doubt,' he added, 'that, had the advance of the cavalry been allowed to continue, the enemy's disorganized retreat would have been turned into a rout.' (21 Mar., 1919, despatch Boraston, 328).

†The cavalry's casualties (other ranks only) for the whole war in the BEF amounted to 19,051, of which 4,421 were killed or died. The proportion of officer casualties compared with the total of other rank casualties was 1:9.4. This was high compared with the infantry where the proportion was 1:23.9. The total casualties of all British fighting arms in *all theatres* were: cavalry, 1.08%; infantry, 86.07%. The percentages of killed and died, wounded, missing and taken prisoner in the cavalry were: k. & d., 23.33%; w., 66.35%; m. & p., 10.32%. In the infantry they were: k. & d., 19.96%; w., 64.23%; m. & p., 14.81% (*Statistics*, 245, 247, 249)

The cavalry sustained on the Western Front the highest proportion of killed to other casualties of all arms. The Tank Corps had the lowest. The proportion of officer casualties from all causes in the cavalry was more than twice the average for all arms: about one to every nine other ranks' casualties. (Badsey, Dr S. 'The Role of the Cavalry on the Western Front', unpublished typescript, 1994, 3–4)

Churchill's view of the use of cavalry in the war

'The vitally important cavalry work of the Retreat from Mons was succeeded by a prolonged period when the trenches stretched from the sea to the Alps, when there were no flanks for the cavalry to turn and no war of movement for their manoeuvring capacity. As the British Army grew, division by division, from the small original Expeditionary Force to a total strength of about two million men, no proportionate increase was made in the cavalry. On the contrary, it became actually smaller, and a single cavalry corps sufficed in the last phase of the war for all the requirements of a British Army of nearly sixty divisions. This unique body of horsemen, with their power of intensely rapid movement across country, became the one mobile reserve on which Lord French and Lord Haig in turn counted to throw into any gap that might be made in the front by the sudden attack of the enemy. As such, the cavalry rendered services of the utmost importance in each successive year of the war. In addition, they took their turn in the trenches whenever it was possible to spare them from their paramount duty.'[24]

11

Top-deck passengers. Interest in the hay ration.

'The cavalry . . . were, for a large part of [the war], responsible for the issue of bread tickets at home.'
— CAPTAIN J.R. KENNEDY in *This Our Army*, 1935

'23 March 1915. Cowans [Quartermaster-General] told me tonight that we have now 160,000 horses in France (every loss being regularly supplied) and send out from here every day 1,000 tons of hay.'
— ASQUITH to Venetia Stanley

'The power of an army as a striking weapon depends on its mobility. Mobility is largely dependent on the suitability and fitness of animals for army work. [I want to stress] the wisdom of

breeding animals for the two military virtues of *hardiness* and *activity*.'
  – HAIG in a fore-note to Capt. S. Galtrey's *The Horse and the War*, September, 1918

'It was a pleasure to me to find . . . that the new armies fully uphold our national reputation as good horse-masters.'
  – GEORGE V to Haig, France, 13 August, 1918

'16 April 1918. Just heard that the question of remounts is acute. There are lots of horses in England, but last winter [due to losses from submarines] the authorities starved them and they are not fit to come out here and work. It all hinges on the decision that our cavalry were no longer worth keeping.'
  – HOME at Cavalry Corps HQ

'In dreary, doubtful, waiting hours,
  Before the brazen frenzy starts,
The horses show him nobler powers;
  O patient eyes, courageous hearts!'
  – CAPTAIN JULIAN GRENFELL in 'Into Battle', Spring, 1915

From the ship to the Remount Depôt. A night-time hurried veterinary examination of the new-comers.

'Innocent victims of man-made madness. They broke your heart, especially when you passed the injured ones, left to die in agony and screaming with pain and terror.'
— TROOPER WILLIAM CLARKE

'There are indications that the use made of mechanical science has rendered possible the passing of the horse in war, in which case we [the Royal Veterinary Corps] have reached our zenith, and, as the horse gradually disappears from the army, our sun will "draw towards its setting".'
— SIR FREDERICK SMITH in *A History of the Royal Army Veterinary Corps*[1]

Horses: forage supply – remounts – types of horse – veterinary service – weights on cavalry horses

'Despite the relatively small number of British cavalry, forage was the largest item of supplies sent overseas, exceeding even ammunition.' Thus Liddell Hart writing in the 1930s.[2] It is unfortunate that an historian, whose numerous books on the war are all wonderfully readable, took so little trouble, in this case, to get at the actual facts.* This sentence was repeated uncritically by David Ascoli, a competent historian of the 1914 campaign, writing as recently as 1981.[3] It is true that forage was 'the largest item',

---

*Alan Clark, in his *The Donkeys* (1961), perhaps the most arrogant and least respectable of writers on the war, was much helped by Liddell Hart who by the late 1950s had become paranoid about the horrors of the war to such a degree as to have lost all sense of proportion. Clark calls him 'that acknowledged master of military history' (p.12). 'Acknowledged' yes; 'master', alas, not entirely!

For a brilliant critique of Liddell Hart's works and his influence on later historians see Strachan, H. '"The Real War": Liddell Hart, Cruttwell and Falls', (ed.) Bond, B. *The First World War and British Military History*, 1991, 41–53. Strachan calls Cruttwell 'an infinitely greater historian' than Liddell Hart (59–60). His influence on later historians has, alas, been much less. The present author has relied a good deal more on Cruttwell than on Liddell Hart. Even Cyril Falls, excellent though he is, is apt to compare unfavourably in some respects with Cruttwell (who, of course, writing in 1934, was deprived of sources of later date). All three were personally engaged in the war – in the infantry.

See also Graves, K. 'Making Sense of the Great War: Regimental Histories, 1918–1923', *JAHR*, LXIX, No. 277, 1991, 6–15.

The forage question

that it exceeded 'even ammunition'* and indeed that it probably took 'more shipping space than was lost to German submarines';[4] but Liddell Hart ought surely to have known that forage for the cavalry was but a very small part of the total required. Without the horse not even the infantry, let alone the artillery – a six-horse team was necessary for drawing every 18-pounder – the engineers, the medical services and above all the vast supply organizations could not have operated at all. Even towards the end of the war, mechanical transport had replaced horse-drawn vehicles of every sort to only a very limited degree. In November, 1918, there were in the BEF 57,460 motor vehicles of all kinds (including 14,464 motor cycles and 3,532 ambulances), whereas there were 382,266 animals, including 76,602 mules.[5]† The forage for mules alone was vastly more than for the whole of the cavalry! Unfortunately it is impossible to discover the numbers of horses employed by all the various arms at different dates. There are, however, official figures giving the animal 'feeding strengths' on 7 December, 1918, for all arms and branches of the BEF including the 'lines of communication'. For the Cavalry Corps, which at that date probably included all but a few regiments of corps and divisional cavalry, there were 25,414 animals to be fed, including those in the RHA and Cavalry Machine Gun Corps, while all the rest of the BEF had 368,492: *a total of 394,443 for the whole BEF, as against 25,414*

---

*Between 9 August, 1914, and 2 August, 1919, the British forces in France received 5,916,104 tons of oats and hay from across the Channel, while the figure for ammunition was 5,269,302 tons. (*Statistical Abstract of Information regarding the Armies at Home and Abroad*, 1 Oct., 1919, IWM, 477).

There was certainly no shortage of forage for export in England, since in 1916 Lloyd George, under pressure from the Jockey Club, overruled the Cabinet and allowed 18,000 lbs of grain a day between July to December for use in training racehorses. This was enough to supply three cavalry regiments! (CAB/23/4, 251, quoted in Badsey, 331)

†On mobilization in 1914 there were only 643 motor vehicles in the whole of the army, including 116 motor cycles. There were no motor ambulances. Four years and three months later there were, in all theatres, 121,702, including 34,865 motor cycles.

Late in 1916 the CIGS was much exercised at the damage being done to stone-flagged roads in the BEF's rear by motor vehicles. He pressed for more transport horses. (Haig notes, 20 Nov., 1916, Acc. 3155.314h, NLS).

In Italy, Salonika, East Africa and Aden, where there were virtually no mounted troops, there were 34,134 horses and 48,503 mules to be fed.

for the Cavalry Corps! The animals on the lines of communication alone, at 48,822, were nearly twice as numerous as those in the Cavalry Corps. The proportion of riding horses to all other types (heavy and light draught and pack) in the BEF on 31 August, 1917, was 122,421 of the former and 245,728 of the latter. One year later there were 96,766 riding horses and of other types 218,115.[6] It is clear that more than half of the total of horses at any one time, except, possibly, during the first few months of the war, were for non-riding purposes. Of course, only a part of the total of riding horses was for the use of the cavalry. A proportion of the officers of all infantry battalions and nearly all staff officers of formations had horses on which to ride. The majority of artillery officers possessed riding horses and officers of the other arms such as the engineers and the RASC were also mostly mounted, as were many senior other ranks. The horse-teams that pulled the field artillery accounted for a large number of the draught horses.

At the war's end there were 1,914,558 men of one sort or another in the BEF and only 27,395 men in the Cavalry Corps, including its supporting services. To be absolutely sure that the statistics do not falsify the contention that the proportion of forage demanded for the cavalry was never anything but very low compared with the total, it might be wise to double the 25,414 December, 1918, figure to 50,828. If this is done, and it must surely be a gross exaggeration, it will be seen that *even then* the animal strength of each of the five armies, not counting the lines of communication, was *above that figure* by: First Army: 24,269; Second Army: 5,724; Third Army: 9,105; Fourth Army: 20,841; Fifth Army: 4,486.[7] If these statistics do not convince future historians that Liddell Hart's statement was, to be charitable, careless, nothing will!*

It is worth noting what the percentages of other ranks of the cavalry to the total strength of the BEF were at various dates. In September, 1914, it was 7.72%. A year later it had declined to 3.20%. In 1916 it was 2.55% and in 1917 2.15%. On 1 March,

---

*The cavalry exhibited its usual helplessness in the field at the beginning of the war on the Western Front. Lieutenant-Colonel Graham Thomas George Edwards of the 20th Hussars in September, 1914, had to point out to his squadron leaders that 'they should have more method in requisitioning, as a quantity of hay and oats within a stone's throw of their billet had not been noticed.' (Edwards, 22).

1918, just when it was most needed, with an effective strength of 15,755, the percentage had dropped to 1.11%. It remained roughly the same until on 11 November, 1918, it was 1.01%.[8] The far-too-often accepted assertion that there were masses of useless cavalrymen and horses eating their heads off to the detriment of the supply situation is obviously groundless. Considering that the cavalry to the very end of the war was the sole force capable of pursuing effectively a finally demoralized enemy it might even be that, had the moment of real breakdown arrived, and the supply situation allowed, there would have been criticism that so little of that force had been kept in being at such small cost.

* * *

When he was twenty Churchill's mother recommended him to make a study of the 'supply of army horses'. He told her that, though there was much to commend the subject to cavalry officers, he felt that it was 'more calculated to narrow and groove one's mind than to expand it'. Alas, this was ever the view of most other cavalry officers. Readers of Volume 4 of this work

HUMOURS OF A REMOUNT DEPÔT
Sergeant (to recruit, lately a motor mechanic). 'Now then, what for are you fumblin' at the back of yer saddle? Looking for the brake?'

(see pp. 279–349) will recollect the situation during the Boer War respecting the provision of remounts. In spite of much continuing indifference in the highest and many lower quarters, the lessons learned and acted upon between 1902 and 1914 were considerable. Conditions, requirements and types of horse on the Western Front were of course different in many respects from those in South Africa, but the organization for supply presented many of the same problems. Two vital lessons learned between the two wars were the need for a remount department which could be speedily expanded and for a comprehensive survey of animals available worldwide. Even more important was the purchase by impressment, mainly in Britain (under a decentralized scheme elaborated since early 1912), of 165,000 horses within twelve or so days of mobilization in 1914. This number included three months' supply 'in order to replace casualties in reserve units behind the armies'.[9]

The reservoir of trans-Atlantic animals had been fully researched before the war. So had the United Kingdom market. In 1909 Haldane, the Secretary of State for War, had required the police to take a census. This revealed that there were some 2,000,000 horses scattered over the country. In the 1911 Army Act

Branding a British Government purchase in North America with the broad arrow.

he directed that the County Associations should prepare lists of the different categories of horse from which the drafts for mobilization could be secured. In the course of the war '17% of the working [horse] population of Great Britain was mobilized for the war effort.'[10]

Already prepared in outline was a purchasing commission in Canada and the United States. This was swiftly constituted as soon as the raising of new armies was decided upon. Its officers were recruited mostly from large landowners, country gentlemen and masters of hounds, many of them beyond military age, thus avoiding the withdrawal of officers from military duties. The chief buying centres were at Chicago, St Paul Minnesota, Sioux City, Des Moines Iowa, St Louis, Kansas City and Toronto and Montreal. The minimum period between purchase and embarkation was seven weeks, and this seems to have been kept to for most of the time.[11]

Except for the 'side-shows' nearly all the remounts for the army came from Britain, Canada and the United States.* The need to scour the world for horses to send to South Africa between 1900 and 1902, entailing vast distances by ship (particularly from Russia and Hungary), was entirely removed between 1914 and 1918. So too was the appalling destruction of horses through the lack of acclimatization periods and the necessity of putting horses to hard work immediately on disembarkation which had characterized the South African experience.[12]

Between 1 August, 1914, and 1 August, 1915, the total of the army's animals rose from 25,000 (with a horse reserve, subsidized and registered, of another 25,000) to 534,951 and the personnel in the Remount Department from 351 to 16,660. The high peak came in August, 1917, when there were 869,931 animals and 20,983 officers and men in all theatres. Landed in the United Kingdom from Canada and North America during the whole of the war were 617,935 animals (including 206,729 mules) and from South America 6,819 horses. Of the total of 510,098 horses in all theatres on 30 November, 1918, 305,664 were with the BEF. (There were also 76,602 mules.) In Britain 467,973 horses were purchased. The total number of *riding* horses bought between 5 August, 1914, and 31 December, 1918, was 174,665. Some of

---

*For Mesopotamia and India the Indian Government bought chiefly from Australasia, China and India itself. Both France and Italy were buying from the United States. The supply from there seems at no time to have been near to drying up.

Testing an alleged riding horse before a British Government purchaser.

the 28,000 horses brought from Australasia were sent to the Western Front, though the majority went to Egypt. The depôts in Egypt and in Salonika were at first supplied from Australasia. Owing to difficulties of transportation, shipment of horses to Egypt from Australasia was stopped and later all direct shipment from across the Atlantic to the Mediterranean also ceased. Hence the supply of remounts to those theatres had to come through Britain and France.

The chief remount depôts were at Bristol, Liverpool and Southampton. Once landed, the animals spent about three weeks 'under veterinary observation'. Nearly every horse on arrival 'was shoeless, long-haired, tousle-maned, ragged-hipped and almost dragged his tail on the ground, so long and full and caked with dirt was it. His neck had gone light and mean, his backbone stuck up like a knifeboard and his ribs were pushing through his neglected hide.'[13] These horses were next apportioned to the smaller depôts or, in the case of the cavalry, direct to the reserve regiments. Here they spent an indeterminate period of conditioning and training* before being sent to base remount depôts

---

*As Private Albert Whitelock of the Bays put it: 'It took twice as long to train a troop horse as it did to train a cavalry recruit.' (Ascoli, 30).

HUMOURS OF A REMOUNT CAMP
Staff Officer: 'I rode this horse you sent me on Tuesday and he was all right. But when I rode him on Wednesday he was much too frisky.'
Remount Officer: 'Well, why not ride him only on Tuesdays?'

abroad. In the French depôts there soon came to be an establishment of about 16,500 animals at any one time. At home accommodation pre-war had been for 1,200 horses. At one period during the war it rose to as many as 60,000.

The total casualties of horses and mules during the war in all theatres and at home came to 529,564, of which 415,979 were horses. This number included, beside animals that died, were killed, destroyed and missing, those that were cast and sold. The percentage of this wastage in France rose from 12.58% for the four months of 1914 to 28.5% for 1917 and 24.24% for 1918.[14]* The total of horses that died, were destroyed, killed and missing in the BEF is hard to compute. However, there are statistics which show that on 1 October, 1917, in France and the United Kingdom,

---

*In the Boer War the wastage worked out at 7.8% *per month*.

The annual wastage of horses 'under peace conditions just before the war' was 14.80%. (Dec., 1918, Birkbeck, Maj.-Gen. W.H., Director of Remounts, quoted in Jessel, 112).

The losses at sea from August, 1914, to January, 1919, came to 11.13% of the 428,608 shipped from America and Canada. Sinking from enemy action accounted for 4,747 of these horses. Compared with the Boer War which lasted from October, 1899, to June, 1902, considering that the submarine menace did not then exist, this record is admirable. The Boer War losses at sea came to 9.72% of the 117,595 shipped from North America alone. (*Statistics*, 399).

225,856 fell into those categories.* The scale of the remount operation in all theatres is well illustrated by the department's expenditure: £67,505,000.[15]†

* * *

As a result of Boer War experiences and in expectation of a continental war, much research into the best types of horses for the various arms was undertaken between the wars. From the point of view of the mounted arm it was realized that the small horses, epitomised by the South African ponies, 'nimble as goats' and able to subsist on minimum forage (see Vol. 4, 341 *et seq.*) were not the

---

*The French army had lost 376,201 by that date. Out of these 165,513 had been cast, while the British figure was only 30,348 cast. The proportion of castings to death in the British army throughout the war was 1 cast to 7 dead. In the French army it was 1 cast to 1.7 dead. (*Statistics*, 397).

Added up, the total horse loss in both armies by 1 October, 1917, comes to 797,918. (*Statistics*, 397). The losses over the last fifteen months are not specified. At a very conservative estimate it cannot have been less than 250,000, which makes a conjectural figure of about a million and a half from both armies for the whole of the war.

†Between 11 November, 1918, and 31 March, 1920, at home and in the Army of the Rhine, 197,181 horses were sold 'for work' and 46,885 'for meat'. (*Statistics*, 397).

Landing of American horses at an English Port.

48. An armoured car held up by fallen trees on the Villers Bretonneux to Brie road, 8 August, 1918. Photograph taken by Australians. (See p.244)

49. Canadian cavalry passing German wounded, September, 1918.

50. 21 August, 1918. The 18th Hussars advancing. (See p.253)

51. 21 August, 1918. An officer of the 18th Hussars steadying his horse under shell fire.

sort chiefly required in France. In 1908 the class required for the cavalry was laid down as: 'A deep, short-legged, short-backed, good-barrelled horse of the hunter stamp, with substance and quality, true action and going without brushing the joints [grazing the fetlock with the shoe or hoof of the fellow foot]. Light, active, well-bred horses that move truly and well in all their paces, well ribbed up with plenty of bone ... Height at four years: 15.0½ to 15.2¼ hands; over four years: 15.1½ to 15.2½ hands.' Because of the great weights that cavalry horses had to carry (see below), stoutness, a certain degree of height and general robustness were indispensable.[16]

It was pretty generally agreed that, though the thoroughbred from the United Kingdom was in many respects unbeatable, the horse from across the North Atlantic was, for general purposes, just about as useful. The ease with which it was managed through its exceptional tractability was much appreciated. The 'higher spirit' of the English and especially the Irish horse was at times on the Western Front, but not very often, a boon not afforded by the American animal.[17] One equestrian authority found the American riding horse 'deceptive. He is usually high in the withers, suggesting that the shoulders are sloping and that he must carry the saddle in the right place. The truth is that the shoulder is straight more often than not and the scapula [shoulder-blade] narrow with a consequent loss of freedom which the riding man well understands. There are of course exceptions and perhaps what is lost in positive correctness of action is compensated for by that measure of comfort to be derived from the "lope" or "tittupping" gait of the Yankee saddle horse.'[18] Major-General Sir John Moore, the Director of the Army Veterinary Services in the BEF throughout the war, thought that 'nothing has ever equalled our Irish horses for cavalry work.'[19]*

The regiments that brought their own mounts to France from India possessed country breds for the most part. 'The offspring of English thoroughbred sires and native mares,' they were 'light of bone and unaccustomed to the climatic conditions of Europe'. Nevertheless they 'thoroughly proved their efficiency,' according to the 17th Lancers' historian. He found them better than the walers from Australia, which formed about a quarter of the horses in the regiment during 1914 and 1915.[20]

In the 11th Hussars it was found at the end of the war that 'the

---

*It is interesting to note that 75% of cavalry troop horses were mares.(Moore: *Vet.*, 122).

old original squadron horses stood the work much the best, some of the old stagers, fifteen years old, coming out best of all. Very few of the hunt horses which had come up on mobilization had been properly fit and they had not the same chance as the others: it was chiefly among these that wastage from sickness occurred.'[21] In peacetime no horse over twelve years old was considered to be capable of active cavalry work. But there were many instances of horses well over that age campaigning efficiently throughout the conflict. An exceptional example was a brown gelding issued to the 5th Dragoon Guards in 1912. He took part in a long-distance ride between London and Aldershot early in 1914, then was present at all the engagements in which the regiment took part. He was said to be 'the first horse to jump the Hindenburg Line [!], in full marching order, after the infantry had broken through. Although wounded on several occasions he never went into the sick lanes and was never "excused duty".' He came back home in April, 1919, as hale as he had left it in 1914. Another veteran was the horse ridden by a NCO of the South Notts Hussars Yeomanry in 1915 in Egypt. It had 'come back from the South African War and he has had it ever since. It is a fat bay, or chestnut, pony.'[22]

Yet another remarkable horse, belonging to the officer commanding the 4th Dragoon Guards, was twice wounded in 1914 and had 'temporarily aped an aeroplane with the assistance of a German "coal box" at Guiscard... He lived to win several jumping prizes in Germany, 1919, and his master owns him still [in 1924]. Despite his age, he still gives a good feel over a country not less than one day a week. He will be remembered in the regiment,' wrote the historian of the 4th, 'as being at one time Sergeant Pettit's horse, no. B.176.'[23]

Others which became famous after the war include Seely's 'Warrior'. He lived to be over thirty, riding to hounds and winning a point-to-point in the 1920s. He and 'Quicksilver', belonging to Sir Percy Laurie, who had been French's Personal Assistant in 1914, were among the veteran horses in the Victory Parade. 'Quicksilver', a large grey charger, was often seen in important London cavalcades, including the funeral processions of distinguished generals, having followed his master, who became Chief of the Mounted Branch at Scotland Yard, when he returned to England in 1919. On these occasions he always wore his 'decorations': the Order of the Blue Cross and the 1916–18 Victory and General

Service medals on his headstall. He was over twenty-eight when he died.[24]*

* * *

Though in all ranks there was considerable love for their steeds, there were many who would have agreed with Lieutenant Alan Lascelles of the Bedfordshire Yeomanry:

'The horse,' he wrote in 1916, 'though a noble animal, is a far more tiresome companion than the Ancient Mariner's Albatross, when you start touring the country with him. He debars you from spending the night anywhere in the neighbourhood of civilization, because he takes up such a lot of room, so that where you might have hoped for a roof, you get only a bivouac; he keeps you standing about two hours longer than you need after a long march, because he is unable to clean or feed himself, and will leave you altogether unless firmly secured; he drags you miles, two or three times a day, through mud that he has churned up with his feet and then refuses to drink at the end of it; he wears a mass of impedimenta with an unlimited capacity for getting dirty and unserviceable; he will bite or kick you on the smallest provocation, and at night he keeps honest men from their beds, because, unless closely watched, he will either hang himself or savage his neighbour. In fact, though he is all very well in peace time, I am beginning to think that the day when he is declared obsolete for war purposes – if it has not already dawned – will be a bright one for the human race.'[25]

As, he might have added, it unquestionably was for the equine one.

* * *

*In 1934 a Parade of Veteran War Horses was staged at the International Horse Show. Twenty-five were traced. They were accommodated in special stabling and 'paraded every evening, carrying shabracques emblazoned with their battle honours. All were aged – the youngest twenty-four and the oldest thirty-two.' One had served with Desert Mounted Corps in the Royal Bucks Hussars and had charged with the regiment at El Mughar (see Vol. 5, 191). (Brereton: *Horse*, 141)

The transport safely docked. Keenness to land in France.

As with the remount service so with the vets, many lessons were learned as a result of the South African War. By August, 1914, numerous improvements had been instituted, most of them stemming directly from War Office committees of various sorts, the earliest being the Hardwicke Committee of 1902. An homogeneous corps, the [Royal] Army Veterinary Corps was formed for the first time in 1906. Among many advances made were proper training in military and technical duties,* research, standardization of dietetics and treatment, a register of civilian veterinary practitioners (of whom about 33% served during the war) and the setting up of centres for the mobilization of veterinary units. In 1909 a

---

*For example, four schools of farriery were set up in France, in which thousands of men were converted into horse-shoers 'by a system of intensive training'. (Smith, 235).

298

The Veterinary Corps

Special Reserve of Veterinary Officers was established for the first time.[26] In 1913 the Veterinary Directorate was removed from the control of the Remount Department and taken under the umbrella of the Quartermaster-General's Department, becoming a separate department like that of the Remount Service.[27] There came into being on mobilization mobile veterinary sections attached to each cavalry brigade and infantry division of the BEF. Like the 1913 *Remount Regulations*, there was produced, but literally not until the last moment, in August, 1914, the painstaking and splendidly complete *Veterinary Manual (War)*. As regards equipment, modifications which took into account the advance of scientific knowledge were made on a comprehensive scale. 'The result of this forethought,' according to Major-General Sir Layton John Blenkinsop, the head of the department and the official veterinary historian, 'was that the equipment as it existed on mobilization was found, on the whole, to be adequate in design and detail during the entire war'. On mobilization 'veterinary equipment for the entire force was perfectly ready.'[28] To bring the establishment of other ranks in the Corps up to that required on mobilization unfit ('Class "D"') cavalry reservists were allotted to it.[29]

The expansion of the Corps during the war was impressive. In all theatres, for instance, 1,668 officers and 41,755 other ranks served in it. In the BEF, including colonials, there were at the war's peak 17,211 officers and men. In August, 1914, there were only 919.[30] The efficiency generated by careful planning and by the placing of the Corps on a level with the other services, (which had never been done before in the army's history), is well illustrated by the astonishing fact that animal sickness in all theatres between 1915 and the Armistice never exceeded 11.44%. In 1914 15.23% had been on the sick list. Then there had been an average strength of 204,628 animals, while in 1915 this figure had risen to 483,134, in 1917 to 966,840 and in 1918 to 827,506. The average daily number of sick during 1917 was 110,000. Throughout the war, on all fronts, the total admissions to hospital were 2,562,549, of which 78%, about two million, were returned to duty. Between July, 1916, and the Armistice, gunshot wounds numbered 58,090 killed and 77,410 wounded. 'On the Western Front by the summer of 1918 a considerable proportion of the wounds were being caused by bombs dropped from aircraft.' In the same period 211 were killed and 2,220 wounded due to poison gas.[31]

The veterinary service

There seems to have been only one blot of any significance on the record. Out of the 768,572 animals purchased in Canada and the United States 42,261 had died or been destroyed *before shipment*. This was chiefly due to disease resulting from poor organization, the depôts being congested, the open stabling, especially in the north during the winter, and, above all, to inadequate veterinary examination for soundness. This was in large part caused by

> 'the arts of the fraudulent horse dealer put into use to deceive the examiner. Sponges for instance are placed up the nostrils to hide unsoundness of wind; animals are "set" in various ways for the purpose of cloaking broken wind; teeth are scientifically "bishoped";* ice is placed in the rectum to hide high temperature; and various dopes are given to stimulate sick animals to temporary activity.'[32]

In the eighteen months between June, 1915, and November, 1916, 108,372 horses were admitted to veterinary hospitals in Canada alone. Of these 15,488 (14.29%) died or were destroyed. This illustrates the scale of the problem. So for the Western front do the 299,082 admissions to hospitals between January and November, 1916. The worst period was the bitter spring of 1917 at a time when the forage ration had to be reduced because of the submarine menace. In April 20,319 animals of the 195,000 in front of Arras were sent to hospital, whereas in March the number was 9,427 and in June only 1,253. Part of the reason for such pronounced feebleness was that clipping as a precaution against mange had been enforced during the winter. For the rest of the war it was not allowed after mid-November.[33] Due to debility it was estimated that for every 10,000 horses in the

---

*This process, designed to make a horse look younger than it is, was invented by a scoundrel called Bishop in the early 18th-century. It consisted of cutting off 'the nippers with a saw to the proper length and then with a cutting instrument the operator scoops out an oval cavity in the corner nippers, which is afterwards burnt out with a hot iron until it is quite black.' (Walsh, J.A., quoted in *Webster's New International Dictionary*, 227).

Equine 'excessive sexual exuberance' dealt with

BEF about 200 reinforcements were required each week to maintain establishments.[34]*

Among the horses which dealers were particularly anxious to sell were those animals which were cryptorchid, the condition in which the testes fail to descend normally into the scrotum from the abdomen, and those described as 'troublesome mares'. Many of these categories found their way into veterinary hospitals. Special instruments were therefore necessary 'for the operation for the relief of animals troubled with excessive sexual exuberance and its resultant annoyance and danger to man and other animals'. Cryptorchids were almost invariably successfully operated upon, while ovariotomy dealt with the vicious propensities of the mares. Their return to duty was thus assured.[35]

During the ghastly weather and mud of the 1917 spring hundreds of horses arrived in hospital 'in an emaciated condition'. Numbers 'died in the trucks and others fell down paralysed in the hind quarters and were shot. . . . Quite a big proportion had paraphimosis [contraction of the orifice of the foreskin] and, indeed, paralysis of the muscles of the penis.' Amputation was avoided by means of a new Swedish operation.[36] All surgery, where possible, was performed under anaesthetics. Chloroform and cocaine were

---

*5,475,202 animal bandages were issued during the whole war. If laid out they would have reached from London to New York and back! (Blenkinsop, 54).

An unforeseen hazard for equines was the puncture of hoofs by nails. This in the BEF accelerated from an average of 400 such casualties a week in 1915–16 to 530 the following year, reaching at times 800. This remarkable increase was 'due to the use on a large scale of regimental field-cookers [chiefly in the infantry and artillery], which used wood from packing cases, complete with nails, for fuel.' Among the measures taken to prevent this type of accident, which usually resulted in lameness arising from quittor [inflammation of the lateral cartilage of the foot] was 'the organization of "nail hunts" by units'! Others proved impracticable, especially the towing behind lorries of 'electromagnetic machines'! (Blenkinsop, 540–1, 557).

Another uncovenanted cause of debility and indeed often mortality was 'greasy heel'. This disease arose from horses standing in the highly manured mud. It quickly developed into a purulent sore.

Yet another unanticipated disorder came from mustard gas. Wherever it fell the ground was infected for a long time afterwards. Horses picketed on it or even walking through it were attacked by 'the irritant poison wherever the hair was thin and caused the most dreadful wounds'. Before long 'an effective curative treatment was found in a dressing of chloride of lime.' (Clarke, Lt-Gen. Sir Travers 'Our Animal Friends in the World War', *Empire Supplement, The Morning Post*, 22 Mar., 1926.)

in abundant supply. This was a great advance. In no previous conflicts had these been available for animals.[37]

Shell and bullet wounds were of course the most common types of injury. Very often bullets passed through the body or a limb, 'leaving a clear-cut hole which did not interfere with the utility of the animal and healed without complications'. The peculiar effects of one shell wound were reported by a veterinary officer in 1915: 'The anus itself of a mare was completely excised as perfectly as if by the surgeon's knife, while the tail, vagina, and buttocks were entirely uninjured. This animal must have been in the act of defaecating when hit by the piece of shell. The horse lived for about four days and was then destroyed, the piece of shell (about 3 inches by 2 inches) being found on post-mortem examination in the region of the mammary gland. The missile must have been deflected immediately upon entry as there were no other wounds anywhere on the body.'[38]

* * *

As in the Boer War (see Vol. 4, 371–5), strenuous efforts were made to reduce the weights carried by cavalry horses. They were all unavailing. Though it came to be accepted that less than eighteen stone was completely unrealistic, considerably more was the norm. The minimum meant that beside the man at, say, ten stone, ten pounds, there had to be carried saddlery, arms, accoutrements, ammunition, clothing, 'necessaries', rations and water.[39]* In practice this minimum was seldom, if ever, achieved. Major Charrington tells how the average officer loaded his mount in 1916:

'My new mackintosh and that invaluable rain-sort-of-sou'wester are rolled up in a mackintosh sheet behind me. With these and the blanket from under the saddle (I carry two there; one for me, one for the horse) and a bundle of straw, I can curl up warmly and comfortably to sleep anywhere....
I have one pair of wire nippers on the saddle, another on me.

---

*On the trooper's saddle alone (from which it was 'nearly impossible to fall off, except sideways') were strapped, on the pommel, 'the cloak, blanket, waterproof-sheet, balaclava helmet and one pair of socks'. On its rear portion were attached 'the mess tin, one nosebag containing corn feed, two shackle pegs, one shackle and one portion of "built up" rope.... The outfit is just about as much as one can lift on to the horse.' (19 Dec., 1914, Case, Tpr R.C., Wiltshire Yeomanry, IWM).

Weights carried by cavalry horses

In my saddle-bag, on the off-side, are maps and emergency food (chocolate, cocoa tablets, sardines). On the near side is my sword, with the watering bucket and picketing peg attached to the scabbard. In front are the wallets containing washing and shaving kit, spare socks and handkerchiefs. Then on me I have everything I really want in case I lose my horse. In the left breast pocket a photograph . . . also my money; in the right, flask, cigarette case, pencils and packet of toilet paper; in right hand bottom pocket, letters, and in left pipe, tobacco, matches, diary and iodine capsules. In flap pocket in lining smoke helmet and field dressing. In trouser pockets any spare cash and silver match box – these are the last line and I borrow matches before I use them. Then on my left are revolver, ammunition pouches, field-glasses and an enormous pocket knife. Hung across my shoulders, to finish with, are map-case, with the map I actually require on the day, and in a flap of this are paper & envelopes. . . . Also, but I don't always carry this, I have a haversack containing plate, cup, woolly waistcoat and probably my lunch. . . . There is nothing I can dispense with.'[40]

The men were not less encumbered than the officers – perhaps even more so. Beside their British Warms, which had replaced the cavalry cloak in 1914,

'they carried a web haversack, containing washing and shaving kit and personal trifles, slung on a brace over the right shoulder; a similar brace over the left shoulder supported a water-bottle – and both haversack and water-bottle banged smartly together whenever the wearer bent forward. On top of these went a leather bandolier with ninety rounds, to which wire-cutters were attached by the few men who carried them. In an emergency a cotton bandolier with fifty rounds was also carried. To this array was added in 1914 a belt, frog and bayonet, and in 1915 first a gas-mask and then a steel helmet. Each man was armed with a lance [if in a lancer regiment], sword, rifle . . ., though sergeants and upwards relied, thankfully enough, on sword and pistol only. The horse, in addition to the man and his equipment, carried a ninety-round bandolier round its neck, two blankets, one saddle blanket and one for the rider, a service saddle with, slung over it, a pair of wallets carrying a spare pair of boots, iron rations, a couple of Mills bombs and a change of washing. Up to 1915 a corn sack was strapped across the wallets. On the near side of the saddle were the sword, which fitted into a shoe-case carrying one fore and one hind shoe fitted to the horse and some nails, surcingle [the narrow leather girth going over the saddle and under the horse] pad, a picketing-peg, hay net and the day's ration of oats. On the off-side were the rifle bucket and rifle, mess tin and canvas water-bucket. Strapped across the rear arch of the saddle was the greatcoat, very neatly rolled indeed.'[41]*

That each horse was required to carry well over eighteen stone cannot be in doubt.

* * *

On 1 April, 1995, the last twenty horses employed by the army on non-ceremonial duties, were put out to grass. These, all of Irish stock, belonging to the Royal Military Police Mounted Troop, had been used for patrolling areas of intractable terrain in Britain, such as gunnery ranges. This task is now performed more economically by motorcycles. Nineteen of the redundant steeds are ending their days at the military animal centre at Melton Mowbray, while the twentieth, Winston, has been transferred to the Aldershot Saddle Club, which is devoted to teaching army families how to ride and look after their horses. The Troop was originally formed in 1855 from men in cavalry regiments who were 'intelligent' and of 'sober habits'. In 1993 it distinguished itself by winning the 'skill at arms' competition at the Royal Tournament.

*Corporal L.M. Lawrence of the 12th Lancers, describes the difficulty of mounting:

'One mounted with the lance, after putting the rifle in the rifle bucket on the off-side. The correct drill was to place the rifle on the off-side of the horse's neck, with a finger of the left hand in the top of the rifle sling, (the left hand used to hold lots [sic]), place the lance in the left hand, take up the reins, put the left foot in the near stirrup-iron, grasp the rear arch of the saddle and mount. Then one placed the rifle in the rifle bucket and forced it home: grasped the lance, threw it in the air so that the butt cleared the horse's withers, caught it and placed the butt in the off-side lance bucket. One had to be supple. Stiff joints were not known.'(Quoted in Stewart, 283).

EPILOGUE

(i)

A chief object of this last volume has been to enable its author to enter the ranks of that small contingent of writers about the Western Front which has been battling to dispel the numerous myths which have grown up concerning the British Army's part in its battles. Such men as John Terraine and Paddy Griffith have been valiantly striving over the last few decades to put the record straight.

These and others have convincingly shown what were the true roles of each of the various arms and of their commanders. The reality, rather than the oft repeated misstatements of the A.J.P. Taylors and the Alan Clarks and of a few more serious students of the war such as Liddell Hart, is gradually entering the consciousness of historians and others.

It is still difficult to disperse the comfortable, facile assumptions so prominently disseminated by these influential commentators. If this volume has helped to do that for the cavalry, the most vilified, despised and misunderstood of the arms, its author will be content. It ought, he hopes, to be no longer possible to sustain the popular view that the mounted arm after 1914 became a large, unwanted, useless and expensive burden kept in being by old-fashioned, stuck-in-the-saddle cavalry generals.

'The Cabinet have given their decision as to the war for which we are to prepare in the future, which is in the East and not in Europe, a war of movement and not of trenches, a mobile war and not a stabilized war.'
– The CIGS to the Secretary of State for War, 1927[1]

(ii)

The period 1919 to 1939 was a depressing one in the history of the armed forces. It was even more depressing for the mounted branch of the army, for when these two decades, known aptly as 'the lean years', came to an end, it had for some time been clear that cavalry as a force in war, everywhere in the world, was facing the same death-throes experienced long ago by the dodo. The background against which they were acted out was complex. Here it is described – much over-simplified.

That the three services had to be drastically reduced as soon as practicable after the war was inevitable. It had produced vastly more men and material and had cost infinitely more than had any of its predecessors.* It left the nation and the Empire greatly impoverished and thoroughly exhausted. Retrenchment was the 'in' word, unhappy though it was after years of trench warfare! How large must be the cuts and in what proportions should they be made? What should be the forces' proper post-war form and functions? These were the problems with which governments and their advisers wrestled for twenty wretched years. The prospects at the Armistice were not happy. At that date there were British troops in France, Belgium, Germany, Italy, Greece, Austria-Hungary, Serbia, Bulgaria, the Ottoman Empire and Russia (see below), yet by November, 1920, demobilization had reduced the army from 3,779,825 to 431,916[2], and the numbers were decreasing steadily.

It is extremely hard for us, living after another gigantic worldwide conflict, as well as a prolonged 'cold war', to put ourselves in the position of those who had to take decisions affecting the

---

*Only 30 per cent of the cost was paid for by taxation. The rest of course came from loans.

defence of the realm at that time. It seemed impossible, at least until fourteen years after the Armistice, when a new major threat was becoming glaringly manifest, to contemplate another world war within a discernible period. The average citizen was understandably reluctant to begin to imagine further large-scale blood-letting within his or even his children's lifetime, or, indeed, ever.* Especially was this so under the economic depressions and slumps which he had to face in the twenties and thirties, and considering that before the war Britain had been a creditor nation and was now a debtor nation. Even had those of his elected leaders who heard and understood the meaning of the initially faint, uncertain ringing of the European and Far Eastern alarm bells actively tried to prompt him to spend his money on reacting to it, they would have been replaced by others less perceptive. Even when the bell-ringing had become a deafening roar†, the powers-that-be were loath to force the electorate to listen to it and to confront the palpable need to prepare for major war. This is easy to censure in retrospect, yet it deserves a measure of understanding. The 'guilty men' were chiefly guilty only in the sense that actors in a Greek tragedy are guilty. Michael Howard sums the situation up: 'After 1918 the reader [of the Committee of Imperial Defence minutes] becomes conscious of a new sound: the heavy and ominous breathing of a parsimonious and pacific electorate,

---

*There were 744,000 British killed in the war. This was not *proportionately* higher than in previous 'big' wars. The great difference was that in those wars only two minority classes had suffered, whereas 'in the Great War the entire nation for the first time had felt the cost of being a great empire'. (Barnett, 412).

†Hitler came to power in 1933. In the same year he withdrew from the Disarmament Conference and the League of Nations (as also did Japan). In 1935 the first three panzer divisions were in being and the existence of an air force was made known, both in blatant contravention of the Versailles Treaty. In the same year the League rejected Abyssinian appeals for help against Mussolini's aggression. In 1935 Hitler recovered the Saar and in 1936 he re-occupied the Rhineland unopposed. In 1937 Japan after six years of disregarding the League's demand that she withdraw from Manchuria, started her conquest of China. In 1938 Hitler annexed Austria and seized the Sudetenland, with, under the Munich pact, the acquiescence of France and Britain. In 1939 Mussolini invaded Albania, while Hitler occupied the rest of Czechoslovakia and later Poland.

to the variations in which the ears of British statesmen were increasingly attuned.'³ Until the Nazi takeover in 1933 it had been first France (for a short time) and then Japan which had been considered the chief threats to peace.*

In defence of the governments' inability to give in good time the necessary priority to rearmament, it is clear that some of the best minds amongst their advisers, especially in the Treasury, believed that the appallingly parlous state of the economy – in mid-1921 there were more than 2,000,000 wholly unemployed – made it totally impossible for the nation to fight another major war until, in the distant future, things returned to 'normality'. 'Not until 1939, when fear of war at last outweighed fear of a financial crash, did the Cabinet ignore Treasury warnings about finance.'⁴ As late as 1936 the Treasury 'believed that the rearmament programme was a far more profound threat to the social and political order than Germany was to the national security.'⁵ Conveniently for the holders of these views there were those who preached as late as the mid-thirties, as Asquith had in July, 1914, the 'limited liability' doctrine of non-intervention by the army in Europe. Neville Chamberlain, both as Chancellor of the Exchequer and as Prime Minister, was chief among the members of the Cabinet who exhorted non-intervention. Liddell Hart, who was becoming an unofficial military guru much attended to in Whitehall – with

---

*'In 1922 when relations with France had reached their lowest point since Fashoda [1898],' a main fear was French bombing attacks on Britain. A sub-committee of the CID warned that 'a French air-force could maintain a continuous series of air attacks on London for several weeks which would so demoralize the population that they would force the government to make peace.' (Howard, 82; 26 Apr. 1922, CID Sub-Committee on Continental Air Menace Report, CID Papers, 1 06–A, CAB 3/3; French, D. *The British Way in Warfare, 1688–2000*, 1990, 183).

It was 'Japan's increasing threat to the Empire in the Far East' that induced the Cabinet to revoke the 'Ten Year Rule' which in secret from 1919 and openly from 1928 had laid it down that until it was revoked it was to be presumed that no major war need be provided for during the next ten years. The rule was reviewed and renewed each year until its cancellation in 1932 at the insistence of the COS Sub-Committee. (Howard, 98; Bond: *BMP*, 23–7, 94–7).

The rule had a baleful effect, especially upon the army. Experiments with new equipment were thought to be unnecessary and 'the spur even to theoretical studies', as Correlli Barnett puts it, was removed. 'The army was thus put back to the 1890s, a colonial gendarmerie with no major role to play or plan for.' (Barnett, 411).

generally unhappy consequences – was foremost of the governments' advisers in propounding it. He urged Britain to 'eschew the idea of landing an army on the Continent', adding that a large air force 'would be more comfort to a threatened neighbour... than any force of the 1914 pattern – a mere drop in the bucket'. This, though hardly what the French expected as a result of the Locarno Treaty of 1925, which promised military support for France if attacked by Germany (and vice versa), was not technically incompatible with its terms. Duff Cooper, when he became Secretary of State for War, pointed out in 1936 how false this attitude was. He said that there were many situations in which the air force could not be used and that a small, efficient 'Field Force' would undoubtedly have a great impact.*[6] During his short sojourn at the War Office he was a sturdy fighter for a strong, small 'Field Force'. Consequently he was sacked by Chamberlain who put Hore-Belisha in his place. Hore-Belisha was vastly influenced by Liddell Hart.

The French, it was said, were led to believe that, since Britain would not face conscription, the next fight against Germany would have to be fought without British help. The British army continued to rely on voluntary recruitment until April, 1939, in spite of serious recruitment problems, a great deal less, incidentally, in the cavalry than in the infantry. In 1936, when the rearmament programme was announced, both the infantry and the territorials were well below their peace establishment, and recruitment was below wastage.[7] In Germany, contrary to the Versailles Treaty, full conscription was restored in 1935.

---

*In 1934 British bombers could hardly reach the Ruhr from home bases. A 'spearhead' expeditionary force was recommended by the RAF for securing air bases. (Peden, 121).

'The Imperial account was already choked with liabilities, and every square yard which accrued to the Empire as a result of the Peace Treaties seemed to bring in more.'
— MICHAEL HOWARD in *The Continental Commitment*[1]

(iii)

The Empire emerged from the war with larger and more complex commitments than ever before.* None of them could be dealt with without military participation. To those in the actual Empire were now added those in the territories mandated to Britain by the League of Nations. There was serious unrest in India, Egypt, Palestine and Iraq, as well as in Ireland and at home. Further there were the (futile) efforts to crush the Bolsheviks, the Chanak crisis in Turkey and the Third Afghan War to be provided for.

A number of these commitments were before long brought to an end through political manoeuvres which in some cases had serious long-term results. The Irish Treaty of 1921 and subsequent truce ended the rebellion there, releasing a considerable number of troops.† The Army of the Rhine was withdrawn for the most part in 1930, the occupation of the rest of Germany having finished in 1922. In that year, too, Egypt, declaring itself an independent state, ceased to be a British protectorate. A military presence was nevertheless still required. This was withdrawn to the Suez Canal in 1926. In Iraq, up to and after the end of the British mandate in 1921, it proved possible to maintain order almost exclusively by the RAF.[2] (But see fn p. 352, Appx 1) The Straits were evacuated in 1923, once the Chanak crisis had

---

**Whitaker's Almanack* for 1922 stated that the British Empire 'extends over one-quarter of the known surface of the globe, and its population exceeds one-quarter of the estimated number of the human race.'

†There were five cavalry regiments in Ireland up to 1922. They were employed in 'sweeps' against the rebels, supported by armoured cars. The rebels blew up bridges and felled trees across roads, 'thus halting the armoured cars and both horsed and mechanical transport, but not in any way holding up the cavalry'. (Oatts: 3DG/6DG, 243). This was a considerable boost to cavalry morale.

The fear of revolution at home

been resolved, while the intervention in Russia did not last much beyond 1922. The Third Afghan War ended in August, 1919, but turbulent tribes of the North West Frontier* and increasing agitation for independence in India still required considerable numbers of troops there. The largest expeditionary force sent overseas between the wars was the Shanghai Defence Force in 1927, the purpose of which was to secure the safety of British nationals in Shanghai from the possible incursions of Chiang Kai-shek's army. Nearly all of these commitments required the inclusion of a mounted element in the forces used.

In short, until a major war became a distinct probability rather than a distant possibility, the priority given to imperial defence was rightly overwhelming, if not absolute. It was clear that any army organization designed for the latter, based on the well tried Cardwell system (see Vol. 3, p.30), was very different from any designed for the former (considerably more so than in 1914). This fact (much more than the influence of the cavalry lobby), combined with the maintenance of over 130 infantry battalions (the bulk of the army and mostly thought to be essential for imperial defence purposes), was a major obstacle to the development of armoured formations.

* * *

At home, until the General Strike of 1926 had been settled, and for some time after, there was a continuing fear of revolution inspired by the Russian example. The War Office, indeed, had been sufficiently alarmed in February, 1919, to send to all commanding officers a questionnaire asking whether their men would remain loyal in case of a revolution. Most replied in the affirmative, without qualifications. So stretched after demobilization were the military forces at home, that Wilson, the CIGS, complained at this time that he had only two spare battalions to deal with potential trouble on Clydebank. After serious rioting had broken out in Liverpool on 2 August, during which shots were fired over the crowds' heads, mounted troops were called upon to patrol the streets.[3] This was almost the last time when mounted troops were used in civil disturbances. Speedy communications and an efficient

---

*In April, 1920, the Indian Government demanded four extra cavalry brigades (*sic*) for the NW Frontier. (Higham, 22)

police force (some of it, of course, mounted to this day) made the cavalry, and, indeed, the infantry too, redundant for this purpose. It was rightly considered that a chief way to mitigate 'bolshie' agitations was to spend more on 'the health and labour of the people'.[4] Throughout the period this consideration was a major disincentive for devoting limited resources to defence.

These widespread and multiform engagements and the financial restrictions imposed, particularly by the draconian economies imposed in 1922 by the Committee of National Expenditure – the famous 'Geddes Axe' – (which hit the army hardest of all the services) and by the slump of 1931 and its lingering consequences, were not the only impediments in the way of a coherent approach to decisions as to what size and what sort of forces should be established – and for what. The League of Nations seemed, for a time, to give real hopes of a prolonged peace, especially in Europe. At the same time there was sweeping over the country a persistent wave of pacifism induced by a feeling that the First World War had been completely unnecessary. Another depressing factor was that the United States required Britain to pay her war debts although her late enemies were unwilling and virtually unable to pay Britain the reparations imposed on them. Further, the United States adopted a strict isolationist policy and banned the export of munitions. However warlike the future seemed, no help was likely from America. Yet another potent influence upon policy was the belief that 'the Maginot Line meant that France would not need assistance by [British] land forces'.[5]

'Concentration on airpower had the advantage, as far as the National Government was concerned, of being fashionable policy. Airpower was relatively new and exciting and a government which concentrated upon it seemed to be forward looking. The preparation of a field force for a Continental war, by contrast, however necessary strategically, inevitably brought back bad memories.'
— J.P. HARRIS in 'The British General Staff and the Coming of War'

'The Cabinets which governed Britain in the 1930s were composed of men who believed that almost any price was too high to pay to avoid another war. The exceptions, curiously enough, were those who had first-hand experience of war, Eden and Duff Cooper; who knew that vile as the experience was, it was not utterly intolerable, and there might be others yet worse.'
— MICHAEL HOWARD in *The Continental Commitment*[1]

(iv)

Throughout the '20s and '30s the army was treated by succeeding Cabinets as the 'Cinderella Service' when it came to expenditure. Limited resources, as Chamberlain put it, 'will be more profitably employed in the air and on the sea, than in building up great armies.'[2] As has been shown, this was also Liddell Hart's view. Even many pacifists saw the need for a strong navy, for 'maritime communications and overseas trading interests have consistently been a very high priority,'[3] especially where food – and now oil – were concerned, while protection from air bombardment every politician and every elector was prepared to pay for. It so happened, too, that to expand the aircraft industry was easier, cheaper and less disrupting to the economy than building up the other defence industries. Thus the RAF's requirements came immediately after the navy's. It was not surprising either that the need for anti-aircraft guns was given top priority when the Army Estimates were formed. This further restricted expenditure on the other requirements of the army.* The preparation of a field or

---

*In early 1936 the government's chief industrial adviser declared that industry could not meet the demands of all three services within five years without controls over industry. These, not surprisingly, were not acceptable in peacetime. (See, especially, Peden, 124).

expeditionary force, therefore, came absolutely at the bottom of the list. 'At the present time,' wrote Lord Hailsham, the Secretary of State for War in 1934, 'if the country went to war the army would not be fit to fight, and it would be mere massacre to send them to do so.'[4] Though in 1933 a force of twelve divisions was being thought of in the War Office, later increased to seventeen and, after the occupation of Czechoslovakia, to thirty-two, the very most that was actually considered possible in the mid-1930s was a force of four or five infantry divisions, one tank brigade and one cavalry division* on the continent, but the resources for even these were thoroughly inadequate. They were still largely so when war came and the force went to France in 1939. Compared with the BEF in 1914, it was pitifully feeble – miserably so in equipment, training and indeed doctrine – and it took longer to ship it over than in 1914. Late in 1938, when the crisis was nearing its climax, the army was told to prepare itself to be able to send two regular infantry divisions and one 'mobile' division to France within twenty-one days and two further infantry divisions within forty days of the declaration of war. Of the intense, long-planned preparation before 1914, there was little sign.† None of this is surprising since in December, 1937, the Cabinet had definitely decided that the army was not to be prepared to fight on the Western Front on the outbreak of war. Nor is it surprising that Britain when she did go to war in 1939 possessed no effective armoured division, nor an agreed doctrine of armoured warfare.

*By the end of 1927 the Cabinet had decided that on mobilization the cavalry element should consist of, beside the two armoured car regiments (see p. 337), nine horsed ones, including a composite Household Cavalry regiment. Five of the nine were to act as divisional cavalry to the five infantry divisions. The regimental establishment decided upon was 'the lowest war establishment ever yet contemplated'. (27 Oct., 1927, AG to SoS, WO 32/2846, 11A; see also 3 Nov., 1927, CIGS to SoS, 16/Gen/5558, 14, WO 32/2846).

None of this, of course, ever came about.

†'The embarkation of this force could commence within fourteen days.
'The force would be at full strength as regards personnel and could be so maintained. Though no longer horsed, it is lacking in modern equipment; it would have no Bren guns, armoured machine-gun carriers or modern field artillery, its tanks, if any, would only be light tanks.' (WO 'Note on the situation ... on 13 March, 1938,' quoted in Pownall, Lt-Gen. Sir H. *Chief of Staff: The Diaries of, 1933–1940,* ed. Bond, B., I, 1972, 378).

It is of interest to note that in 1932 defence accounted for 12% of government expenditure, in 1936, 21%, in 1938, 38% and in 1939, 48%. (Shay, 297).

'The horse is doomed; it is no longer an argument of fire-arms *versus* the *arme blanche*, but of a change in the element of movement itself.'

* * *

'There is at present moment a school of thought, unthoughtful in the main, which considers that the cavalry "idea" is part of an obsolete doctrine.'
— BREVET-COLONEL J.F.C. FULLER in 'The Influence of Tanks on Cavalry Tactics (A Study in the Evolution of Mobility in War)', 1920

'So long as the masses of the infantry march, the existence of cavalry is probable, but once these masses become motorised, even if only for logistical purposes, they will disappear ..., for though it is easy to motorise a man, it is unprofitable rather than difficult to motorise a horse.'

* * *

'The cavalry will certainly not die. It will live on in the form of the motorised trooper and the mechanized one as well.'
— J.F.C. FULLER *Armoured Warfare*, 1943[1]

(v)

The mounted force of the British Army at the Armistice numbered twenty-eight regular, over fifty yeomanry (see p. 344) and forty-five Indian native regiments. In 1933 there were still fifty-seven horsed regiments in the British Empire: twenty regulars, sixteen yeomanry and twenty-one of the Indian Army. At the outbreak of war in September, 1939, the only mounted formation mobilized was a yeomanry division, which was sent to Palestine. It was not mechanized until 1941, by the end of which year only the Cheshire and Yorkshire regiments remained mounted. (For the fate of the yeomanry between the wars see p. 344)

During the post-war years at least four of the regulars were always stationed, as in the past, in India and another two or three in Egypt or elsewhere in the Middle East. Of the twelve at home, six were nominally grouped into two brigades, while the other six were stationed in different parts of the country at single-unit stations.

The one really important modernizing change, beside the gradual substitution of Armoured Fighting Vehicles (AFV) for horses, was the rather less gradual mechanization (or motorisation) of all the regimental transport as well as of the machine-gun squadrons (see below).*

* * *

When the 5th Earl of Yarborough, Colonel of a distinguished yeomanry regiment and an old 11th Hussar, asked his yeomen to gather round for a momentous announcement, he stood 'on a table with tears streaming down his face'. 'He told us,' remembers one of his men, 'that he had just heard the regiment had to give up the horses.' His love of the horse was not shared by his men. 'The cheer that went up was deafening.'[2] Love of horses was always tempered in the minds of the rank and file, especially, perhaps, of the

*Though the lance was finally abolished by AO 392 of 1927, except for ceremonial purposes, it is interesting to note that a new design was recommended in the previous year. (23 November, 1926, Cav. Comm. Interim Report, WO 32/2841, 24)

For the history of the lance in the British cavalry, see Vol. 1, 98–101; Vol. 2, 416–7; Vol. 4, 410–11.

'Don't you worry. It'll be a long time before they can do without us.'

Officers' and ORs' attitudes towards 'mechanicalization'

yeomanry, by experiences of the tiresomeness of the animal, so often referred to, love and hate well mixed, as that 'long-faced bugger'. A trooper in an Indian cavalry regiment, asked for his views on mechanization, replied: 'On Sunday I pat my tank and tell it to sit still. I do not have to take it to be fed and watered five times a day,'[3] and, worse, he might have added, to be mucked out, groomed and exercised every day of the year. Though there is further evidence of other ranks welcoming the equine demise, most, especially the young ones, seemed to be indifferent. After the last mounted parade of the 11th Hussars on 10 April, 1928, for example, a trooper was heard to say, 'We got a name for picking cherries. I suppose that now, with our bleeding tanks [in fact, in his case, armoured cars], we'll get a name for picking nuts.' 'Before long,' wrote a 12th Lancer soon after the regiment had taken over its armoured cars in 1928, 'the talk was all of differentials, carburettors and all the many parts which go to make up a car. . . . In addition to the enthusiasm the next most favourable point was the youth and flexibility of mind of the majority of the men. They were able to absorb the new technical training with little difficulty and many and long were the discussions in canteens and messes on the relative merits of the various cars and proprietary parts of those days.'[4]*

One of the great tank men, Major (later Lieutenant-General Sir) Giffard Le Quesne Martel, who attended the first post-war two-year Staff College course in 1921, discovered to his surprise that in heated discussions about 'mechanicalization', as for a time it was inelegantly called, 'the students who were cavalrymen were very open-minded as a whole. In particular Rollie Charrington†

---

*When, in 1936/7, the 7th Hussars were mechanized, only sixteen of the 530 other ranks volunteered to transfer to regiments still horsed. (Brereton: 7H, 168).

†Major (later Lieutenant-Colonel) H.V.S. Charrington, was the historian of the 12th Lancers during the war, and author of a slim volume *Where Cavalry Stands Today*, 1927. In this, though generally progressive, he stands out for the need to retain a small proportion of cavalry. His chief reason was one that in the '20s had some force: 'Armoured fighting vehicles go farther and faster, and afford a considerable amount of protection to their crew, but even the most efficient of them is more likely to break down than the horse.' (Charrington, H.V.S. *Where Cavalry Stands Today*, 1927, 50). This should be borne in mind as a very real factor when considering the slow pace of mechanization, and, *(continued over)*

was quite ready to be convinced that the cavalry would use tanks in the future.... The cavalry instructor, on the other hand, was a die-hard and determined to do all he could to retain horsed cavalry.'

An example of the extreme die-hard was the cavalryman Lieutenant-General Sir Raleigh Gilbert Egerton (see Vol. 6, 145) who, in 1927, said:

'if we turn to the introduction of mechanical transport into the Army to replace the horse, and look into the faces of individuals who deal with the horse and the faces of men who deal with the machine, you will see in the latter what, I might almost call a lack of intelligence! Many of us remember the old hansom cab driver and the bus driver, cheery men who seemed to enjoy driving their horses. Now, what you see is a hunched-backed man leaning over a wheel looking like Cerberus. I consider that the horse has a humanising effect on men, and the longer we can keep horses for artillery and for cavalry the better it will be for the Army, because thereby you keep up the high standard of intelligence in the man from his association with the horse.'

---

indeed, of instruction in what some cavalry officers called 'the garage school of warfare'. (Nicol, G. *Uncle George* [Milne], 1976, 264). It took a number of years before AFVs, indeed any motor vehicles, reached the state of reliability required, and which only after the Second World War began to be taken for granted.

Those tank men and historians who condemn wholesale the cavalry officers of the day for their conservatism forget this. That the situation allowed it to be argued that the horse was still the better for close-in reconnaissance does not surprise. Such an argument was persuasive to a greater degree than with hindsight is often accepted. Without a great increase of speed and stout armour, tanks were almost as vulnerable to artillery and especially anti-tank guns as horses were to shrapnel and bullets. This, of course, could not be proved until anti-tank guns and tanks had come into actual contact. There was, thus, much uncertainty, making clear cut assertions difficult, though that did not stop them being made. During the debate of the Army Estimates in 1934 a member stated that 'everybody knows that cavalry is out of date altogether....' Duff Cooper, by no means a die-hard, replied, 'I have had occasion during the past year to study military affairs both in my public and in my private life [he was at the time writing his biography of Haig], and the more I study them the more impressed I become by the importance of cavalry in modern warfare.' (15 Mar., 1934, *Hansard (C)*).

This is what the Cavalry thought they would do.

This is what would really have happened.

'Rollie Charrington drew the picture [top] . . . I produced the second picture . . . These sketches v. like the earlier type of MG carrier of 1927.'
–Lieut-Gen. Sir Giffard Martel.

Among infantry officers there were quite a few who were 'horse-minded'. The most important and persistent was Major-General Sir Harry Knox, who, between 1926 and 1930 was Director of Military Training at the War Office. The most surprising view of a senior officer was that of Elles, the first great tank commander who had led the tanks at Cambrai and had nursed the infant Tank Corps through its difficult childhood. When he became head of the Ordnance, 'the department that had through its history shaped the offensive power of the Army, he reached in 1936 the astonishing conclusion that tanks would "still be of some good to the Army" but only at a secondary level from past experience.'

There were die-hards even as late as 1940. A young officer of the 3rd Hussars joined the Oxford University OTC in that year. 'I knew already,' he wrote, 'that I wanted to go into the Armoured Corps, so applied to join the appropriate branch of the OTC. But, far from learning about armoured warfare, I was given a lance, a sword and a horse, and well remember, during the fighting in France, listening to a lecture on horsed cavalry as the "decisive weapon" in battle. The lecturer was a regular cavalry officer attached to the OTC to train its members for modern war.' In 1942, nineteen-year old Oliver Ormrod, a pilot in the RAF, serving in Malta, had

> an interesting conversation with his new commanding officer, who, to his great joy, had started his career as a trooper in the Life Guards. "I was overjoyed to find that my C.O.'s views exactly coincided with mine, in that though each of us considers that the Air Force is the service to be in today in modern war, each wishes that times might go back to days of old, when we might have taken the field with the cavalry. That we would have loved more than this. . . . Oh for the days that had gone! Oh for a horse not a Hurricane!" [5]

As has been shown it was not only cavalry officers who had firm views on the horse in war. Major Leonard Dent, an infantryman, insisted, enigmatically, in a newspaper article published in the 1920s, that 'the tank would never replace the horse until a sporting use could be found for it'.[6]

Unprofessionalism and snobbery still remained to some degree in the cavalry well into the Second World War. The cavalry regiments of the 7th Armoured Division, for example, rebelled

'Blokes', 'tankees' and 'donkey wallopers'

(unsuccessfully) when asked to face a full working week, which meant the virtual abandonment of polo, while 'before the battle of El Alamein a cavalry brigadier attempted (again unsuccessfully) to refuse the attachment of an extra field regiment of the Royal Artillery. "We only accept support from the Royal *Horse* Artillery," he said loftily.' Other instances of snobbery were the tendency by reactionary officers to refer to people in the technical branches as 'blokes' and 'tradesmen'. The 'tankees' got their own back by calling cavalrymen 'donkey wallopers'. Rudyard Kipling, attending an early mechanized exercise, described it as smelling 'like a garage' and 'looking like a circus'. Greasy overalls also helped to 'provoke an attitude of snobbish disdain'.[7] The present author enjoyed the inverted snobbery implied when, as a Blue, he was greeted on entering a pub by: 'Chippy, chippy, Guardee; *I'm* tanks!' uttered in a strong cockney accent.

THE PASSING OF THE CAVALRY, 1939

No more the dung pit's reek perfumes the Breeze,
No more the Squadron-Leader shouts out 'March at Ease',
No more the Troop horse searches in his manger
Oblivious to any thought of danger.

Gone are those chestnuts, browns and bays
From all except those lucky 'Royals' and 'Greys';
And Household Cavalry, who when at home
Still use the hoof-pick and the curry comb.

Hussars, Dragoons, and Lancers still bear ancient names,
The men content to play dismounted games
While Tanks and Lorries grimly thunder past
Replacing those dear Gees that have been cast.

Of petrol now they draw a daily ration
Instead of oats and hay which were in fashion.
Gone is the Farrier and the skilful Vet.;
Who knows but we may want them badly yet?

CYRIL STACEY, Major.
Formerly 14th King's Hussars.
(*Cavalry Journal*, XXIX, 566)

'The proposed re-organization is a vast upheaval of old ideas.'
— LIEUTENANT-COLONEL A.W. PARSONS, 19th Hussars, in 1921

'I think the time has come when we can take the Cavalry into our confidence in regard to their own future. I feel that the good cavalryman will welcome this, and he is the man we want to carry with us. The man who only goes into the cavalry for a few years to have a good time may talk large on the subject, and possibly get silly questions asked in Parliament, but I think we can ignore him and the hypothetical member that he may get to represent his view in Parliament.'
— GENERAL SIR WALTER BRAITHWAITE, Adjutant-General, commenting on the Cavalry Committee Report, 1927[1]

(vi)

The process of bringing the regular cavalry into the second quarter of the twentieth-century began with a War Office suggestion early in 1921, that it should be converted to a mechanized force wholesale. This was rejected out of hand.[2] There followed a paper by the DAAG of 22 February, 1921: 'Scheme for Reducing Cavalry Regiments'. This made it clear that the War Office assumed that, if drastic cuts had to be made, the disbanding of regiments was the only other way to proceed, and that the cavalry should be the first arm of the regular Army to have to face disbandments or, indeed, any other forms of reduction.* The official reason given

---

*In late 1927, according to the CIGS, 'all the great military nations' were proposing 'to retain a considerable proportion of cavalry even in cases where a European war is considered'. (31 Oct., 1927, CIGS Memo. 'The Substitution of Armoured Vehicles for Cavalry', 16/Gen.5558, WO 32/2846). In the US Army and in the Russian Red Army, the mounted proportion was actually being *increased*, while 'during a recent visit to London [May, 1927], the President of the French Republic stated that a reaction was taking place in France in favour of cavalry.' (30 June, 1927, Memo. by the Military Members of the Army Council, WO 32/2846). This was six years before Hitler came to power.

In April, 1921, according to Worthington-Evans, France had then been reducing her cavalry by 29% and Italy by 20%, while, had four British regular cavalry regiments been abolished at that time, this would have been a reduction of 12½%. (20 Apr., 1921, Worthington-Evans, *Hansard (C)*).

Most mounted regiments of the US Army remained unmechanized until 1940. Cooperation with mechanized troops was up to then still believed in. The 'Portee' system had been devised. Horses and men were carried in trucks until action was imminent or until going became unsuitable for vehicles. (Brereton: *Horse*, 145).

Which cavalry regiments should be disbanded first?

was that the money saved should be devoted to 'the new mobile services whose development the experience of war has proved to be so important'.[3] This is evidence that very early on the War Office was thinking seriously about mechanization.* The Household Cavalry was at that time presumed to be sacrosanct.† Twenty-three of the line regiments had been in existence without interruption since they were raised in the 17th and 18th centuries (see Vol. 4, 512–3). This left what were considered by nearly everyone to be the five most junior regiments: the 5th and 21st Lancers and the 18th, 19th and 20th Hussars, all of which had been disbanded and re-raised for various reasons during the 19th century.§ These were thought to be the obvious choices for abolition. It was not, though, as simple as that. The 5th Lancers, for example, were placed high in the Army List, while the other four were at the bottom of it. That ought, it was thought, especially by the 5th Lancers (!), to have made that regiment safe.††

Yet there was another problem, which, incidentally, bedevilled

---

*For a full, convincing study of the Chiefs of Staffs' continuity of thought in this respect throughout the inter-war years, see Harris.

†Though, since it was much the most expensive part of the arm, and did 'not affect drafting considerations' (see below), the disbanding of the 2nd Life Guards 'would leave the 1st Life Guards and the Royal Horse Guards to carry out the necessary escort duties for which these Regiments are mainly used.' (22 Feb., 1921, WO 32/5959, 17). For what happened to the Household Cavalry later, see p. 327.

§The 5th Lancers, raised in 1689, were disbanded in 1799, on discovery of a plot by the men to murder their officers. Like the 18th Lancers the regiment was re-raised in 1858 (see Vol. 2, 282). The 19th and 20th Hussars and the 21st Lancers, all raised in 1759, were disbanded in 1763 and re-raised in 1779. The 19th and 20th were again disbanded in 1783, the 19th was re-raised in 1786, the 20th in 1791 and the 21st in 1794. All three were once again disbanded in 1818, 1819 and 1821. All three were re-raised as 1st, 2nd and 3rd Bengal Cavalry in 1858 and re-absorbed with their original titles into the Crown forces in 1860, 1861 and 1862. (See Vol. 2, 346).

††Indeed, in spite of a break of fifty-nine years, there was something to be said for this assumption, the 18th Hussars having been raised seventy-three years later than the 5th Lancers and disbanded for only thirty-six years. (16 Mar., 1921, Lt-Col J.R. Harvey to Allenby, 20/Cav/452, 14B, WO 32/5959).

the whole question of what form the post-war army was to take. The paper outlines it. 'So long as Cavalry Regiments are required for Garrisons abroad, at least an equal number of Regiments must be maintained at Home as are required Abroad, for purposes of draft finding.' This meant that, if abolition were to take place, an equal, not an odd number of regiments must be expunged from the army, otherwise 'the whole drafting and link Regiment machinery' would be upset. Since the abolition of only two regiments was not considered to be sufficient, the number suggested was four: two lancer and two hussar regiments. It so happened that all four selected (the 18th Hussars (as senior to the 19th* and 20th) being the regiment left out) were stationed overseas: three were in India and the 20th Hussars were dealing with the Chanak crisis (see p. 351). The 5th and 21st Lancers were 'linked' with the 12th and 9th Lancers which were at home, while the 19th and 20th were 'linked' with the 15th in Dublin and the 14th Hussars, about to come home from the Rhine. The disbandment of the four would entail upsetting the foreign service roster and also the location of regiments at home and, of course, the re-'linking' of regiments. Tiresome though all this would be, it could be faced.

There were alternative arrangements which would avoid these difficulties, but nearly all of them were too complicated or involved getting rid of regiments senior in the Army List and were therefore ruled out on grounds of fairness. However, when the Military Members of the Army Council considered the proposal and agreed to it they suggested that the entity and traditions of the disbanded regiments might be retained 'by eventually transferring their names and numbers to new Tank units, of which seven are being proposed for 1922'. As regards the 'disposal of personnel', since there were few regiments up to establishment, transference of other ranks was no problem. It was thought that senior officers would probably resign or retire and that subalterns who wanted

---

*French, as Colonel of the 19th Hussars, pressed on Worthington-Evans, the Secretary of State, the fact that, unlike his regiment, there were two or three regiments which 'never served in any of the theatres of war during the recent campaign' and 'in the interests of fighting efficiency' these should be the first to be disbanded having not 'enjoyed such unique war experience'. (15 Mar., 1921, French to SoS, WO 32/5959, 20/Cav/453.) Though urged in parliament (and by others elsewhere), this idea was not taken seriously. The Hansards of the first half of 1921 are full of speeches making suggestions on behalf of the four regiments.

to go to other regiments to fill the many gaps in them would do so.*

The abolition of the four regiments was never implemented, though the necessary Army Order was actually issued.[4]† In April, 1922, it was revoked.[5] The influence of the Commons debates, of senior cavalry officers and of Chetwode, who became DCIGS in 1920 and who was the highest ranking cavalry officer at the War Office, were responsible in part for swaying opinion against disbandments. Nevertheless the abolition principle had powerful adherents. These included Henry Wilson, who, just before he retired from the post of CIGS, believed that any schemes of amalgamation (see below) would 'ruin the soul and the regimental esprit-de-corps of every cavalry regiment in the army'.[6] One of the alternatives put forward was that the cavalry should be 'treated as a complete Corps in the sense that the Gunners are now'. The Royal Horse and Field Artillery had for some years been reorganized on a battery as opposed to a regimental basis. Chetwode, totally contradicting Wilson, believed that 'a Corps of Cavalry' would do away 'at one swoop with twenty-eight regimental traditions and names, some of them of great antiquity'.[7]

---

*Officers were asked to choose between transfer to other regiments, leave on half-pay or retirement with two extra years' service added for pension. (ffrench-Blake, 2–3).

Throughout the late 1920s and early 1930s there was a chronic shortage of all ranks in the army, though considerably less in the cavalry than elsewhere. 'The unsettlement due to the reorganization past and prospective is having its effect. The class which supplies officers for the Army is losing all confidence in the Service as a career for its sons . . . while recruitment for the ranks is getting steadily worse.' (30 June, 1927, Memo. by the Military Members of the AC, WO 32/2846). Nevertheless a War Office paper of late 1927 stated that 'in spite of the protests of parents [of potential officers] the number of first commissions to be given annually in cavalry regiments has been reduced by over 50%' (7 Nov., 1927, 'Memo. on the Reorganization of the Cavalry', WO 32/2846, 5B). In an article in the JRUSI of two years later it was stated that there could be 'no doubt that the officer class is decreasing; the Cadet Colleges are under strength; battalions are under strength; in fact . . . the only corps that is up to strength in officers is the cavalry.' (Anon. 'The training of the Regimental Officer,' JRUSI, 1929, 259, 261.)

†The process of disbandment had progressed a long way. In January, 1922, for instance, the 20th Hussars consisted of only the commanding officer, second-in-command, adjutant, quartermaster, RQMS, one SQMS and the officers' mess sergeant! (Oatts: 14H/20H, 417.)

The origins of the system of amalgamated regiments – the first truly revolutionary cavalry reorganization ever undertaken and one which still holds today – are to be found in an outline paper produced at 1st Cavalry Brigade, Aldershot, July, 1921, and in two others resulting from meetings of the Colonels Commandant of the three cavalry brigades, one at the War Office in August and the other at the Cavalry Club in January, 1922.[8]

The initial reactions of the Colonels Commandant and the commanding officers of the regiments in their three brigades to the scheme as adopted (see AO 133 below) were varied. A considerable majority were in favour of some sort of 'complete Corps' plan. They felt, as did Wilson, that 'by attempting to save the four regiments' they were 'losing the "esprit de corps" of the whole' and that 'the identity of regiments could not be maintained by squadrons'. Further, since there would have to be 'a very big reduction in officers, it was better to let the unfortunate regiments die.'*
Colonel Harman (see p. 189), the senior Brigade Commandant, added: 'In all fairness, it must be remembered that the regiments at home (except 17th Lancers) are all senior regiments, and a very large reduction in cavalry regiments would have to take place before any of these regiments would be affected.'[9]

While what threatened to be prolonged debates continued to rage between the various War Office departments and between them and the three brigades and the regiments, it suddenly became clear that it was a matter of urgency to come to a decision. The dreaded 'Geddes Axe' (see p. 312) began to descend upon nearly

---

*Lieutenant-Colonel F.C. Pilkington, commanding the 15th Hussars, wrote: 'Even if it means my regiment going, it seems infinitely preferable for a regiment to be temporarily disbanded than for it to be lost in a Corps of Hussars. [One suggestion was that there should be three corps, one of each of the three types of cavalry with all ranks interchangeable within them.] It dies for the present with the finest of records to rise again when the country needs it.' Lieutenant-Colonel Henry Cecil Lloyd Howard, 16th Lancers, on the other hand, was in favour of amalgamation because '"the cut" of four regiments is unlikely to be a final one. Policy will entail further "cuts" perhaps year by year.' Lieutenant-Colonel Sir Berkeley Vincent of the Inniskillings reported that 'the senior NCOs, especially, are in favour of disbanding whole regiments (even their own) rather than upset the existing organization of those that remain'. However, 'unofficial' discussions at the Cavalry Club produced, according to the Director of Operations, 'the general feeling that almost any sacrifice is preferable to wiping four regiments off the Army List'. (7, 4, 21 Aug., 1921, Pilkington, Howard, Vincent to Harman; n.d., DO Memo., WO 32/5960).

52. General Kavanagh, Cavalry Corps Commander, watching his troops passing through Spa, the General Headquarters of the German Army, on 29 November, 1918.

53. The 9th Lancers enter Spa, the General Headquarters of the German Army, on 29 November, 1918.

54. Five 'bull-nosed' Morris motor cars bought and converted into machine-gun carriers by an officer of the Inns of Court Regiment, 1933. Private enterprise mechanization! (See p.344)

55. Serving and former Life Guards officers during the Cavalry Memorial Weekend, 1988.

all government departments, upon none more hardly than the War Office. Consequently the Cabinet decided, as soon as the Geddes Report came before it, that a further reduction of the equivalent of five cavalry regiments must be made as soon as possible. The Earl of Cavan, soon to succeed Wilson as CIGS, put forward a potent argument: 'The power of expansion in an emergency,' he wrote to him, 'is undoubtedly greater by the adoption of a scheme of compression instead of extermination, and this power is vitally important at a time when the state of India and the Middle East is disquieting.' It was important, too, because, if it came to mobilization for another world war, the married regiments, it was supposed, could then be divorced, reverting to their original status and titles. This, of course, never came about.[10]

It is probable that Sir Charles Harris, the dynamic Financial Secretary to the War Office, with whom Chetwode was in day-to-day consultation, was the man who first suggested the double-title amalgamation scheme.[11] By the middle of April, 1922, Army Order 133 had been issued. It read in part:

> '3. Household Cavalry. – The 1st and 2nd Life Guards will be amalgamated to form one regiment consisting of four squadrons, the existing regiments providing two squadrons each. The composite regiment will be designated "The Life Guards". A further reduction of two Hotchkiss troops each in the Royal Horse Guards and the Life Guards will be effected.
>
> 'Cavalry of the Line. – Regiments of the Cavalry of the Line will be amalgamated as follows:-
>
> | | | |
> |---|---|---|
> | 3rd Dragoon Guards | 2 squadrons | To form 3rd/6th Dragoon Guards. |
> | The Carabiniers | 1 squadron | |
> | 4th Dragoon Guards | 2 squadrons | To form 4th/7th Dragoon Guards |
> | 7th Dragoon Guards | 1 squadron | |
> | 5th Dragoon Guards | 2 squadrons | To form 5th/6th Dragoons. |
> | The Inniskillings | 1 squadron | |
> | 13th Hussars | 2 squadrons | To form 13th/18th Hussars. |
> | 18th Hussars | 1 squadron | |

14th Hussars	2 squadrons	To form 14th/20th
20th Hussars	1 squadron	Hussars.
15th Hussars	2 squadrons	To form 15th/19th
19th Hussars	1 squadron	Hussars.
16th Lancers	2 squadrons	To form 16th/5th
5th Lancers	1 squadron	Lancers.
17th Lancers	2 squadrons	To form 17th/21st
21st Lancers	1 squadron	Lancers.

'Other cavalry regiments not referred to above will remain as at present constituted.

'4. A composite regiment will be treated for all purposes as a complete regiment, but each squadron will retain the name of its original regiment in order to preserve the identity of the latter, e.g., 1st Life Guards Squadron, The Life Guards; The 6th Dragoon Guards Squadron, 3rd/6th Dragoon Guards, &c.'[12]*

It will be seen that a compromise had been arrived at which did not, of course, satisfy everyone. It was to prove, though, remarkably durable. Twelve regiments remained untouched.† Although there

---

*In the case of the Carabiniers and the Inniskillings, as a result of pressure from both regiments, their squadrons were later re-named 'The Carabinier Squadron, 3rd/6th Dragoon Guards' and 'The Inniskilling Squadron, 5th/6th Dragoons'. (AO 261, Jul., 1922). Of those amalgamated, five were dragoon guard, one dragoon, four lancer and six hussar regiments.

It is clear that little sensitive thought had been applied to the question of nomenclature by the mandarins of the War Office. Fancy calling a regiment of Dragoon Guards Dragoons! It was understandable though that squadrons should not retain, on the grounds of unwieldiness, their regimental prefixes such as 'Royal Irish' and 'Princess Royal's'. Nevertheless, these omissions were resented. An officer of the 4th/7th Dragoon Guards commented: 'We become a very vulgar fraction.' (Brereton, 348).

†1st The Royal Dragoons; The Royal Scots Greys (2nd Dragoons); 1st King's Dragoon Guards; The Queen's Bays (2nd Dragoon Guards); 3rd The King's Own Hussars; 4th Queen's Own Hussars; 7th Queen's Own Hussars; 8th King's Royal Irish Hussars; 9th Queen's Royal Lancers; 10th Royal Hussars (Prince of Wales's Own); 11th Hussars (Prince Albert's Own); 12th Royal Lancers (Prince of Wales's Own).

were a few minor changes in names of regiments, there were no further amalgamations until the 1950s, 1960s, 1970s and 1990s.

There were, of course, numerous problems to be solved as a result of the creation of composite regiments. These ranged from the questions of bands, uniforms, mess plate, barrack accommodation, seconds-in-command and composition of regimental headquarters to how to deal with redundant personnel. All these were solved in due course, more or less satisfactorily. Even those, most difficult of all, relating to the perennial dilemmas connected with 'trooping' to and from India were disentangled without too much disruption. Whether Haig, who, when consulted, 'gave it as his opinion that whatever happens we should retain the identity of the regiments somehow,'[13] was content is not known. What is certain is that nearly all cavalry officers thought that the new system, which made the squadron instead of the regiment a self-accounting unit and which gave its leader new and desirable responsibility for training and administration (as would also have been the case in the 'Corps' system), was a good thing. The saving effected for the cavalry of the line was not, in fact, all that great: somewhere between £820,000 and £650,000 out of a total of about £3,700,000. This did not include the expense of regiments in India, which were as always paid for by the government of India.[14]

Each regiment, whether amalgamated or not, consisted of three squadrons of four troops each and a machine-gun troop. In 1927, though, the number of sabre squadrons was reduced to two with a third squadron comprising eight machine guns carried on lorries. This alteration was not liked by commanding officers: 'If he deployed one squadron as advanced guard he deployed half his horsemen and had too small a "mass of manoeuvre" left in hand; if he deployed less he broke up the normal organization.'[15] This lack of tactical balance was remedied in 1932 when a third sabre squadron was added. At the same time one sabre troop per squadron was replaced by a machine-gun troop of four guns carried on pack horses, the lorry-borne machine-gun squadron being done away with. This temporary reorganization came about because the lorries proved during exercises too conspicuous and could not be replied upon, especially cross-country, to keep within supporting distance of the sabre squadrons.

> 'The 19th Lancers were the last regiment of horsed cavalry – except of course the Viceroy's Bodyguard. They kept their horses until November, 1940, when they held their last parade with horses. Their commanding officer addressed the regiment, recalling its good name and reputation, expressing confidence that the spirit of the regiment would go on. But "let us remember", he added, "how much of our good name we owe to our horses. For the last time – 'Make much of your horses!'" And with that familiar cavalry command the parade, and an epoch, ended.'
> – PHILIP MASON in *A Matter of Honour*[1]

(vii)

The principle of regimental pairing had already been established in the Indian cavalry. Between 1920 and 1923 the forty-five native regiments of 1919 had been reduced to twenty-one (excluding the four Bodyguards), chiefly by the amalgamation process.* This had proved comparatively easy, since 'linking' and 'trooping' problems did not apply. Further, already during the war, especially on the Western Front, the silladar system (see Vol. 2, 237–42), which in the past had been largely responsible for the *élan* of the Indian Army's mounted arm, had proved almost impossible to maintain in the field, but it was not formally abolished until 1921. The only two non-silladar regiments and one other, the Guides Cavalry, retained their separate identities. The Governor-General's Bodyguard and the Madras, Bombay and Bengal Bodyguards, as well as the Aden Troop, also remained in being. (For regimental titles of 1922, see Note on p. 332).†

---

*The regimental establishments had to be drastically reduced. About half the British officers were sent home. (See Sandhu, 403).

    Twenty-one 'regular' regiments cost about the same as had thirty-nine silladar regiments. (Sandhu, 400).

†'The regiments were grouped in threes, the racial class composition of each group being identical, so that a pool of trained reservists would be available to serve in any regiment of the group on mobilization, when group depots would be formed. This was carried a stage further in 1937, when the groups were reduced to three of seven regiments each, one of which became permanently located as a training regiment to serve as a depot (*continued over*)

Mechanization in the Indian Army

The first glimmering of mechanization in the Indian Army came in 1931 when two signallers in each native cavalry regiment were provided with motor cycles. Six years later there were six. At the same time a few light cars, ambulances and 15-cwt trucks were introduced for trial purposes. Early in 1938 two regiments became – on paper – armoured car regiments. The Expert Committee on Indian Defence, chaired by Admiral of the Fleet Lord Chatfield,† recommended in early 1939 a mechanization plan which meant that four of the regiments were to be given light tanks, four armoured cars, while six were to be converted into motor cavalry regiments. Only the Poona Horse and the 19th Lancers were to keep their horses, but even these were mechanized in November, 1940, showing that horsed troops were no longer thought to be much needed for internal security purposes. The increased costs of mechanization were offset by the reduction of two British cavalry regiments, five British and five native infantry battalions.

---

unit for the whole group.' (Jackson, 6; for details, see Sandhu, 401–02, 427–9 and O'Donnell, Maj. B.H. 'The Indian Cavalry Group System', *Cav. Jnl*, XX, 1930, 269).

By 1933 Indianization of the officer cadre had taken place in three cavalry regiments.

'The Indian Military Academy for the training of Indian gentlemen as officers independently of the Royal Military College at Sandhurst, was established in 1931. . . .

'The Indian soldier [as the author of an Indian Army pocket book wrote in 1940] is fed, clothed, housed and horsed entirely by centralized services, in direct contrast to the unit arrangements, often inadequate, before the Great War. . . . His arms and equipment are identical with those of his British comrades and now no longer one step behind, as was formerly the case.' (Jackson, 6–7: see also articles in the *Army Quarterly*, XIII, 1927, 307–17, XVIII, 1929, 387, 391–2).

In 1920 the pre-war Volunteer Corps became the Auxiliary Force. It included ten mounted units. The Imperial Service Troops (see Vol. 5, p. 2), which included twenty cavalry regiments, were renamed the Indian State Forces.

†It is said that the admiral, when inspecting the 17th/21st Lancers in their AVFs, was heard to ask: 'Do these things go astern?'! (Filose, Brig. A.A. *King George V's Own Central India Horse*, II, 1950, 191).

NOTE
Indian cavalry amalgamations, 1922

1st Duke of York's Own Lancers (Skinner's Horse) 3rd Skinner's Horse	1st Duke of York's Own Skinner's Horse
2nd Lancers (Gardner's Horse) 4th Cavalry	2nd Lancers (Gardner's Horse)
5th Cavalry 8th Cavalry	3rd Cavalry
9th Hodson's Horse 10th Duke of Cambridge's Own Lancers (Hodson's Horse)	4th Duke of Cambridge's Own Hodson's Horse
11th (King Edward's Own Lancers (Probyn's Horse) 16th Cavalry	5th King Edward's Own Probyn's Horse
13th Duke of Connaught's Lancers (Watson's Horse) 16th Cavalry	6th Duke of Connaught's Own Lancers
28th Light Cavalry	7th Light Cavalry
26th King George's Own Light Cavalry 30th Lancers (Gordon's Horse)	8th King George's Own Light Cavalry
20th Deccan Horse 29th Lancers (Deccan Horse)	9th Royal Deccan Horse
Queen Victoria's Own Corps of Guides (Frontier Force) (Lumsden's) Cavalry	10th Queen Victoria's Own Corps of Guides Cavalry (Frontier Force)
21st Prince Albert Victor's Own Cavalry (Frontier Force) (Daly's Horse) 23rd Cavalry (Frontier Force)	11th Prince Albert Victor's Own Cavalry (Frontier Force)
22nd Sam Browne's Cavalry (Frontier Force) 25th Cavalry (Frontier Force)	12th Cavalry (Frontier Force)

31st Duke of Connaught's Own Lancers 32nd Lancers	13th Duke of Connaught's Own Bombay Lancers
35th Scinde Horse 36th Jacob's Horse	14th Prince of Wales's Own Scinde Horse
17th Cavalry 37th Lancers (Baluch Horse)	15th Lancers
27th Light Cavalry	16th Light Cavalry
33rd Queen Victoria's Own Light Cavalry 34th Prince Albert Victor's Own Poona Horse	17th Queen Victoria's Own Poona Horse
6th King Edward's Own Cavalry 7th Hariana Lancers	18th King Edward's Own Cavalry
18th King George's Own Lancers 19th Lancers (Fane's Horse)	19th King George's Own Lancers
14th Murray's Jat Lancers 15th Lancers (Cureton's Multanis)	20th Lancers
38th King George's Own Central India Horse 39th King George's Own Central India Horse	21st King George's Own Central India Horse
40th Cavalry Regiment 41st Cavalry Regiment 42nd Cavalry Regiment 43rd Cavalry Regiment 44th Cavalry Regiment 45th Cavalry Regiment	Disbanded

(Jackson, 541–5).

> 'When you introduce improvements, you need to be quite sure that they are improvements and that they will not have to be scrapped again in a year or so, because they have been made too hastily.'
> – MAJOR CLEMENT ATTLEE in the House of Commons, 1924

> 'Should a war come, an army with many tanks of not quite the latest pattern will be superior to an army possessing only a few tanks of the latest design.'
> – MAJOR B.C. DENING in 'Obstacles in the Way of Mechanization', 1927

> 'Replacement of mounted troops by mechanized forces must be gradual and will therefore take time. The capital expenditure will be great, machines have to be purchased, garages constructed or stables converted, mechanics and drivers trained and repair installations set up. Meanwhile we cannot dispense with the mobile arm we have and must proceed by evolution and not by revolution. Wholesale reductions of cavalry and their replacement by necessarily inefficient mechanical units would not only cost a large amount of money but would place the country in danger in event of war.'
> – Memorandum by the Military Members of the Army Council, 1927[1]

(viii)

In June, 1927, Baldwin, in the middle of his second term as Prime Minister, wrote to Worthington-Evans, Secretary of State for War, that it would be difficult to 'justify heavy expenditure on recruiting and training men for the cavalry' if that arm was to be 'abolished in the near future'.[2] Obvious though this was, and pre-empting a decision not yet taken, it avoided the question of how and when to replace horsed units by what some reactionaries called 'tin-can units'. Worthington-Evans, whilst agreeing with the Prime Minister, also assured him that 'so far from there being any opposition in the higher ranks of the army to mechanization and new weapons, they are one and all thinking of nothing else'. He added: 'The real facts of the case are that owing to the requirements of economy, the Chancellor of the Exchequer [Churchill] or myself are continually being placed in the unfortunate position of having to negative expenditure which is essential to progress.'[3] This very well sums up the situation at that time, half way between the slumps of the early 1920s and those of the early 1930s, and in

The Montgomery–Massingberd Cavalry Committee, 1926/1927

face of a reduction each year in the money allotted to the Army Estimates.* It is tragic in the light of later lack of action to read Worthington-Evans's more or less truthful statement that he had spent all that he possibly could 'on experiment' and that he had 'produced the best fighting tank, the best cross-country transport vehicle and the best artillery "dragon" in the world,'[4] a statement which, though also a little economical with the truth, may perhaps be allowed a politician!

* * *

As has been shown, 1926/1927 was an important year in the history of the horsed cavalry's demise. In the winter of that year the Montgomery–Massingberd Cavalry Committee had produced two reports. Of these the chief results were the establishment of the principles that no regiments would be abolished and that no further amalgamations would take place. The Cavalry Depot at Canterbury was to be abolished, and, amongst other measures, each squadron at home would be reduced by one troop – a total of 560 all ranks and 448 horses – thus saving nearly £150,000 a year.† Further, on the positive side, the gradual mechanization of the first-line transport by lorries and motor cycles was approved.§ This was welcomed by all ranks, since it was certain to solve in part the age-old problem of excessive weight on the horse by relieving it of some of the impedimenta hitherto carried by it. The equine load by late 1930 had been reduced by 32 lbs, 11¼ ozs.[5] Also approved were the full mechanization of the machine-gun squadron and an increase in the number of guns in it. There was also

---

*The 1927 Army Estimates provided £607,000 for forage and only £78,900 for petrol, oil and lubricants. Considering how little actual mechanization had by then taken place – for instance none of the field artillery had yet relinquished their horses – this should not be made too much of. In 1933 the figures were: forage: £363,800; p, o and l: £108,200. In 1938: forage: £139,000; p, o and l: £1,735,000 (Winton, 250).

†'Since 1914 ... the total reduction [in the cavalry of the line] amounts to 6,373 all ranks and a large number of horses.' (30 June, 1927, Memo by Military Members of the AC, enclosed in Worthington-Evans to Baldwin, WO 32/2846).

§By September, 1939, the British army could claim to have a greater proportion of its transport mechanized than that of any other considerable country.

The Salisbury CID sub-committee, May, 1928

agreement to 'partial replacement of mounted men by cross-country armoured cars . . . within the existing cavalry regiments and not by raising new Royal Tank Corps units'.

In November, 1927, the Cabinet set up a CID sub-committee, chaired by the Marquess of Salisbury and including Churchill and Haig, amongst others. When the question of making provision for an expeditionary force was raised, it was agreed that only the ten cavalry regiments at home and the one on the Rhine could be made available. The report, issued on 3 May, 1928, stressed that 'another European war like the last, in which static conditions might obtain, is not by any means the only war for which we have to be prepared, and that in some of the possible theatres further afield, the employment of a large proportion of mounted troops might be necessary.' Thus it was concluded that to further reduce the army's only truly mobile fighting troops would be dangerous. Haig, typically, suggested that a cavalry reduction might be even more detrimental than would be a reduction of equivalent cost in either the infantry or artillery. General Sir Alexander Godley, known in military circles as 'Lord God' and before the war the great mounted infantry guru (see Vol. 4, 412), recently Commander-in-Chief of the Army of the Rhine, told the sub-committee that

> 'if cavalry were abolished, instead of being transformed, there would be a great danger of losing the type of officer, non-commissioned officer and man that has hitherto gone to the cavalry, and that will be equally necessary in the new mechanized cavalry; men who were to a great extent by birth and upbringing, and by their habits in boyhood, natural leaders with an eye for country, quickness of decision, habit of command and all the attributes required in connection with highly mobile forces.'[6]

He asserted, too, that 'cavalry officers and the class which provides them are quite ready to look facts in the face and, with whatever natural regret, to take no exception to the change from horses to machine*.'[6]

*The Salisbury sub-committee report also stated that 'mechanical vehicles have a greater radius of action than horses so long as the going is good, but they cannot reach an enemy who occupies woods, buildings or marshy ground and they are inevitably stopped (until a substantial bridge can *(continued over)*

Still the Same Spirit
From the drawing by Gilbert Holiday

Though none of the decisions taken to date could be made really effective until further experiments had been undertaken and more finance provided, the 11th Hussars and the 12th Lancers, the two junior regiments by date of raising which had not been amalgamated, were converted, largely at Churchill's insistence, into armoured car regiments on 4 April, 1927, They were the first regular cavalry in the world to be mechanized. Only a tiny number

---

be built) by streams which cavalry can ford in a few minutes.' The report recommended that an armoured force be built up which could after a couple of years or so take its place in an expeditionary force and which could 'strengthen as far as possible with mechanical means the existing cavalry formations'. The sub-committee prided itself on this proposal as being 'well in advance of that of any foreign power. All the great military nations propose to retain a considerable proportion of cavalry even in cases where a European war is considered to be the most likely danger to be apprehended.' (PRO CAB 2 (5), 15 Encl. No. 1, 2 (a), 2(b), 2(c) and (2d). Francis, A. 'The Early Mechanisation of the Cavalry Arm: 1925–1931', History Dissertation (unpublished), University of Westminster, 1995, is useful on the Salisbury sub-committee)

The 11th Hussars and 12th Lancers converted to armoured cars

of officers resigned or asked to be transferred – against expectations.* This speedy conversion was made possible by transferring two armoured car companies from the Royal Tank Corps.† Since subsequent conversions were to be either to tanks, troop-carrying

---

*For most of the officers it was the disposal of the horses which was distasteful. After an examination to determine their future use, most of those over fifteen and those between twelve and fifteen which were deemed unfit, were destroyed. The rest were distributed to other cavalry regiments. (Conversation between Maj. C.H. Bromfield and Andrew Francis. Jan., 1995)

†There had been twelve companies in 1918.

Crossleys, Lanchesters and the '1920–1924' pattern Rolls Royces were the vehicles used. These were gradually brought up to date, or replaced by more modern types, such as 'the Morris armoured reconnaissance car', which the 12th received in September, 1939, but which was described as 'under-engined, under-armed and under-armoured'. (Stewart: *XII L*, 348).

Armoured cars were well suited to Imperial policing and were therefore favoured above slow-moving tanks. 'There was a gap in the military ecology which armoured cars comfortably fitted.' (Lewin, R. *Man of Armour: a Study of Lt-Gen. Vyvyan Pope*, 1976, 52)

Wireless and modern machine guns were soon procured, while, at Martel's suggestion, numbers of Austin Sevens (the famous 'Baby Austins'), as well as Triumph motor-cycles were also provided. (Lumley, 438–45; Clarke, Brig. D. *The Eleventh at War* . . . *1934–1945*, 1952; Stewart, *XII L*, 320–22).

The 'Baby Austins', according to an officer of the 7th Hussars, 'in the hands of a dashing hussar subaltern could be relied upon to put up prodigies of cross-country performance, as well as high road-speed, and "special reconnaissance" tasks were pressed home with astonishing *élan* in the face of heavy fire from blank cartridges and to the fury of impotent umpires.' This was an up-to-date variation of the old cavalry custom of 'galloping up the hills and riding down the umpires'. (Evans: *7H*, 187).

The first mechanical vehicles received by the Indian cavalry in 1940 were 'Baby Austins'. In one regiment 'the burly Rajput Risaldar-Major' took over the first one received. 'Almost bulging out of his pony-sized mount', he was seen 'grinning like a child with a new toy.' (Brereton; *7H*, 165).

'Being extremely light, the machine had a surprisingly good cross-country performance and after a little training the two men could "heave" it over quite difficult obstacles. . . . The machine was the prototype of the American Jeep.' (Martel, 64).

How armoured cars were to be tactically employed was an as yet unresolved question. An infantryman, Colonel William Denman Croft, who between 1929 and 1931 was to command the Royal Tank Corps Centre, wrote in 1926:

> 'For reconnaissance the horse is undoubtedly the best means, even if the armoured cars are working alone; and if . . . [they] are ordered to carry out a long distance reconnaissance, which will carry them far beyond the
>
> *(continued over)*

trucks ('pick-ups' as they were then called), or other forms of AFVs, these two regiments, (fully equipped with thirty-four armoured cars each by the end of 1930), until after the outbreak of war, were the sole units in the regular army equipped with armoured cars only.*

---

nearest cavalry, it will be necessary to provide horse-box trailers which can be hauled by the first line transport [by horses].

'When actually working with cavalry it is essential for the armoured car commander to be mounted, for he must be with the cavalry commander....

'There are still those who cannot or will not see the necessity for providing an armoured car unit with horses....

'It is . . . just as unreasonable to say that cavalry are unnecessary as to say that the armoured car commander need not be mounted.'(Croft, Col W.D. 'Notes on Armoured Cars', *Cav. Jnl*, Apr., 1926, 160)

*In May, 1927, the short-lived Experimental Mechanized (in 1928 renamed Armoured) Force was formed as recommended by the Salisbury sub-committee (see above). At its two annual manoeuvres on Salisbury Plain cavalry was used, in part, in opposition to it. This was meant to bring out the merits and the limitations of both. To try to harmonize horses and motors was, of course, bound to end in failure. As Brian Bond has put it, it was astonishing that 'the lingering belief that tank and horsed cavalry could work together' persisted for so long. (Bond: *PMP*, 171. Professor Bond's book is the most truly reliable and comprehensive study of inter-war military policy. Winton, Lt-Col Harold R. (US Army) 'The Evolution of British Mechanised and Armoured Doctrine, 1919–1938' *JRUSI*, Mar., 1985, 60–1 is a distillation of his excellent Winton (see List of Abbreviations) and is an essential source. For a short summing up Keegan, J. *Six Armies in Normandy, from D-Day to the Liberation of Paris . . .*, 1982, 194–7 cannot be bettered.)

The EMF was the result of the positive thinking of Milne, who became CIGS in 1926. He insisted upon 'a mechanized division capable of covering at least 100 miles per day across country'. (Mallinson, 218).

General Sir F. Pile asked by Winton why he thought Milne had dispersed the EMF, 'answered without hesitation that the old cavalrymen were responsible.' (Winton, 105). Bungling by its commander on manoeuvres was, perhaps, another reason.

At the end of 1935 a 'Mobile Division' was decided upon. It consisted of the Tank Brigade and one mechanized cavalry brigade. It eventually became the 1st Armoured Division. (8 Dec., 1934, 20/Cav/831, SD2, WO 32/2847).

There is conclusive evidence that about this time the futility of including a mounted division in the expeditionary force was unanimously recognized by the General Staff. (Harris, 204; see also Minute by Montgomery-Massingberd, WO 32/2847, 15 Oct., 1934)

"THE ARMOURED CAR-BINIERS"

By "Nomad"

(Trooper Thomas Atkins hears that his regiment has been converted into an armoured car unit.)

They say there ain't no difference and we are still 'ussars
And lancers (in the Army List) equipped with armoured cars,
But now the order's come to us and clearly it appears
That 'enceforth we shall just be called the Armoured Car-biniers.

The Colonel's on the sick list with an apoplectic fit.
The Sergeant-Major's temper 'asn't modified a bit.
And the subalterns are swearin' that they'll call for volunteers
To shoot the bloke wot changed us into Armoured Car-biniers.

The Adjutant's a "dressy" bloke; 'is face a sight will be
When 'e meets a squadron dressed in overalls of dungaree.
The Ridin'-Master's orf 'is chump and calls us "pretty dears,"
For 'is job – and language – fails 'im in the Armoured Car-biniers.

The ridin'-school's a garidge and the forage-store a dump
And squadrons goes and draws their "feeds" from orf a petrol pump
And they'll issue us with goggles to prevent the wind-swept tears
And with greatcoats made of leather for the Armoured Car-biniers.

The silver trumpets' notes are still and trumpeters forlorn
Are tryin' to blow "stables" on a blinkin' motor-'orn
And "honking" Fords salute the day like brazen chanticleers
To sound a new "revelly" for the Armoured Car-biniers.

With our tossin' plumes and pennons and our scarlet, blue and gold,
Well, we made a pretty picture in the 'appy days of old,
But now a reek of petrol and a cloud of dust appears
And that's the bloomin' march-past of the Armoured Car-biniers.

It's a fate in store for many. It's the writin' on the wall,
But they'd get a better move on if they "mechanised" White'all,
And a bloke wot's fond of 'orses and been soldierin' for years
Don't want to be a "shuvver" in the Armoured Car-biniers.

"Nomad"

(Cavalry Journal, July, 1928, p. 469)

* * *

The Cabinet decides on mechanization of most cavalry regiments

No significant actions occurred in the saga of the dying of the horsed cavalry until 1936/1937, nine years after the flurry of activity prompted by the Geddes Axe. In 1935 the Inspector General of Cavalry had informed all cavalry colonels that he could no longer see any future for horsed cavalry as such. He therefore recommended that the bulk be converted to armour. The process started in the spring of 1936.*

Late in 1937 the Indian Government, after years of pressure from Whitehall, agreed to the mechanization of the cavalry of the line regiments stationed there.† This decision much simplified the 'trooping' and 'linking' problem. It also allowed the Cabinet to resolve to mechanize all but three of the remaining horse regiments as soon as money for AFVs became available, now that interchangeability between home and India of different types of regiment was no longer a difficulty. The three units which were to remain horsed were the Household Cavalry Composite Regiment and the Royals and the Greys, the two senior regiments of the cavalry of the line.§

---

*The year, incidentally, in which 'battle dress' was first issued.

By June, 1937, the Bays had made sufficient progress for a troop to demonstrate an attack with its light tanks in cooperation with the RHA, before Prince Chichibu of Japan. (Mann, M., *The Regimental History of the 1st Dragoon Guards*, 1993, 384).

Though very far from being a reactionary, Duff Cooper, Secretary of State for War at the time, apologized for the decision. 'It is like,' he said, 'asking a musical performer to throw away his violin and devote himself in future to the gramophone.' (H. of C. speech, quoted in Lunt, J. *The Scarlet Lancers: the Story of 16th/5th The Queen's Royal Lancers . . .*' 1993, 124).

†In 1923 Worthington-Evans had made a special trip to India to persuade Birdwood, then Commander-in-Chief, to adopt the same cavalry organization as at home. Birdwood accepted the two squadron organization, but not the mechanization of machine-gun squadrons. (8 Mar., 1928, *Hansard: (C)*, 12/2–/3).

§Suspecting, wrongly, that the Greys, Scotland's only cavalry regiment (which had the best recruiting record of any regiment, largely because, it was said, of the glamorous grey horses), was to be mechanized, its Colonel wrote a public letter to Scottish MPs, deploring so awful a fate. He telephoned Chetwode saying that 'he had got reasons in writing from the Home [?] Office for doing so'. Chetwode told him ('an idiot') 'exactly what I thought of him and that he had probably spoilt the whole thing', adding that 'his only chance was to grovel' to the War Office. (2 Nov., 1937, Chetwode to Knox (AG), WO 32/4633). The Army Council confined themselves 'to an expression of "severe displeasure" at the Colonel's action.' (9 Nov., 1937, Hore-Belisha to Hardinge, WO 32/4633, 33B).

The 22nd Dragoons and 23rd Hussars resurrected

These were to act as 'individual units in any particular theatre for which horsed cavalry may be specially useful', or as 'Corps cavalry for close reconnaissance duties' or, 'as a cavalry brigade'.[7] It was decided to tell all commanding officers what was to be their regiments' fate without delay, since recruiting was being affected owing to the uncertainty of men as to which type of unit they were enlisting in.

The frustrating lack of vehicles led to regiments taking the matter into their own hands, especially respecting training. In 1939 the War Office magnanimously offered a grant of £10 so that the 13th/18th Hussars could equip a Driving and Maintenance School. 'It was only by the generosity and patriotism of the Rootes Group, Lucas Ltd and the local garages, who gave freely almost everything necessary [sectionalized engines and mechanical parts] that it was possible to set up a school at all.'[8] The 7th Hussars bought their own engines and chassis of old cars and lorries and dismantled and cut them up for instructional purposes.[9]

In 1939 the Royal Armoured Corps was formed. It was to have precedence immediately before the Royal Regiment of Artillery. Twenty cavalry of the line regiments were 'associated' with the Royal Tank Corps in the new corps. Included were the Greys and the Royals. By then they, too, had been mechanized.[10]*

In the early 1940s, at a time when numerous extra tank regiments were being raised, a few 'new' 'cavalry' regiments were brought into being – the 22nd Dragoons, 23rd Hussars, etc. In fact regiments with these numbers had been raised in 1794–5 and later disbanded. (See Vol. 1, 44, 65, 296). They were now resurrected. Churchill, Prime Minister and Secretary of State for Defence since 1940, incensed, wrote to the CIGS: 'Surely it was a very odd thing to create these outlandish numbered regiments . . . when there exist already telescoped up the 18th, 20th and 19th Hussars, 5th and 21st Lancers. Surely all these should have been revived before creating these unreal and artificial titles.'[11] He was told that since re-amalgamation of the regiments he cited would inevitably have recurred once the war was over, this resurrection seemed the proper course to take.

*At the outbreak of war the regiments of the Household Cavalry became, for the first time in history truly composite. Personnel of the three regiments were mixed indiscriminately within the squadrons of the 1st and 2nd Household Cavalry regiments. The 1st went mounted to Palestine in 1940, became 'motorized' in 1941 and was converted to armoured cars just before Alamein in October, 1942. At home the 2nd Regiment was thus named when in early 1941 it too became an armoured car regiment in the Guards Armoured Division.

The disposal of troop horses

When on mechanization the troop horses had to be dispensed with they were sent to remount depots or sold, many of them to the contractors who supplied the yeomanry. Officers were allowed to keep one charger each. This extraordinary Army Council decision was come to largely because it was still feared that officers would resign when the regiments were mechanized. 'Even courses at Bovington Tank School were "sweetened" by allowing the charger to accompany the officer. The Quartermaster-General pointed out forcefully that this was not even-handed, so the Tank Corps were allocated five horses there too!'[12]

* * *

'I don't care if you have been mechanised . . . you can't leave that there 'ere!'

The yeomanry transformed

While the regulars were going through major transformations, so were the yeomanry. Since radical post-war changes in the reserve army were obviously needed, a conference was called at the War Office in 1920 by Churchill, the then Secretary of State for War. It considered how best to reorganize the Territorial Force (later to be renamed the Territorial Army) and its affiliated yeomanry units. It was attended by the Lords Lieutenant of counties, the Territorial Associations' chairmen and all the yeomanry commanding officers. The result of three meetings was that the fourteen senior regiments were to remain mounted and that the Lovat Scouts and the Scottish Horse were to serve as mounted 'scouts'. The remainder were given some measure of choice and a year in which to decide which they preferred of the alternatives the War Office proposed. Twenty-four regiments chose to become field artillery. Since there were then no plans to mechanize that arm, this meant that they would still be dealing with horses. One regiment became horse artillery. Eight regiments, reduced in strength, became armoured car companies of the Tank Corps ('Royal' from 1923). One was subsumed in its local infantry battalion and another became a signals regiment attached to the cavalry division. Only two were disbanded.[13] Though a few rearrangements of regimental roles took place up to 1939, this was virtually how the yeomanry stood at the outbreak of war.

The general chronic deficiency of all sorts of modern equipment was even greater than for the cavalry of the line. To some degree it was overcome, as in the case of the regulars, by private enterprise. The Inns of Court Regiment, for instance, which in 1936 was converted into a cavalry regiment of one horsed and two mechanized squadrons, had to build at its own expense garages for its five Morris 'bull-nosed' 15 cwt trucks. Further, since there was a long delay in supplying wireless sets, two of these, costing £25 each, were made by a Lance-Corporal in the regiment who was on the technical staff of HMV.[14] The difficulties of proper training without adequate resources were compounded by the fact, as Worthington-Evans wrote to Churchill (now Chancellor of the Exchequer) in 1927, that

> 'The old yeomanry class has ceased to exist and the yeomanry is nowadays composed almost entirely of business men as officers and clerks and artisans as other ranks. Their occupations make it impossible for these men to devote more than

The provision of yeomanry mounts

a very small proportion of their time to military training or to the country pursuits which help develop "an eye for ground". Whereas formerly the yeoman had his own horse, which he used in every-day life, now the horses of yeomanry regiments are either provided by County Territorial Associations or hired by individual men. In either case the animal is, from a military standpoint, almost untrained.'[15]

Eight mounted yeomanry regiments went to the Middle East as part of the 1st Cavalry Division later designated the 10th Armoured Division. For their actions in the Syrian campaign see p. 350.

ENVOI

The last hundred years of the British cavalry have turned out to be far more extraordinary than I thought they would be when I first decided to undertake a chronicle of them. I never, for instance, until I embarked on the necessary research, thought that there would be much to say about the First World War, (except, of course, for the great campaign in Palestine). That it would take four volumes to record never entered my head. The long and fascinating journey from, so to say, Aliwal to Amiens, Chilianwala to Cambrai became more and more depressing, though more and more full of surprises as it proceeded.

War has always been a beastly, brutish business, but when engagements were mostly confined to a day or two, when weapons were more or less inefficient and when combatants were gloriously dressed, there was glamour too, even a measure of glory. These declined from the Great Boer War onwards. When troops no longer went into winter quarters as a matter of course, to the other horrors of war was added the curse of fighting in filthy weather.

As the life of fighting men during war became more detestable, there developed during the twentieth century certain compensations. The peacetime living conditions of the other ranks, for example, improved to a considerable degree, while, though wounds became more frightful, their treatment became, as a rule, more skilful and speedy. The same applied to horses, upon which all branches were completely dependent. Further, in the last half of this century the shocking cruelties which war from time immemorial had imposed upon them has at last come to an end. For these mercies humanity can be grateful.

* * *

The first words of Volume 1 of this work, published nearly a quarter of a century ago, were 'The cavalry is dead, except for ceremonial purposes.' The truth of this is even more evident now than then. It has been my intention to present a fair and detailed account of the peacetime life and the wartime actions of the British mounted arm in the course of its protracted descent into the grave.

Envoi

Though certainly flawed, the attempt has been an earnest and I hope an honest one.

*   *   *

'Farewell the neighing steed and the shrill trump;
The spirit-stirring drum, the ear-piercing fife,
The royal banner, and all quality,
Pride, pomp and circumstance of glorious war!
Farewell! Othello's occupation's gone.'
— SHAKESPEARE, *Othello*, III, 3

APPENDIX 1

'The Last Charge'

It is almost as certain as are death and taxes that there will never be another cavalry charge against an enemy. Over the years that the present author has been cobbling together his chronicle of the British cavalry, he has received a number of correspondents' information about the last cavalry charge of British mounted troops; about the last time that they rode into action (without charging) and about the last time that mounted troops anywhere in the world were operationally employed. As regards the British there can be a considerable degree of certitude. From a massive file of these letters, published accounts and press cuttings it is possible to come to some conclusions which it is hoped will clinch the matter for all time. (See below).

In the case of other nations – not really the concern of this work, but nevertheless interesting – it is difficult to be equally positive. Some South American states still (1995) retain mounted troops for internal patrol work, but it appears likely that the squadron or two of Portuguese dragoons which were employed in 1971–2 against the guerrillas in Angola can claim to be among the last mounted soldiers used in real anger, though there seems to have been nothing more than skirmishing and patrolling.*

The last occasion on which British troops were attacked by enemy cavalry was at the action of Agordat [or Keru] in early 1941. The charge was made, according to an officer of the recently mechanized Skinner's Horse, who was at its receiving end, 'by an Italian "Bande" or troop of Eritrean soldiers [about sixty in number]

---

*Israel abolished its horsed units in 1956. In the Second World War the Eastern Front saw the employment of a number of horsemen, especially in rough terrain. The 18th Pomorze Lancers of the Polish army threw themselves against a German panzer division in a hopelessly gallant charge at Krojanty on 3 September, 1939. There were also other charges made by the eleven Polish cavalry brigades, but this is the most famous.

On 24 August, 1942, at Jbuschenskij, Siberian infantry was charged by the Italian 3rd Gorizia Regiment which managed to take the infantry's standards. (See Caporilli, P. *Sette Anni di Guerra*, 1959.) In that year the Red Army included thirty-five mounted divisions. Two corps took a useful part in the counter-offensive to free Moscow in December, 1941. In the following November cavalry formations helped to close the ring round the German Sixth Army at Stalingrad, *(continued over)*

'The Last Charge'

during the advance to Keren and Asmara. The Italians were led by a young officer on a grey horse and he, with about twenty-five men and several horses, were mown down by our gunners (the Surrey and Sussex Yeomanry) who turned their 25-pounders round and fired point blank at the ponies galloping at the British position. 'We were full of admiration for the Italian troops,' says an officer who was present, 'and were sad that we had to kill them.'[1]

It has been claimed that the last British troops to ride into battle, *without* indulging in a charge, were two of the yeomanry regiments which formed part of the 5th Cavalry Brigade. These crossed into Syria from Palestine to deal with the Vichy French in June, 1941. On three separate occasions the regiments were literally on the point of charging when the enemy decided to fly before the yeomanry's swords could perform their task.[2] However, it has also been claimed that an *ad hoc* troop of the King's Dragoon Guards, which scraped together local horses and performed patrol work in the final part of the Italian campaign in 1944-5, was the last non-charging British cavalry to ride horses on active service. Yet neither of these claims quite holds water, for as late as 1979 there went into combat some 250 men of Grey's Scouts of the Rhodesian Army. There is no evidence of their charging.[3] Yet the KDG troop was undoubtedly the last of any part of the regiments of the cavalry of the line to ride on active service, while the regiments in Syria were the last of the yeomanry to do so.

* * *

As for the last actual British charge, there are three claimants. None of these involved regular or yeomanry troops. The earliest

---

while the final advance into Germany saw three corps taking part. In 1943 the Germans raised about two cavalry divisions to fight the Russian partisans behind the lines. One of the junior officers, whose squadron had found its way to Italy, surrendered it to a British division in Austria in 1945. (Lunt, 35.) The Russians may still have a horsed unit or two. Until recently the Chinese and Turkish armies possessed some mounted units.

In the 1941 actions against the Vichy French in Syria a mounted force of 1,000 was raised by the British from the Jebel Druze. That it was little employed in a mounted role seems certain.

Between the wars, in the Wars of Intervention and in the Russo-Polish War, much use was made of horsed troops between 1919 and 1922. At the battle of Zomosc, for instance, it is believed, unlikely though it seems, that the advance of 25,000 of Marshall Budenny's cavalry 'was checked by two "concentrated" Polish cavalry divisions', which were less than half the Russians' strength. (Shea, Gen. Sir John 'Swan Song of the Sword', *Daily Telegraph*, 27 Aug., 1955, quoting from a book by M. Paul Zaremba. See also Badsey, 352.)

'The Last Charge'

took place on 19 March, 1942. A detachment of some fifty Sikhs of the Burma Frontier Force on reconnaissance duties north of Rangoon rode into an ambush set by a large force of Japanese infantry. The detachment was led by Captain Arthur Sandeman of the Central Indian Horse who decided that, rather than surrender, he would charge. Neither he nor his men reached the enemy. They were largely wiped out by machine-gun fire, a few wounded surviving only to die in prison camps later on.[4]

The next 'last charge' is attributed to a squadron of Gwalior Lancers which made it in the Arakan early in 1944. This regiment was, of course, not of the Indian Army, but belonged to an Indian State force. The very last charge, though, was made in Africa by a section of the Northern Frontier Tribal Police, employed on anti-Mau Mau operations near Isiolo in 1953. Chenevix Trench tells what happened: 'They came upon a large, well-armed gang... armed only with rifles. They should have dismounted and opened fire, but Sergeant Yusuf Abdulla, with a well-founded distrust of his men's markmanship, ordered a charge. They galloped down the gang and killed the lot, shooting from the saddle at point-blank range or bashing them with rifle-butts. Their only loss was one broken rifle.'[5]

There can be no shadow of a doubt that the last proper charge launched by *a complete regiment* of British regular cavalry against well-armed troops took place in Turkey in 1920 during the Chanak crisis. The Allies had dealt rather harshly with the Turks at the Peace Conference. The empire had been dismembered and Anatolia, the Turkish heartland, had been divided into spheres of influence. A Nationalist uprising resulted, led by Mustapha Kemal (see Vol. 5, p. 244). To counter this, Allied troops were despatched to Constantinople. Ironside (see p. 196) commanded the British contingent which in June occupied the Izmid Peninsula. Communications with this were severed by the Nationalists when they captured the village of Gebze and blew up the connecting bridge. The British line of communications ran along the coast and the bridge was a vital link in the chain. Consequently on 12 July a battle group, consisting of the 20th Hussars, the 39th Royal Garhwal Rifles and accompanying artillery and engineers, set out to recapture the village and repair the bridge. The village was retaken on the 13th, but not before a minor engagement had taken place. The Garhwalis made a frontal attack watched by the hussars who were drawn up in mass on the Turkish right flank. As the attack developed the Turks occupied prepared positions in front of the village, about 1,000 yards across open ground from the hussars' position. An officer of the Garhwalis recorded what he saw happen next:

'Our artillery opened fire and I could see the shells falling on the enemy position. Suddenly, as I watched, I saw movement on the ridge to the north. Over the crest of the ridge came the whole of the 20th Hussars, two squadrons abreast in columns of troops with the third squadron in depth, nearly three hundred men in all. Their sabres were drawn and glistened in the early morning sunlight, their trumpets sounded as they moved, slowly at first, but gathering speed as they approached the enemy's flank. Our artillery stopped firing. The Turks huddled together as best they could in small groups facing the on-coming horsemen. Some lay down and fired, some knelt, a few fired standing. All stood their ground, though lamentably positioned and with little hope of checking the cavalry. The Turk was always a dour fighter.

'Now the Hussars reached the Turkish flank. We could see their sabres flashing in the sun as they struck, withdrew, and struck again. All the time the trumpets echoed, fierce and thrilling, lifting one's spirits in some form of savage exultation. The charge swept clean through the Nationalists' line. Beyond it the Squadrons rallied, regrouped, turned and charged back through the bewildered Turks, now making off for the cover of the vineyards round the village itself. Not more than thirty minutes after appearing over the ridge the Hussars had vanished whence they came, leaving huddled bodies on the plain to bear testimony to their passage.

'The last of the Nationalists disappeared into the thick country behind Gebze and it was time for me to advance with my company to take possession and to complete the job begun so competently by the cavalry. There was no more resistance.'

Though several horses were wounded, the sole human casualty in this charge was one officer wounded.[6]*

The last charge of British mounted troops on the scale of a whole brigade was that at El Mughar in Palestine. (See Vol. 5, p. 191).

---

*During the Arab Rebellion in Iraq of 1920–1921 the 35th Scinde Horse made a number of charges against the Arabs, especially during the retreat after 'the Hillah Column Disaster' in July–August, 1920. (Maunsell, Col E.B. *Prince of Wales's Own, The Scinde Horse*, 1926, 264–310; information from Mr Peter Chapman)

APPENDIX 2

Old Soldiers

In 1930 there died at the age of eighty-nine Major-General Sir Henry Augustus Bushman. In the 1860s he had been Adjutant of the 7th Hussars. In 1879 he had commanded the 9th Lancers in the 2nd Afghan War. He 'had brought with him from England a sling which permitted the carbines to be slung on the man's back when going into action.' He had also arranged for the sword to be 'fastened to the saddle instead of round the man's body'. This was officially adopted by all mounted troops in 1891. (See Vol. 3, p. 235.) In 1926 he presented the 7th Hussars with a silver-mounted swagger-stick inscribed 'from the Adjutant, 1863–72'. This he specified was to be 'carried by the best-turned-out man on guard during his tour of duty as C.O.'s Stick Orderly.'[1]

Colonel Sir Fitzroy Maclean, Bart, was 101 when he died in 1936. He had joined the 13th Hussars in 1852. He missed the charge of the Light Brigade because he was sick, but had taken part in the cavalry affair at the Bulganak on 19 September, 1854. (See Vol. 2, 46–7.) He commanded the 13th from 1871 until his retirement in 1872. Troop-Sergeant-Major Edwin Hughes, also of the 13th, was ninety-six when he died in 1927. He was said to be the very last of those who took part in the Light Brigade charge.[2]

On 16 January, 1932, the funeral took place of Troop-Sergeant-Major John Stratford of the 14th Light Dragoons. He was 103 and the oldest pensioner of the army. After leaving the 14th in 1871, he had served for sixteen years as Troop Sergeant Instructor of the Staffordshire Yeomanry. He had fought at Ramnagar, 1848, Chilianwala, 1849, in the Persian War, 1856–7 and the Central India campaign, 1858–9. (See Vol 1, 266, 288, 176–84, Vol. 2, 126–30, 178–214.) 'He retained his faculties to the end.'[3]

Brigadier W.G. Carr died in 1982, 'happily out hunting', at the age of eighty. When the 12th Lancers were converted to armoured cars in 1928 (see p. 337) he became adjutant to the regiment. He was one of a small group of cavalry officers who pioneered the conversion to armour. He was responsible for training two yeomanry armoured regiments just before the Second World War. He later commanded the 22nd Armoured Brigade and later still the 4th Light Armoured Brigade in the early desert battles of 1941 and 1942.[4]

353

ABBREVIATIONS USED IN THE FOOTNOTES AND SOURCE NOTES

Some important sources which have been consulted but not quoted from are also included here. They may be useful for further reading.

AFV	Armoured Fighting Vehicle
Anon: 'E.P.'	Anon 'E.P.' [Lt-Col E. Paterson, temp. cmdr, 7 Cav. Bde in battle of Amiens, Aug., 1918], 'The Door Ajar', *Cav. Jnl*, Oct., 1921
Anon: *Mhow*	Anon 'Operations Carried Out by the Mhow Cavalry Brigade on December 1st, 1917', *Cav. Jnl*, Jan., 1928
AO	Army Order
Arthur	Arthur, Capt. Sir George *The Story of the Household Cavalry*, III, 1926
Ascoli	Ascoli, David *The Mons Star: the B.E.F. 5 Aug–22 Nov. 1914*, 1981
Atkinson	Atkinson, C.T. *History of the Royal Dragoons, 1661–1934*, 1934
Badsey	Badsey, Dr S.D. 'Fire and the Sword: The British Army and the *Arme Blanche* Controversy, 1871–1921' (MS Doctorial Dissertation), 1981
Bickersteth	Bickersteth, Lt J.B. *History of the 6th Cavalry Brigade 1914–1919*, [1920]
Bidwell & Graham	Bidwell, S. & Graham, D. *Fire-Power: British Army Weapons and Theories of War 1904–1945*, 1985
Blake: *Haig*	Blake, R. *The Private Papers of Douglas Haig, 1914–1919*, 1952
Blaxland	Blaxland, Gregory *Amiens: 1918*, 1968
Blenkinsop	Blenkinsop, Maj.-Gen. Sir L.J. & Rainey, Lt-Col J.W. *History of the Great War based on Official Documents: Veterinary Services*, 1925
BM	British Museum
Bolitho	Bolitho, H. *The Galloping Third*, 1963
Bond	Bond, Brian 'Doctrine and Training in the British Cavalry, 1870–1914', (ed.) Howard, Michael *The Theory and Practice of War: Essays Presented to Captain B.H. Liddell Hart on his 70th Birthday*, 1967
Bond: *BMP*	Bond, Brian *British Military Policy between the Two World Wars*, 1980

355

Abbreviations

Bond: WWI/BMH	Bond, Brian *The First World War and British Military History*, 1992
Boraston	Boraston, J.H. (ed.) *Sir Douglas Haig's Despatches (December 1915–April 1919)*, (Foreword by Terraine, J.), (1919), 1979
Boyle	Boyle, Capt. R.C. *A Record of the West Somerset Yeomanry 1914–1919*, n.d.
Brereton	Brereton, J.M. *A History of the 4th/7th Dragoon Guards and Their Predecessors, 1685–1980*, 1982
Brereton: *Horse*	Brereton, J.M. *The Horse in War*, 1976
Brereton: *7H*	Brereton, J.M. *The 7th Queen's Own Hussars*, 1975
Brunton	Brunton, Sgt D. MS diary, 1914–1919, XV/XIX R. Hussars Regimental Museum, Newcastle upon Tyne.
Buchan	Buchan, John *A History of the Great War*, 4 vols, 1921–2
Burrows	Burrows, J.W. *The Essex Yeomanry*, 1926
CAB	Cabinet Papers
Cardew	Cardew, Maj. F.G. *Hodson's Horse, 1857–1922*, 1928
Carnock	Carnock, Lord *The History of the 15th The King's Hussars, 1914–1922*, 1932
Cav. Jnl	*The Cavalry Journal*
Cav. Trng	[Official] *Cavalry Training* (various dates)
Charrington	Charrington, Maj. H.V.S. *The 12th Royal Lancers in France, 1914–1918*, 1921
Charteris	Charteris, Brig.-Gen. J. *Field-Marshal Earl Haig*, 1929
Churchill: *GW*	Churchill, W.S. *The Great War*, 3 vols, 1933
Churchill: *'16–'18*	Churchill, W.S. *The World Crisis, 1916–1918*, 1927
CID	Committee of Imperial Defence
CIGS	Chief of the Imperial General Staff
Clabby	Clabby, Brig. J. *The History of the Royal Veterinary Corps, 1919–1961*, 1961
Clarke	Clarke, Tpr Wm 'Random Recollections, 1914–1918', IWM (87/18/1)
Coleman	Coleman, Frederic *From Mons to Ypres with French: A Personal Narrative*, 1916
Connolly	Connolly, Lt-Col C.E. 'The Action of the Canadian Cavalry Brigade at Moreuil Wood and Rifle Wood – March and April, 1918' *Canadian Defence Quarterly*, III, Oct., 1925, and July, 1926
Cooper	Cooper, Duff *Haig*, 2 vols, 1935
COS	Chiefs of Staff
Crichton	MS letter, 17 April 1917, from Kavanagh to Lt-Col C.W.H. Crichton, 10th Hussars, who had been wounded in 1915 (kindly made available by B.J. Crichton Esq.)
Croft	Croft, Maj. the Rev. John 'Horsed Cavalry in the 1914–1918 War', *The Army Quarterly and Defence Journal*, Apr., 1985

Abbreviations

Cruttwell	Cruttwell, C.R.M.F. *A History of the Great War, 1914–1918*, 1934
Daniell	[See Scott Daniell]
Darling	Darling, Maj. J.C. *20th Hussars in the Great War*, 1923
De Groot	De Groot, G.J. *Douglas Haig 1861–1928*, 1988
Dent	Dent, Capt. Geoffrey, letters (20 Sep., 1914–23 Dec., 1918), IWM, (PP/MCR/226)
De Pree	De Pree, Maj.-Gen. H.D. 'The Battle of Cambrai: November 20th to 30th, 1917', *Journal of the Royal Artillery*, LV, 1928–9
DNB	*Dictionary of National Biography*
Dundonald	Dundonald, Lt-Gen. The Earl of *My Army Life*, 1926
Durand	Durand, Sir H. Mortimer *The Thirteenth Hussars in the Great War*, 1921
Edmonds	Edmonds, Brig.-Gen. Sir James [The Official History] *Military Operations: France and Belgium, 1915*, 2 vols: I (with Wynne, Capt. G.C.), 1927; II, 1928; *1916*, 2 vols: I, 1932; II, (compiled by Miles, Capt. W.), 1938; *1917*, 3 vols: I, 1940; II, 1948; III (compiled by Miles), 1948; *1918*, 5 vols: I, 1935; II (with Davies, Maj. H.R. & Maxwell-Hyslop, (Lt-Col R.G.B.), 1939; III (with Davies & Maxwell-Hyslop), 1939; IV (with Davies & Maxwell-Hyslop), 1947; V (with Maxwell-Hyslop), 1947
Essame	Essame, H. *The Battle for Europe, 1918*, 1972
Evans: *4H*	Evans, Capt. H.H.D. and Laing, Maj. N.O. *The 4th (Queen's Own) Hussars in the Great War*, 1920
Evans: *5DG*	Evans, Maj.-Gen. Roger *The Story of the Fifth Royal Inniskilling Dragoon Guards . . .*, 1951
Evans: *7H*	Evans, Maj.-Gen. Roger *The Years Between: The Story of the 7th Queen's Own Hussars, 1911–1937*, 1965
Falls: *WWI*	Falls, Cyril *The First World War*, 1960
Farndale: *WF*	Farndale, Gen. Sir M. *History of the Royal Regiment of Artillery: Western Front, 1914–18*, 1986
Farrar-Hockley	Farrar-Hockley, A. *Goughie: The Life of General Sir Hubert Gough*, 1975
Fellows	Fellows, G. and Benson Freeman *Historical Records of the South Nottinghamshire Hussars Yeomanry, 1794 to 1924*, 1928
ffrench-Blake	ffrench-Blake, Lt-Col R.L.V. *A History of the 17th/21st Lancers, 1922–1957*
Fuller	Fuller, Bt-Col J.F.C., 'The Influence of Tanks on Cavalry Tactics (A Study in the Evolution of Mobility in War)', *Cav. Jnl*, X, 1920
Furse	Furse, Maj. Sir Ralph Dolignon, MS 'Hoofmarks: A Cavalry Officer's Memories of the Great War,

Abbreviations

1914–1918', in the possession of his daughter, Mrs Theresa Whistler

Galtrey	Galtrey, Capt. S. *The Horse and the War*, 1918
Gibb	Gibb, Rev. Harold *Record of the 4th Royal Irish Dragoon Guards in the Great War, 1914–1918*, 1925
Godwin-Austen	Godwin-Austen, Bt-Maj. A.R. *The Staff and the Staff College*, 1927
Gough	Gough, Gen. Sir Hubert *The Fifth Army*, 1931
Gough: *March*	Gough, Gen. Sir Hubert *The March Retreat*, 1934
Graham	Graham, H. *History of the 16th, the Queen's, Light Dragoons (Lancers), 1912 to 1925*, 1926
Gray	Gray, Randal *Kaiserschlacht 1918*, 1991
Griffith	Griffith, Paddy *Battle Tactics of the Western Front: The British Army's Art of Attack, 1916–1918*, 1994
Haig: diary	Haig's various WWI diaries and orders, NLS
Hansard: (C)	*Hansard's Parliamentary Debates*, House of Commons
Hansard: (L)	*Hansard's Parliamentary Debates*, House of Lords
Harris	Harris, J.P. 'The British General Staff and the Coming of War, 1933–9', *Bulletin of the Institute of Historical Research*, Nov., 1986
Harvey	Harvey, Col J.R. and Cape, Lt-Col H.A. *The History of the 5th Lancers, 1689–1921*, 1921
Harrison-Ainsworth	Harrison-Ainsworth, E.D. *The History and War Records of the Surrey Yeomanry (Queen Mary's Regt), 1797–1928*, 1928
Haslam	Haslam, Lt P.L.C. MS diary, IWM (7612-21)
Higham	Higham, R. *Armed Forces in Peacetime: Britain, 1918–1940, a case study*, 1962
Hobart	Hobart, Maj.-Gen. Sir Percy, unpublished account of the battle of Cambrai, 1935, Tank Museum
Holmes	Holmes, Richard *The Little Field-Marshal: Sir John French*, 1981
Home	Home, Brig.-Gen. Sir Archibald Home *The Diary of a World War I Cavalry Officer* (ed. Briscoe, Diana), 1985
Howard	Howard, Michael *The Continental Commitment . . .*, 1972
HRAVC	Smith, Maj.-Gen. Sir Frederick *A History of the Royal Army Veterinary Corps, 1796–1919*, 1927
Hudson	Hudson, Gen. Sir H. *History of the 19th King George's Own Lancers, formerly 18th King George's Own Lancers and 19th Lancers (Fane's Horse), amalgamated in 1921*, 1937
'Instructions'	'Instructions to officers i/c wire pulling companies, HQ 3rd Bde, Tank Corps, 15 Nov., 1917', Tank Museum
IOL	India Office Library

Abbreviations

IWM	Imperial War Museum
Jackson	Jackson, Maj. D. *India's Army*, 1940
JAHR	*Journal of the Society for Army Historical Research*
Jeffery	Jeffery, K. *The British Army and the Crisis of Empire, 1918–22*, 1984
Jenkins	Jenkins, R. *Asquith*, 1964
Jessel	Jessel, Col Sir H.M. *The Story of Romsey Remount Depot* [1919]
Jones	Jones, H.A. *The War in the Air . . .*, IV, 1934, VI, 1937
JRUSI	*Journal of the Royal United Service Institution*
Kearsey	Kearsey A. *The Battle of Amiens 1918 & Operations 8 August–3 September 1918*, 1950
Keith-Falconer	Keith-Falconer, Adrian *The Oxfordshire Hussars in the Great War*, 1927
Kennedy: *Army*	Kennedy, Capt. J.R. *This, Our Army*, 1935
Lascelles	Hart-Davis, Duff (Ed.) *End of an Era: Letters and Journals of Sir Alan Lascelles, from 1887 to 1920*, 1986
LHC	Liddell Hart Centre
L.I.	L.I. 'Cambrai, 1917 – The Impressions of an Infantryman', *Royal Tank Corps Journal*, 1927
Liddell Hart	Liddell Hart, Sir Basil Henry *A History of the World War*, 1934
Liddell Hart: *Outline*	Liddell Hart, Sir Basil Henry *The War in Outline*, 1936
Liddell Hart: *Real*	Liddell Hart, Sir Basil Henry *The Real War, 1914–1918*, 1930
Liddell Hart: *Tanks*	Liddell Hart, Capt. B.H. *The Tanks: The History of the Royal Tank Regiment and its Predecessors*, Vol I, 1959
Liddle	Liddle, Peter H. *The 1916 Battle of the Somme: A Reappraisal*, 1992
Ludendorff	Ludendorff, Gen. von *My War Memories, 1914–1918*, 2 vols., 1919
Lumley	Lumley, Capt. L.R., MP *History of the Eleventh Hussars (Prince Albert's Own) 1908–1934*, 1936
Lunt	Lunt, James *Charge to Glory! A Garland of Cavalry Exploits*, 1961
Luvaas	Luvaas, Jay *The Education of an Army: British Military Thought, 1815–1940*, 1965
Macdonald	Macdonald, Lyn *1914–1918: Voices and Images of the Great War*, 1988
Macdonald: *Somme*	Macdonald, Lyn, *Somme*, 1983
Macksey	Macksey, Maj. K.J. *Armoured Crusader: A Biography of Maj.-Gen. Sir Percy Hobart*, 1967
Macpherson	Macpherson, Maj.-Gen. Sir W.G. *History of the Great War . . . Medical Services, General History*, 3 vols, 1924

Abbreviations

Mallinson	Mallinson, A. *Light Dragoons: the Origin of a New Regiment*, 1993
Marshall-Cornwall	Marshall-Cornwall, Gen. Sir J.H. *Haig as Military Commander*, 1973
Martel	Martel, Lt-Gen. Sir G. *An Outspoken Soldier* [1949]
Maunsell	Maunsell, Col E.B. 'Cambrai', *Cav. Jnl*, Apr. 1926
Maurice: *Last*	Maurice, Maj.-Gen. Sir F. *The Last Four Months: The End of the War in the West*, 1919
Maurice: *Raw*	Maurice, Maj.-Gen. Sir F. *The Life of General Lord Rawlinson of Trent from his Journals and Letters*, 1928
Micholls	Micholls, Maj.G. *A History of the 17th Lancers (Duke of Cambridge's Own), Vol. II, 1895–1924*, 1931
Middlebrook	Middlebrook, M. *The Kaiser's Battle, 21 March, 1918: the First Day of the German Spring Offensive*, 1978
Montgomery	Montgomery, Maj.-Gen. Sir Archibald *The Story of the Fourth Army in the Battle of the Hundred Days, August 8th to November 11th, 1918*, 1919
Moore	Moore, W. *A Wood Called Bourlon: The Cover-up after Cambrai, 1917*, 1988
Moore: *Vet.*	Moore, Maj.G. Sir J. *Army Veterinary Service in War*, 1921
Moyne	Bond, B. (ed.) *Staff Officer: The Diaries of Lord Moyne 1914–1918*, 1987
Murray	Murray, Rev. R.H. *The History of the VIII King's Royal Irish Hussars, 1693–1927*, 2 vols, 1928
Nalder	Nalder, Maj.-Gen. R.F.H. *The Royal Corps of Signals: A History of its Antecedents and Development*, 1958
NAM	National Army Museum
Nicholls	Nicholls, Jonathan *Cheerful Sacrifice: The Battle of Arras 1917*, 1990
Nicholson	Nicholson, Col G.W.L. *Canadian Expeditionary Force 1914–1919 (Official History of the Canadian Army in the First World War)*, 1962
NLS	*National Library of Scotland*
Norman	Norman, Terry *The Hell they called High Wood: The Somme, 1916*, 1984
Oatts: *3DG/6DG*	Oatts, Lt-Col L.B. *I Serve: Regimental History of the 3rd Carabiniers*, 1966
Oatts: *14H/20H*	Oatts, Lt-Col L.B. *Emperor's Chambermaids: The Story of the 14th/20th King's Hussars*, 1973
OTC	Officers' Training Corps
Otley	Otley, C.B. 'The Social Origins of British Army Officers' *Sociological Review*, XVIII, No. 2 (New Series), July 1970
Parry	[Parry, D.H., 'H.P.H.' and others] *The History of the*

Abbreviations

	Third (Prince of Wales's) Dragoon Guards, 1914–1918, (priv. ptd) [1922]
Paterson	Paterson, Lt-Col, officer commanding the Fort Garry Horse, letter in *Cav. Jnl*, XIII, October, 1923
Pease	(ed.) Pease, Howard *The History of the Northumberland (Hussars) Yeomanry, 1819–1919,* 1924
Peden	Peden, G.C. *British Rearmament and the Treasury: 1932–1939,* 1979
Philipps	*Philipps, Colwyn Erasmus Arnold, Captain, Royal Horse Guards,* 'Extracts from letters from the Front written chiefly to his mother, Nov. 1914 to April 1915', 1916
Pitman	Pitman, Col Cmdt T.T. 'General Outline of Cavalry Operations on the Western Front', *Cav. Jnl*, XIII, 1923
Pitman: 'Amiens'	Pitman, Maj.-Gen. T.T. 'The Operations of the Second Cavalry Division (with Canadian Cavalry Brigade attached) in the Defence of Amiens, March 30–April 1, 1918', *Cav. Jnl*, Oct., 1923
Pitman: 'Cambrai'	Pitman, Maj.-Gen. T.T. 'The Part Played by the British Cavalry in the Surprise Attack on Cambrai, 1917' *Cav. Jnl*, XIII, July, 1923
Pitt	Pitt, Barrie *1918: The Last Act,* 1962
Pomeroy	Pomeroy, Maj. Hon. R.L. *The Story of the 5th Princess Charlotte of Wales's Dragoon Guards,* 2 vols, 1924
Pomeroy: 2D	Pomeroy, Maj. Hon. R.L. [and others] *History of the Royal Scots Greys (the Second Dragoons) August 1914–March 1918,* 1928
Powell-Edwards	Powell-Edwards, Lt-Col H.I. *The Sussex Yeomanry ... 1914–1918,* 1921
Preston: *Arras*	Preston, Maj. T. 'The Cavalry at Arras, 1917', *Cav. Jnl*, Oct., 1930
Preston: 'Loos'	Preston, Col. T. 'The Third Cavalry Division at Loos', *Cav. Jnl*, 1937, 17–30
Preston: 'MG'	Preston, Capt. T. 'The Machine Gun Corps (Cavalry) in France, 1916–1918', Parts I, II, III, IV, V, VI, VII, VIII, IX, X, *Cav. Jnl*, 1920; XI, 1921; XII, 1922; XIII, 1923
Preston: '1918'	Preston, Lt-Col T. 'The Cavalry in France, March-April, 1918', Parts, I, II, III, IV, V, VI, VII, *Cav. Jnl,* Apr., 1932, 170–83; Jul., 1932, 326–41; Oct., 1932, 484–96; Jan., 1933, 11–29; Apr., 1933, 161–178; Jul., 1933, 336–52
Preston: '1918'(2)	Preston, Lt-Col T. 'The Cavalry in France, August–November, 1918', Parts, I, II, III, IV, V, VI, VII, *Cav. Jnl*, Apr., 1934, 167–82; Jul., 1934, 338–58; Oct., 1934, 496–514; Jan., 1935, 7–27; Apr., 1935, 165–86; Jul., 1935, 332–50; Oct., 1935, 489–508
Price	Price, Capt. J.A.T., 5th Lancers, diary IWM (7511-80-77-359)
PRO	Public Record Office

Abbreviations

Prior & Wilson	Prior, R. & Wilson, T. *Command on the Western Front: The Military Career of Sir Henry Rawlinson, 1914–1918*, 1992
Prior & Wilson: 'Dawn'	Prior, R. and Wilson, T. '15 September 1916: The Dawn of the Tank', *JRUSI*, Autumn, 1991
RA	Royal Archives, Windsor Castle
RCHA	Royal Canadian Horse Artillery
Repington	Repington, Lt-Col C. à Court *The First World War, 1914–1918*, 2 vols, 1920
Robbins	Robbins, Keith *The First World War*, 1984
Robertson	Robertson, FM Sir William *From Private to Field-Marshal*, 1921
Robertson: *S & S*	Robertson, FM Sir William *Soldiers and Statesmen 1914–1918*, 2 vols, 1926
Rowcroft	Rowcroft, Lt-Col C.H. 'The 9th Hodson's Horse at Cambrai 1917' *Cav. Jnl*, XIII, 1923
Royals	War Diary of 'C' Sqn, Royals, 1914–1919, IWM DS/MISC/50
Sandu	Sandu, Maj. Gen. G.S. *The Indian Cavalry*, 1981
Scott	Scott, Capt. F.J. *Records of the Seventh Dragoon Guards (Princess Royal's) during the Great War*, 1923
Scott: 'Cambrai'	Scott, P.T. 'The Battle of Cambrai – November 1917', *Army Quarterly*, April, 1964
Scott Daniell	Scott Daniell, D. *4th Hussar: the Story of the 4th Queen's Hussars, 1685–1958*, 1959
Seely	Seely, J.E.B. *Adventure*, 1933
Shay	Shay, R.P. *British Rearmament in the Thirties...*, 1977
Sheppard	Sheppard, Maj. E.W. *The Ninth Queen's Royal Lancers, 1715–1936*, 1939
Smith	Smith, Maj.-Gen. Sir Frederick *A History of the Royal Army Veterinary Corps, 1796–1919*, 1927
Smithers: *Cambrai*	Smithers, A.J. *Cambrai: The First Great Tank Battle, 1917*, 1992
Sparrow	Sparrow, W. Shaw *The Fifth Army in March 1918*, 3rd edn, 1923
Spears: *Prelude*	Spears, Maj.-Gen. Sir Edward *Prelude to Victory*, 1939
Statistics	[Official] *Statistics of the Military Effort of the British Empire during the Great War, 1914–1920*, 1922
Stewart: *XII L*	Stewart, Capt. P.F. *The History of the XII Royal Lancers (Prince of Wales's)*, 1950
Strachan	Strachan, Major H., VC, 'A Squadron on its own', *Cav. Jnl*, Apr., 1927

Abbreviations

Tegner	Tegner, H. *The Northumberland Hussars Yeomanry*, 1969
Tennant	Tennant, Lt-Col E. *The Royal Deccan Horse in the Great War*, 1939
Terraine	Terraine, J. *The First World War 1914–1918*, 1965
Terraine: *Haig*	Terraine, J. *Douglas Haig: the Educated Soldier*, 1963
Terraine: *Impacts*	Terraine, J. *Impacts of War 1914 and 1918*, 1970
Terraine: *Pass.*	Terraine, J. *The Road to Passchendaele: the Flanders Offensive of 1917: A Study in Inevitability*, 1977
Terraine: *S and F*	Terraine, J. *The Smoke and the Fire: Myths and Anti-Myths of War, 1861–1945*, 1980
Terraine: *White*	Terraine, J. *White Heat: the New Warfare 1914–1918*, 1982
Terraine: *Win*	Terraine, J. *To Win a War, 1918: the Year of Victory*, 1978
Thomas	Thomas, Hugh *The Story of Sandhurst*, 1961
Toland	Toland, John *No Man's Land: the Story of 1918*, 1980
Travers	Travers, Tim *How the War Was Won: Command & Technology in the British Army on the Western Front, 1917–1918*, 1992
Travers: 'Evolution'	Travers, Tim 'The Evolution of British Strategy and Tactics on the Western Front in 1918: GHQ, Manpower and Technology' *Journal of Military History*, LIV, Apr., 1990
Tylden	Tylden, Maj. G. *Horses and Saddlery . . .*, 1965
Verdin	Verdin, Lt-Col Sir Richard *The Cheshire (Earl of Chester's) Yeomanry, 1898–1967*, 1971
Warner	Warner, Philip *Field Marshal Earl Haig*, 1991
Watson	Watson, Maj.-Gen. W.A. *King George's Own Central India Horse: the Story of a Local Corps*, 1930
Wavell	Wavell, Gen. Sir A. *Allenby: a Study in Greatness*, 1940
Whitmore	Whitmore, Lt-Col F.H.D.C. *The 10th (PWO) Royal Hussars and the Essex Yeomanry during the European War 1914–1918*, 1920
Whitworth	Whitworth, Capt. D.E. *A History of the 2nd Lancers (Gardner's Horse)*, 1924
Whyte & Atteridge	Whyte, F. and Atteridge, A.H. *A History of the Queen's Bays (the 2nd Dragoon Guards), 1685–1929*, 1930
Willcox	Willcox, Lt-Col W.T. *The 3rd (King's Own) Hussars in the Great War (1914–1919)*, 1925
Williams	Williams, Capt. S.H. *'Stand to Your Horses': through the First Great War with the Lord Strathcona's Horse*, 1961
Winton	Winton, Lt-Col H.R. (US Army) *To Change an Army: General Sir John Burnett-Stuart and British Armored Doctrine, 1927–1938*, 1988

Abbreviations

WO	War Office
Woollcombe	Woollcombe, Robert *The First Tank Battle: Cambrai 1917*, 1967
Young	(ed.) Young, Lt-Col F.W. *The Story of the Staff College, 1858–1958*, 1958

SOURCE NOTES

PREFACE (pp. xix–xxv)

1. Lloyd George *War Memoirs*, 1936, I, 76
2. Taylor, A.J.P. *The First World War*, 1963, 20
3. Graves, R. *Promise of Greatness: The War of 1914–1918*, (ed.) G.A. Panichas, 1968, 6
4. Terraine: *S & F*, 163, 168. The statistics concerning generals all come from this first-class book.
5. Sassoon, S. *Memoirs of an Infantry Officer*, 1930, 163
6. Messenger, C. *The Art of Blitzkrieg*, 1976, 11; Dixon, N. *On the Psychology of Military Incompetence*, 1976, 307
7. Wavell, 158–9
8. Falls, *WWI*, 149

CHAPTER 1 (pp. 3–18)

1. Macdonald: *Somme*, 316
2. Feb., 1915, Daniell, 257–8
3. Willcox, 161; Parry, 4, 26; Lumley, 192; Whyte and Atteridge, 359
4. Durand, 68; Arthur, 121; Micholls, 95
5. Keith-Falconer, 107–8
6. Keith-Falconer, 105; Carnock, 125; Whyte and Atteridge, 341; Stewart: *XII L*, 277; Charrington, 11; Pomeroy: *?D*, 75, 76; Durand, 86; Stewart: *XII L*, 276
7. Arthur, 120; Lumley, 194; Graham, 70–1; Edmonds, 1915, I, 29
8. Tegner, 28; Keith-Falconer, 106, 145–6, 148
9. Keith-Falconer, 97, 137; 13 Jan., 1915, Philipps, 106, 119; Pomeroy 301, 311; Gibb, 44
10. Stewart: *XII L*, 269; Keith-Falconer, 114
11. Keith-Falconer, 99, 211; Oatts: *3DG/6DG*, 217; 18 Dec., 1914, Haslam; Micholls, 101; the Sub-Editor for Yeomanry 'The Yeomanry with the Cavalry Corps', *Cav. Jnl*, X, 1920, 99; Pomeroy, 319; Stewart: *XII L*, 278, 288; Tennant, 57

365

12 Brereton, 324; Keith-Falconer, 103–4, 325–6; 23 Feb., 1914, Haslam; Whitmore, 61, 72; Harvey, 345; Lumley, 241
13 Whyte and Atteridge, 344; Durand, 86
14 Micholls, 102–3
15 Whitmore, 60
16 Keith-Falconer, 135; Whitmore, 118; Oatts: *3DG/6DG*, 227; Parry, 67
17 Pomeroy, 306; Stewart: *XII L*, 273, 275; Home, 88; Willcox, 161, Lumley, 258; Whitmore, 76; Atkinson, 440; Scott, 85; Brereton, 329

CHAPTER 2 (pp. 19–24)
1 Stone, N. *The Eastern Front, 1914–1917*, 1975, 132; 25 Mar., 1915, Rawlinson to Wigram, quoted in Wilson, T. *The Myriad Faces of War . . .*, 1986, 125; 1 April, 1915, Rawlinson Papers, NAM 5201/33/17; 25 Apr., 1915, Price
2 Blake: *Haig*, 90; 14 Mar., 22 Mar., 1915, Rawlinson's Diary, Rawlinson Papers, NAM 5201/33/17
3 Quoted in Cooper, I, 228
4 Quoted in Holmes, 273; Prior and Wilson, 35
5 Wavell, 153
6 Pomeroy: *2D*, 80; Brereton, 324; Gibb, 33, 36; Hudson, 146; Lumley, 201; Oatts: *3DG/6DG*, 217; Blenkinsop, 540–1
7 13 May, 1915, Brunton; Atkinson, 420

CHAPTER 3 (pp. 25–32)
1 Home, 83; 'G.S.O.' [Sir Frank Fox], *G.H.Q. (Montreuil-sur-Mer)*, 1920; Keith-Falconer, 134; Atkinson, 417; Robbins, 63
2 Terraine, 91; Robbins, 49
3 Edmonds, *1915*, II, 140, 156; Badsey, 304, quoting Haig Diaries, 8 Sep., 1915; Pease, 122
4 Edmonds, *1915*, II, 140; Preston: 'Loos', 18; 26 Sep., 1915, Whyte and Atteridge, 352; Scott, 58; Pease, 112
5 Atkinson, 431; 2 Oct., 1915, Home, 88
6 Atkinson, 434; 20 Oct., 1915, 24 Feb., 1916, Home, 91, 101
7 Durand, 87
8 Quoted in De Groot, 273
9 Jenkins, 382
10 1 and 14 Jan., 1916, Haig, diaries, quoted in Terraine: *Pass*, 12
11 Taylor, A.J.P. *English History, 1914–1945*, 1965, 47
12 Magnus, Sir P. *Kitchener: Portrait of an Imperialist*, 1958, 367
13 Home, 93, 95

CHAPTER 4 (pp. 33–64)
1 18 Mar., 1916, 'Notes on Conference of Army Commanders', Haig Papers, NLS; Whyte and Atteridge, 364; Middlebrook, M. *The First Day of the Somme*, 1970 quoted in Fussell *The Great War and Modern Memory*, 1975, 32; Maurice: *Raw*, 166, 167; Terraine: *Pass.*, 16; Churchill: *'16–'18* I, 180; CAB/22/65 4–5; see also Stone, N. *The Eastern Front, 1914–1917*, 1975, 50, 80; Brereton, 328

Source notes (pp. 34–54)

2. Watson, 335–6; see also Whitworth, 84, 85 and Hudson, 155; Terraine, 117; see also Ludendorff, I, 244 and *Die 27 Infanterie Division im Weltkrieg*, quoted in Churchill: *'16–'18*, I, 1927, 184
3. Pomeroy: 2D, 96–7
4. Robbins, 55
5. De Groot, 225; 19, 20, 29 May, 7 June, 1916, Haig: diary, incl. letters between Robertson and Haig and vice versa, NLS; Badsey, 310
6. 23 Nov., 1916, Haig: diary, and Memo. on cavalry of same date, NLS; CAB/23/1, p.82; CAB/22/73 pp. 1–7 and p.3 of conclusion; Badsey, 313
7. CAB/22/73 p.5; Memo. on cavalry by Curzon, 14 Nov., 1916, CAB/22/78, p.6; Badsey, 313, 315; Edmonds, *1917*, I, 64; Carnock, 138; Arthur, 162
8. 8, 18 Jan., 1916, Haig: diary, and paper 32(b), NLS, 31
9. Seely, 247; Farrar-Hockley, 183; 9 Apr. and 18 June, 1916, Haig: diary, NLS; Badsey, 306–7
10. 30 June, 1916, Rawlinson diaries; Badsey, 307; see also Edmonds, *1916*, I, 266–7
11. 16 June, 1916, GHQ OAD 12, quoted in Edmonds, *1916*, I, Appx 13, (Appx vol., 86); 'Report of Army Commander's remarks at conference at IV Army HQ, 22 June 1916', IVth Army Papers, Vol 6, quoted in Prior and Wilson, 154–5
12. 1 July, 1916, Rawlinson diaries, Prior and Wilson, 151; Gough, 138; Badsey, 307; June, 1916, Diary of Money, R.C., 15 Bn, D.L.I., quoted in Liddle, 34
13. Hudson, 157; *Lascelles*, 203
14. 'An officer of 15th The King's Hussars' 'Somme Battle', MS a/c, 2–3, XV/XIX R. Hussars Museum; Bolitho, 221
15. Scott, 77
16. Carnock, 137, 143
17. Stewart: *XII L*, 279–80
18. Pomeroy, 307; Pomeroy: 2D, 100–101
19. Keith-Falconer, 170
20. Edmonds, *1916*, I, 20
21. quoted in Norman, 61; Farndale: *WF*, 149
22. Edmonds, *1916*, II, 83
23. Letter from Potter to Edmonds in PRO, quoted in Norman 94; 2 July, 1916, Kiggell to Montgomery, in IV Army Summary of Operations, WO 158/234, quoted in Prior and Wilson, 194
24. Norman, 90
25. 14 July, 1916, Rawlinson diary, Maurice: *Raw*, 167; Moreham, T. 'The Dawn Assault – Friday 14th July, 1916', *JAHR*, LXXI, 287, (Autumn, 1993), 181
26. Norman, 89
27. Scott, 72–3
28. Norman, 100
29. Farrar-Hockley, 162
30. Macdonald: *Somme*, 137; Scott, 73
31. Scott, 73–4; Preston: 'MG', 268

32 Scott, 74; see also Lieutenant Stallibras's RFC log, Liddle, 76
33 Tennant, 47–50
34 Scott, 74–5
35 Edmonds, *1916*, II, 89
36 Quoted in Seely, 250; *Lascelles*, 205; LHC, 7/1916/22; Dewar G.A.B. and Boraston J. H. *Sir Douglas Haig's Command*, 115
37 1 Sep., 1916, Home, 119
38 Churchill: *'16–'18*, I, 344; Terraine, 119, 120; Liddell Hart, B.H. *The Tanks...*, I, 67
39 18 Nov., 1916, Moyne, 131; 8 Sep., 1916, Home, 120; Prior and Wilson, 62
40 13 Sep., 1916 Wright's diary, Brereton, 328
41 Quoted in Terraine: *WWI*, 121
42 15 Sep., 1916, Home, 120
43 14 Sep., 1916, Rawlinson diaries; see also 14 Sep., 1916, Haig: diary, NLS; both quoted in Badsey, 309
44 Edmonds, *1916*, II, 291–2, 303
45 18 Sep., 1916, Home, 121
46 Hudson, 162
47 Edmonds, *1916*, II, 385
48 Hudson, 162–3; Edmonds, *1916*, II, 385
49 25 Sep., 29 Oct., 4 Nov., 6 Nov., 1916, Home, 122, 124, 125
50 Edmonds *1916*, II, 448, 541

CHAPTER 5 (pp. 65–96)
1 Terraine: *Haig*, 276; Terraine, 136; Murray, 599; Nicholls, xi; Spears: *Prelude*, 219; Terraine: *Haig*, 289; Whitmore, 106
2 20 Dec., 1916, Haig: diary, Note 79 of Army Commanders' Conference, 3 Feb., 1917, and entry 1 Feb., 1917, quoted in Badsey, 318; Harvey, 352
3 Nicholls, 3
4 Falls: *WWI*, 242
5 Churchill: *GW*, II, 991
6 18 Mar., 1917, 133, Edmonds, *1917*, I, 137, 154; Furse, 87, 88, 91
7 Murray, 601
8 Murray, 602–03
9 Liddell Hart, 507; Nicholson, 242; Seely, 259–6
10 De Montmorency, Hervey *Sword and Stirrup: Memories of an Adventurous Life*, 1936, 276
11 Haig: diary, Note 337, quoted in Badsey, 317
12 Article by Lynch, C. in *12th Lancers' Regimental Journal*, Dec., 1935, quoted in Stewart: *XII L*, 284
13 Willcox, 174
14 Edmonds, *1917*, I, 237; Croft, W.D. *Three Years with the 9th Scottish Division*, 1919, 117
15 Arthur, 166; Edmonds, *1917*, I, 224; see also Spears: *Prelude*, 594; quoted in Nicholls, 132
16 Darling, 78

Source notes (pp. 78–98)

17 Pomeroy: 2D, 107–08
18 Parry, 51
19 Burrows, 127; Edmonds, *1917*, I, 252; Macdonald, 202
20 Quoted in Falls: *WWI*, 255; quoted in Preston: 'Arras', 537
21 Preston: 'Arras', 529; Parry, 53; Preston: 'Arras', 530
22 Preston: 'Arras', 530; Burrows, 131
23 Nicholls, 145–6
24 Nicholls, 144–5
25 Edmonds, *1917*, I, 264
26 Harvey, 350
27 Whitmore, 95–8; Crichton, 3
28 Burrows, 130
29 Burrows, 131
30 Preston: 'Arras', 533; Burrows, 134
31 Burrows, 135; Edmonds, *1917*, I, 266
32 Cuddeford, D.W.J. *And All for What? Some War Time Experiences*, 1933, 162
33 Whitmore, 105
34 Crichton, 3; Whitmore, 101
35 Whitmore, 102–03
36 Burrows, 136
37 Crichton, 3–4; *10th Royal Hussars Gazette*, Vol. 21, 1959, quoted in Nicholls, 147
38 Haig: diary, quoted in de Groot, 312
39 Thomas, Alan *A Life Apart*, 1968, 97
40 Macpherson, III, 80
41 Macpherson, III, 80–1
42 Macpherson, III, 81
43 Macpherson, III, 86, 88–9
44 'Medical Arrangements for "Z" Day, 8 April 1917', Macpherson, III, 82
45 Macpherson, III, 84
46 Macpherson, III, 84–6
47 Macpherson, III, 88, 194
48 Pomeroy: 2D, 109; Preston: 'Arras', 539
49 Stewart: *XII L.*, 287
50 Burrows, 140
51 Edmonds, *1917*, I, 273
52 Lumley, 266
53 Folder in Chetwode papers, IWM, quoted in Badsey, 317; Crichton, 5
54 Edmonds, *1917*, I, 263; for an assessment of the part played by the cavalry machine-gun squadrons at Monchy, see Preston: 'MG', 494–7; Blake: *Haig*, 325
55 Home, 139

CHAPTER 6 (pp. 97–160)
1 Quoted in Fuller, 121; Terraine: *Haig*, 378; Churchill: ''16–'18', I, 343; Boraston, 152; Woollcombe, 90; Fuller, 316; 23 November, 1925, Blakiston, Georgina *Letters of Conrad Russell, 1897–1947*, 1987, 81;

369

Source notes (pp. 98–122)

    Boraston, 171; Smithers: *Cambrai*, 7–8; Liddell Hart: *Real*, 369; Griffith, 86

2   Falls: *WWI*, 280
3   Terraine, 147
4   Charteris: *GHQ*, 270; Smithers: *Cambrai*, 80
5   25 Dec., 1917, Haig's Despatch, Boraston, 130
6   Robbins, 69
7   15 Nov., 1917, Haig to Robertson, quoted in De Groot, 350; Charteris: *GHQ*, 269; 20 Dec., 1917, Hansard: (C), quoted in Moore, 169
8   Charteris: *GHQ*, 267, 269; Marshall-Cornwall, 252
9   Fuller, 1920, 150
10   Falls: *WWI*, 303
11   Terraine: *Haig*, 379
12   Kiggell, private letter, PRO WO 95/367; Edmonds, *1917*, III, 18; Third Army No. GS56/35, quoted in Woollcombe, 32
13   Edmonds: *1917*, III 306
14   Haig: diary, 24 Sep., 1917, 48/Acc.3155, 117; Edmonds: *1917*, III, 322; Third Army Instruction to III Corps, Cavalry Corps, Tank Corps, 17 Nov., Third Army No. GS 56/154, quoted in Woollcombe, 46–7; see also Brereton, 332
15   'Third Army Instructions to Cavalry Corps, 13 Nov., 1917', Edmonds, *1917*, III, 309
16   Haig's diary quoted in De Groot, 350
17   Whyte and Atteridge, 393
18   Edmonds, *1917*, III, 40–1
19   Farndale: *WF*, 221; Pitman: *Cambrai*, 242 (this emanated from the Cavalry Corps 'diary of events'); Maunsell, 132
20   Liddell Hart, 443; Scott: 'Cambrai', 97
21   Hobart, Brig. P.C.S. 'A Complete Narrative of the Battle of Cambrai', Tank Museum; Browne, D.G. *The Tank in Action*, 1920, quoted in Woollcombe, 92
22   Watson, 415–6, 418
23   Instructions, 1
24   'Report on Wire Pulling Operations, 20 November, 1917', Tank Museum
25   Fuller, 213
26   Whitworth, 100–1
27   Quoted in Fuller, 210
28   PRO WO 95/1097 (1 Can. Div. Box) quoted in Woollcombe, 128. Most of the following information respecting 1 Cav. Div. comes from this source.
29   Pitman: *Cambrai*, 243
30   Furse, 136
31   Brereton, 333
32   De Pree, 221; L.I., 255; 6 Division's account, quoted in Woollcombe, 128; Home, 157
33   Narrative of 2 Cav. Bde, quoted in Woollcombe, 131
34   'Report on the action of 4th Dragoon Guards', quoted in Woollcombe, 132

35 Blake: *Haig*, 269
36 IV Corps War Diary, quoted in Woollcombe, 133
37 Quoted in Woollcombe, 133; De Pree, 221
38 Woollcombe, 134
39 Gibb, 51
40 IV Corps War Diary, quoted in Woollcombe, 134
41 Brereton, 333
42 Gibb, 52
43 Pitman: *Cambrai*, 243; Maunsell, 132
44 Pitman: *Cambrai*, 244
45 Scott, 105. Other sources say 2 p.m., e.g. Pitman: *Cambrai* 244
46 Edmonds, *1917*, III, 76; Scott, 106; Brereton, 334
47 Anon. 'Cambrai – the First Day', *Royal Tank Corps Journal*, July, 1936, 71; Hamond Papers, Tank Museum
48 Hobart, 70; L.I., quoted in Woollcombe, 102; Prigg C. (ed.) *The War Despatches – Sir Philip Gibbs*, 1964, 296
49 Smithers: *Cambrai*, 114
50 Hobart, 70
51 Strachan, 241–51; Paterson, 464; See also Pitman: *Cambrai*, 255–7; Maunsell, 133; Williams, 158; Nicholson, 336; Edmonds, *1917*, III, 70; Scott, 107
52 Edmonds, *1917*, III, 31, 70, 364
53 Pitman: *Cambrai*, 245
54 Edmonds, *1917*, III, 71
55 Pitman: *Cambrai*, 245; Woollcombe, 87
56 Maunsell, 130–2
57 Terraine: *Haig*, 351–2
58 Maunsell, 232–3; Rowcroft, 49–50; Cardew, 47; Darling, 90; Scott: 'Cambrai', 105; 27 Nov., 1917, Haig: diary, Blake: *Haig*, 269
59 Furse, 154
60 Farndale: *WF*, 250
61 Whitworth, 103
62 Whitworth, 104, 105
63 Cav. Corps Order for 1 Dec., issued 30 Nov., 1917, Edmonds, *1917*, III, 374
64 4 Cav. Div. Op. Order, No. 22, Anon: *Mhow*, 47
65 Edmonds, *1917*, III, 232
66 Whitworth, 104; Anon: *Mhow*, 48
67 Whitworth, 104
68 Whitworth, 185
69 Anon: *Mhow*, 48
70 Edmonds, *1917*, III, 233
71 Whitworth, 105
72 Whitworth, 106
73 Anon: *Mhow*, 51
74 Whitworth, 106–07
75 Anon: *Mhow*, 51; Whitworth, 107
76 Whitworth, 107

77 Anon. *Mhow*, 51
78 Maunsell, 354
79 Whitworth, 112
80 Edmonds, *1917*, III, 234; Anon: *Mhow*, 49
81 Maunsell, 355
82 Evans: *5DG*, 150; Anon: *Mhow*, 50
83 Edmonds, *1917*, III, 237
84 Whitworth, 112
85 Maunsell, 356
86 Whitworth, 186
87 Fuller, 188
88 Fuller, 189–91
89 Hobart, 41–2
90 Churchill: '*16*–'*18*, 348
91 Smithers: *Cambrai*, 116
92 Terraine: *Haig*, 380
93 Terraine: *S & F*, 165
94 Colville, J.R. *Man of Valour: FM Lord Gort, VC*, 1972, 35–6; Cruttwell, 473
95 IV Corps Order No. 320, 15 Nov., 1917, Edmonds, *1917*, III, 319
96 Maunsell, 134
97 Terraine: *White*, 317
98 Edmonds, *1917*, III, 281–4
99 Edmonds, *1917*, III, 281–2
100 Smithers: *Cambrai*, 117
101 Home, 159, 160
102 Liddell Hart: *Real*, 380
103 Churchill: '*16*–'*18*, 348
104 Repington, II, 164

CHAPTER 7 (pp. 161–219)

1 PRO WO 95/1100, quoted in Middlebrook, 130; quoted in Edmonds, *1918*, I, 40–1; Charteris, 282; quoted in Farrar-Hockley, A. 'Sir Hubert Gough and the German Breakthrough, 1918', Bond, B., (ed.), *Fallen Stars*, 1991, 74; Micholls, 117; Atkinson, 453; Churchill: '*16*–'*18*, 426; Keith-Falconer, 271; Sparrow, 218
2 Grieves, K. *The Politics of Manpower, 1914–18*, 1988, 174; CAB/23/13, 187; CAB/27/14, 14 of report, 3–4, 4th Mtg; CAB/1/25/26, Memo by Churchill, 4; CAB/23/13, 187, all quoted in Badsey, 331–2
3 CAB/22/78, 6; Robertson, 324; 27 Jan., 1918, Haig diary, 39, & 23 Oct., 1918, Acc. 3155.128 & 3155.132, all quoted in Badsey, 332–3; Edmonds, *1918*, I, 114
4 27 Jan., 1918, Home, 160
5 Gough, 254
6 Edmonds, *1918*, I, 185
7 See, especially, Terraine: *Haig*, 4–08
8 Churchill, '*16*–'*18*, 403
9 Falls: *WWI*, 317

10 Terraine: *Haig*, 420
11 Pitt, 97
12 Edmonds, *1918*, I, 457, 458, 498
13 Carnock, 164; Edmonds, *1918*, II, 33
14 Edmonds, *1918*, II, 79; 26 Mar., 1918, Keith-Falconer, 269
15 Oatts: *3DG/6DG*, 232
16 Keith-Falconer, 267–8. Very few such lucid accounts were kept amidst the turmoil of battle
17 Stewart: *XII L*, 204–05
18 Harvey, 402–03
19 Preston: '1918', V, 164; Keith-Falconer, 266–7
20 Bickersteth, 93; see also Oatts: *3DG/6DG*, 234–5
21 Whitmore, 155
22 Atkinson, 456–7; Micholls, 123
23 Edmonds, *1918*, I, 190
24 Gough, 266
25 Parry, 70, 73
26 23 Mar., 1918, Brunton
27 Edmonds, *1918*, I, 347
28 Murray, 624
29 Carnock, 166
30 Murray, 625
31 Carnock, 166
32 23 Mar. 1918, Brunton
33 Carnock, 166; Preston: '1918', VII, 505
34 Edmonds, *1918*, I, 334, 339
35 Goes, Capt. G. *Der Tag X. Die grosse Schlacht in Frankreich 21 März – 5 April, 1918*, 118–9, quoted in Edmonds *1918*, I, 406
36 Atkinson, 453
37 Edmonds, *1918*, I, 405
38 Atkinson, 453
39 Oatts: *3DG/6DG*, 229, 230; Whitmore, 152
40 Scott, 125; Bickersteth, 85
41 Oatts: *3DG/6DG*, 230 see also Whitmore, 152 and Bickersteth, 85
42 Bickersteth, 85
43 Oatts: *3DG/6DG*, 230
44 Atkinson, 454
45 Bickersteth, 85
46 Bickersteth, 86
47 Bickersteth, 86
48 25 Mar., 1918, Home, 162
49 Edmonds, *1918*, I, 406
50 25 Mar., 1918, Home, 162
51 Churchill: *'16–'18*, 426; Blake: *Haig*, 272
52 Terraine: *Haig*, 410
53 Prior and Wilson, 278
54 Edmonds, *1918*, II, 28
55 25 Mar. 1918, Maurice: *Raw*, 213

Source notes (pp. 198–217)

56 Quoted in Farrar-Hockley, 306
57 Cooper, II, 267
58 Farrar-Hockley, 359
59 30 Mar, 3 Apr, 1918, Maurice: *Raw*, 113, 215
60 Liddell Hart, 507
61 Seely, 299
62 Edmonds, *1918*, II, 89
63 Pitman: 'Amiens', 362; see also Edmonds, *1918*, II, 88–9
64 Pitman: 'Amiens', 362
65 Seely, 300–01
66 Seely, 301
67 Connolly, 12
68 Connolly, 12
69 Pitman: 'Amiens', 363
70 Seely, 302
71 Edmonds, *1918*, II, 90
72 Connolly, 12
73 Seely, 302
74 Seely, 302–03
75 Seely, 303
76 Quoted in Seely, 304
77 Related by 'a man with him', Seely, 304
78 Toland, 109–10
79 Seely, 304-5
80 Jones, 342
81 Pitman: 'Amiens', 366
82 Seely, 308
83 Seely, 305–06
84 Daniell, 272
85 Pitman: 'Amiens', 365
86 Seely, 306
87 Pitman: 'Amiens', 365
88 Seely, 306
89 Lunt, 237
90 21 Mar., 1919, Despatch, Boraston, 328
91 Edmonds, *1918*, II, 482
92 Gough, 323
93 Rogerson, S. *The Last of the Ebb*, 1937, 112
94 Toland, 45
95 Croft, 217
96 Pitt, 103
97 Terraine: *Impacts*, 132; Gibbs, P. *Open Warfare: The Way to Victory*, 1919, 183; quoted in Liddell Hart: *Outline*, 206
98 Cruttwell, 511
99 Cruttwell, 511; Edmonds, *1918*, II, 15; Fuller, 316
100 Furse, 242
101 Edmonds, *1918*, II, 260

Source notes (pp. 217-236)

102 11 Oct., 1921, on receiving the freedom of Canterbury, quoted in Preston: '1918', VII, 516
103 Home, 167
104 Gray, 88
105 *Lascelles*, 249-50
106 Home, 175; Preston: '*1918*',(2), I, 168; Preston: '1918'(2), VI, 334-5

CHAPTER 8 (pp. 220-246)
1 Quoted in Edmonds: *1918*, III, 306; Churchill: *'16-'18*, 458; Fuller, 127-8; Home, 178; Falls: *WWI*, 357; Willcox, 272-3; Lascelles, 250; Gibb, 56
2 Churchill, *'16-'18*, 501
3 17 May, 1918, Blake, 311
4 Montgomery, 11
5 Jones, VI, 435-6; Essame, 124; Montgomery, 24
6 Falls: *WWI*, 355
7 Haig diary, 1, Acc.3155., NLS, 130; Home, 178
8 Terraine: *Haig*, 453
9 Lumley, 365; Preston: '1918' (2) I, 173
10 8 Aug., 1918, Home, 179
11 Parry, 90
12 Preston: '1918' (2), I, 173; Lumley, 366; see also Montgomery, 29 and Anon: 'E.P.', 401-02
13 Edmonds, *1918*, IV, 51
14 Anon: 'E.P.', 395
15 Preston: '1918' (2), I, 174
16 Williams, 239; Anon 'E.P.', 401
17 Anon: 'E.P.', 398
18 Preston: '1918' (2), I, 175-6
19 Whitmore, 185; Preston: '1918' (2), I, 176
20 Williams, 240-1
21 8 Aug., 1918, MacPherson, Lieut., RCHA, diary, vol. 10, Public Archives, Ottawa, Canada, quoted in Travers, 121; Edmonds *1918*, IV, 53
22 Edmonds: *1918*, IV, 53
23 Scott, 148
24 Anon: 'E.P.', 402; see also Scott, 149-50; Brereton, 339
25 Edmonds: *1918*, IV, 53; Fuller, 317
26 Anon. *The War History of the 6th Tank Battalion*, 97, quoted in Badsey, 336; Fuller, 316-19; Fuller to Fourth Army HQ, Fourth Army Papers, vol. 49, quoted in Prior and Wilson, 307
27 Preston: '1918' (2), I, 177
28 Preston: '1918' (2), I, 178
29 Anon., 'E.P.', 403
30 Preston: '1918' (2), I, 179
31 Anon: 'E.P.', 404
32 Edmonds: *1918*, IV, 54
33 Preston: '1918' (2), I, 179

34 Preston: '1918' (2), II, 339
35 Carnock, 187; 8 Aug., 1918, Brunton
36 Carnock, 186
37 Preston: '1918' (2), II, 340; Carnock, 188
38 Preston: '1918' (2), II, 340; Edmonds, 1918, IV, 55
39 Carnock, 188
40 Whyte & Atteridge, 440-1
41 Whyte & Atteridge, 441; Preston: '1918' (2), II, 341
42 Preston: '1918' (2), II, 341; Whyte & Atteridge, 442
43 Preston: '1918' (2), II, 341
44 Whyte & Atteridge, 444
45 Preston: '1918' (2), I, 342
46 Jones, IV, 437-8; see also Lumley, 370-1
47 Preston: '1918' (2), II, 343-4
48 Pomeroy, I, 151, 329-30
49 Preston: '1918' (2), II, 345; Willcox, 274; Jones, IV, 439
50 Fourth Army Op. O, 6 Aug., 1918, Edmonds: *1918*, IV, 575; Edmonds: *1918*, IV, 55; Lumley, 368; Preston: '1918' (2), II, 347-8
51 Preston: '1918' (2), II, 346-7; Edmonds: *1918*, IV, 58
52 Edmonds: *1918*, IV, 68
53 Edmonds: *1918*, IV, 68-9; quoted in Blaxland, 172; Essame, 150
54 13 Aug., 1918, Haig diary, Acc. 3155.130, NLS; 8 Aug., 1918, Rawlinson diary; 5 Aug., 1918, 9, Acc. 3155.130, NLS; Byng, quoted in Haig diary, 29 Nov., 1918, 54, Acc. 3155.131, NLS; 11 Nov., 1918, Rawlinson diary, all quoted in Badsey, 335
55 8 Aug., 1918, Home, 179
56 Home, 181; Official German account, quoted in Terraine: *Haig*, 458; Liddell Hart: *Real*, 457
57 Home, 180

CHAPTER 9 (pp. 247-269)
1 Churchill, *'16-'18*, 516; quoted in Travers, 43; Preston: '1918' (2), IV, 10; Haig to Wilson, 20, Acc. 3155.131; Blake, 326; c. 29 Aug., 1918, Churchill: *'16-'18*, 518; Haig's diary, Terraine: *Haig*, 467
2 Bolitho, 230
3 Bolitho, 230; Sheppard, 303
4 Falls: *WWI*, 359
5 Except in articles in obscure professional journals, particularly *Cav. Jnl*
6 Preston: '1918' (2), II, 13
7 Preston: '1918' (2), II, 18; see also Home, 180
8 Haig diary, 46, Acc. 3155.130, NLS
9 C-in-C's telegram to Army & Cavalry Corps commanders, 22 Aug., 1918, Edmonds: *1918*, IV, 588
10 Edmonds: *1918*, IV, 187
11 Pease, 201-02 in which a full first-hand account of this charge is given; see also Tegner, 30-4, Preston: '1918' (2), 504 and Edmonds: *1918*, IV, 200
12 Preston: '1918' (2), 513-4

13   Charrington, 26
14   Keith-Falconer, 315
15   17 Sep., 1918, Haig diary, 29, Acc. 3155.131, NLS
16   24 Sep., 1918, Terraine: *Haig*, 472
17   21 Dec., 1918, Despatch, Boraston, 285
18   Preston: '1918' (2), IV, 12–17; Haig to First, Third and Fourth Armies, Edmonds: *1918*, V, 172
19   Anon., quoted in Preston: '1918' (2), IV, 26
20   Lumley, 390–2; 8 Oct., 1918, Brunton; Darling, 120
21   Edmonds: *1918*, V, 173
22   Preston: '1918' (2), V, 167
23   Preston: '1918' (2), V, 168
24   Atkinson, 465
25   Bickersteth, 114
26   Atkinson, 465
27   Parry, 101
28   Oatts: *3DG/6DG*, 238
29   Parry, 102, 103; Edmonds: *1918*, V, 217
30   Edmonds: *1918*, V, 218
31   'Canadian Cavalry Brigade Narrative of Operations . . . 8–10 October, 1918', 1, Appx 'D' to Bde Diary, quoted in Nicholson, 463
32   'Narrative of Operations Lord Strathcona's Horse (RC) 9/10/18', Appx 1 to Unit Diary, Oct., 1918, quoted in Nicholson, 463; Preston: '1918' (2), V, 172
33   'Narrative of Operations, FGH (Canadian Cavalry Brigade Narrative)', 2, Appx 'D' to Bde diary, quoted in Nicholson, 463–4; Preston: '1918' (2), V, 172
34   Edmonds: *1918*, V, 216
35   Preston: '1918' (2), V, 174
36   9 Oct., 1918, War Diary, RCD, Nicholson, 464
37   Nicholson, 464
38   Edmonds: *1918*, V, 235

CHAPTER 10 (pp. 270–283)
1   Cooper, II, 386; Home, 187; Terraine: *Haig*, 471; Keith-Falconer, 329; Preston: '1918' (2), VII, 491; Home, 189; quoted in Preston: '1918' (2), VII, 501; Edmonds: *1918*, V, 574; Keith-Falconer, 337
2   Home, 187–8
3   Quoted in Cruttwell, 551
4   26 Oct., 1918, Home, 188
5   Maurice: *Last*, 228, 230
6   1 Nov., 1918, Home, 189; Preston: '1918' (2), VII, 499
7   Edmonds: *1918*, V, 535
8   For a detailed account see Preston: '1918' (2), VI, 332–50, VII, 335, 489–508; see also Edmonds: *1918*, VIII, 8–9
9   Furse, 280
10   Furse, 285, 287
11   Pomeroy: *2D*, 169–70; Darling, 126; Stewart: *XII L*, 305–06; Preston:

'1918' (2), VI, 343-5
12 Edmonds: *1918*, VIII, 533; Preston: '1918' (2), VI, 346-7, 350
13 Preston: '1918' (2), VI, 349
14 Preston: '1918' (2), VII, 496-7
15 Preston: '1918' (2), VII, 505
16 7 Nov., 1918, Fifth Army Order: 'Rôle of the Cavalry Corps', Preston: '1918' (2), VIII, 2
17 Scott, 173-4; Singleton-Gates, P. *General Lord Freyburg VC*, 1963, 80-1; Brereton, 341-3; Preston: '1918' (2), VIII, 12; Edmonds: *1918*, V, 556-7
18 Preston: '1918' (2), VII, 507-8
19 Micholls, 134
20 Keith-Falconer, 338
21 Carnock, 207; Daniell, 278; Lumley, 413; Keith-Falconer, 339; 10, 11 Nov., 1918, Brunton
22 Edmonds: *1918*, 558
23 3 Dec., 1918, Brunton
24 Foreword to Evans: *4H*, vii

CHAPTER 11 (pp. 284-304)
1   Kennedy: Army, 136; Brock, 503; Galtrey, 11; 13; Home, 168; quoted in Gilbert, M. *First World War*, 1994, 161; Clarke, 5; Smith, 4
2   Liddell Hart, 62
3   Ascoli, 30
4   Taylor, A.J.P. *English History, 1914-1945*, 1965, 59
5   *Statistics*, 877, 878
6   *Statistics*, 400, 401
7   *Statistics*, 91
8   *Statistics*, 65-68
9   1895, Gilbert, M. *Churchill: A Life*, 1991, 55; *Statistics*, 861
10 Spiers, E.M. *Haldane...*, 1980, 155; Tylden, 39
11 Bate, Brig.-Gen. T.R.F. in Galtrey, 27, 30
12 The sixty pages of *Remount Regulations, 1913*, are a good example of the thorough, detailed work applied to the whole range of mobilization questions
13 *Statistics*, 396; Galtrey, 24
14 *Statistics*, 879
15 *Statistics*, 397. The statistical information in the five foregoing paragraphs is gleaned chiefly from *Statistics*, 396-7, 399, 400-01
16 Board of Agriculture and Fisheries 'Types of Horses suitable for Army Remounts' *Journal of the Board of Agriculture*, Aug., 1908, 2; Moore: *Vet*, 123
17 Jessel, 6-7
18 Galtrey, 22
19 Moore: *Vet.*, 122
20 Micholls, 89-90
21 Lumley, 117
22 'An "Old Contemptible"' *The Veterinary Record*, 23 August, 1919, 89.

Souce notes (pp. 296-312)

      This article was kindly brought to the author's notice by Dr T.J. Schadler, DVM, Columbus, Ohio, USA
23 Gibb, 32
24 Hammerton, Sir John (ed.), *The Great War . . . I was There*. n.d. II, 79–81
25 *Lascelles*, 210
26 Information kindly supplied by Dr T.J. Schadler, DVM, Columbus, Ohio, USA; Blenkinsop, 4
27 Blenkinsop, 2–3
28 Blenkinsop, 5, 6
29 Blenkinsop, 5
30 Smith, 240; Blenkinsop, 23–25, 47, 69–70
31 Information kindly supplied by Dr T.J. Schadler, DVM, Columbus, Ohio, USA; Clabby, 16, 17
32 Blenkinsop, 461
33 Blenkinsop, 514; see also 1 Nov., 1927, Allenby to Robertson, 'The Future of Cavalry', WO 32/2846
34 Blenkinsop, 509
35 Blenkinsop, 555
36 Blenkinsop, 556
37 Blenkinsop, 558
38 Blenkinsop, 550–1. The 702 pages of Blenkinsop make fascinating reading. But for lack of space, much more use of them would have been made in the present work
39 Moore: *Vet.*, 123
40 Letter, Dec., 1916, quoted in Stewart: *XII L*, 281–2
41 Stewart: *XII L*, 283

EPILOGUE *(pp. 305–345)*
(ii)
1 3 Nov., 1927, WO 32/2846
2 WO, 73/111, 113
3 Howard, 79
4 Peden, 149; Shay, 159–60
5 Shay, 159–60
6 Shay, 80–1
7 Liddell Hart, Capt. B.H. *Europe in Arms*, 1937, 78 *et seq*.: See also his *The British Way in Warfare*, 1932 and other works. See also Dennis, P. *Decision by Default: Peacetime Conscription and British Defence, 1919–39*, 1972, 62–65; Stone, Brig.-Gen. F.G. 'Man Power in the Next War', *The Nineteenth Century and After*, LXXXVII, Apr., 1920, 638–45; Peden, 168

(iii)
1 Howard, 99
2 See Jeffery, 68–9
3 Higham, 21, 39, 40
4 5 Aug., 1919, Lloyd George, War Cabinet meeting, CAB 23/15/606A
5 23 Nov., 1937, Maurice Hankey's memorandum, quoted in Peden, 11

Source notes (pp. 313–330)

(iv)

1. Harris, 200; Howard, 99
2. Feiling, K. *The Life of Neville Chamberlain*, 1946, 314
3. Jeffery, 11
4. Quoted in Shay, 41

(v)

1. Fuller, 109, 530; Fuller, J.F.C. *Armoured Warfare*, 1943, 9
2. 11 Oct., 1990, *Grimsby Evening Telegraph*
3. Mason, P. *A Matter of Honour*, 1974, 469
4. Walters, J. *Aldershot Review*, 1970, 222; letter of Fenton, Capt. W., Stewart: XIII, 320
5. Martel, 32; Remarks after lecture by Maj.-Gen. Percy Hambro, 'The Horse and the Machine in War', Feb., 1927, *JRUSI*; Higham, 87; Divine, D. *The Blunted Sword*, 1964, 157; Bolitho, 243; Perowne, Stewart *The Siege Within the Walls: Malta, 1940–1943*, 1970, 107
6. Obituary, 24 July, 1987, *The Times*
7. Macksey, K. *Armoured Crusader: Maj.-Gen. Sir Percy Hobart*, 1967, 159; personal communication to Bidwell from Gen. Sir S. Kirkman, then Brig., RA, 8th Army, Bidwell & Graham, 228, 306; Lunt, J. *The Scarlet Lancers*, 1993, 126; Liddell Hart, *Memoirs*, I, 1965, 79–80; see also Bond: *BMP*, 132

(vi)

1. Parsons to Harman, Aug., 1921, WO 32/5960; AG to CIGS, 21 Sep., 1927, WO 32/2842
2. See 30 Jul., 1921, Asst DMO to Chetwode, WO 32/5960
3. 8 Jun., 1921, Sec., WO to Harvey, Col. J.R., WO 32/5959, 19b; see also n.d., Memo., WO 32/5959, 1
4. AO 319, 1921
5. AO 133, 1922; see also 20/Cav/482, WO 32/5960
6. 12 Feb., 1922, WO 32/5960
7. 16 Jan., 1922, Chetwode to Cavan, WO 32/5960; 8 Aug., 1921, Chetwode to Harris, WO 32/5960, 2a; see also 10 Aug., 1921, Harman, Col Commandant, 1 Cav. Bde to Chetwode, WO 32/5960
8. 31 Jul., 8 Aug., 1921; 21 Jan., 1922, WO 32/5960, 1, 2, 3
9. 10 Aug., 1931, Harman to Chetwode, WO 32/5960
10. Mar., 1922 'Precis for Army Council – Reduction of the Cavalry', No. 1091, 20/Cav/482, WO/32/5960, 20A; Cab. Papers, 3868, XX,22,13, 26A, WO 32/5960
11. 31 Jan., 1922, Cavan to Wilson, WO 32/5960; ffrench-Blake, 4
12. AO 133, 1922
13. 8 Aug., 1921, Chetwode to Harris, WO 32/5960, 4A
14. 31 Jul., 1921, 1 Cav. Bde's 'Proposal . . .', WO 32/5960, 7
15. Evans: *7H*, 102

(vii)

1. Mason, Philip *A Matter of Honour*, 1974, 470

Source notes (pp. 334-353)

(viii)
1. Hansard (C), 1924; *JRUSI*, Nov., 1927, 788; WO 32/2846
2. 20 June, 1927, WO 32/2846
3. 1 July, 1927, WO 32/2846
4. 30 June, 1927, memo. by Military Members of the AC, enclosed in Worthington-Evans to Baldwin, WO 32/2846
5. Anon. 'The Mounted Trooper in 1918 and 1930', *Cav. Jnl*, Oct., 1930
6. 22 Feb., 1927, NE 45, 20/Cav/592, WO 32/2841; 3 May, 1928, CID, 'Report of the Sub-Committee on the Strength and Organization of Cavalry', Cab. Papers 178(28), [Cab. 24/195]
7. 3 Nov., 1937, CIGS to Hardinge, WO 32/4633
8. Miller, C.H. Maj.-Gen. *History of the 13th/18th Royal Hussars, 1922-1947*, 1949, 27-8
9. Evans: *7H*, 224
10. AO 58, 1939
11. Churchill to Sir A. Brooke, Dec., 1941, quoted in Mallinson, 211-12
12. Mallinson, 220-1
13. Mileham, P.J.R. *The Yeomanry Regiments*, 1985, 45-51
14. Hatton, D.M. *The Devil's Own: A History of the Inns of Court Regiment*, 1992, 90
15. 27 Sep., 1927, Worthington-Evans to Churchill, Note on letter from WSC, WO 32/2846

APPENDIX 1 (pp. 350-352)
1. Information from Lt-Col C.R.D. Gray. See also Smith, F.G. 'The Last Cavalry Charge: Eritrea, 1941' supplement to *One Gunner's War*, 1990; Anon. 'Gazelle Force and II Grupps Bande Amhara a Cavallo', *Bulletin, Military Historical Society*, May, 1977, 124-31, and Keown-Boyd, H. *A Good Dusting*, 1986, 277-8
2. Verdin, R.B., Lt-Col, letter to *Daily Telegraph*, 7 April, 1971; Slimming, A.L., letter to *Daily Telegraph*, 1 Aug., 1955; obit., Dunn, Brig. Keith, *Daily Telegraph*, 19 Feb., 1985 and numerous correspondents. See also Preface, Brereton, J.M. *Duke of Lancaster's Yeomanry*, 1993
3. Mollo, A., McGregor, M., Smith, D. and Chappell, M. *World Army Uniforms since 1939*, 1981, 145-6
4. Crawford, R., Research Officer, IWM, 'Cavalry Charges', letter to *Daily Telegraph*, 3 May, 1971 and numerous private letters
5. Chenevix Trench *History of Horsemanship*, 1970, 181
6. Oatts: *14/20 H*, 415/6. See also Perrett, B. *The Hawks: A Short History of the 14th/20th King's Hussars*, 1984, 110 and Walder, D., *The Chanak Affair*, 1969, 73

APPENDIX 2 (p. 353)
1. Evans: *7H*, 103
2. Miller, Maj.-Gen. C.H. *The History of the 13th/18th Royal Hussars, 1922-1947*, 1949, 11, 22
3. Oatts: *14/20H*, 423
4. 30 Jan., 1982, obituary, *Times*

INDEX

BATTLES; BRITISH, FRENCH AND GERMAN FORMATIONS and REGIMENTS appear under these headings

Aizlewood, Maj.-Gen. (1895-), 4DG, at Cambrai, 124
Albert I, King of the Belgians (1875-1934), 251
Allenby of Megiddo, FM Edward Henry Hynman, 1st Viscount (1861-1936), 20, 160, 163; i/c Third Army, at Arras, 80
Allison, Lt, 5L, 280
Anson, Lt, 7DG, 54
Armistice signed, 5 a.m., 11 Nov., 1918, 273
armoured cars, 24, 337; at Amiens, 226; at Honnechy, 265
Ascoli, David, 286
Ashwell, Lena (d. 1957), 14
Asquith, Herbert Henry, 1st Earl of Oxford and (1852-1928), 32, 308

Bailey, Tpr Sam, 1LG, 76
Baldwin of Bewdley, Stanley, 1st Earl (1867-1947), 334
Batchelor, Pte P.J., Oxfords H Yeo, 12, 80

BATTLES (including wars, campaigns, expeditions, actions, combats, engagements, skirmishes, sieges and unopposed entries)
Agordat (Keren), early 1941, 349
Affaire Nivelle, L', 66
Afghan War, 2nd, 1878-80, 353
Afghan War, 3rd, 1919, 310, 311
Aisne, 3rd, 27 May, 1918, 176
Alamein, El, 1942, 321
Amiens, 8 Aug., 1918, 178, 222
Arras, Apr., 1917, 66, 68
Balaklava, 25 Oct., 1854, 353
Bapaume, 21 Aug., 1918, 251, 253
Bazentin Ridge, 14 July, 1916, 52
Beaumont, 1794, 269
Bulganak, 19 Sep., 1854, 353
Cambrai, 20 Nov., 1917, 21, 59, 66, 93, 100, 228
Cambrai, 2nd, 27 Sep., 1918, 251, 259
Caporetto, 24 Oct., 1917, 101
Central India campaign, 1858-9, 353
Champagne, 25 Sep., 1915, 25
Champagne, 2nd, 26 Sep., 1918, 251
Chilianwala, 1849, 353
Collézy, (Villeselve), 24 Mar., 1918, 191
El Mughar, 13 Nov., 1917, 352
Epéhy, 10 Sep., 1918, 251
Falvy, 23 Mar., 1918, 186
Festubert, 15 May, 1915, 19
Flanders, 14 Oct., 1918, 251
Flers-Courcelette, 15 Sep., 1916, 59, 104
Gattigny Wood, 9 Oct., 1918, 266
Gebze, 12 July, 1920, 351
German Spring offensives, Mar.-Apr., 1918, 9, 168
Guyencourt, 27 Mar., 1917, 73
Hamel and Vaire, 4 July, 1918, 177

383

Index

Harbonnières, 8 Aug., 1918, 241
Hazebrouck, 12 Apr., 1918, 216
Hébutene, 'gap' at, 4 Apr., 1918, 216
Honnechy, 9 Oct., 1918, 263

Jena, 1806, 37
Lassigny, 9 June, 1918, 177
Lassigny, 2nd, 9 Aug., 1918, 251
Le Cateau, 1914, 269
Le Cateau, 2nd, 7 Oct., 1918, 251, 261
Lessines, 11 Nov., 1918, 279
Longueval, 'gap' at, 24 Mar., 1918, 215
Loos, 25 Sep., 1915, 19, 25
Messines, 7 June, 1917, 99
Monchy (Arras), 11 Apr., 1917, 13, 81
Montdidier, 'gap' at, 27 Mar., 1918, 215
Moreuil Wood, 30 Mar., 1918, 183, 199
Morval, 25 Sep., 1916, 62
Neuve Chapelle, 10 Mar., 1915, 19, 20
Passchendaele - see Ypres, 3rd
Persian War, 1856-7, 353
Ramnagar, 1848, 353
Reumont, 9 Oct., 1918, 267
Rifle Wood, 1 Apr., 1918, 199
Roye, 10 Aug., 1918, 252
St Quentin, 24 Mar., 1918, 190
St Quentin, 2nd, 27 Sep., 1918, 251
St Mihiel, 12 Sep., 1918, 251
Sambre, 2 Nov., 1918, 273
Scarpe, 26 Aug., 1918, 251
Selle, 17 Oct., 1918, 269
Somme, 1 July, 1916, 17, 36
South African War, 181
Suzoy, 26 Mar., 1918, 182
Syrian campaign, 1941, 350
Valenciennes-Guise, 4 Nov., 1918, 273

Vauvillers, 9 Aug., 1918, 252
Verdun, 21 Feb., 1916, 36
Villers-Bretonneux, 1st, 4 Apr., 1918, 184
Villers-Bretonneux, 2nd, 24 Apr., 1918, 176
Villers Faucon, 27 Mar., 1917, 71
Waterloo, 18 June, 1815, 168
Ypres, 1st, 25 Jan., 1915, 3, 5, 180
Ypres, 2nd, 22 Apr., 1915, 21
Ypres, 3rd (Passchendaele), 1917, 66, 98, 100

Beadle, 2nd-Lt F.W., RA, 52
Beale-Browne, Brig.-Gen. Desmond John Edward (1870-1953), i/c 2 Cav. Bde at Cambrai, 122
Beddington, Brig. Sir Edward Henry Lionel (1884-1966), 198
Bell, Lt-Col R.C., CIH, i/c special cav. track body at Cambrai, 113
Bell-Smyth, Brig.-Gen. John Ambard (1868-1922), i/c 3 Cav. Bde at Moreuil Wood, 202
Bethell, Maj.- Gen. Sir Keppel (1882-1947), i/c small mobile force to keep touch with enemy, 9 Nov., 1918, 275
'Bethell's Force', 276
Bickersteth, Lt John Burgon (1888-1979), 1D, at Honnechy, 263
Bingham, Lt-Col Hon. Denis, (d. 1940), i/c wire-cutting tanks at Cambrai, 116
Birdwood of Anzac, FM William Riddell, 1st Lord (1865-1951), i/c Fifth Army, 278
Bishen Singh, Armourer Dafadar, 2L, 17
Blenkinsop, Maj.-Gen. Sir Layton John (1862-1942), 299
Blücher, Marschall Gebhard Leberecht von (1742-1819), 168
Bolitho, Hector (1897-1974), 248

384

Index

'Bonham's Detachment', 181
Bovington Tank School, 343
Boyles, Tpr J. Oxfords H Yeo, 12
Broadway, Lt N.H., 2L, 148
Brooke, Maj.-Gen. Geoffrey Francis Heremon (1884-1966), in 1918 retreat, 183; at Moreuil Wood, 210
'Brooke's Detachment', 183
Brunton, Sgt D., 19H, 23, 186, 188, 189, 237, 260, 281
Bulkeley-Johnson, Brig.-Gen. Charles, 79; k. at Arras, 89
Bushman, Maj.-Gen. Sir Henry Augustus (1841-1930), 353
Byng, FM Hon. Julian, 1st Viscount (1862-1935), 95, 245, 271; i/c Third Army at Cambrai, 104; in 1918 retreat, 168

Campbell, Capt., Fort Garry Horse, at Cambrai, 131
Carr, Brig. William Greenwood (1901-1982), 353
Carter, Lt-Col E.J., i/c 17 Armoured Car Bn at Amiens, 245
Carton de Wiart, Lt-Gen. Sir Adrian (1880-1963), 22, 74
Cavalry Benefit Association, 15
Cavalry Depot, Canterbury, abolished, 1927, 335
Cavalry Field Ambulances at Arras (Monchy), 91
cavalry tracks, 26, 42, 62; at Arras, 74; at Amiens, 227
Cavan, FM Frederic Rudolph Lambart, 10th Earl of (1865-1946), favours amalgamation of cav. regts, 327
Chamberlain, Neville (1869-1940), 308, 313
Chanak crisis, 1920, 310
Charrington, Maj. H.S.V., 12L, 6, 302, 318; in 1918 retreat, 182
Charteris, Brig.-Gen. John (1877-1946), 101, 140; misleads Haig before Cambrai, 102

Chatfield, Admiral of the Fleet Alfred Ernle Montacute, 1st Lord (1873-1967), chairs Expert Committee on Indian Defence, 1938-9, 331
Chetwode, FM Sir Philip Walhouse, 7th Bt and 1st Baron (1869-1950), 95, 327; as DCIGS uses influence against disbandment of cav. regts, 1921, 325
Chiang Kai-shek (1886-1975), 311
Churchill, Sir Winston Spencer, (1874-1965), 32, 68, 155, 160, 166, 196, 222, 259, 289, 334, 336, 344, 432; orders production of tanks, 1915, 59; suggests disbandment of cav., 162, exculpates Gough after his dismissal, 198; sums up cav's part in the war, 283; insists on 11H and 12L being converted to armoured cars, 337; calls conference on yeomanry's future, 1920, 344
Clark, Alan (1928-), 305
Clemenceau, Georges (1841-1929), at Doullens conference, 26 Mar., 1918, 173
Cochrane, Lt-Gen. Lord Douglas Mackinnon Baillie Hamilton, 12th Earl of Dundonald (1852-1935), 21
Cockerill, Lt, 15H, at Amiens, 240
Colville, Sir John (1915-1987), 156
Connaught, Prince Arthur of (1883-1938), 32
Connolly, Maj., i/c Lord Strathcona's Horse at Moreuil Wood, 200
'Cook's Detachment', 179, in 1918 retreat, 181
Cooper, Alfred Duff, 1st Viscount Norwich (1890-1954), 198; as Sec. of State for War presses for a 'Field Force', 1936, 309

Index

Cowan, Lt, Fort Garry Horse, 136
Cox, Maj.-Gen. Charles Frederick (1863-1947), 142
'crows feet' (caltrops), 69
Cruttwell, Charles Robert Mowbray Fraser (1887-1941), 156
Curell, Maj. Andrew Cotteril, 8H, in 1918 retreat, 186
Curragh 'mutiny', 1914, 197
Currie, Gen. Sir Arthur William (1875-1933), i/c Canadian Corps, 280
Curzon of Kedleston, George Nathaniel, 1st Marquess, wants Indian cav. sent to Egypt, 38; believes few opportunities for cav., Jan., 1918, 163

Darling, Maj. Hon. John Clive (1887-1933), 20H, at Arras, 77
Davis, L/Cpl G.W., 10H, at Monchy, 90
Debeney, Gén. Maries Eugène (1864-1943), i/c French First Army, 1918, 222
Dent, Maj. Leonard Maurice Edward (1888-1987), 320
Derby, Edward George Villiers Stanley, 17th Earl of (1865-1948), 196
Dhara Singh, Woordi Maj., 2L, at Cambrai, 148
Doullens conference, 26 Mar., 1918, 173
Dundonald - see Cochrane

Egerton, Lt-Gen. Sir Raleigh Gilbert (1860-1931), 318
Elles, Gen. Sir Hugh Jamieson (1880-1945), i/c Tank Corps at Cambrai, 103; in 1936 thinks tanks 'still of some good' but only at 'secondary level', 320
Eve, Capt. W.H., 13H (-1917), 6, 29

Falkenhayn, Gen. Reich von (1861-1922), replaced as Chief of General Staff by Hindenburg, 36
Falls, Capt. Cyril Bentham (1888-1971), 172
'Fane's Composite Regiment', in 1918 retreat, 182
Fayolle, Gén. Marie Emile (1852-1928), 172
Fishlock, L/Cpl, King Edward's Horse, 272
FitzGerald, Capt., 19L, 62
Fleming, Bt-Col Peter (1907-1971), 13
Fleming, Commander Ian Lancaster (1908-1964), 13
Fleming, Lt, Fort Garry Horse, at Cambrai, 136
Fleming, Maj. Valentine (1882-1917), 13
Flowerdew, Lt Gordon Muriel, Lord Strathcona's Horse, at Moreuil Wood, 205
Foch, Mareschal Ferdinand (1851-1929), 30, 203, 253, 271; co-ordinates action of allied armies in France, 26 Mar., 1918, 173; assumes full command, 175; his first counter-offensive begins, 12 June, 1918, 222; places French First Army under Haig, 222; agrees that Haig should close down Amiens, 12 Aug., 1918, 249; tells German armistice delegates Allied terms must be accepted by 11 a.m. 11 Nov., 1918, 273
forage, supplies of, historians' inaccuracies regarding, 286
Franks, Lt-Col George Despard, 19H, 188; k. at 2nd Cambrai, 260

Index

FORMATIONS, BRITISH, FRENCH, GERMAN, etc. (excluding regiments, squadrons, etc.)

BRITISH

First Army, 20, 251; in 1918 retreat, 175

Third Army, 261; at Cambrai, 104; in 1918 retreat, 172; at Bapaume, 253

Fourth Army, at Somme, 41; at Amiens, 223; at 2nd Le Cateau, 261; halted for lack of supplies, 9 Nov., 1918, 275

Army of the Rhine, 310

Fifth Army, 64, 164, 278; in 1918 retreat, 172

III Corps, 226; at Cambrai, 104; in 1918 retreat, 178

IV Corps, 20; at Cambrai, 102

VI Corps, 76

IX Corps, at 2nd Le Cateau, 261

XI Corps, 260

XIII Corps, at 2nd Le Cateau, 261

XIV Corps, 18

XVIII Corps, in 1918 retreat, 178

XIX Corps, in 1918 retreat, 178

Canadian Corps, 280; at Amiens, 226

Australian Corps, at Ameins, 226

Royal Armoured Corps, 342

Tank Corps (later Royal), 249, 336, 338, 342; originally Heavy Branch, MG Corps, retitled July, 1917, 60; at Cambrai, 102

CAVALRY

Cavalry Corps, 3, 28, 269; Dec., 1915, 28; re-formed, Sep., 1916, 58; at Arras, 74, 96; at Cambrai, 106; in 1918 retreat, 178; its casualties, 21 Mar. to 7 Apr., 1918, 217; at Amiens, 223; pulled out, 1 Sep., 1918, 256; at 2nd Le Cateau, 261; its casualties, 8-10 Oct., 1918, 267

Indian Cavalry Corps, 3, 26, 32

1st Cavalry Division, 23, 26, 40, 45, 64, 253, 345; at Cambrai, 108; in 1918 retreat, 178; at 2nd Cambrai, 260; at 2nd Le Cateau, 261

2nd Cavalry Division, 26, 164; at Cambrai, 110; in 1918 retreat, 178; split up, 255; does useful work, split up, late Oct., 1918 to Armistice, 272

3rd Cavalry Division, 23, 26, 40, 64; at Arras, 77; in 1918 retreat, 178; at Amiens, 228; at 2nd Cambrai, 260; at 2nd Le Cateau, 261

4th Cavalry Division, at Cambrai, 108; cavalry track body formed from, 113

5th Cavalry Division, at Villers Faucon, 71; at Cambrai, 110

Yeomanry Division, in Palestine, 163

2nd Indian Cavalry Division, 40, 45, 48, 50

4th Indian Cavalry Division, 143; reformed in Palestine, 163

5th Indian Cavalry Division, 143

1st Cavalry Brigade, 4, 5, 326; at Cambrai, 117; at Amiens, 237

2nd Cavalry Brigade, 252, 258; at Amiens, 237

3rd Cavalry Brigade, 28; at Arras, 77

4th Cavalry Brigade, 164; in 1918 retreat, 181; at Amiens, 243

Index

5th Cavalry Brigade, 269, 276, 350; at Arras, 77; in 1918 retreat, 181; split up at 2nd Cambrai, 260

6th Cavalry Brigade, at Arras, 77; in 1918 retreat, 179; 500 cases of 'flu in, 218; at Amiens, 236; at 2nd Le Cateau, 261; at Honnechy, 9 Oct., 1918, 265

7th Cavalry Brigade, 26, 39, 278; in 1918 retreat, 185; at Amiens, 230; at 2nd Le Cateau, 261; at Honnechy, 9 Oct., 1918, 265

8th Cavalry Brigade, 27, 39; at Arras, 77

9th Cavalry Brigade, 26, 47, 74, 278; in 1918 retreat, 186; at Amiens, 237; at 2nd Le Cateau, 260

Canadian Cavalry Brigade, at Somme, 48, 73; at Cambrai, 125; in 1918 retreat, 183; at Amiens, 230; at 2nd Le Cateau, 263; on 9 Oct., 1918, 265; its final action, 267

Ambala Cavalry Brigade, at Villers Faucon, 71; at Cambrai, 141

Lucknow Cavalry Brigade, at Cambrai, 108

Meerut Cavalry Brigade, 38; at Cambrai, 143

Secunderabad Cavalry Brigade, 48, 49; at Cambrai, 126

INFANTRY
9th Division, 54, 76
12th Division, 76
13th Division, 255
14th Division, 191, 194
51st Division (Highland) Division, 123, 128
4th Canadian Division, at Amiens, 232
5th Australian Division, at Amiens, 244

88th Brigade, 131, 279
112nd Brigade, 255
South African Brigade, 266, 276

ARMOURED
7th Armoured Division, 320
10th Armoured Division, 345
1st Tank Brigade, at Cambrai, 112
22nd Armoured Brigade, 353
4th Light Armoured Brigade, 353

OTHER ARMS
Royal Air Force (Royal Flying Corps), becomes from RFC, 207; has local superiority of 7 to 1 at Amiens, 226
Royal Army Veterinary Corps, formed 1906, 298
Shanghai Defence Force, 1927, 311
Territorial Army (earlier Force), 344

FOREIGN
2nd American Corps, 255, 261
First French Army, 261; at Amiens, 226
German Second Army's Caudry Group, at Cambrai, 111
German LI Corps, at Amiens, 245
German Alpine Corps, 248
German 3rd Guard Division, at Cambrai, 102
Portuguese brigades (three), at Neuve Chapelle, 176, 216

Freer, 2nd-Lt, 12L, 43
French, FM John Denton Pinkstone, 1st Earl of Ypres (1852-1925), 20, 283; at Neuve Chapelle, 21; at Loos, 26; succeeded by Haig, 29; C-i-C, Home Forces, 30; Lord-Lieutenant, Ireland, 30;

Index

recommends Robertson as his successor, 32
Freyberg, Bernard, 1st Lord (1889-1963), 279
Fuller, Maj.-Gen. John Frederick Charles (1878-1966), 102, 154, 234
Furse, Maj. Sir Ralph, King Edward's Horse, 273, 274

Gafur, Jemadar Abdul, Poona Horse, 50
Ganga Ram, Trumpet-Major, 2L, at Cambrai, 148
Garnett, Tpr Clarence, Essex Yeo., 85
gas, poison, 22, 28
'Geddes Axe' (1922 Committee of National Expenditure), 312, 326, 341
George V, King of England (1865-1936), 37; thinks French should be replaced, 29
Gerard, Capt. Frederic John, 3rd Lord (1883-1953), RHG, 88
Gibbs, Sir Philip (1877-1962), 128, 214
Gobind Singh, 2L, gains VC at Cambrai, 149
Godley, Sir Alexander John (1867-1957), 336
Gort, John Standish Surtees Prendergast Vereker, 6th Viscount (1886-1946), wounded at Cambrai, 156
Gough, Gen. Sir Hubert Poer (1870-1963), 20, 156, 165; i/c 'striking force', Somme, 40; replaces Plumer after Messines, 99; i/c Fifth Army in 1918 retreat, 168; dismissed, 195
Greenly, Maj.-Gen. Walter Howorth (1875-1955), 178, 199; i/c 2 Cav. Div. at Cambrai, 137
Gregory, Maj.-Gen. Charles Levigne (1870-1944), 49

Haig, FM Douglas, 1st Earl (1861-1928), 9, 21, 38, 66, 68, 165, 166, 212, 213, 222, 251, 278, 283, 336; at Neuve Chapelle, 20; at Loos, 26; succeeds French, 29; largely responsible for final vistory, 30; gets on well with Joffre, Pétain and Foch, 30; his relations with Lloyd George, 30; promoted FM, 31; at Somme, 36, 37; thoughts on strategy, 1916, 39; criticized for not waiting for large numbers of tanks, Sep., 1916, 58; at Arras cautions careful handling of cav., 74; replaces Plumer by Gough after Messines, 99; gives reasons for launching Cambrai, 100; maintains to War Cabinet value of cav. as mobile infantry, 163; faces German March, 1918 offensives, 168; ordered to take over 28 miles of French trenches, 1918, 169; alleged differences between handwritten and typed versions of diary of, Mar., 1918, 174; meets Pétain, 23 and 24 March, 1918, 174; fears for Channel ports and issues 'backs to the wall' proclamation, 13 Apr., 1918, 176; and Gough's dismissal, 197; offers to resign, 197; gets Foch's agreement to close down Amiens, 12 Aug., 1918, 249; orders Byng to use cav. to fullest extent at Bapaume, 253; urges Wilson to send more mobile troops, 258; directs Kavanagh to avoid heavy losses at 2nd Cambrai, 260; favours retaining cav. regts identities, 329
Haig, Brig.-Gen. Neil Wolseley (1888-1926), i/c Mhow Cav. Bde at Cambrai, 146
Hailsham, Douglas McGarel Hogg, 1st Viscount (1872-1950), 314

Index

Haldane, Richard Burdon, 1st Viscount (1856-1928), in 1909 requires police to take horse census, 290
Hamond, Maj. Philip, Tank Corps, at Cambrai, 127
Hardwick, Lt-Col Philip Edward (1875-1919), i/c 10H at Monchy, 87
Hardy, Maj. 'Duddy', 88
Harman, Lt-Gen. Sir Wentworth (1872-1961), 326; i/c 6 Cav. Bde at Arras, 77; i/c 3 Cav. Div. in 1918 retreat, 178; at Amiens, 230; at 2nd Le Cateau, 261; at Honnechy, 265
'Harman's Detachment', 181
Harvey, Lt F.M.W., Lord Strathcona's Horse, wins VC at Guyencourt, 73; at Moreuil Wood, 205
Harris, Sir Charles (1864-1943), 327
Hartley, Lt D.J., 7DG, 53
Hawkins, L/Cpl T.H., 3H, 256
Hidayat Ali, 2L, at Cambrai, 148
Hindenburg, FM Paul Ludwig Hans Anton von Benckendorff und (1847-1934), replaces Falkenhayn as Chief of Staff, 36
Hindenburg Line, German withdrawal to, 1917, 68
Home, Brig.-Gen. Sir Archibald Fraser (1874-1953), 28, 61, 63, 69, 195, 217, 226, 245, 271, 272; thinks tanks 'wonderful machines', 60; depressed about cav. after Cambrai, 159; on 11 Aug., 1918, points out to Fourth Army HQ that terrain impossible for cav., 252
Hore-Belisha, Leslie, Lord (1898-1957), succeeds Duff Cooper as Sec. of State for War, 309
horses - (*see also* remounts) - enter 1917 debilitated, 67; freeze to death before Arras, 76; heaps of dead at Monchy, 91; losses, Mar. to Aug., 1918, 246; Haldane requires police to take census of in 1909, 290; during the war, 17% of GB's working horses mobilized, 291; wastage in BEF, 293; types for cav. on Western Front, 294; distinguished veterans of the war, 296; statistics of health of, 300; types of wounds inflicted on, 302; weights carried by cav., 302; mechanization of transport reduces weights carried by cav., 335
Howard, Sir Michael (1922-), 307
Howell, Brig.-Gen. Philip (1877-1916), 20
Hughes, TSM Edwin (1831-1927), 13H, 353
Humphriss, Lt, Northamptonshire Yeo., 84
hunting in France, 11

'infantry-ization' of cav., 6
influenza epidemic, 1918, 218
Irish Treaty, 1921, 310
Ironside, FM William Edmund, 1st Lord (1880-1959), 166, 196, 351
Irwin, Capt. T.S., 1D, 41

Jarvis, Capt. F., 7DG, 55
Jenkins of Hillhead, Roy Harris, Lord (1920-), 29
Joffre, Mareschal Joseph Jacques Césaire (1852-1931), 59; at Loos, 26; Haig gets on well with, 30; replaced by Nivelle, 67
Joscelyne, RQMS, Essex Yeo., 13

Kavanagh, Lt-Gen. Sir Charles Toler McMorrough (1864-1950), i/c Cav. Corps, 58, 62, 63, 212, 256, 278; at Cambrai, 106; in 1918 retreat, 195; at Amiens, 226; at Bapaume, 253; ordered by Haig to avoid heavy

Index

losses at 2nd Cambrai, 260; at 2nd Le Cateau, 261
Kennedy, Maj.-Gen. Alfred Alexander (1870-1926), i/c 4 Cav. Div. at Cambrai, 146
Kiggell, Lt-Gen. Sir Launcelot Edward (1862-1954), 45, 105, 155
King, Cpl, Seely's orderly at Moreuil Wood, 209
Kipling, Rudyard (1865-1936), 321
Kitchener of Khartoum, Horatio Herbert, Earl (1850-1916), 25; disillusioned with Sir J.French, 29; loses power, 32; dismisses tanks as 'pretty mechanical toys', 60
Knowles, Maj. G., 2L, at Cambrai, 147
Knox, Gen. Sir Harry (1873-1971), 320
Kuhl, Gen. von, Chief of Staff to Prince Rupprecht, 215

Lane, Capt. C.W.T., 7DG, 126
Lascelles, Sir Alan Frederick (1887-1981), 42, 58, 218, 297
Laurie, Brig. Sir Percy Robert (1880-1962), 296
Law, Andrew Bonar (1858-1923), 101; thinks French should retire, 29
Lawrence, Gen. Hon. Sir Herbert Alexander (1861-1943), 142, 172, 271
Lawson, Brig.- Gen. Algernon (1869-1929), 258
League of Nations, 310, 312
leave, home, 8
Liddell Hart, Sir Basil Henry (1895-1970), 58, 246, 305, 308, 313; draws lesson from Cambrai, 160; on Moreuil and Rifle Woods, 199; his gross inaccuracy respecting forage supply, 286; strong influence on Hore-Belisha, 309

Lloyd George of Dwyfor, David, 1st Earl (1863-1945), 9, 140, 162, 165, 173; thinks French should be replaced, 29; his relations with Haig, 30; his determination to deprive Haig of manpower, 1918, 169; and Gough's dismissal, 197
Locarno Treaty, 1925, 309
Ludendorff, Gen. Erich Friedrich Wilhelm (1865-1937), 30, 80, 273, 281; points to opportunity afforded by Russian collapse, 166; commands 1918 offensives, 168; fails to exploit gap, 21 Mar., 1918, 172; launches Flanders offensive, 9 Apr., 1918, 176; his disbelief in utility of cav., 215; believes initiative still his, July, 1918, 221; describes 8 Aug., 1918 as the 'black day of the German army', 222; resigns, 26 Oct., 1918, 251; decides to give 'not a foot's breadth of ground', 271
Lunt, Maj.-Gen. James Doiran (1917-), 212

MacAndrew, Maj.-Gen. Henry John Milnes (1866-1919), 20, 50
Maclean, Col Sir Fitzroy, 10th Bt (1835-1936), 353
McConnachie, Pte, 2D, 36
McCreery, Gen. Sir Richard Loudon (1898-1967), 275
Maillard, Mons., 11
Malcolm, Maj.-Gen. Sir Neill (1869-1953), 196
Marson, Lt L.F., 4DG, at Cambrai, 124
Martel, Lt-Gen. Sir Giffard Le Quesne (1889-1958), 317
Maunsell, Col E.B., 152
Miles, Capt. Wilfred (1885-1962), 137, 158

Milner, Alfred, 1st Viscount (1854-1925), 198; at Doullens conference, 26 Mar., 1918, 173

Misa, Brig. Lawrence Edward (1896-1968), 4DG, at Cambrai, 122

Moltke, Gen. Count Helmuth von (1848-1916), 30

Montgomery-Massingberd Cavalry Committee, 1926/7, 335

Moore, Maj.-Gen. Sir John (1864-1940), Director, AVS, 295

Morgan. Lt, Lord Strathcona's Horse, 204

Morrell, Pte, Fort Garry Horse, at Cambrai, 134

Mugford, L/Cpl Harold, Essex Yeo., 85

Mukand Singh, Risaldar, 2L, at Cambrai, 148

Mullens, Maj.-Gen. Richard Lucas (1871-1952), at Cambrai, 119; i/c 1 Cav. Div. in 1918 retreat, 178; at Amiens, 237; at 2nd Cambrai, 260

Mustafa Kemal Pasha (Kemal Ataturk), (1881-1938), 351

'mutinies' in French army, 67

Napoleon I, Emperor (1769-1821), 152

Newcomen, Maj. R. Canadian Dragoons, at Moreuil Wood, 203; at Gattingny Wood, 266

Nicholas II, Czar of Russia (1868-1918), 32

Nihal Chand, Kote Dafadar, 2L, at Cambrai, 149

Nivelle, Gén. Robert Georges (1856-1924), 67, 98

Nordheimer, Capt., R. Canadian Dragoons, at Moreuil Wood, 203

Northcliffe, Alfred Charles William, Viscount (1865-1922), 165

Orléans, Capt. Prince Antoine, ADC to Seely at Moreuil Wood, k. 1918, 200

Ormrod, Oliver, Pilot Officer, RAF, (1923-), 320

Paterson, Brig.-Gen. Ewing (1873-1950), i/c 2L at Cambrai, 151; at Amiens, 233; at 2nd Le Cateau, 261

Paterson, Brig.-Gen. Robert Walter (1876-1936), 48; i/c Fort Garry Horse at Cambrai, 131; in 1918 retreat, 191; at Amiens, 235

Pembroke and Montgomery, Maj. Reginald Herbert, 12th and 15th Earl of (1880-1960), at Monchy, 88

Pershing, Gen. John Joseph (1860-1948), 175

Pétain, Mareschal Henri Phillippe (1856-1951), 99; Haig gets on well with, 30; replaces Nivelle, 67; gives Haig assurances of aid before 1918 retreat, 168; relations with the British, Mar., 1918, 173; meets Haig, 23 and 24 Mar., 1918, 174

Pettit, Sgt, 4DG, 296

Philipps, Capt. Colwyn Erasmus Arnold, RHG, 8

Pitman, Maj.-Gen. Thomas Tait (1868-1941), 178; i/c 2 Cav. Div. at Moreuil Wood, 199

Plumer, Sir Herbert Charles Onslow, 1st Viscount (1857-1932), 17; Haig replaces by Gough after Messines, 99

Poincaré, Raymond (1860-1934), at Doullens conference, 26 Mar., 1918, 173

Pope, 2nd-Lt H.W., 7DG, at Somme, 51

Proby, Maj. Sir Richard George, 1st Bt (1886-1979), at Arras (Monchy), 87

Index

Pulteney, Lt-Gen. Sir William Pulteney (1861-1941), 104

Rawlinson, Gen. Henry Seymour, 1st Lord (1864-1925), 30, 177, 197, 245, 271; at Neuve Chapelle, 20; i/c Fourth Army at Somme, 40; impressed by tanks, Sep., 1916, 60; takes over Fifth Army (re-numbered Fourth) from Gough, 175, 195, 198; his part in genesis of Amiens, 222; at Amiens, 223; tells cav. senior officers what expected of them at Amiens, 228

Rees, Pte Frank at Moreuil Wood, 206

REGIMENTS (and other units, e.g. independent squadrons, battalions, batteries, companies)

British Cavalry
amalgamated regiments (1922), a list of, 327-8
1st Life Guards, 327
2nd Life Guards, 7, 327
Royal Horse Guards (Blues), 39, 327; at Monchy, 81
Household Cavalry Composite Regiment, 163, 323, 327, 341; become machine gunners, 1918, 166
King's Dragoon Guards, 350; leaves for India, 1917, 163
2nd Dragoon Guards (Bays), 14, 27; at Cambrai, 108; in 1918 retreat, 186; at Amiens, 239
3rd Dragoon Guards, 327; at Arras, 77; in 1918 retreat, 185; at 2nd Cambrai, 261; at Honnechy, 9 Oct., 1918, 264
4th Dragoon Guards, 13, 22, 254, 258, 296, 327; at Cambrai, 119; in 1918 retreat, 180

5th Dragoon Guards, 8, 9, 17, 44, 296, 327; at Cambrai, 119; in 1918 retreat, 180; at Harbonnières, 241
6th Dragoon Guards (Carabiniers), 327; in 1918 retreat, 179
7th Dragoon Guards, 18, 27, 42, 327; at Somme, 49; at Cambrai, 126; at Amiens, 233
1st Royal Dragoons, 28, 341, 342; in 1918 retreat, 185; at 2nd Cambrai, 261
2nd Dragoons (Royal Scots Greys), 36, 45, 276, 341, 342; at Arras, 77; in 1918 retreat, 181; severe 'go' of 'flu in, 219; at Sains, 9 Nov., 1918, 275
3rd Hussars, 18, 74, 255, 320; at Amiens, 243
4th Hussars, 3, 280; in 1918 retreat, 183; at Moreuil Wood, 209
5th Lancers, 14, 323, 328; in 1918 retreat, 179; at Moreuil Wood, 210; 1st regt to re-enter Mons, 11 Nov., 1918, 280; selected for abolition, 1921, 324
6th (Inniskilling) Dragoons, 327; at Cambrai, 146; at Amiens, 233; at 2nd Cambrai, 263; at Honnechy, 265
7th Hussars, 342, 353
8th Hussars, 26, 254; at Villers Faucon, 71; in 1918 retreat, 186; at Amiens, 237; at Vauvillers, 252
9th Lancers, 252, 324, 353
10th Hussars, 13, 39; at Monchy, 77; in 1918 retreat, 185; at 2nd Cambrai, 261
11th Hussars, 7, 18, 95, 280, 295, 317; in 1918 retreat, 186; converted to armoured cars, 1927, 337

393

Index

12th Lancers, 6, 9, 11, 17, 74, 275, 317, 324, 353; at Arras, 77; in 1918 retreat, 182; converted to armoured cars, 1917, 337
13th Hussars, 4, 6, 15, 327, 353
14th Hussars, 324, 328
15th Hussars, 26, 42, 280, 324, 328; in 1918 retreat, 180; at Amiens, 237
16th Lancers, 7, 183, 328; at Moreuil Wood, 209; in last charge of war, 11 Nov., 1918, 278
17th Lancers, 4, 15, 280, 295, 326, 328; in 1918 retreat, 185; at Amiens, 233
18th Hussars, 13, 323, 327; at 2nd Le Cateau, 269
19th Hussars, 26, 281, 323, 328; in 1918 retreat, 186; at Amiens, 237; at 2nd Cambrai, 260; selected for abolition, 1921, 324
20th Hussars, 7, 272, 275, 323, 328; at Arras, 77; at Cambrai, 141; in 1918 retreat, 181; put under II American Corps, 255; at 2nd Cambrai, 260; selected for abolition, 1921, 324; at Gebze, 12 July, 1920, 351
21st Lancers, 323, 328; selected for abolition, 1921, 324
22nd Dragoons, 342
23rd Hussars, 342
King Edward's Horse, 70, 255, 273; at Cambrai, 120; in 1918 retreat, 216
13th Australian Light Horse, 255; at Amiens, 244
19th Alberta Dragoons, 64
1st Canadian Hussars, 64
Canadian Light Horse, 255
Fort Garry Horse, at Somme, 48; at Cambrai, 124; at Moreuil Wood, 205; at Amiens, 230; at Roye, 10

Aug., 1918, 252; at 2nd Le Cateau, 265; at Gattigny Wood, 266
2nd King Edward's Horse, 48
Lord Strathcona's Horse, 48, 73; at Moreuil Wood, 204; at Amiens, 230; at 2nd Le Cateau, 265; at Gattigny Wood, 266
Royal Canadian Dragoons, 48; at Moreuil Wood, 203; at Amiens, 232; at Gattigny Wood, 266
Bedfordshire Yeomanry, 164
Cheshire Yeomanry, 315
Essex Yeomanry, 13, 164; at Monchy, 77
Inns of Court Regiment, 344
Leicestershire Yeomanry, 11, 23, 164
Lovat Scouts, 344
Northamptonshire Yeomanry, at Arras, 76
North Somerset Yeomanry, 164; at Arras, 83
Northumberland Hussars Yoemanry, 7, 27; in 1918 retreat, 190; at Bapaume, 254
Oxfordshire Hussars Yeomanry, 5, 7, 8, 9, 12, 13, 17, 45, 164, 166, 256, 276, 281; in 1918 retreat, 181; 1st regt to enter Maubeuge, 275
Scottish Horse, 344
South Irish Horse, 63, 73
South Nottinghamshire Hussars Yeomanry, 296
Staffordshire Yeomanry, 353
Surrey Yeomanry, 350
Sussex Yeomanry, 350
Wiltshire Yeomanry, 70
Yorkshire Yeomanry, 315

Indian Cavalry
2nd Lancers (Gardner's Horse), 16, 116; at Cambrai, 143
18th Lancers, 72
19th Lancers, 62, 331

Index

Aden Troop, 330
Bengal Bodyguard, 330
Bombay Bodyguard, 330
Central India Horse, 34, 351; at Cambrai, 150
Deccan Horse, 11; at Somme, 50
Governor-General's Bodyguard, 330
Guides Cavalry, 330
Gwalior Lancers, 351
Hodson's Horse, at Cambrai, 142
Madras Bodyguard, 330
Poona Horse, 331
Skinner's Horse, 349

British Artillery
Royal Horse Artillery
'A' Battery, 164
'C' Battery, at Arras, 83; at 2nd Le Cateau, 263
'D' Battery, at Moreuil Wood, 208
'E' Battery, at Arras, 77
'J' Battery, 18
'K' Battery, at Amiens, 233
'N' Battery, 164; at Somme, 48, 54
'Q' Battery, 164; at Cambrai, 146
'U' Battery, at Cambrai, 146
'X' Battery, 164; at Villers Faucon, 71
Chestnut Troop, at Cambrai, 146
Royal Canadian Horse Artillery, at Moreuil Wood, 208; at Amiens, 232

Miscellaneous
4th MG Squadron, at Monchy, 94
6th MG Squadron, at 2nd Le Cateau, 263
8th MG Squadron, at Monchy, 90
Cavalry Track Battalion, at Cambrai, 113
6th Cavalry Field Ambulance, 268
9th Light Armoured Car Battery, at Somme, 48
17th Armoured Car Battalion, at Amiens, 244
11th Cyclist Battalion, in 1918 retreat, 216
Royal Military Police Mounted Troop, disbanded, 1995, 304
Welsh Guards, 62
Burma Frontier Force, 351
39th Royal Garhwal Rifles, 351
Grey's Scouts, Rhodesian Army, 350
North Frontier Tribal Police, Rhodesian Army, 351
16th Bavarian Regiment, 56

remounts, provision of, 290; purchasing commission for in Canada and USA, 291; personnel in Remount Dept rose during war from 351 to 16,660, 291; depots for, 292
Repington, Lt-Col Charles A'Court- (1858-1925), 160
'Reynolds' Force', in 1918 retreat, 190
Reynolds, Lt-Col Alan Boyd (1879-1940), 12L, 190
Robbins, Prof. Keith Gilbert (1940-), 26, 36
Robertson, FM Sir William Robert, 1st Bt (1860-1933), 37, 101; becomes CIGS, 32; sends cav. recruits to other arms, 1916-17, 66; 'in substantial agreement' with Churchill's suggestion for cav. disbandment, Dec., 1917, 162; succeeded by Wilson as CIGS, Feb., 1918, 173
Rome, Brig. Charles Leslie (1878-1936), at Honnechy, 9 Oct., 1918, 264

Index

Rupprecht, FM Crown Prince of Bavaria (1869-1955), 68

Sahib Singh, Acting L/Dafadar, 2L, at Cambrai, 148
Salisbury, James Edward Hubert Gascoyne-Cecil, 4th Marquess of (1861-1947), 336
Salkeld, Maj., 2L, 149
Salmond, Air Chief Marshal Sir Geoffrey (1878-1933), promises Haig 300 low-flying aircraft, Sep., 1918, 258
Sandeman, Capt. Arthur, CIH, 351
Scott, Capt. F.J., 7DG, at Somme, 51
Seely, John Edward Bernard, Lord Mottistone (1868-1947), 48; at Guyencourt, 73; at Moreuil and Rifle Woods, 199
Sewell, Brig.-Gen. Horace Somerville (1881-1953), 4DG, 120
Smith-Dorrien, Gen. Horace Lockwood (1858-1930), 269
Smithers, A.J., 155, 159
Snow, Lt-Gen. Sir Thomas D'Oyly (1855-1940), 143
steel helmets, first issued early 1916, 34
Stokes, Capt., 10H, at Monchy, 91
Strachan, Lt-Col Henry (1884-1982), Fort Garry Horse, at Cambrai, 131
Stratford, TSM John (1830-1932), 14LD, 353
Sutherland, 2nd-Lt J.W., 3H, 256
Swinton, Maj.-Gen. Sir Ernest Dunlop (1868-1951), told by Haig tanks saved lives, 1916, 60

tanks, 1st time used in history, 15 Sep., 1916, 58; description of Mark I, 60; at Cambrai, 102; co-operation with cav. Haig's hopes for before Cambrai, 106; wire cutting at Cambrai, 114; 1st Whippets employed near Hebuterne, 4 Apr., 1918, 216; 530 of at Amiens, incl. Marks V and V*, 223-4; Whippets at Amiens, 231
Taylor, Alan John Percivale (1906-1990), 305
Taylor, Tpr Bertie, Northamptonshire Yeo., 84
Taylor, Tpr, Oxfords H. Yeo., 12
Tennant, Lt-Col E., Deccan Horse, 54
Tennyson, Alfred, Lord (1809-1892), 254
Terraine, John (1921-), 26, 59, 103, 140, 155, 172, 197, 214
Timmis, Col Reginald Symonds (1884-1968), R. Canadian Dragoons, at Moreuil Wood, 203
trench conditions, 4, 8
Trotter, Lt, Lord Strathcona's Horse, at Moreuil Wood, 204
Tudor, Maj.-Gen. Sir H. Hugh (1871-1965), responsible for new artillery doctrines at Cambrai, 104
Turner, Lt-Col H.H.F., i/c 2L at Cambrai, 147
Tweedmouth, Lt-Col Dudley Churchill Marjoribanks, 3rd Lord (1874-1935), i/c RHG at Monchy, 89

Van der Byl, Brig. John (1878-1953), 8H, at Villers Faucon, 72
Vanwilderode, Pte, Fort Garry Horse, at Cambrai, 134
Versailles, Treaty of, 1919, 309

Warter, Capt. H. de Gray, 4 DG, at Cambrai, 124
Watts, Lt-Gen. Sir Herbert Edward (1858-1934), 201
Weldon, Capt. Edric George, 8H, 72

Index

Wellesley, Lt G.V., Oxfords Yeo., 276

Wellington, Arthur Wellesley, 1st Duke of (1769-1852), 168

Weygand, Gén. Maxime (1867-1965), Chief of Staff to Foch, 211

Whitmore, Col Sir Francis Henry Douglas Charlton, 1st Bt (1872-1962), i/c Essex Yeo. at Monchy, 86

Whitworth, Capt., 2L, at Cambrai, 147

Wiley, Capt. Henry Ormsby, 5DG, at Harbonnières, 241

William II, Friedrich Wilhelm Viktor Albert, Emperor of Germany (the Kaiser) (1859-1941), 248

Williams, Bt-Col Evelyn Hugh Watkin, 10H (1884-1934), 190

Wilson, FM Sir Henry Hughes (1864-1922), 197, 223, 259, 311; as CIGS at Doullens conference, 26 Mar., 1918, 173; urged by Haig to send mobile troops speedily, 258; against amalgamation of cav. regts, 325

Woollcombe, Lt-Gen. Sir Charles Louis (1857-1934), 104

Wormald, Brig.-Gen. Frank, k. 1915, 17

Worthington-Evans, Sir Laming, 1st Bt (1868-1931), Sec. of State for War, 334, 344; claims in 1927 to have produced 'best fighting tanks . . . in the world', 335

Wright, Capt. Archibald, 4DG, 60

Yarborough, Lt-Col Sackville George Pelham, 5th Earl of (1888-1948), OC Nottinghamshire Yeo., 1936-1940, 316

Young, Lt-Col, R. Canadian Dragoons, at Moreuil Wood, 208

Yusuf Abdulla, N. Frontier Tribal Police, 351